The Public Policy Process

The Public Policy Process

MICHAEL HILL

Fifth edition

PEARSON
Longman

Harlow, England • London • New York • Boston • San Francisco • Toronto • Sydney • Singapore • Hong Kong
Tokyo • Seoul • Taipei • New Delhi • Cape Town • Madrid • Mexico City • Amsterdam • Munich • Paris • Milan

Pearson Education Limited
Edinburgh Gate
Harlow
Essex CM20 2JE
England

and Associated Companies throughout the world

Visit us on the World Wide Web at:
www.pearsoned.co.uk

First published 1997
Fourth edition published 2005
Fifth edition published 2009

ISBN: 978-1-4058-7352-9

British Library Cataloguing-in-Publication Data
A catalogue record for this book is available from the British Library

Library of Congress Cataloging-in-Publication Data
A catalog record for this book is available from the Library of Congress

10 9 8 7 6 5 4 3 2 1
14 13 12 11 10 09

Typeset in Stone Serif by 3
Printed and bound in Malaysia (CTP-KHL)

The publisher's in policy is to use paper manufactured from sustainable forests.

Contents

Part 1   Introduction

Part 2   Policy theories

Part 3   Analysis of the policy process

Preface

The roots of this book lie in a book I published with Chris Ham in 1984, *The Policy Process in the Modern Capitalist State*. That underwent a substantial revision when I produced *The Policy Process in the Modern State* on my own in 1997. In 2005 I produced a fundamental revision of the later book, not only updating it to introduce more recent theory and research, but also reshaping the text. This is yet another update of the text, taking into account my experience – and that of various anonymous referees – of using it in teaching.

This is a book about the process by which public policy is made. Efforts to influence the policy process, the concern of much policy analysis writing, need to be grounded in an understanding of it. Making policy embraces the emergence of policies on the agenda, policy formulation and policy implementation. It is a continuous process, with many feedback loops, carried out by diverse actors. This is something that was recognised in the earlier books but is made much more explicit here.

The book starts with an introductory chapter (Part 1) which sets the study of the policy process in the context of the wider policy studies literature and examines some of the key underlying concepts and methodological issues. It is then followed by five chapters (Part 2) which set out the various theoretical approaches to policy process analysis. Part 3 comprises eight chapters which explore the application of those approaches. These start with an examination of the implications of policy diversity for any analysis. This is followed by separate explorations of agenda setting, policy formulation and policy implementation. Two chapters then look explicitly at issues about the roles of organisations in the policy process (making a distinction between inter- and intra-organisational issues). After that one chapter pays special attention to issues about the roles of 'street-level' workers in the policy process. The book ends by exploring the impact of concerns about evaluation and accountability for the operation of the policy process.

Despite all the changes, the book obviously still owes a great deal to the original collaboration with Chris Ham, and I am very grateful to him for his original contribution and for then letting the book evolve in my way. We developed *The Policy Process in the Modern Capitalist State* when we worked together on a teaching programme on the policy process for the master's course in public policy studies at the School for Advanced Urban Studies at Bristol University.

Over the years that I have been engaged on writing about the policy processes my debts to colleagues and students, both in the institutions in which I have worked and in many other places at home and abroad, have accumulated to the extent that I cannot acknowledge them all. I will confine myself to some of those who have been particularly helpful in the recent past. After I left Bristol I used the book for undergraduate teaching at the University of Newcastle. During that period I revised the original book twice. Also during that period I developed collaborative work with Pieter Degeling and with Peter Hupe. Subsequently I wrote *Implementing Public Policy* with Peter Hupe. That collaboration has had a big impact upon my thinking about how to analyse the policy process. I have learnt a great deal from Peter, who brings an analytical eye to the subject and a Dutch scepticism about some of the things the British take for granted. This book draws heavily on recent work with him. I would also like to thank Peter Knoepfel, Corinne Larrue and Frédéric Varone for involving me in the production of an English version of their book on public policy analysis.

Teaching at Goldsmiths College and at the University of Brighton enabled me to develop my ideas further, as have a variety of guest lecturing opportunities in Britain and abroad. Then in 2004 Wayne Parsons invited me to contribute to a master's course on public policy at Queen Mary College. The lively group of students at Queen Mary, combining varied work experience and a wide range of national perspectives, has contributed greatly to my recent thinking.

I would like to thank Philip Langeskov at Pearson for his support and Nicola Chilvers and Lorna Cullen for their work on the preparation of the manuscript.

Finally, I must thank my wife for her tolerance of the extent to which inroads have been made into my half-retirement as I have become increasingly preoccupied with the book over the past few months.

Acknowledgements

We are grateful to the following for permission to reproduce copyright material:

Figures
Figure 7.1 and 10.1 adapted from Synthesizing the implementation literature: The ambiguity-conflict model of policy implementation, *Journal of Public Administration Research and Theory*, 5 (2), p.160, Table 4.1 (Matland, R.E. 1995), Public Management Research Association, by permission of Oxford University Press.

Tables
Table 13.1 adapted from *Bureaucratic Justice*, Yale University Press (Mashaw, J.L. 1983) p.31, (c) Yale University Press; Table 14.1 adapted from Fairness in Context, *Journal of Law and Society*, 33 (4), p. 622 (Adler, M. 2006), Copyright 2006 Blackwell Publishing Ltd. Reproduced with permission of Blackwell Publishing Ltd.

Text
Box 1.5 from *Governance and Public Policy in the UK*, Oxford University Press (Richards, D. and Smith, M.J. 2002) p. 36, Table 2.2, by permission of Oxford University Press; Box 12.5 adapted from Joined-up government in the Western world in comparative perspective, *Journal of Public Administration Research and Theory*, 14 (1), p.108 (6, P. 2004), Public Management Research Association, by permission of Oxford University Press.

In some instances we have been unable to trace the owners of copyright material, and we would appreciate any information that would enable us to do so.

Part

1

Introduction

1 Studying the policy process

SYNOPSIS

After this introductory chapter the book is divided into two further parts. Part 2 (Chapters 2–6) explores a range of theories that have been developed to explain all of, or key aspects of, the policy process. Then Part 3 (Chapters 7–14) looks at various aspects of the policy process, essentially developing and applying some of the main ideas from the first part. Connections between the theories in the first part and the discussions of the issues in the second part will be made in various ways, including summarising observations at the ends of chapters.

This introductory chapter looks at some important overall considerations about the study of the policy process. It explores the implications of the three key words in the title in reverse order. Thus it starts with an exploration of what is implied in examining the policy *process*. This examines the relationship between the 'descriptive' aim of this book and the 'prescriptive' objectives that motivate much policy analysis. A particular aspect of this that requires some introductory exploration here is the fact that many prescriptive approaches involve very explicit views about the 'staged' shape that the policy process should take whilst a descriptive approach involves a much more agnostic perspective on that. This leads on to a general exploration of the relationship between the study of the policy process and political science, and other social science disciplines. Two policy examples are used at the end of this discussion to illustrate these points. They are then also used to illustrate the examination of what may be meant by *policy*. Here it will be shown again that a distinction may be drawn between approaches to this concept – often from a prescriptive perspective – that endeavour to use a very precise meaning and the stance taken in this book that political and ideological contests make that activity difficult and/or contentious. Finally there is consideration of what is distinctive about the study of *public* policy. The examination of this topic involves a recognition of the extent to which there are problems with identifying a distinctive public sector, something which is emphasised in modern stresses upon the extent to which 'government' needs to be seen as 'governance'.

Introduction

We are all critical of public policies from time to time. Most of us have ideas about how they could be better. When we engage in ordinary conversations about the defects of policies we put forward, or hear advanced, various propositions about why they are defective. Those propositions tend to involve views about policy makers as ignorant or misled or perhaps malign. They often embody views that policies would be better if only different people had more influence on policy, including, of course, perhaps ourselves.

This book is based on the belief that before you can really start to suggest alternative policies to the ones we have, or to suggest alternative ways of making policy, it is essential to try to understand how policy is made. Many of the popular prescriptions for improving policy rest upon essential mis-understandings of the nature of the policy process. For example:

- Views about the need for policy makers to be more aware of 'the facts' often disregard the way the facts are actually matters of dispute between different 'interests'.
- Suggestions for taking 'politics' out of policy making disregard the fact that politics is much more than simply the interplay of politicians.
- Statements about the roles of politicians (including many they them-selves make) suggest that they have much more influence over the policy process than in fact they do.

The view taken in this book is that the policy process is essentially a complex and multi-layered one. It is essentially a political process, but in the widest sense of that term. The policy process is a complex political process in which there are many actors: politicians, pressure groups, civil servants, publicly employed professionals, and even sometimes those who see them-selves as the passive recipients of policy.

To explore further what studying the policy process implies it is appro-priate to start with an examination of the place of this approach in the context of the many different approaches adopted to what can be generically called 'policy analysis'. This then leads on to some more specific consider-ations about adopting a process perspective. From there we can then go to what that implies for the way public policy is examined in this book.

Description and prescription in policy analysis

Some policy analysts are interested in furthering understanding of policy (analysis *of* policy); some are interested in improving the quality of policy (analysis *for* policy); and some are interested in both activities (see Parsons, 1995, for an overview of the many approaches). Further, cutting across the distinction between 'analysis of' and 'analysis for' policy are concerns with *ends* and concerns with *means*.

The typology set out in Box 1.1 identifies a range of different kinds of policy analysis.

Box 1.1	Different kinds of policy analysis

Analysis *of* policy

- *Studies of policy content,* in which analysts seek to describe and explain the genesis and development of particular policies. The analyst interested in policy content usually investigates one or more cases in order to trace how a policy emerged, how it was implemented and what the results were. A great deal of academic work concentrates on single policies or single policy areas (social policy, environment policy, foreign policy, etc.).

- *Studies of policy outputs,* with much in common with studies of policy content but which typically seek to explain why levels of expenditure or service provision vary (over time or between countries or local governments).

- *Studies of the policy process,* in which attention is focused upon how policy decisions are made and how policies are shaped in action.

Analysis *for* policy

- *Evaluation* marks the borderline between analysis *of* policy and analysis *for* policy. Evaluation studies are also sometimes referred to as impact studies as they are concerned with analysing the impact policies have on the population. Evaluation studies may be either descriptive or prescriptive.

- *Information for policy making,* in which data are marshalled in order to assist policy makers to reach decisions. An important vein of contemporary studies of this kind manifests a pragmatic concern with 'what works', trying to ensure that policy and practice are 'evidence based' (Davies, Nutley and Smith (eds), 2000).

- *Process advocacy,* in which analysts seek to improve the nature of the policy-making systems through the reallocation of functions and tasks, and through efforts to enhance the basis for policy choice through the development of planning systems and new approaches to option appraisal. Much of the academic work in the sub-fields of 'public administration' and 'public management' has this concern.

- *Policy advocacy,* which involves the analyst in pressing specific options and ideas in the policy process, either individually or in association with others, perhaps through a pressure group.

Typology based upon ones offered by Gordon, Lewis and Young (1977) and by Hogwood and Gunn (1981, 1984).

This book's concern is with the third of the varieties of policy analysis identified in Box 1.1. However, many studies of policy outputs contribute to our understanding of the policy process. Similarly, evaluation studies give much attention not merely to what the policy outputs or outcomes were but also to questions about how the policy process shaped them. Much the same can be said of studies that seek to offer information for policy making, since 'what works' may be determined by the way the policy process works. Overall, to reiterate the point already made, it is often not easy to draw a clear line between 'analysis of' and 'analysis for' policy.

The desire to examine how the policy process works was in many respects a minor concern in the period between 1950 and 1980 when policy studies in their own right mushroomed dramatically. If the right policies could be found, and their design difficulties solved, then progress would be made towards the solution of society's problems. Only a minority – radical analysts on the 'Left' who doubted that modern governments really had the will to solve problems, and radical analysts on the 'Right' who were sceptical about their capacity to do so – raised doubts and suggested that more attention should be paid to the determinants of policy decisions. While many of the leading figures in the development of policy analysis certainly moved between prescription and description, endeavouring to ground solutions in political and organisational realism, prescription was dominant in policy studies.

This book's original predecessor (Ham and Hill, 1984) was, when it was first published, comparatively unusual in asserting that it was appropriate to concentrate on description, to explore the nature of the policy process, to help to ensure that proposals about policy content or about how to change policy should be grounded in the understanding of the real world in which policy is made. Nowadays that is a much less exceptional stance to take towards the study of policy. Rather, the problem may instead be that scepticism is so widespread that it is hard to make a case for the development of more sophisticated approaches to the policy process. That contributes to a widening gulf between the practical people – politicians, civil servants, pressure group leaders, etc. – whose business is achieving policy change and the academic analysts of the policy process.

This book's stance, then, is to assert that we must continue to try to understand the policy process – however irrational or uncontrollable it may seem to be – as a crucial first step towards trying to secure effective policy making. The stance taken here can be compared to one in which effective engineering needs to be grounded in a good understanding of physics. While – at least in the past – many successful engineers have operated pragmatically, using trial and error methods and accumulating experience with only an intuitive understanding of physics, the latter can inform their activities. However, as we will indicate below, there is a need to be cautious about use of the word scientific in relation to the study of political and social life. In reality, much of the so-called knowledge of the policy process derives from the observations of practical people, much more interested in prescribing than in describing. The aim here is merely to try to stand back critically from their eagerness to prescribe, leading often to either complicity with the goals of the powerful or, as Rothstein has put it, to 'misery research' (1998, pp. 62–3) reflecting how often what is prescribed fails to be realised.

Does a process perspective need to start with any assumptions about the shape it takes?

If you are engaged in one of the prescriptive forms of policy analysis you are likely to be relating your activity to one of the stages of the policy process: helping agenda setting or policy formulation through the provision of information, advising how actors might seek to steer or control the implementation process or evaluating policy outcomes. But if you are engaged in description you may even need to be sceptical about notions that policy development follows a staged process. There seem to be common sense reasons why we should expect there to be stages in a policy process. Many human activities are staged in this way. Take for example going on a journey; you may typically:

- Determine where you want to go
- Work out the best way to go there
- Go on the journey
- (And perhaps) reflect on that process for future reference.

However, this activity does not always take that shape. You may go for a walk in which choices of the route and even the ultimate destination emerge as you engage in the process, depending on how you feel and what you see as you go along. Hence, it is important not to assume that policy processes will necessarily take the shape embodied in the journey model set out systematically above. The problem is then that much of the activity observed by the student of the policy process is presumed by key actors to take that form, and that (as suggested above) much analysis of it takes that for granted.

The issues about the extent to which the 'stages model' of the policy process is, can or should be used will be explored further in Chapter 7. However, there is one point about it that must be mentioned here. Readers of the last paragraph may have said to themselves that, while apparently presenting an open-minded view of whether the policy process involves stages, several of the chapter headings of this book seem to take some of those stages for granted. The defence against a charge of inconsistency here is that any text book, or teaching activity, needs a structure. The topic examined needs to be divided up in some way. The justification for the divisions adopted – as John, one of the stages model's severest critics, has recognised – is that there is a pragmatic case for the model as it 'imposes some order on the research process' (1998, p. 36). What had to be recognised in shaping this book was that, if every process is continuously seen as interacting with every other process, there is no way to divide up discussion into separate chapters or sections. Hence, limited use is made of the stages model by recognising rather that there are somewhat different things to say about agenda setting, policy formulation and implementation respectively. At the same time, interactions are regularly stressed. Moreover the view taken here is not quite as radical as John's: very many policy processes do take shape along staged lines (albeit often with feedback loops).

Studying the policy process

As an issue for academic study, the exploration of the policy process is most evidently a part of political studies or political science. We are concerned here with the explanation of the outputs of politics – the 'how' aspect of Lasswell's terse definition of the study of politics as being about 'who gets what, when, how' (1936). At the same time, much of the study of politics is about how power is acquired and used, without reference to outputs, inasmuch as it is concerned with elections, legislative processes and so on.

Any discussion of the public policy process needs to be grounded in an extensive consideration of the nature of power in the state. Any consideration of how the process works will tend to involve propositions about who dominates. Omission of this, in statements about the policy process, will tend to have the implication that there are no dominant elements in the state. That is in itself a stance on this much debated subject, congruent with the pluralist perspective that power is evenly spread and openly contested. This has been widely opposed by views which draw upon Marxist theory or elite theory, which see power as very distinctively structured or which suggest that dominance is very much embedded in the nature of the machinery of the state itself.

An important element in the controversy about control over the state concerns the nature of power itself. This will be explored further in the next chapter. Controversy about the state and about power is closely related to the debate about democracy. Broadly, there is a conflict about the extent to which it is possible to identify, in the society that is under scrutiny – in much of the English language literature it is of course the United States or Britain – a system of power over the state which can be regarded as reasonably according with some of the criteria for a democracy. While modern political scientists recognise problems about the realisation of any ideal model of democracy, there are differing views about the scope any specific system offers for public participation. Sometimes these differences seem like little more than debates about whether the bottle is half full or half empty. However, there has been a strong division between a pluralist camp, taking an optimistic view of democracy, particularly American democracy, and a neo-Marxist or elitist camp emphasising, for example, the dominance of the 'military–industrial complex' (Mills, 1956).

Having identified the study of the policy process as so closely related to the study of politics, it is pertinent to note, without going too deeply into the argument, the problems about adopting too restrictive a view of the 'political'. Hay, in exploring what is meant by 'political analysis', makes the following point:

> . . . the political should be defined in such a way as to encompass the entire sphere of the social. The implication of this is that events, processes and practices should not be labelled 'non-political' or 'extra-political' simply by virtue of the specific setting or context in which they occur. All events, processes and practices which occur within the social sphere have the potential to be political and, hence, to be amenable to political analysis. The realm of government is no more innately political, by this definition, than that of culture, law or the domestic sphere. (Hay, 2002, p. 3)

Hay goes on from that to argue for the need for political analysis to include 'extra-political variables', to be concerned with economic and cultural processes, for example. He thus argues: 'Political analysts cannot simply afford to leave the analysis of economics to the economists, history to historians and so forth' (ibid., p. 4). But there is also a need to turn that argument the other way about and acknowledge that economists, historians, etc. can make a contribution to the understanding of the policy process.

In some parts of this book attention will be paid to arguments about the nature of the policy process that derive from economics: arguments about the extent to which it can help us to understand the policy process if we identify some or all of those engaged in it as 'rational actors' following their interests, and engaged in forms of gaming, that have much in common with the way economists analyse human behaviour in the 'marketplace'. We will also have to examine a very different kind of economics which sees decision making as determined by powerful economic forces.

Another discipline which contributes to the understanding of the policy process is sociology. It may be argued that analysis of political behaviour is political sociology. But quite apart from that, the sociology of organisations makes an important contribution to the study of the policy process, inasmuch as most policy making occurs within institutions. The sociology of organisations is particularly important for the interpretation of the translation of policy into action, exploring issues about the behaviour of workers within complex organisations (among which state bureaucracies loom large).

It is important to stress that there is no reason to suggest that the study of policy processes is any different from any other social science research enterprise. However, a little more needs to be said about the way in which the characteristics of the policy process pose certain problems for research.

The object of study is normally a unique sequence of events. This means that there will be little scope for testing earlier research by looking for a situation in which a process is replicated. Policy experiments are rare, and when they occur they are not necessarily set up in ways which make research evaluation easy (Bulmer (ed.), 1987; Booth, 1988). The political environments in which they are conducted mean that they are very unlikely to run their course without ongoing adjustments. When they do occur, the very fact that they are atypical limits the lessons that can be drawn from them. Furthermore, the impact of the presence of researchers on the behaviour of the researched will also distort the impressions they give of processes.

Policy process studies are very often case studies, using qualitative methods. Where quantitative methods are used they are likely to deal with impact, from which deductions can be made back to process. Perhaps the ideal here is some combination of qualitative observation of process with quantitative work on impact.

There are many relevant activities that are very hard to observe. This brings us back to the issue of power. The fact that many power processes are covert – indeed, their very success may depend upon their being so – is acknowledged in many colloquial expressions ('the power behind the throne', the 'kitchen cabinet', the '*éminence grise*'). Official secrecy is openly used as a justification for restricting access to situations or data necessary to evaluate policy processes. Very much more is just kept secret without any attempt to offer a justification for doing so.

Analysts of policy processes are thus thrown back on methods which must involve inference from the data they can secure. They also find themselves in situations in which – like journalists – they cannot validate their findings by revealing their sources. All social scientists are open to accusations that their theories and ideologies predispose them to particular interpretations of their data. Those who study the policy process are particularly vulnerable to this charge.

One interesting way of trying to deal with this problem is to openly acknowledge the validity of competing frames of reference and then to explore a case study using each as an alternative lens (likely to amplify some parts of the subject and obscure others). Allison's (1971) use of this approach is described in Box 7.1. A number of other writers have followed Allison's lead, using different models. A particular concern has been to try to evaluate the evidence for the interpretations of policy processes to be discussed in the next chapter, as fairly open and competitive ones or as ones that are strongly structured or biased in favour of particular actors or interests (Ham, 1992; Blowers, 1984; Hill, Aaronovitch and Baldock, 1989).

In the social and political sciences we recognise how complexity, change and the consciousness of the actors we are studying limit our scope for the establishment of generalisations. We also recognise how, particularly in a field like the study of policy, we cannot use experimental methods and we must often use qualitative techniques to study phenomena. Hence, whilst the study of the policy process is claimed to be an academic discipline (Lasswell, 1951, 1968, 1970) upon which the more active contributions to policy analysis need to be based, there is a need not to overwork that distinction. People describe because they want to prescribe. Conversely, people who dedicate themselves directly to prescription will always want to root what they have to say in a realistic appreciation of what 'is', whether derived from academic studies or from their own practical experience.

A number of books have taken this observation further to pose a challenge to efforts to generalise about the policy process. This is not a book on methodology, let alone one which will extend into some of the difficult questions about the philosophy of the social sciences. But the fact that even the cautious empiricism set out above is challenged by some writers, including some who have discussed policy processes, cannot be left entirely without comment. Some theorists (who are here labelled 'postmodernist') argue that it is impossible to draw a distinction between 'analysis of' and 'analysis for' policy. The starting point for their argument is a view that few realistic social scientists will contest, namely that when we attempt to study a topic on which we have strong views on what 'ought' to happen this may distort our interpretation of what does happen. That distortion is then even more likely if we have difficulties in developing a methodology for our work which enables the establishment of undisputable facts. What we face here, of course, are the issues about the extent to which social or political studies can be called 'scientific'.

In debates in English about the claim that social sciences are scientific, the core of the argument is about the extent to which 'positivist' methods can be used, involving the formulation and testing of hypotheses. The difficulties about doing this are partly practical problems about the extent to which it is possible to set up experimental situations and control some of the variables so that the impact of others may be tested. These problems are tackled by those who subscribe to positivist approaches by seeking situations in which there are variations between research sites in the extent of the presence of key variables. Sophisticated statistical methods are used to sort out the impact of a complex mix of variables. But there are other problems. When we try to develop explanations of what people do we need to be aware that they have their own explanations of their behaviour; and their behaviour is influenced by the way they think and speak about what they are doing. Then we must also not forget that researchers themselves are people developing hypotheses about other people. Hence, not only do they bring biases to their studies but they are also likely to be in situations in which their views and what they are doing will be communicated to those whose activities they are researching and thus will be influencing future behaviour. While even in the physical sciences there are some problems about the relationship between researchers and the 'matter' they study, in the social sciences these problems are fundamental. The objects of studies can understand what is being hypothesised and can react to that.

Postmodernist theorists go further to argue that when reporting 'facts' the observer is an active shaper both of the message sent and of the message received. For postmodernists, the language with which evidence is reported is important. The social construction of reality involves discourses and the presentation of 'texts' in which issues about language usage are at the core of the postmodern argument (Farmer, 1995).

At its strongest, the postmodernist perspective challenges all attempts to generalise about the policy process. It is often not clear in this 'post-modernist' writing whether it is only being argued that more attention needs to be paid to discourse, and the need to deconstruct dominant discourses, or whether an entirely relativist stance is being taken. In much postmodernist writing there is an emphasis on the need for the 'democratisation of discourse' (Drysek, 1990; Fox and Miller, 1995; Fischer, 2003). This is particularly important for the issues about evidence in political analysis.

The position taken in this book is to support the positivist 'project' inasmuch as it involves the systematic search for truth, in a context in which there are great difficulties about either accumulating good evidence or avoiding biases. But there must be a concern to recognise the significance of discourse (see further discussion in Chapter 4, pp. 75–6 and 80–1) and to allow for the possibility of alternative interpretations of evidence. This position has been described as 'critical modernist', explained by Pollitt and Bouckaert as still holding to 'the importance of the empirical testing of theories and hypotheses, although accepting that this is only one kind of test, and that arguments concerning whether the appropriate conditions for falsification will be met will never cease' (2000, p. 23). They go on to emphasise that 'reality is socially constructed, but not all constructions have equal claim to our credulity', and that there is a need to 'discriminate between more – and less – adequate descriptions and explanations' (ibid.).

 ## Focusing on the policy process: exploration through examples

Box 1.2	The right to roam

The roots of the quest for wider rights of access to the countryside than embodied in the long-standing English and Welsh 'rights of way' goes back to efforts by ramblers to gain access to privately owned moorland in the 1930s. In its 1997 manifesto the Labour Party promised: 'Our policies include greater freedom for people to explore our open countryside. We will not, however, permit any abuse of a right to greater access'.

That promise was kept and a right of access to specifically designated land was included in the Countryside and Rights of Way Act 2000. That Act contains very specific provisions on the land involved. This is designed to exclude cultivated land, parks and gardens, golf courses, military land etc.; in other words, it confines the right to roam to open, comparatively wild country. The land remains in private ownership, and owners have rights to make use of it in various ways (including putting animals to graze on it); conversely there are also limitations on the things the public can do on it (horse riding, camping, driving a vehicle on it). The land in question has to be designated on official maps, and 'access authorities' (local governments or National Parks Authorities) have explicit powers to manage it (setting up entrance points, fences, notices etc.).

This section will use two examples to clarify the issues that have been discussed so far and to introduce the issues about the definition of policy that are the concerns of the rest of this chapter. The examples have been chosen to offer a clear contrast between example 1 (Box 1.2), a case where a comparatively straightforward process analysis is possible, and example 2 (Box 1.3), a case that is difficult and may be controversial.

Both the policy examples are set out in the boxes in terms which can be seen as descriptive rather than prescriptive. But both developments can be seen in terms of wider goals, which can be (and in the case of the poverty issue very much are) the concerns of policy analysts. The chain of events following Blair's poverty pledge involved the translation of that into something to which actual government activity might be related; prescriptive analysts have much to say about how that has been done. But from a descriptive point of view there is also much to be said. In the case of the right to roam the original manifesto commitment may be seen, from its cautious terms, to be a product of an agenda-setting process in which the influence of interests contrary to those eager to open up the countryside can be detected. The actual elaborate designation process set up testifies to the

Box 1.3	The reduction of child poverty

The attack on child poverty is of course a topic that is a widespread subject of policy advocacy. Pressure groups exist that address themselves wholly or partly to this; note for example the Child Poverty Action Group in the UK. Unlike the legislation discussed in Box 1.2, the 1997 Labour manifesto contained no specific commitment to an attack on child poverty but did include a variety of measures that might be expected to make a contribution to that goal either quite directly (the reduction of unemployment, the introduction of a minimum wage, reduction of taxes that imposed heavy burdens on lower income families) or indirectly (measures to improve health, education, housing, for example). However, in 1999 the then Prime Minister, Tony Blair, proclaimed that the government had a '20 year mission' 'to end child poverty for ever' (see Stewart in Seldon ed. 2007, p. 411; also Hills and Stewart, 2005, for wider discussion of this policy issue). That pledge was followed by the specification of interim targets, and various official indications about how the pledge might be interpreted. Crucial here has been the use by the government of a definition of poverty in terms of below 60% of 'equivalised' (meaning a technique for taking into account household composition) median income after meeting housing costs.

That pledge has been followed up by various official assessments of progress towards the goal. There has also been extensive academic activity to track progress, and of course pressure groups have paid careful attention to evidence on that subject. More specific policy changes (in particular the development of tax credits) have been evaluated in terms of the contributions they make to the proclaimed goal.

further importance of this. What is then interesting is the extent to which the freedom of access acquired in practice has depended upon a quite complex, and indeed expensive, implementation process concerned with the designation, mapping and setting out of the access land. The anti-poverty pledge offers a much more extreme example of how complex a policy process may be. It was itself quite meaningless until accompanied by an official definition and until a very long-run goal was accompanied by interim goal statements (note pledges to cut emissions to combat global warming in similar terms). But even then, where the countryside access pledge implied a quite specific measure, the poverty pledge required realisation in terms of the development of a sequence of activities (in fact further policies, which we will come back to in the next section).

In terms of what was said earlier about the notion of policy as 'staged' it may also be noted that it is quite easy to separate out agenda setting, more detailed policy formulation and implementation in respect of the 'right to roam'. The logical sequence predicted by stages models was followed. But then it was a comparatively low-profile measure (it is not even mentioned in Seldon's two edited volumes on the Blair governments) with fairly low implications either for those opposed to it or for other public policies. On the other hand, actually following through the events since Blair's anti-poverty pledge takes us down a tortuous path of interacting policies, some of which advanced the nation towards that goal while others led away from it.

At this point some readers may protest that comparing 'right to roam' with 'anti-poverty' policy is not comparing like with like. Some may even want to say that the first is a policy, the second just an aspiration. It does indeed seem probable that Blair's famous pledge may have been meant as a vague rhetorical aspiration, and may have been followed by angry recriminations from his Chancellor, Gordon Brown (along the lines of 'look what you have let us in for now, Tony'). But the point is that the word 'policy' is regularly used about both. This obviously leads us to the issues about the definition of policy.

The meaning of 'policy'

Chambers's dictionary defines policy as 'a course of action, especially one based on some declared and respected principle'. That definition clearly sees policy as something more than simply a decision: it embodies the idea of action – indeed, rational action – inasmuch as some 'principle' is involved. In everyday speech we sometimes say things like 'my policy is always to . . .'. This book is, of course, about *public* policy. Interestingly, the *Oxford English Dictionary* describes the following as 'the chief living sense' of the word 'policy': 'A course of action adopted and pursued by a government, party, ruler, statesman . . .'. We come back to this issue below.

These definitions do not get us very far towards identifying a policy. Perhaps we can do no more than adopt the very British pragmatism of Cunningham, a former top British civil servant, who argued that 'Policy is rather like the elephant – you recognise it when you see it but cannot easily define it' (1963, p. 229). A rather similarly vague approach is adopted by Friend and his colleagues, who say: 'policy is essentially a *stance* which, once articulated, contributes to the context within which a succession of future decisions will be made' (Friend, Power and Yewlett, 1974, p. 40). However, others have sought to do better than that. Box 1.4 sets out some examples.

The definitional problems posed by the concept of policy suggest that it is difficult to treat it as a very specific and concrete phenomenon. Policy may sometimes be identifiable in terms of a decision, but very often it involves either groups of decisions or what may be seen as little more than an orientation. The attempts at definition also imply that it is hard to identify particular occasions when policy is made. There is a temptation here to adopt a more specific definition of policy for the purposes of this textbook, since there are grounds for seeing some usages as too vague for systematic analysis. This is perhaps the case with the poverty policy example discussed above. But it is unhelpful for social scientists to give terms in wide general use specific meanings for the purposes of their own analyses. In analysing the policy process it is important to recognise that different actors will be using the word policy in different ways, often with the specific objective of influencing how others view their actions.

Let us look a little more at the implications of the fact (emphasised in Easton's and Jenkins's definitions in Box 1.4) that policy involves a course

---

Box 1.4   **Definitions of policy**

- Heclo's definition of policy, like the Chambers's dictionary one set out in the text, emphasises action: 'A policy may usefully be considered as a course of action or inaction rather than specific decisions or actions' (1972, p. 85).

- Easton offers a variant of this, noting that 'a policy . . . consists of a web of decisions and actions that allocate . . . values' (1953, p. 130).

- Bill Jenkins sees policy as 'a set of interrelated decisions . . . concerning the selection of goals and the means of achieving them within a specified situation . . .' (1978, p. 15).

- Smith suggests that 'the concept of policy denotes . . . deliberate choice of action or inaction, rather than the effects of interrelating forces': he emphasises 'inaction' as well as action and reminds us that 'attention should not focus exclusively on decisions which produce change, but must also be sensitive to those which resist change and are difficult to observe because they are not represented in the policy-making process by legislative enactment' (1976, p. 13).

of action or a web of decisions rather than just one decision. There are several aspects to this. First, a decision network, often of considerable complexity, may be involved in producing action. A web of decisions, taking place over a long period of time and extending far beyond the initial policy-making process, may form part of the network. Both of the examples above (Boxes 1.2 and 1.3) involve this; this is very clear in respect of the issue of anti-poverty policy but even the right to roam policy was shown to imply a quite elaborate pattern of implementation actions.

A second aspect is that policy is not usually expressed in a single decision. It tends to be defined in terms of a series of decisions which, taken together, comprise a more or less common understanding of what policy is. That is, of course, crucial for the anti-poverty policy example, where from the very start a pragmatic response to the core issue of how to define poverty was of fundamental importance.

Third, policies invariably change over time. Yesterday's statements of intent may not be the same as today's, either because of incremental adjustments to earlier decisions, or because of major changes of direction. Also, experience of implementing a decision may feed back into the decision-making process. This is not to say that policies are always changing, but simply that the policy process is dynamic rather than static and that we need to be aware of shifting definitions of issues. Again the way in which a decision that something should be done about poverty led on to a sequence of other decisions is quite evident. But the much more concrete policy making around the right to roam also had implications for related actions. There remain issues about the extent to which the originally designated access land can be extended, and a related issue has now become more prominent in the debate: access to the coast.

Fourth, it is therefore important not to fall into the trap of seeing the policy process as if it exists on a desert island. Most of the policies that are likely to be studied in the modern world are changes to existing policies. Even when they seem to address a new issue or problem they will neverthe-less be entering a crowded policy space, impacting upon and being influenced by other policies. Hence, as Wildavsky puts it, 'any major move sets off a series of changes, many of which ... inevitably transform any problem they were originally supposed to solve' (1979, p. 71). The complex issues around anti-poverty extend more widely to redistributional issues in society as a whole. Someone has to pay for any gains made by the poor. Furthermore, the concentration on raising incomes close to the poverty threshold has implications for the situations of those further up the income 'ladder'. Perhaps most significantly of all, the fact that the incomes of many who secure state benefits are below the officially defined poverty level generates a dilemma for the government, which they find easier to respond to in terms of efforts (often controversial) to get people off benefits than to change the rates of benefit.

Fifth, a development of this point is that much policy decision making is concerned, as Hogwood and Gunn (1984) have stressed, with attempting the difficult task of 'policy termination' or determining 'policy succession' (see also Hogwood and Peters, 1983). In this sense the anti-poverty pledge may be seen as crucial for partial shifts in the benefit system from basic social assistance guarantees to tax credits only available to those in work.

Sixth, the corollary of the last three points is the need to recognise that the study of policy has as one of its main concerns the examination of non-decisions. This is what Heclo and Smith are pointing to (see Box 1.4) in their references to inaction. It has been argued that much political activity is concerned with maintaining the status quo and resisting challenges to the existing allocation of values. Analysis of this activity is a necessary part of the examination of the dynamics of the policy process.

Finally, the definitions cited raise the question of whether policy can be seen as action without decisions. It can be said that a pattern of actions over a period of time constitutes a policy, even if these actions have not been formally sanctioned by a decision. Dery takes this point even further to argue that often we can write of 'policy by the way . . . the by-product of policies that are made and implemented to pursue objectives other than those of the policy in question' (1999, pp. 165–6). In this sense policy may be seen as an outcome, which actors may or may not want to claim as a consequence of purposive activity. Having proclaimed that they had an anti-poverty policy, the government was able to claim credit for reductions of the numbers of those below the poverty line whether or not this was a result of their interventions.

Writers on policy have increasingly turned their attention to the action of lower-level actors, sometimes called 'street-level bureaucrats' (Lipsky, 1980), in order to gain a better understanding of the policy process. It has been suggested that in some circumstances it is at this level in the system that policy is actually made. It would seem to be important to balance a decisional, top-down perspective on policy with an action-oriented, bottom-up perspective. Actions as well as decisions may therefore be said to be the proper focus of policy analysis. The success of the right to roam policy rested heavily upon the actions of local implementers, who might well have varied in respect of the zeal with which they sought to identify potential open access land.

Later we will explore some of the issues surrounding the evolution of policy, noting writers who see the policy process as involving distinctive stages or a cycle and a literature which draws a stronger distinction between policy making and implementation. Such an approach rests very much upon a taken-for-granted version of the Chambers's definition set out above. It may be contrasted with a view that in many respects policy needs to be seen as what happens, rather than as what politicians say will happen.

The view that policies may simply be outcomes of political and bureaucratic processes as opposed to courses 'of action adopted and pursued' leads to two important themes for the study of the policy process: (1) the relationship between policy and politics, and (2) the dominance in much that is said and written about policy of the view that political action is (or should be) purposive.

A deeper exploration of the *Oxford English Dictionary* reveals that the word 'policy' has an interesting history in English. Among usages of the word that are now obsolete are the notions of policy as a 'prudent, expedient or advantageous procedure' and as a 'device, expedient, contrivance ... stratagem, trick'. Parsons points out that Shakespeare used 'policy' in various ways:

> Policy encompassed the arts of political illusion and duplicity. Show, outward appearance and illusions were the stuff of which power was made. Shakespeare employed the terms of Machiavellian philosophy ... Power cannot be sustained purely with force. It needs, in a Machiavellian sense, *policy*: and 'policy sits above conscience', as the bard tells us in *Timon of Athens*. (Parsons, 1995, p. 14)

Furthermore some languages, including French and Italian, do not draw a clear distinction between 'policy' and 'politics'. Richard Jenkins argues that the 'apparently objective distinction between politics and policy is actually likely to be deeply political in its own right; in this sense, the other European languages have definitely got it right' (2007, p. 27). Thus he attacks the 'technocratic illusion of 'rational policy' (ibid.). We have here another aspect of the distinction between descriptive and prescriptive approaches to the policy process. Much prescriptive writing depends upon taking an explicit stance on what policy *should* be, but in the study of the policy process it is important to be aware of the complexity and ambiguity of the concept of policy. Hence, the purpose of this very brief excursion into linguistic history is to emphasise not merely that policy has been seen as a simple and expedient, even duplicitous, ingredient in political strategy but also that this may still be an appropriate way to think of it. We need to ask: what is being said when someone stresses that they have a policy? May they not simply be trying to convince us that they are acting effectively and purposefully? Edelman (1971, 1977, 1988) has devoted considerable attention to the 'symbolic' uses of the concept of policy. Further, even if people can convince us, we still need to ask: what are the implications of their policy? Phenomena like proclaimed 'anti-poverty policy' particularly need unpacking in this way. The notion here that policies are 'claims' takes us back to the simplest of the dictionary definitions, that is, that when we (and by the same token politicians) say we have a 'policy' we are in a sense making a claim to have a 'property'. And, of course, then – as has been shown in respect of anti-poverty policy – such claims may provoke challenges.

It is a particular feature of the modern discourse about policy that it is seen as desirable that politicians should have policies – so that electorates may make choices – and that governments should enact those policies in a systematic way. It was suggested above that the very rise of the study of policy was dominated by that perspective, and that many contributions to policy analysis are motivated by a desire to assist a rational policy-making process. Yet politicians do not necessarily see their roles in this way – power may be more important to them than policy, and power may be used for personal ends rather than to try to solve problems in the way presumed in discussions of policy analysis.

What, then, needs to be understood as we examine the policy process is that, although the concept of policy is vague and elusive, it is nevertheless widely used to suggest a rational process. Readers need to be sceptical about writing which takes it for granted that a policy-making process is organised and has specific goals. It may be desirable that it should be like this, but whether it actually is or not must be an issue for research.

Public policy

The *Oxford English Dictionary* definition of policy quoted above refers to action 'by a government, party, ruler, statesman, etc'. But it goes on to note the more private usage of 'any course of action adopted as advantageous or expedient'. It was noted that individuals sometimes talk of adopting 'policies'. Organisations of all kinds regularly do so. This book is about 'public policy'. Is there anything intrinsically different about the definition arising from the fact that it is the state or state organisations that are seen as the makers of the policy? The answer to that is surely 'no' as far as the simple characteristics of policy are concerned, but 'yes' inasmuch as special claims are made about the legitimacy of state policy and its primacy over other policies. This takes us into two difficulties – one about the nature of the state, the other about the special justifications used for the role of the state as a provider of policies.

The basic definition of the state is as a set of institutions with superordinate power over a specific territory. It can be defined in terms of both the institutions that make it up and the functions these institutions perform. State institutions comprise legislative bodies, including parliamentary assemblies and subordinate law-making institutions; executive bodies, including governmental bureaux and departments of state; and judicial bodies – principally courts of law – with responsibility for enforcing and, through their decisions, developing the law. State institutions are located at various levels – national, regional and local.

However, there are also supra-state institutions which act, to some degree, as superordinate states. These include both international organisations – the United Nations, the World Trade Organisation, etc., which may seek to impose policies on nation states – and organisations like the European Union, which operate quite specifically as supra-national law makers. The very fact that this superordinate power is controversial and is to some degree challenged by nation states offers a reminder of the fact that many states have gone through a process of struggling to achieve a legitimate superordinate role.

The identification of a complex of institutions as making up the state introduces another complication. This is that the state may operate through institutions which have many features that are regarded as private rather than public. In the past, particularly in the early years of state formation, states hired mercenary armies, subcontracted tax collection and delegated law enforcement to local, quasi-autonomous barons. In many of the early nation states the whole apparatus of government was initially no more than an extension of the royal household. In other societies the establishment of a centralised governmental system was very much a partnership between the sovereign and a religious body.

The modern manifestation of the phenomena discussed in the last paragraph has been a deliberate shift to the delegation of what had become accepted as governmental functions. What this implies is a contract between government and a 'private' body to operate all or part of a public service. This is often presented as simply a mechanism for policy 'implementation' with policy making remaining in government hands, but it will be shown later in this book that this policy making/implementation distinction is not easily drawn. The delegation of a major activity, particularly a monopoly activity, tends to involve some shift of control over policy. A related phenomenon is a public/private partnership where resources are drawn from both publicly collected revenues and private sources; policy control is obviously particularly likely to be shared in these circumstances. Finally, in introducing this subject the word 'private' was deliberately put in inverted commas. Like the concept 'public', this is hard to define when there is a complex partnership between different elements, including state ones. Furthermore, 'private' does not necessarily imply a private profit-making organisation – in this respect institutions bringing voluntary organisations into association with the state may be seen as ways of further integrating state and society and increasing democratic participation.

These complications, arising both from the increasing importance of supra-state bodies and from changes within the nation state (sometimes described as the 'hollowing out' of the state – see Milward, Provan and Else, 1993) – have led many contemporary writers to speak of a movement from 'government' to 'governance'. Richards and Smith thus say:

> 'Governance' is a descriptive label that is used to highlight the changing nature of the policy process in recent decades. In particular, it sensitizes us to the ever-increasing variety of terrains and actors involved in the making of public policy. Thus, it demands that we consider all the actors and locations beyond the 'core executive' involved in the policy making process. (Richards and Smith, 2002, p. 2)

That definition perhaps gives insufficient emphasis to the supra-state issues, that is, that the key actors may be outside as well as inside the nation state. There is a debate about the extent to which globalisation and the development of international governing institutions are important for contemporary governance (see Pierre, 2000).

Pierre and Peters explore the use of the term 'governance', suggesting that it is confusing since it is used both to describe empirical phenomena and to explore how those phenomena operate (2000, p. 12). Some writers empha-sise a need for a shift from government to governance because of new realities, while others use this terminology to analyse how processes are actually changing.

Richards and Smith (2002) also portray the way these developments make the policy process more complicated as a shift to a 'postmodern state' (see Box 1.5). This usage has been adopted by others (see, for example, Bogason, 2000). However, readers need to be careful about the expression 'postmodern'. In this context it simply refers to new sources of complexity for the analysis of the policy process, not to the methodological challenge to traditional political science discussed above, except inasmuch as some writers link what they see as increasing complexity to difficulties in developing generalisations.

To sum up then, there is an obvious objection to seeing the public policy process as only about policies delivered and/or enforced by governments. Private actors may do this for governments. But that still leaves a problem about identifying governments in situations of over-lapping supra-national and sub-national governments, even perhaps competing governments. To return to the example of anti-poverty policy: the European Union, the United Kingdom government, the devolved governments in Scotland and Wales and many local authorities all claim to have anti-poverty policies (the actual terms may vary – for example, in the European Union case the issue is often embraced within the notion of 'social exclusion'). Moreover since, as has already been stressed, effective action in this area depends upon many different activities it is implicit that this may involve different governments, whose actions may or may not be consistent with each other.

Box 1.5	The Weberian state vs. the postmodern state

Weberian bureaucratic state	**A postmodern state**
Government	Governance
Hierarchy (Weberian)	Heterarchy (networks, etc.)
Power (1): zero-sum game	Power (1): positive-sum game
Power (2): concentrated	Power (2): diffuse
Elitist	Pluralist
Unitary, centralised, monolithic state	Decentralised, fragmented, hollowed state
Strong, central executive	Segmented executive
Clear lines of accountability	Blurred/fuzzy lines of accountability
State central control	State central steering
Single homogeneous public service ethos	Heterogeneous service cultures

Note: the notions implicit in the idea of the Weberian state are explained on pp. 218–21.

Source: Richards and Smith, 2002, p. 36, Table 2.2. By permission of Oxford University Press.

CONCLUSIONS

This chapter has stressed that this book deals with the description of the policy process. It will proceed from a discussion of the relevance of competing theories of power to the examination of various aspects of the policy process. In doing this it will not attempt to offer prescriptions for policy making and implementation. However, it has been noted that it is impossible to maintain a rigid distinction between description and prescription because so many of those who have written about the policy process have combined the two. Descriptions have been offered in order to justify or criticise the way policies are made and implemented. Some of the most important controversies in policy analysis have been between analysts who differ on what they observe and what they want to observe.

One widely quoted proposition from Karl Marx is: 'The philosophers have only *interpreted* the world in various ways; the point, however, is to *change* it' (1845, in Marx, 1958, vol. 2, p. 405). Marx was clear that he needed to offer a realistic description of the world in order to establish his political programme. The study of policy processes has been dominated by people concerned to show how power is concentrated or how politicians may be called to account or how administrators distort the intentions of their political chiefs and so on. While this account attempts to achieve a measure of neutrality in that respect, it would be foolish of its writer to pretend that his prescriptive biases will not show through from time to time. And in the last resort Marx is right – the justification for trying to understand is a desire to do things better.

Part 2

Policy theories

2 Theories of power and the policy process

SYNOPSIS

This chapter, the first of five exploring theoretical approaches to the analysis of the policy process, deals with the general issues about power in society, of importance for explaining the policy process. It shows how a pluralist perspective on representative government was developed, which saw power as fragmented yet relatively equally distributed. That view of power challenged, and was in turn challenged by, perspectives that saw power as concentrated in unrepresentative hands.

The chapter goes on to examine theories that stress power inequalities, particularly Marxist theories. It shows that these often take a structurally determinist form: seeing state action as determined by the economic order. That leads on to a consideration of forms of structural determinism, the most important of which is globalist theory. Many aspects of this raise questions about the nature of the relationship between social structure and political action. Reasons are suggested for recognising other structural constraints, moving beyond narrow economic determinism to embrace considerations about inequalities introduced by analysts of gender and ethnic inequalities, but avoiding a narrowly determinist approach to them.

Introduction

The study of the policy process is essentially the study of the exercise of power in the making of policy, and cannot therefore disregard underlying questions about the sources and nature of that power. These questions have been the subject of widespread controversy. In that controversy there are two particularly important themes: about the extent to which systems have power distributed in a relatively egalitarian way and about the extent to which power is concentrated or fragmented. Figure 2.1 expresses these as

Figure 2.1   A simplified representation of the main approaches to the policy process

	Power structured	**Power fragmented**
Power distributed relatively equally	1. Representative government in which a unified executive is responsive to popular will	2. Pluralist government in which popular will prevails through competition between groups
Power distributed unequally	3. Government by an unrepresentative elite, or in the grip of external influences	4. Unpredictable and chaotic government, buffeted by multiple pressures

two dimensions. All four positions represent generalised versions of different theoretical positions which will be discussed further here and in the following chapters. The two top positions (1 and 2) show what are often presented as alternative models of democracy, but the concern here is the extent to which power is structured, not with the arguments about what constitutes a democratic system of government. The diagram has been deliberately drawn to involve four quadrants rather than axes, but of course in reality different theories take different positions about the extent of the structuring (or conversely the fragmentation) of power or about the extent to which its distribution is egalitarian. In the process of arguments between theorists, new modified positions are adopted. This means that contemporary exponents of any of these perspectives are likely to take positions closer to the axes than their predecessors. For example, a classical Marxist position would be way out on the margins of quadrant 3 if a continuum was used, and a classical pluralist one would be at an alternative extreme position in quadrant 2, but many modern theorists will be much closer to the axis. A great deal of the literature on power and theories of the state does indeed focus upon the arguments between theorists who are broadly in quadrants 2 and 3. The perspective represented by quadrant 1 has come under considerable attack from all sides, while in quadrant 4 will be found some recent writers who see the political process as exceptionally incoherent (see Chapter 4, pp. 79–82).

Origins of pluralist theory: rescuing the theory of representative democracy

Reference was made in Chapter 1 to the way in which descriptions of the nature of the policy process are often very much linked with prescription of how it should work. That mixture lies right at the centre of the debate about pluralism. Defenders of democratic ideals have had to come to terms with the large and complex institutional structures of states. An Athenian ideal of democracy – that is, one involving direct participation – has been seen to offer an unworkable model. The alternative has been to see democracy as a representative system. A limited number of people participate in the day-today business of government but they may be the representatives of the people as a whole. The early model for this representation was still seen to involve a relatively personal relationship between the elected politician and the comparatively small electorate that elected him (it was almost always 'him' at that stage of the development of political institutions). With the enlargement of the electorate and the increasing need to organise within the legislature, another institution developed to make the connection between elector and elected more indirect – the political party. Schumpeter (1947) defines democracy as 'that institutional arrangement for arriving at political decisions in which individuals acquire the power to decide by means of a competitive struggle for the people's vote' (p. 269).

However, in addition, the processes of government increasingly began to involve other groups, organisations of public interests who might try to influence voting decisions at elections or the legislative programmes of political parties. Once established, moreover, these 'pressure groups' were likely to try to influence the policy process at any stage – negotiating the details of legislation, establishing links to influence the implementation process, monitoring policy outcomes and so on. Thus, it is argued that the pressure groups that have grown up alongside the formal institutions of government have come to play an important direct part in representing the views of specific interests. Talking about the United Kingdom, Beer (1965) notes the development of a collectivist theory of representation legitimising a much greater role for groups than earlier conceptions of representative government. Beer argues that as governments sought to manage the economy they were led to bargain with organised groups of producers, in particular with worker and employer associations. Governments of both political parties sought the consent and cooperation of these associations, and needed their advice, acquiescence and approval. Similarly, the evolution of the welfare state stimulated action by organised groups of consumers, such as tenants, parents and patients. The desire by governments to retain office led them to consult and bargain with these consumer groups in attempts to win support and votes. Beer's thesis has been developed in the work of Richardson and Jordan (1979; see also Jordan and Richardson, 1987), who have argued that the United Kingdom is a 'post-parliamentary democracy' in which policies are developed in negotiation between government agencies and pressure groups organised into policy communities. According to Richardson and Jordan, pressure groups influence public policy from the point at which issues emerge on to the agenda to the stage of implementation.

What has been described here, then, is a replacement of the view of government portrayed in quadrant 1 of Figure 2.1, 'representative democracy', in which an executive responsible to a legislature was seen as making policy on behalf of the people, by a more complex pluralist model (as in quadrant 2). As far as some countries are concerned, particularly the United Kingdom, this perspective on the system is still contested – if not by political scientists then at least by some politicians – inasmuch as claims are made that the government 'in parliament' is still paramount, with a mandate to legislate. The empirical question to which we will need to return, therefore (particularly in Chapter 8), is the extent to which policies emerge directly and untainted by the influence of pressure groups from political manifestos and promises in some societies.

The pluralist school of thought in political science described and charted the developments described above, exploring how political parties really worked and the roles played by pressure groups. But many in this school also argued that this was how a modern democracy should work. Theorists like Truman (1958) and Bentley (1967) gloried in the institutional complexity of their society, contrasting it favourably with less open societies where they perceived much group activity to be limited or even suppressed. Hence pluralism should be seen, in Schwarzmantel's words, 'both as a normative theory and as a way of explaining and analysing the power structure of the liberal-democratic system' (Schwarzmantel, 1994, p. 48). Schwarzmantel amplifies this as follows:

> Because pluralism takes its starting point to be a modern society in which there are different interests, popular power is realised through group activity, the working of political parties and pressure groups or interest groups, each of which represents one of the many interests into which a developed society is split. Pluralist perspectives salute and emphasise this diversity of interest, and like liberal theorists they see this variety as a necessary and positive dimension of social life. (Schwarzmantel, 1994, p. 50)

Clearly, then, opposition to the pluralist perspective can take two forms. One of these is to argue that this is not a satisfactory model for democracy (it is too indirect or it is impossible to realise the 'general will' through such diversity). This is not the concern of this discussion. The other is to argue that pluralism provides a misleadingly optimistic picture of the way power is organised in those societies described as pluralist. This may, of course, then lead back to a critique of the ideal, or, as in the case of the work of the socialist pluralist Herbert Laski (1925), to a set of proposals for strengthening pluralism by countering the biases in the system (see also Cohen and Rogers, 1995, for a modern version of this approach).

Dahl and his followers

Perhaps the most influential exponent of pluralist theory, and certainly a very important one for the study of policy processes, has been Robert Dahl. Dahl (1958) argues that power in many Western industrialised societies is widely distributed among different groups. No group is without power to influence decision making, and, equally, no group is dominant. Any group can ensure that its political preferences and wishes are adopted if it is sufficiently determined. Dahl's main empirical contribution to the study of power is described in Box 2.1.

Box 2.1	Dahl's study of power

Dahl analysed power in the town of New Haven, and reported the study in his book Who Governs? (Dahl, 1961). In asking 'Who governs?' in New Haven, Dahl examined a number of more specific questions, including whether inequalities in resources of power were cumulative or non-cumulative, how important decisions were made, and if the pattern of leadership was oligarchic or pluralistic. He concluded that, in the period from the 1780s to the 1950s, the town had gradually changed from oligarchy to pluralism. No one person or group was dominant.

What Dahl did in New Haven was to select a number of key political issues and examine who won on those issues. One of the criteria used in identifying key issues was that there should be disagreement among two or more actors about what should be done. An issue was key, in other words, if there was open conflict. Analysis of the handling of three key political issues in the 1950s – urban redevelopment, public education and political nominations – revealed a situation in which power was not concentrated in a single group. Rather, because the resources that contributed to power were widely dispersed in the population, power itself was fragmented between different actors. Different interests were active on different issues, and there was no consistent pattern of success or failure. Indeed, one of the points Dahl notes is that interests opposed on one issue might join together on another. The only actor consistently involved was the mayor, but he was by no means dominant. Only a few people had direct influence over key decisions, but most people had indirect influence through the power of the vote.

Dahl and colleagues such as Nelson Polsby (1963) argued that their position is not that power is equally distributed. Rather, pluralist theory argues that the sources of power are unequally though widely distributed among individuals and groups within society. Although all groups and interests do not have the same degree of influence, even the least powerful are able to make their voices heard at some stage in the decision-making process. No individual or group is completely powerless, and the pluralist explanation of this is that the sources of power – like money, information, expertise and so on – are distributed non-cumulatively and no one source is dominant. Essentially, then, in a pluralist political system power is fragmented and diffused, and the basic picture presented by the pluralists is of a political marketplace where what a group achieves depends on its resources and its 'decibel rating'.

There is an issue here, to which we will return in the next three chapters, about the way that pluralist theory deals with the role of government agencies. In much pluralist work the state, as such, is little investigated. While some writers argue that government is neutral and acts essentially as a referee in the struggle between groups (Latham, 1952), the dominant theme in the work of Dahl is that government agencies are one set of pressure groups among many others. According to the latter interpretation, government both pursues its own preferences and responds to demands coming from outside interests.

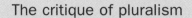

The critique of pluralism

In the discussion in the previous section, the case for the pluralist perspective was made without acknowledging that much of the theoretical work, and particularly Dahl's contribution, was an attack on earlier work which stressed power concentrations. In an article published in 1958 Dahl argues that 'the evidence for a ruling elite, either in the United States or in any specific community, has not yet been properly examined so far as I know' (p. 469). Dahl's article and the criticisms it contains were aimed explicitly at two studies which had claimed to find a ruling elite in the United States. In Dahl's view, there is a need for researchers interested in the power structure to examine neither power reputation nor organisational position, but rather to focus on actual decisions and to explore whether the preferences of the hypothetical ruling elite are adopted over those of other groups. Only in this way is it possible to test the assertion that a ruling elite exists. As the studies summarised in Box 2.2 had not adopted this test, Dahl maintains that the ruling elite model has not been examined properly.

Box 2.2	Studies stressing power concentrations criticised by Dahl

The first study, by Floyd Hunter (1953), examined the distribution of power in Atlanta, Georgia. By analysing the reputation for power of local leaders, Hunter concluded that control rested with a small group of key individuals. The second study, by C. Wright Mills (1956), focused on the United States as a whole, and argued that a power elite drawn from the military, from business corporations and from state agencies governed American society. Dahl contends that the research methods used by Hunter and Mills were not sufficiently rigorous to justify their conclusions. In particular, Hunter's approach of examining the 'reputation' for power of local leaders, and Mills's strategy of identifying those in key positions in large-scale organisations, did not meet the test Dahl proposes should be required of those claiming to find a ruling elite.

Underpinning Dahl's critique is a straightforward definition of power which states: 'A has power over B to the extent that he can get B to do something that B would not otherwise do' (Dahl, 1957, p. 203). This draws attention to the fact that power involves a relationship between political actors. These actors may be individuals, groups or other human aggregates, and Dahl emphasises that power must be studied in cases where there are differences of preferences between actors. Actors whose preferences prevail in conflicts over key political issues are those who exercise power in a political system. It follows that the student of power needs to analyse concrete decisions involving actors pursuing different preferences. Careful study of these decisions is required before the distribution of power can be described adequately.

The problem with this is that it treats the exercise of power as something that is likely to be very visible. Critics of Dahl have pointed out that much power is exercised more covertly and through the subtle cultural processes which influence how people determine their activities and interests. Attempts have been made to deal with this issue by using other words – 'authority', 'influence' and 'domination', for example. Changing the words does not really solve the problem, but it does draw attention to the variety of ways in which power is exercised. Knoke offers a useful approach, using 'influence' to describe what 'occurs when one actor intentionally transmits information to another that alters the latter's actions' (Knoke, 1990, p. 3) and 'domination' where 'one actor controls the behaviour of another actor by offering or withholding some benefit or harm' (ibid., p. 4). This helps to get away from a simple model of the way power is exercised, but it does not deal with the problem of deeply structured power.

Dahl came under attack from Bachrach and Baratz, who, in an article published in 1962, argue that power does not simply involve examining key decisions and actual behaviour. Bachrach and Baratz assert that 'power is also exercised when A devotes his energies to creating or reinforcing social and political values and institutional practices that limit the scope of the political process to public consideration of only those issues which are comparatively innocuous to A' (1962, p. 948). Borrowing a term from Schattschneider, Bachrach and Baratz describe this as 'the mobilisation of bias' (Schattschneider, 1960, p. 71), a process which confines decision making to safe issues. What this suggests is the existence of two faces of power: one operating, as Dahl indicates, at the level of overt conflicts over key issues; the other operating, through a process which Bachrach and Baratz term 'nondecision-making', to suppress conflicts and to prevent them from entering the political process. The implication of Bachrach and Baratz's analysis is that the methodology adopted by researchers such as Dahl is inadequate, or at least partial. A more complete analysis needs to examine what does not happen as well as what does happen, and to unravel the means by which the mobilisation of bias operates to limit the scope of debate.

But what does nondecision-making actually involve? Bachrach and Baratz define nondecision-making as 'the practice of limiting the scope of actual decision-making to "safe" issues by manipulating the dominant community values, myths, and political institutions and procedures' (p. 642). Bachrach and Baratz argue that a nondecision-making situation can be said to exist 'when the dominant values, the accepted rules of the game, the existing power relations among groups, and the instruments of force, singly or in combination, effectively prevent certain grievances from developing into full-fledged issues which call for decisions' (ibid.). In this respect

Bachrach and Baratz distinguish nondecision-making from negative aspects of decision making such as deciding not to act and deciding not to decide. In their view, nondecision-making differs from these other phenomena in that, when nondecision-making occurs, issues do not even become matters for decision. That is, issues remain latent and fail to enter the decision-making process because of the impact of the mobilisation of bias.

Bachrach and Baratz emphasise the means by which vested interests are protected by nondecision-making. In their model of the political process, Bachrach and Baratz argue that demand regulation is not a neutral activity, but rather operates to the disadvantage of persons and groups seeking a reallocation of values. These may be expected to be those who are disadvantaged by the status quo.

The pluralists responded to Bachrach and Baratz's critique by claiming that nondecision-making was unresearchable (Merelman, 1968; Wolfinger, 1971). How, they asked, could nondecisions be studied? On what basis could social scientists investigate issues that did not arise and conflicts that did not emerge? Bachrach and Baratz replied by amplifying and to some extent modifying their position. In their book, *Power and Poverty* published in 1970, they maintain that the second face of power operates to keep grievances covert. A nondecision – defined as 'a decision that results in suppression or thwarting of a latent or manifest challenge to the values or interests of the decision-maker' (p. 44) – can be investigated through the identification of covert grievances and the existence of conflicts that do not enter the political arena. If no grievances or conflicts can be discovered, then a consensus exists and nondecision-making has not occurred (see Box 2.3).

Box 2.3	**Bachrach and Baratz's examples of the different forms that nondecision-making can take**

- The use of force to prevent demands from entering the political process. For example, the terrorisation of civil rights workers in the southern United States.
- The use of power to deter the emergence of issues. The co-optation of groups into decision-making procedures is an illustration.
- Rules or procedures used to deflect unwelcome challenges. Referring issues to committees or commissions for detailed study is one example; labelling demands as unpatriotic or immoral is another.
- Reshaping rules and procedures to block challenges.

Bachrach and Baratz also argue that power may be exercised by anticipated reactions. That is, an actor, A, may be deterred from pursuing his or her preferences because he or she anticipates an unfavourable reaction by another actor, B. Anticipated reactions may operate when a community group fails to mobilise because it anticipates an unfavourable response by decision makers, or when decision makers themselves do not act because they expect opposition from key political actors. Although these examples involve an exercise of power, Bachrach and Baratz note that this 'is not non-decision-making in the strict sense' (1970, p. 46). This last point is explored in a study of air pollution policies in the United States, described in Box 2.4.

Box 2.4	Different approaches to air pollution policy in the United States

Matthew Crenson (1971) compared two cities with respect to action taken to control dirty air. The cities, Gary and East Chicago in Indiana, are adjacent steel towns. While East Chicago passed a law controlling air pollution in 1949, Gary did not act until 1962. Crenson explains the differences between the two cities in terms of the existence in East Chicago of many different steel companies and the domination of Gary by a single corporation, US Steel. The delay in legislating in Gary resulted, Crenson suggests, from the power reputation of US Steel. Although the company was not politically active, the economic power of US Steel, which was exercised through anticipated reactions, was decisive. Thus, indirect influence was important, with political leaders anticipating that US Steel might move from Gary and adversely affect its prosperity if restrictive legislation were passed. In contrast, in East Chicago the fragmentation of the steel industry meant that it was easier for those seeking to control pollution to secure favourable action.

Crenson observes: 'if indirect influence can work for ordinary community residents, then there is no reason why it cannot work for US Steel or General Motors or bank presidents or members of families in the Social Register' (1971, p. 108). Crenson maintains that observable action provides an incomplete guide to the distribution of political power. The comparative method as used in Crenson's study, described in Box 2.4, and the operation of indirect influence through anticipated reactions, illustrate the way in which the nondecision-making thesis can be tested.

The debate about power was taken a stage further by Lukes (1974), who argues that power must be studied in three dimensions. First, there is the exercise of power that occurs in observable, overt conflicts between actors over key issues: the pluralists' approach. Second, there is the exercise of power that occurs in covert conflicts between actors over issues or potential issues: Bachrach and Baratz's method. Third, there is the dimension of power that Lukes adds, which involves the exercise of power to shape people's preferences so that neither overt nor covert conflicts exist. In other words, when the third dimension of power operates, there is latent conflict.

Lukes states that latent conflict exists when there would be a conflict of wants or preferences between those exercising power and those subject to it, were the latter to become aware of their interests. In this context, the definition of power employed by Lukes is that 'A exercises power over B when A affects B in a manner contrary to B's interests' (1974, p. 27). In Lukes's view the existence of a consensus does not indicate that power is not being exercised, for as he argues:

> is it not the supreme and most insidious exercise of power to prevent people, to whatever degree, from having grievances by shaping their per- ceptions, cognitions and preferences in such a way that they accept their role in the existing order of things, either because they can see or imagine no alternative to it, or because they see it as natural and unchangeable, or because they value it as divinely ordained and beneficial? To assume that the absence of grievance equals genuine consensus is simply to rule out the possibility of false or manipulated consensus by definitional fiat. (Lukes, 1974, p. 24).

The difficulty with Lukes's formulation is that it suggests that 'true interests' can readily be identified, and that in this sense the researcher can identify something that the objects of his or her study cannot. While there is some- thing to be said for this when what is at stake are policies (like pollution) that may actually poison us and shorten our lives, there is otherwise a problem about this approach. Hay suggests that one way out of this problem is not to follow Lukes in identifying a third dimension of power but to suggest that there are two uses of power which he describes as 'conduct shaping' and 'context shaping'. He argues about the latter that:

> To define power as context-shaping is to emphasise power relations in which structures, institutions and organisations are shaped by human action in such a way as to alter the parameters of subsequent action. (Hay, 2002, pp. 185–6)

Hay's formulation fits with the way in which Lukes's third dimension of power suggests for Gaventa (1980) and others a 'deep structure' condi- tioning policy options. It also draws attention to identifiable actors in the policy process whose indirect influence is difficult to chart, in particular the mass media.

The shaping of power can be studied, for example through the examin- ation of 'social myths, language, and symbols and how they are manipulated in power processes' (Gaventa, 1980, p. 15). In his elaboration of Lukes's work, Gaventa explores the way in which power is exercised in all three dimensions and stresses the need to see how successful operation on one 'dimension' affects another:

> the total impact of a power relationship is more than the sum of its parts. Power serves to create power. Powerlessness serves to reinforce powerless- ness. Power relationships, once established, are self sustaining. (Gaventa, 1980, p. 256)

Identifying a 'shaping' activity in respect of power can, however, also suggest scope for activities that do not take existing power structures for granted. From the point of view of Marilyn Taylor, exploring the possibilities for the empowerment of disadvantaged communities, it carries a 'more positive message that power is not fixed and immutable and that it is possible to seize opportunities to redefine assumptions and divert the flow of power into new directions' (2003, p. 102).

In an edition of the original book published in 2005, Lukes has reproduced the first edition in its entirety but added chapters that (a) offer some qualifications of his original argument and (b) respond to his critics. He defends his approach but modifies his position in the following way:

> Following others in the 'power debate' it focuses on the *exercise* of power, thereby committing the exercise fallacy': power is a dispositional concept, identifying an ability or capacity, which may or may not be exercised. Secondly, it focuses entirely on the exercise of 'power over – the power of some A over some B and B's condition of dependence on A. Thirdly, it equates such dependence-inducing power with *domination*, assuming that A affects B in a manner contrary to B's interests, thereby neglecting ... the manifold ways in which power over others can be productive, transformative, authoritative and compatible with dignity. Fourthly ... it offers no more than the most perfunctory and questionable account of what such interests are and, moreover treats an actor's interests ... And, finally, it operates (like most of the literature on power) with a reductive and simplistic picture of binary power relations ...
>
> What is clear is that the underlying concept here defined is not 'power' but rather the securing of compliance to domination (pp. 109–10).

The issues about the faces of power have been given considerable attention by theorists who have explored issues about the role of discourses in the power structure. Habermas (1987) has emphasised the importance of communication in securing the acceptance of the unequal distribution of power, and of the policy consequences that flow from it. Foucault (1980) goes further, to see power relations as flowing from taken-for-granted discourses. In his 2005 commentary on his earlier work, Lukes argues that in some respects the work of Foucault and his disciples adopts a deeply deterministic perspective, rendering power unchallengeable in ways which Foucault (at least in his later work) did not espouse. Lukes calls this an 'ultra radical' fourth face of power. If it is not that then it does no more than restate some 'sociological commonplaces' that 'Individuals are socialized: they are oriented to roles and practices that are culturally and socially given; they internalize these and may experience them as freely chosen ...' (p. 97). We return to these issues about the structuring of power later.

What seems to have been given relatively little attention before the development of discourse analysis is the role of the media (newspapers, radio, television). It is surprising that there are not indexed references to the media in either Bachrach and Baratz's book or Lukes's book (including the recent edition). The balance is redressed by writers like Fischer who says that discourse analysis requires attention to be given to 'the distribution of discourse capabilities across society' (2003, p. 80). He then goes on to point out:

> A key aspect of modern society is the role of the media, particularly how it is controlled. As is well documented the media in the United States and Europe is increasingly controlled by smaller numbers of people and the content is more and more influenced by the advertisers who pay for the programmes. This strongly supports the ideological complex with a distinctive consumer-oriented business bias. Moreover much of the news is limited in the perspectives it offers (ibid.)

The pluralists rethink?

It is important to note again that all of the more sophisticated exponents of the pluralist position, and in particular Dahl, do not claim that power is likely to be equally distributed. Their theory has two crucial components: one is that the political stage is accessible to all, the other is that the elites who mount that stage do so largely as the representatives of larger groups of people.

Such statements need to be located in times and places: they cannot be taken to be generalisations about everywhere. They might only be applicable to the places that were studied. Indeed, it is not without relevance that Floyd Hunter's study which Dahl set out to refute was carried out in a city in the south of the United States in the 1950s, whilst Dahl's was carried out in a northern city, host to a major university. Bachrach and Baratz's study was conducted in Baltimore, a 'border' city between North and South where the black population has become very much more politically assertive in the years since that research was carried out. However, much of the debate was carried out in terms which applied it to the whole of the United States, and often beyond.

That is not to belittle the important methodological and conceptual issues that figured in this debate, but it is to stress that the degree of concentration of power and the extent of suppression of interests ought to be regarded as empirical questions not simply resolvable by taking sides in the debate. The contributions from Bachrach and Baratz and from Lukes have raised issues about how power should be studied that cannot be disregarded.

It is interesting to note, therefore, a significant shift in position adopted by some of the key protagonists in the debate on the pluralist side. Dahl and Lindblom's 1953 collaboration *Politics, Economics and Welfare* was revised in 1976 and prefaced with a strong statement on political inequality. Parsons describes it as reflecting on

> many of the failures of policy-making which were becoming evident in the 1970s ... After Vietnam, Watergate, the 'imperial presidency', the

growth of urban decay, and social and economic inequality, Dahl and Lindblom confessed to changing their minds on the question of who governs. (Parsons, 1995, p. 253)

Lindblom's *Politics and Markets* (1977) also offered powerful evidence on the limitations imposed upon pluralist democracy by the working of business and markets.

In terms of the quadrants in Figure 2.1, these qualifications to pluralist theory can be seen as bringing it closer to the perspective embodied in the third quadrant, emphasising inequalities and recognising, as Schattschneider so memorably put it, that 'The flaw in the pluralist heaven is that the heavenly choir sings with a strong upper-class accent' (Schattschneider, 1960, pp. 34–5).

However, there are two rather different ways of conceptualising a revised pluralist position, both of which represent compromises between the pluralist perspective and other perspectives, though they are rather different in character. One is to reconceptualise pluralism as 'democratic elitism' (Bachrach, 1969), which involves a sort of reconciliation between Dahl and the writers like Hunter and Wright Mills whom he originally set out to attack. The other is to take the arguments about the limitations upon pluralism in a much more structuralist direction. The next section addresses the first of these options, leading discussion on towards the stronger statements about power concentration that are associated with Marxism. The latter leads on to the discussion of structuralist perspectives.

The elitist perspective

The classical elitist position was set out at the end of the nineteenth century by an Italian, Gaetano Mosca:

> Among the constant facts and tendencies that are to be found in all political organisms, one is so obvious that it is apparent to the most casual eye. In all societies – from societies that are very meagerly developed and have barely attained the dawnings of civilisation, down to the most advanced and powerful societies – two classes of people appear – a class that rules and a class that is ruled. The first class, always the less numerous, performs all political functions, monopolises power and enjoys the advantages that power brings, whereas the second, the more numerous class, is directed and controlled by the first, in a manner that is now more or less legal, now more or less arbitrary and violent. (Mosca, 1939, p. 50; original publication in Italian, 1896)

The classical elitist thesis maintains that political elites achieve their position in a number of ways: through revolutionary overthrow, military conquest, the control of water power (a key resource in oriental societies: see Wittfogel, 1963), or the command of economic resources. It is a perspective that most obviously applies to pre-democratic states. However, it may be argued that in the modern state the position of elites is related to the development of large-scale organisations in many areas of life, with the result that there are different kinds of elites, not just those holding formal political power. Bottomore makes a distinction between the political *elite*, which is made up of 'those individuals who actually exercise power in a society at any given time' and which 'will include members of the government and of the high administration, military leaders, and, in some cases, politically influential families of an aristocracy or royal house and leaders of powerful economic enterprises', and the political *class*, comprising the political elite but also leaders of political parties in opposition, trade union leaders, businessmen and politically active intellectuals (1966, pp. 14–15). Defined in this way, the political elite is composed of bureaucratic, military, aristocratic and business elites, while the political class is composed of the political elite together with elites from other areas of social life. What this suggests is that elite power may be based on a variety of sources: the occupation of formal office, wealth, technical expertise, knowledge and so on. To a certain extent, these resources may be cumulative, but power is not solely dependent on any one resource.

In the twentieth century, the growth of large firms, the establishment of trade unions, and the development of political parties – all institutions in which effective power is likely to rest with an oligarchic leadership – underline the significance of organisational control and institutional position as key political resources. Of particular importance in this context was the creation of bureaucratic systems of administration to carry out the increasing responsibilities taken on by the state from the nineteenth century onwards. As Weber (1947) notes, bureaucracies have both positive and negative aspects: positive, in that they offer an efficient way of organising administration; negative, because they open up the possibility of power being vested in officials who are accountable neither to the public nor to politicians. The growth of bureaucracies may, in Weber's view, lead to control of the economy by bureaucrats. In this line of argument, elite theory draws attention to the need to look at the state itself. This theme has been echoed by various writers who have seen the modern state as a technocracy (Ellul, 1964; Meynaud, 1965). We will also see other variants on this theme in theories stressing the importance of policy communities in Chapter 3 and institutions in Chapter 4, and in some aspects of the rational choice theory explored in Chapter 5.

C. Wright Mills (1956) draws attention to institutional position as a source of power, and suggests that the American political system is dominated by a power elite occupying key positions in government, business corporations and the military. The overlap and connection between the leaders of these institutions helps to create a relatively coherent power elite. Reference has already been made to Mills' book and to the work of Hunter on local power. But can a realistic distinction be drawn between the sort of modified pluralist perspective set out in the last section and the elitist one? The elitist case is not helped by the fact that many alternative sources of elite power have been suggested. This tends to reinforce the pluralist case, and may be seen as the basis of the theory of 'democratic elitism' mentioned above. That theory argues that regular elections based on competition between the leaders of political parties, together with participation by pressure group elites in between elections, and interaction between these elites and the bureaucratic elites, are the ways in which democracy operates in the modern state. The fact that different elites operate in different issue areas is a protection against domination by one group.

There is a problem with sustaining a simple elite theory position inasmuch as there are difficulties in specifying the mechanisms by which power is seized and the techniques used to hold on to it. One now very unfashionable elite theorist, Pareto, who worked in Italy around the same time as Mosca, offered an answer to that question inasmuch as he saw elite domination as based upon the special qualities possessed by the elite (Pareto, 1966). In this respect it is relevant to bear in mind that Pareto belonged to a generation that attached more importance to immutable genetic characteristics than do most modern theorists. But even he posited a kind of pluralist process by which the 'circulation of elites' occurs as old elites weaken and new ones arise.

There are, however, two ways in which the debate about how power is exercised needs to be taken further. One, as indicated above, is to bypass the question about how power is acquired but to argue that once that has happened then the institutions of the state offer the means for an elite to perpetuate its power. The detailed examination of this will have to await Chapter 4. The other approach to this question is to emphasise the importance of economic power. Where it does this, elite theory begins to merge with another very important approach to the study of power, Marxist theory, to the extent that some of the key exponents of the position set out above (for example, Wright Mills) are only distinguishable from Marxists by their comparative reluctance to quote Marx in their support. The next section therefore picks up on those aspects of Marxist theory that concentrate on the role of individual actors in the pursuit of power.

Elite theory, in both classical and modern guises, represents an important alternative to pluralism. Yet, while some writers have attempted to reconcile elitism and pluralist democracy, others have used the findings of elitist studies to argue that the power elite is but a ruling class by another name. That is, it is suggested that institutions may well be run by minority groups, but that these groups come from similar social backgrounds and are therefore exercising power in the interests of a dominant group.

It must be noted that the bridging concept between elitism and Marxism is the idea of a 'ruling class'. However, until recently this class analysis has led to a disregard of the extent to which other forms of social stratification, particularly stratification in terms of gender and ethnicity, may be significant for the distribution of power. Now, both within feminist literature and in the analysis of racism, a lively debate has developed about the extent to which these other forms of stratification may operate independently of, or in association with, class divisions, to structure and bias the policy process. We will return to this later.

Marxism

When the original book from which this version has developed was published (Ham and Hill, 1984) Marxist theory was much more influential than it is today; Karl Marx's own propositions had been developed by a wide variety of theorists. One of those with things to say particularly pertinent for the examination of the policy process was Ralph Miliband. In his book *The State in Capitalist Society* (1969), Miliband takes as his starting point not the political process itself but the form of economic organisation or the mode of production. In advanced Western industrialised societies the capitalist mode of production dominates, giving rise to two major social classes – the bourgeoisie and the proletariat. Miliband's analysis of the distribution of income and wealth, and changes in this distribution over time, demonstrates the continued concentration of wealth in a small section of the population. The question Miliband then asks is whether this economically dominant class exercises decisive political power. In other words, he explores the relationship between economic power and political power.

Taking their cue from Karl Marx, writers like Miliband argue that the state is not a neutral agent, but rather is an instrument for class domination. Marx expressed this view in the *Communist Manifesto*, where he wrote that 'The executive of the modern state is but a committee for managing the common affairs of the whole bourgeoisie' (quoted in McLellan, 1971, p. 192). Miliband suggests three reasons why the state is an instrument of bourgeois domination in capitalist society. First, there is the similarity in social background between the bourgeoisie and members of the state elite – that is, those who occupy senior positions in government, the civil service, the military, the judiciary and other state institutions. Second, there is the power that the bourgeoisie is able to exercise as a pressure group through personal contacts and networks and through the associations representing business and industry. Third, there is the constraint placed on the state by the objective power of capital. In these ways, Miliband contends, the state acts as an instrument which serves the long-term interests of the whole bourgeoisie.

Marxism is today seen, above all, as the ideology that sustained the Soviet empire until its collapse and – increasingly unconvincingly – is argued to continue to hold sway in China. But it must be remembered that Marx's original purpose was to analyse the system of economic power dominant within capitalist societies and to show how that system contained within it the seeds of its own downfall. The fact that it has not fallen in the way Marx predicted does not necessarily invalidate the whole of his analysis, particularly those parts relating to the significance of ownership or control of the means of production for power within the state. It should be added that continuing to give attention to that argument does not necessarily imply an acceptance of the model of ownership and control over economic enterprise, involving primarily individual entrepreneurship, that prevailed in Marx's time. In the modern world key controllers may well not be, formally speaking, the owners of economic enterprises.

The original theory set out by Karl Marx, though complicated and stated in rather different ways at different times in his life, postulated a theory of history in which the means of production is a dominant and determining force. The 'executive of the modern state' was a committee to manage the 'affairs of the whole bourgeoisie' not because the latter was able to control it, but because it could be nothing else so long as society remained capitalist. In other words, mainstream Marxist theory takes the issues about the determination of policy in a very different direction from the concerns of this chapter so far, to suggest that a power *structure* determined by the means of production is of dominant importance.

Structuralist aspects of the Marxist perspective

This section will deal fairly briefly with Marxist structuralism since direct use of this form of analysis has declined significantly in recent years. Yet it is worth a little attention as an alternative approach to the explanation of unequal power in the policy process, seeing what may be called 'economic imperatives' as a crucial influence, a view that we will then see echoed by some theorists who would not see themselves as Marxists.

According to classical Marxist theory, the social structure of a capitalist society is essentially a 'class structure'. The two classes that confront each other in a capitalist society (at least in the last resort) are the bourgeoisie (the owners of the means of production) and the proletariat (who work for the bourgeoisie). Some of Marx's work deals with other classes, but his logic indicates that they will eventually be sucked into the fundamental class struggle. That struggle will then intensify, as the nature of competitive production forces the bourgeoisie to systematically reduce the rewards going to the proletariat. This process of 'immiseration' will eventually lead the increasingly unified proletariat to rise up to overthrow the bourgeoisie. That revolution will lead to the replacement of capitalism by socialism, just as earlier the logic of industrial change led capitalism to replace feudalism. In other words, at the core of classical Marxist theory there is an essentially determinist argument. Our position in relation to the means of production determines our long-run political interests. Our fate is set by the working out of that dialectic. Notwithstanding that position, Marx urged the proletariat to organise politically, to work towards the ultimate revolution. In that sense there is a contradiction at the core of classical Marxism, which has left it open for some to reinterpret the theory in a very much less deterministic way.

Our concern here is with the role of the state in the determinist model. The idea, set out above, of the state as 'the executive committee of the bourgeoisie' is, in this interpretation, the only thing it can be. Its role is a supportive and subsidiary one in relation to capitalism. In his determinist 'mood' Marx was not very interested in the role of the state. The problem is that in his more activist 'mood' he urged the organisations of the proletariat to mobilise to try to take over the state. This engendered an argument within Marxism about the purpose of such activity. Was it just to prepare for, or practise for, or advance, the revolution, since the state could neither be transformed nor transform capitalism? Or was there a peaceful road to revolution by way of securing control over the state? It was this alternative that engendered a social democratic form of Marxism which the revolutionary followers of Marx repudiated.

Hence, while generating an elaborate controversy about the state within Marxist ranks (which became increasingly complicated as the role of the state changed in the twentieth century in ways that did not seem to accord with Marxist predictions), the classical Marxist position is to suggest that the capitalist state's main function is to assist the process of capital accumulation. This means creating conditions in which capitalists are able to promote the production of profit. The state is seen as acting to maintain order and control within society.

Twentieth-century Marxist theory has elaborated this in a variety of ways, partly to explain phenomena that Marx had not expected to occur. In specific terms, assisting accumulation means providing physical resources such as roads and industrial sites, while maintaining order is carried out both through repressive mechanisms like the police and through agencies such as schools, which perform an important legitimation function. The accumulation process is further assisted through state intervention in the provision of services such as housing and health to groups in the working population. One of the functions of these services is to reduce the cost of labour power to capital and to keep the workforce healthy.

O'Connor (1973) classifies these different forms of state expenditure as social investment, social consumption and social expenses. Social investment increases labour productivity through the provision, for example, of infrastructure and aid to industry; social consumption lowers the cost of reproducing labour power as, for example, in the provision of social insurance; and social expenses serve to maintain social harmony. In practice, nearly all interventions by the state perform more than one of these functions.

O'Connor's analysis suggests that state expenditure serves the interest of monopoly capital, and that the state is run by a class-conscious political directorate acting on behalf of monopoly capitalist class interests. In a similar vein, Gough (1979) makes use of O'Connor's typology to show how the modern welfare state serves the long-term interests of the capitalist class.

The key point overall is that Marxist theory tends to take a stance which treats state action as to a considerable extent constrained and *determined* by economic institutions. It will be suggested below that this simple proposition is restated today by many who would certainly not wish to be portrayed as Marxists.

Other structuralist perspectives

Thompson puts the underlying theoretical issue about the relationship between explanations of social action that emphasise actions and those that emphasise structure as follows:

> The problem of the relation between the individual and society, or between action and social structure, lies at the heart of social theory and the philosophy of social science. In the writings of most major theorists ... this problem is raised and allegedly resolved in one way or another. Such resolutions generally amount to the accentuation of one term at the expense of the other ... the problem is not so much resolved as dissolved. (Thompson, 1989, p. 56)

Structuralist theories that see political action as determined by powerful forces outside human control have a long history in the social sciences. Writers have postulated distinct patterns of human evolution or a determinist approach to history which have challenged the view that individuals have the capacity to determine their own social and political institutions. Theories of this kind have taken forms that suggest a need to accept the status quo, and/or to regard political choices as predetermined by demographic, social and economic factors. They have also come in 'critical' forms – concerned to analyse what are seen as powerful constraints upon human action which have to be attacked in order to achieve fundamental change. That contrast draws attention to the problem within much of this theory: that in dealing with the factors that determine social stability in changing societies it has to try to specify conditions under which change can occur. Its proponents have, particularly in its critical forms, to try to answer questions about the conditions under which actions to effect social change may be appropriate.

Structuralist theory has, in short, to take a stance on the relationship between structure and action. The former determines the latter, yet the latter feeds back to alter the former. All but the most simplistic forms of structural theory – with which we need not bother ourselves because they are so unrealistic – acknowledge some measure of scope for action to secure change. Further distinctions can be made between different kinds of structural theory about the extent to which they are totally determinist. These differences particularly concern the extent to which there are strong evolutionary forces in societies.

Related to this issue of variations in the extent to which theories are determinist is the issue of what is seen as the source of that determinism – demography, technological evolution and economic forces being perhaps the most widely identified sources. A sort of determinism which lies at the very weakest end of structural theory sees the institutional and ideological configurations that have been established as imposing strong constraints upon future actions.

Hence, structuralist Marxism sits alongside other structuralist perspectives. In sociology 'structure functionalist theory' has been influential but is now seen as fairly dated. Yet it is worth a brief mention (a) because of the way in which it poses questions about structural influences that – at least when postulated in a very weak form – still need attention, and (b) because as a theoretical perspective it occupies an important place in relation to Marxism as a set of propositions which partly support and partly offer a contradiction of that perspective.

Structural functionalism involves a fusion in sociological theory between propositions from early anthropological studies – which suggested that social institutions reinforce each other in ways which support the status quo in allegedly 'static' societies – and propositions from social Darwinism, which traced processes of social evolution. Sociologists in this tradition in the United States or Western Europe saw their own societies as 'progressing', with their institutions adapting in response to evolving social needs. Where Marxists saw an evolutionary process leading towards social crisis, these theorists saw a progressive adaptation occurring.

What this perspective implied for political choices – and thus for the policy process – was a series of imperatives to which the political system would respond. The evolutionary element in this perspective led some scholars to proclaim that their own societies had reached 'the end of ideology' (Bell, 1960) – in which political battles would be muted by a common acceptance of the benefits of the status quo – and less 'developed' societies would follow to evolve along the same progressive path. Economic development is seen as the generator of a wide range of social changes (Kerr, 1973). In addition to its contribution to the growth of the standard of living it is a source of urban development. These changes are then held to have influenced patterns of social behaviour, including choices about marriage and family size.

Comparative studies have thus aimed to explain the emergence of public policies – particularly social policy – by correlating their incidence with the phenomena of economic growth, industrialisation, urbanisation and demographic change linked together in a package of ingredients of 'modernisation' (Hofferbert, 1974; Wilensky, 1975).

Some versions of the modernisation thesis go beyond these issues to try to identify a postmodernist or a post-industrial order with its own distinctive policies. We will find some traces of this approach later in the book when we examine organisational arrangements and find that there are suggestions that we are now in a postmodernist, or more specifically post-Fordist, era in which old bureaucratic and hierarchical models for the organisation of industrial and administrative life are giving way to new forms. Clearly, technological changes – the development of computers and other electronic control devices – facilitate the development of these new forms of organisation. Readers should be suspicious of arguments about these phenomena which come in deterministic forms, however. It is one thing to say that people are trying new approaches to the organisation of complex activities, aided by new technology, but quite another to dress this up in a technologically determinist form which seems to deny any role for human choice.

The question is: have we here a set of determinist theories suggesting that public policy developments can be read off from these economic and social developments? Or are these theories merely making the point that there is

(a) a general association between economic growth and state growth across the broad band of prosperous nations in the past, together with (perhaps)

(b) a certain critical threshold that nations have to pass before significant levels of public services, imposing high costs on the nation, become feasible in developing societies, and

(c) further – picking up on the last part of this section – that there is a later generation of technological developments which are further transforming some of the record keeping and surveillance options open to governments?

To go further would be to pay too little attention to the choices made by actors or to variations in response from place to place (Ashford, 1986).

Economic determinism without Marxism

Perspectives can be identified on economic determinism which either diverge so far from classical Marxism that it is inappropriate to call them Marxist, or which involve propositions about the dominance of economic considerations in the policy process of a kind that have no foundations in Marxist theory. The most important of these propositions are those that stress the significance of 'global' economic forces. These will be discussed separately following this comparatively brief look at other theories that embody forms of economic determinism.

There is a perspective which suggests that there is built into the politics of any but the poorest societies a set of concerns about the need for advances in the standard of living that any politicians will disregard at their peril. Related to this – particularly since the collapse of communism – is the view that only capitalist economic institutions can provide those advances. This perspective is obviously advanced in philosophical works which celebrate capitalist economic institutions (Hayek, 1944, 1960), and is more generally taken for granted in much contemporary political analysis. The pronouncement by the Chinese leader Deng Xiaoping – to justify his flirtations with capitalism – that it does not matter what colour the cat is so long as it can catch mice (Shambaugh, 1995, p. 88), perhaps sums up this post-Marxist consensus.

It is interesting to note how implicit economic determinism crops up in the ranks of thinkers from all parts of the ideological spectrum. Arguably, there is a thread of thinking from the 'Right' which is very like Marxist structuralism, but without any theory of change or revolution. This is the view that there has been a process of evolution to the ideal economic order (capitalism) and the ideal political order (representative democracy) and that the kind of 'directional history' embodied in the theories of Hegel and Marx has come to an end (Fukuyama, 1992). Such a perspective suggests that:

> All countries undergoing economic modernisation must increasingly resemble one another: they must unify nationally on the basis of a centralized state, urbanize, replace traditional forms of social organisation like tribe, sect and family with economically rational ones based on function and efficiency, and provide for the universal education of their citizens ... the logic of modern natural science would seem to dictate a universal evolution in the direction of capitalism. (Fukuyama, 1992, pp. xiv–xv)

Fukuyama explores this theme with a caution not evident in the quotation, but he does in many respects advance a 1990s version of Bell's earlier 'end of ideology' thesis (see p. 43).

More pragmatic versions of this perspective involve taken-for-granted assumptions about the need to limit public expenditure or taxation – with the implicit consequences of this for other policies – in the interests of the maintenance of the capitalist economy. Clearly there is here a kind of structuralist perspective, specifying a distinct limit to the extent to which politicians can disregard economic forces.

Globalism

A closely related kind of determinist theory, deserving of a section of its own because of the wide attention it is given, is globalism. This sees a sequence of worldwide economic developments as of determining importance for contemporary policy making. Globalist theory has developed on a massive scale, and in the process branched in many directions. It embodies various themes – the development of global financial markets, the cross-national diffusion of technology, the emergence of transnational or global corporations (and the increasing economic pressure upon large corporations to 'think globally') and the emergence of global cultural flows. It is given particular relevance for the policy process by policy problems – pollution, conflicts over scarce resources, poorly regulated international trading, movements of people as economic migrants and refugees – that have global implications. All these trends offer challenges to state autonomy and stimulate new political formations beyond the nation state. More cautious statements on this topic stress the extent to which this is in some respects a gradual change, acknowledge that complex supra-national economic developments have a long history and recognise that the speed of modern communications heightens awareness of the phenomenon.

There are variants of globalism that are close to classical Marxism, in that they see the processes described by Marx as now taking place on a world scale (Wallerstein, 1979; Cox, 1987). This is a view that George and Wilding describe as 'Marxissant', with 'the fundamental premise that the driving logic of capitalism for constantly increased profitability has been the major force behind globalisation' (2002, p. 7). This is a view that is not particularly new: it was set out originally by Lenin in 1917. It suggests that there is a complicated working through of the postulated conflict between capitalists and proletariat across the world, postponing the eventual crisis and raising difficult tactical problems for international Marxists who have to face difficulties in getting the proletariat to think globally rather than to accept national interpretations of exploitation.

Within Marxist thinking there are distinctions to be found between those who see capitalism as an increasingly international phenomenon and those who argue that companies are rather more supra-national than global (that is, they spread out from a national base) and that their power is not necessarily an external imposition upon nation states but something established within them (see Panitch, 1994). As Panitch puts it in a rhetorical question:

> Is it really to international finance that governments in London or Ottawa are accountable when they prepare their budgets? Or are they accountable to the City of London or to Bay Street? (Panitch, 1994, p. 74)

Alternatively, globalist theory may accept that capitalist economic relationships are increasingly organised on a world scale but not set out that view in Marxist terms. The question that emerges for this discussion is then to what extent a globalist position is really a determinist one. Is globalist theory saying that here is a series of structural developments about which politicians can do little? Or is it merely saying that the issues about the power of economic interests – which even pluralist writers like Lindblom have come to accept as critical for the policy process – need to be analysed in supra-national terms? In other words, this is not so much a determinist point of view as one which emphasises *either* that national policy makers must increasingly be able to deal with interests organised outside their country *or* that effective policy processes need to be supra-national too (Hirst and Thompson, 1992). The latter position may lead to a pessimistic stance on the feasibility of achieving solutions to political problems in the face of institutional complexity, but it is not ultimately a determinist stance.

This is certainly the position reached by analysts of issues about pollution policy (see, for example, Hurrell and Kingsbury, 1992), energy policy (see Yergin, 1991) and monetary policy (Walter, 1993).

Hay offers a useful alternative slant on the determinist element in the globalist perspective arguing that:

> Whether the globalist thesis is 'true' or not may matter far less than whether it is *deemed* to be true – or, quite possibly, just useful – by those employing it. (Hay, 2002, p. 258)

Hence, Hay argues that decision makers may believe either that there is no alternative but to respond to perceived global economic forces, or that globalisation 'may provide a most convenient alibi, allowing politicians to escape the responsibility they would otherwise bear for reforms which might otherwise be rather difficult to legitimate' (ibid., p. 259). That puts a very interesting slant on the structure/action relationship, seeing decision makers as active 'agents' within structures. But those structures are not all determining, and how those structures are perceived or 'used' may be crucial.

This observation on globalism leads to two others. First, it is obviously not a determinist approach in itself to pay attention to the extent to which pressures upon policy decisions come from sources outside the nation state. In that sense it is quite feasible to adopt a pluralist analysis (whether modified or not by concerns about power concentrations), taking into account the extent to which interest groups organised outside the nation state or across several nation states have an impact upon policy in any specific state. Second, if governments are more aware of international developments then this may affect how they respond to economic interests within their own country. Hence, as Pierre and Peters put it:

> The need to develop closer links ... with private industry is driven by a strategy to maintain or increase the international competitiveness of the domestic industry. (Pierre and Peters, 2000, p. 60)

Other variants of structuralism

Some of the structuralist arguments originating from feminism link very closely with Marxist theory. For some writers, gender divisions in society are seen as further ways in which the proletariat are divided and controlled. The growth of a female workforce which is poorly paid and insecure is seen as a particularly insidious development in the 'reserve army of labour' that keeps the proletariat cheap and weak (Barrett, 1980).

Other feminist theory focuses rather more upon male domination of economic and political institutions *per se*, not seeing it in the Marxist context of class divisions (Millet, 1970; Delphy, 1984). Inasmuch as this perspective is structuralist in nature, it opens up a very important issue with ramifications beyond the relations between the genders. What is involved is an argument that there is a range of institutions – the family, the church, the economy, the state – that are linked together in a structure that has a powerfully determining impact upon what gets on the agenda. We are back here with Lukes's third face of power. This structure influences culture, discourse and behaviour, defining the political agenda. As such it *defines out* many female concerns. Schwarzmantel makes a direct parallel with Marxism using the concept of 'deep structure':

> Both feminism and Marxism take a common stance, in that both are concerned to reveal . . . a 'deep structure' or power dimension which exists in the liberal-democratic state and the society that surrounds it, and in other forms of state and society as well. The power dimension is in both cases seen as a 'fault line' or basic division which is to some extent hidden from view. (Schwarzmantel, 1994, p. 115)

Rhetorics of equality are seen as masking real inequalities of power. An ideology of male domination is seen as embodied in a division between the 'public' sphere and the 'private' sphere. The public sphere for long excluded women, whilst, in the private sphere, behaviour within the household was regarded as outside the realm of political interference. This has had the effect of keeping issues about domineering behaviour by men within the household off the policy agenda.

Schwarzmantel perhaps takes the parallels between feminist theory and Marxist theory too far. What the general feminist position brings into the discussion is a good example of how policy processes have been structured with the effect that they support the status quo and suppress certain issues in the way described by Lukes. They take us into a very much looser and more general approach to the way in which policy processes are structured.

Before we look at that it is important to recognise that the arguments deployed here also apply to ethnic divisions. The equivalent of radical feminism's development of Marxist theory is a body of work that stresses the way ethnic divisions function to keep the proletariat divided (Solomos *et al.*, 1982). The term 'ethnicity' needs to be interpreted widely here – going far beyond recognised biological differences (which are in any case ambiguous and contestable) to comprise national, linguistic, cultural and religious divisions which create or are used to create divisions of an 'ethnic' kind. In this case there is a connection back, too, to the issues about globalism. There are economic differences associated with divisions between countries, where the 'national interest' is invoked to both attack and defend inequalities. The world 'division of labour' has ethnic dimensions. Migration has then further complicated this by contributing to the reproduction of these divisions within countries (Cohen, 1987).

Just as there is a conflict within feminist theory between those who link gender and class issues and those who focus primarily on gender, so in the analysis of ethnic divisions there are those whose analyses are embedded in

Marxist theory and those who see that perspective as too limiting for a satisfactory analysis of the exploitation of ethnic groups (Rex, 1986). In the analysis of ethnic divisions, as in the exploration of gender divisions, there is a need to analyse structural constraints upon political action in historical terms, examining both the establishment of institutions which privileged some and disadvantaged others, and the development of ideologies which set out to justify inequalities. In the case of ethnicity, the establishment and maintenance of cohesive nation states involves the deployment of rules to define who do and who do not belong, and ideologies to justify those rules.

In this section, as in the last, it is open to question whether the phenomena being explored should be described as 'structural'. What is being described are divisions within societies, which are maintained and reinforced in various ways. It is implicit in feminist theory and in attacks upon ethnic divisions that there is a politics of challenge to these divisions. Where the structuralism comes in is in regarding challenging such divisions as a difficult political task. It is a task, moreover, where policy processes have to involve not just changing distributive or regulatory rules but also challenging the ideologies that have underpinned those rules. Here we are back to the point made by Hay in relation to globalism, that we have here ideas about society and its culture – discourses, if you like (and here the postmodernist approach discussed on pp. 11–12 is very relevant) – that sustain patterns of power.

It is very important to recognise how the perspective set out in the last paragraph embodies cultural concepts and ideologies within 'structural' influences. With this in mind we can go back to the objection to Lukes' suggestion that the third face of power is in evidence when people are seen to act in ways that conflict with their true interest, that this involves an 'Olympian' condescension on the part of the scholar who claims to know better than the actors what their interests are. If a policy change with implications for the reduction of some disadvantage is rejected by many who would gain from it, we cannot necessarily know whether this is because of 'false consciousness' or of a consciousness which for some reason has not been articulated because the disadvantaged know, or assume, that efforts to secure it would in the end be frustrated (or worse). There is then a need to look more widely at the things that seem to help us explain events if we look (as has been characteristics of work inspired by Foucault) into the cultural context of the arguments, the forms that arguments take, the uses made of ways (education, media presentations etc.) that structure it and so on. In such circumstances we do not need to impute particular forms of false consciousness.

Faced with a policy issue on which a disadvantaged group has something specific to gain, the counter-argument may come from elite groups who deploy a wide and general argument as to why they should *instead* be supported. This may be seen as the use of a general 'conservative' ideology. There are three obvious forms of this:

- Traditional conservatism – we are the best guardians of society.

- Neo-conservatism – we can protect you from big dangers out there.
- Neo-liberalism – the maintenance of market arrangements are the least worst ways of dealing with social problems.

Opposed to these are ideas for change advocated by 'radical' groups whom so-called 'false conscious' people may recognise good reasons to distrust. After all, the history of the twentieth century is littered with false dawns, false prophets and false expectations offered by socialist, radical, populist etc. movements. As Tilly notes, in one item in a check list of answers to the question 'why do people not rebel' this may be: 'As a result of mystification, repression, or the sheer unavailability of alternative ideological frames . . .' (1991, p. 594). He might have added words like 'convincing' or 'acceptable' before 'alternative' there.

This discussion of structural determinants of policy processes has moved from theories which seem to be strongly determinist – structural function-alism and classical Marxism – to perspectives that many would not call structuralist at all since they merely spell out factors which are likely to have a strong influence on political choices. Parsons (1995, pp. 608–9) argues that some of these may simply be incorporated into accepted constraints:

> The distinction between politics and economy and society . . . needs to be revised to take account of the argument that the world of 'facts' and social and economic forces is not simply 'out there'.

He goes on:

> it may well be that external environments are better understood as mirrors or projections of the values, beliefs and assumptions which frame the internal policy-making process.

That is, however, perhaps to make too little of some powerful forces at work. The case for a discussion of structuralist theory lies not primarily in a need to outline what are in many respects rather over-deterministic theories, but in a need to stress that there is running through any policy process a series of strong biases or influences on action. This may be described as an influential 'deep structure' (Schwarzmantel, 1994) or in terms of Lukes' 'third face of power' or Hay's 'context-shaping power' (see p. 34). Social change – in which the policy process plays an important part – involves a dynamic in which structure influences action and is at the same time altered by that action.

It has been shown that structural perspectives do not necessarily put 'class interests' and 'economic forces' as the only kinds of determining agents. Implicit in the concept of structure is a system which gives domi-nance to a range of powerful groups (see Degeling and Colebatch, 1984). Such groups will include professional and bureaucratic elites, males, specific ethnic, religious, linguistic groups, and so on. This dominance is given struc-tural form by customary practices and modes of organisation. It may well be built into language, and manifested symbolically in a variety of ways.

Structures are not fixed and immutable. In giving attention here to formalised political institutions, it must not be forgotten that they vary considerably in strength and in the extent to which they are formalised. A distinction may perhaps be drawn between structures and institutions, where the latter are seen as 'regularized practices *structured* by rules and resources deeply layered in time and space' (Thompson, 1989, p. 61). They are changed by action, and some actions may be specifically directed at trying to change structures. The prevailing order is continually being renegotiated. This is clearly not an easy process, but in addressing the determinants of decision making it is one that must not be entirely disregarded (this sort of approach to the relationship between structure and action is explored in the sociological writings of Giddens, 1976, 1984). In this context the word that has become widely used in relation to action is 'agency', expressing the extent to which people are able to operate autonomously.

CONCLUSIONS

This long chapter started by outlining a simple way to classify discussions of power in terms of four quadrants illustrating arguments about the extent to which it is structured and the extent to which it is distributed equally. It rather quickly dismissed the 'representative government' model (Figure 2.1, quadrant 1) which sees power as, broadly speaking, structured but not unequally distributed.

The discussion showed that the main arguments seem to have been between pluralists who see power as fragmented but relatively evenly distributed, and a variety of theorists who identify ways in which it is concentrated in the hands of small groups, often described as elites. Identifying Marxism as, at least historically, the most important version of the latter theory, it went on to explore the way in which Marxists have been split between those who identify capitalists as actors in their own interests and those who adopt a more structuralist explanation of the (for them temporary) dominance of capitalism.

Interestingly, then, it is this structuralist version of Marxism that tends to continue to exert influence, detached from its origins in an evolutionary theory, in the variety of ways in which economics is seen as exerting a deterministic influence upon the policy process. The most important modern form of this determinism is globalist theory.

The chapter ended by looking at challenges to determinism, seeing the extent to which it involves discourses used to support the existing distribution of power or to enhance the power of specific interests. In the end it needs to be conceded that actions occur within structures, and are influenced by those structures, but that what this implies in practice is very complex. The next three chapters pick up this theme in different ways, since much of the theoretical work considered is concerned with the relationship between structure and action.

3

From pluralism to networks

SYNOPSIS

Chapter 2 showed how classical pluralist theory came under attack both from those who emphasised power inequalities and from those who saw the system of power as in various respects structured. In this chapter, particular attention will be given to approaches to the modification of pluralism which accepted the force of these criticisms without at the same time accepting either the very unitary vision of much Marxist work or going very deeply into the sources of structuration. The chapter will start with a consideration of a body of theory which can be seen as in many respects a precursor of network theory, the theory of corporatism. While it will be argued that much of this theory has been discredited, it is important to look at it, not merely because of the place it occupies in the evolution of theory but also because corporatist tendencies can still be identified in the policy-making systems of some countries. But what is then given primary attention is a variety of approaches to the examination of the policy process which stress the extent to which interest groups are aggregated into networks or policy communities to provide more coordinated systems of power.

Corporatist theory, or corporatism

Schmitter describes corporatism as a system of interest representation. He goes on to put this more specifically as one:

> in which the constituent units are organised into a limited number of singular, compulsory, non-competitive, hierarchically ordered and functionally differentiated categories, recognised or licensed (if not created) by the state and granted a deliberate representational monopoly within their respective categories in exchange for observing certain controls on

their selection of leaders and articulation of demands and supports. (Schmitter, 1974, pp. 93–4)

In Schmitter's analysis there are two forms of corporatism: state and societal. State corporatism is authoritarian and anti-liberal. The label is applied to the political systems of Fascist Italy and Nazi Germany. In contrast, societal corporatism originated in the decay of pluralism in western European and North American political systems. Schmitter hypothesises that in the latter systems changes in the institutions of capitalism, including concentration of ownership and competition between national economies, triggered the development of corporatism. The need to secure the conditions for capital accumulation forced the state to intervene more directly and to bargain with political associations. The emerging societal corporatism came to replace pluralism as the predominant form of interest representation.

Much of the English language literature on corporatism has explored that concept's applicability to the United States and Britain. Its use to encapsulate the policy process in some of the continental European countries – particularly Scandinavia, Austria and the Netherlands – has been rather more taken for granted. For example, writing about the last-named country, Kickert and van Vucht say:

> The threat of labour revolt and rising socialism was countered at the end of the 19th century by the creation of 'corporatism': the institutionalisation of socio-economic cooperation between ... organised capital, organised labour and government. Based on this ... the Netherlands developed into an extreme example of the modern non-statist concept of *neo-corporatism*. This concept emphasises the interest representation by a number of internally coherent and well-organised interest groups which are recognised by the state and have privileged or even monopolised access to it. (Kickert and van Vucht, 1995, p. 13)

This emphasis upon an organised and legally recognised system certainly highlights a difference from the rather uncertain evolution of the 'Anglo-Saxon' systems in this direction. In the 1960s and 1970s various writers suggested that such an evolution was occurring. Winkler (1976), for example, argued that the state had come to adopt a more directive and interventionist stance as a result of a slowing down of the process of capital accumulation. He pointed to industrial concentration, international competition and declining profitability in the British economy as examples of significant changes in the economic system which prompted the shift towards corporatism.

The political history of corporatism in Britain has been outlined most fully by Middlemas (1979, 1986). Middlemas argues that a process of corporate bias originated in British politics in the period 1916–26, when trade unions and employer associations were brought into a close relationship with the state for the first time. As a consequence, these groups came to share the state's power, and changed from mere interest groups to become part of the extended state. Effectively, argues Middlemas, unions and employers' groups became 'governing institutions' (1979, p. 372), so closely were they incorporated into the governmental system. By incorporation, Middlemas means the inclusion of major interest groups into the governing process and not their subordination. The effect of incorporation is to maintain harmony and avoid conflict by allowing these groups to share power.

The impact of Margaret Thatcher's policies led some British writers to dismiss British applications of corporatist theory as merely a description of a passing phase (see, for example, Gamble, 1994). During the 1980s the trade unions were dismissed from the 'triangular' relationship, and at times even the role of business seemed to be downgraded. But this evidence surely only discredits those who proclaimed, borrowing Marxist historicism, that we entered, in the 1970s, the 'age of corporatism'. Corporatism remained in other countries, and could return in Britain, as a way in which the state may 'manage' its relations with key economic actors.

In the United States the relevance of the corporatist thesis has been questioned by observers such as Salisbury (1979), who have argued that Schmitter's model of societal corporatism does not fit the American experience. A different stance is taken by Milward and Francisco (1983), who note important trends towards corporatism in the United States (see Box 3.1).

Box 3.1	Milward and Francisco's (1983) theory of 'corporatist interest intermediation'

This perspective, applied to the United States, stresses the development of corporatist institutions in some policy sectors and particularly those based on government programmes. In these sectors, state agencies support and rely on pressure groups in the process of policy formulation. The result is not a fully developed corporate state but rather 'corporatism in a disaggregated form'. In Milward and Francisco's view, neither federalism nor the separation of powers has precluded the development of corporatist policies because corporatism is based on policy sectors which cut across both territorial boundaries and different parts of government.

Reviewing different approaches to the use of the concept of corporatism, Panitch (1980) argues for a limited definition. In his view, corporatism is not a total economic system, but rather a specific and partial political phenomenon. More concretely, corporatism is a political structure within advanced capitalism which 'integrates organised socio-economic producer groups through a system of representation and cooperative mutual interaction at the leadership level and mobilisation and social control at the mass level' (ibid., p. 173).

This rather cautious approach to the formulation of corporatist theory contributed to generating other ways of conceptualising relationships between interest groups and the state. Grant has summed up the fate of corporatist theory in Britain under the impact of political change and academic elaboration:

> By the time they had developed a conceptual apparatus to analyze the phenomenon, and had managed to organize large-scale research projects, the object of study was already dwindling in importance. The corporatist debate did, however, help to stimulate a new wave of theoretical and empirical work on pressure groups promoting a re-examination of pluralist theory, and thereby encouraging the development of new forms of pluralist analysis such as the idea of policy communities. (Grant, 1989, p. 36)

It seems on balance as if 'corporatism' is more a descriptive label than a theory. Whilst some corporatist theorists have adopted the Marxist-like argument that there are inevitable tendencies operating in this direction, few have accepted that view, and events in places like the United Kingdom have suggested that corporatist tendencies may come and go as matters of political choice rather than be inevitable developments. Corporatist theory highlights the way in which interests may be aggregated, and the extent to which the state may play a role in bringing capital and labour together in ways which may (and this is very much a hypothesis) limit the power of the former. But it paid little attention to interests outside the key productive processes. It belonged to a world in which political conflict could still be seen as involving interaction between the state and the two big organised groups highlighted by Marxist theory: capital and labour. It may be seen as dated, if not by a realisation that the world was more complicated than that, then at least by a recognition that the structure of interests in the modern 'post-industrial' world is rather different. However, this theoretical work thus draws our attention to the possibility that collaboration within networks may be a feature of the policy process. This brings us to the next section.

Policy networks and policy communities

Corporatist theory indicates that there is a need to pay attention to the ways in which powerful interest or pressure groups outside the state and groups within the state relate to each other. But it tends, in a rather generalised way, to develop a single model which gathers the 'parties' to this relationship into three overarching groups: capital, labour and the state. Much other pluralist theory, however, sees neither capital nor labour as single interests, easily brought together in all-embracing institutions. The same point may be made about the state. Analysts of government have recognised that it is very difficult to get departments to act corporately. Many policy issues are fiercely contested between departments, even within relatively unitary systems of government, between central and local governments and between the many different elements in complex systems like that of the United States.

It has been suggested, therefore, that there may be, rather than corporatist systems, a variety of separate linking systems between interests within government and those outside. One such formulation postulates the existence of a variety of 'iron triangles' embracing the state and both sides of industry and operating in specific industrial sectors and not necessarily across the economy as a whole (Jordan, 1986; Thurber, 1991; Salisbury, 1979).

A related alternative formulation, using the concept of corporatism, comes from Dunleavy (1981), who argues that it is possible to identify systems of 'ideological corporatism' (p. 7) in operation in policy communities. These systems derive from 'the acceptance or dominance of an effectively unified view of the world across different sectors and institutions' (ibid.). In many cases the unified view of the world emanates from a profession – the medical model is a good example – and provides 'ideological cohesion' (ibid.). Dunleavy goes further, suggesting that:

> underlying apparent instances of policy shaped by professional influences it is possible on occasion to show that structural parameters and dynamics shaped by production relations and movements of private capital play a key role in shifts of welfare state policy. But I doubt if fairly specific policy changes can ever be reduced to explanation in such terms alone. (Dunleavy, 1981, p. 15)

These formulations suggest relatively strong links between actors: *iron* triangles or policy *communities*. Others have borrowed from transaction theory (see Chapter 12, pp. 247–8 for a discussion of this) and from the sociological study of inter-organisational relationships to suggest that where powerful institutions need to relate to each other over a period they develop a variety of ways of doing business which assume a measure of stability (see Knoke, 1990). Furthermore, it should not be assumed that these relationships are simply one-way. Pluralist theory can be seen as stressing the amount of competition between groups to try to influence the state. Marxist theory goes to the other extreme of regarding the state as the 'creature' of capitalism. An alternative view is that both sides need each other – the pressure groups need to influence policy, the institutions of the state need support from powerful groups outside it. The exchanges may even be more explicit than that – when the two sides need to trade knowledge, expertise and influence over other actors. Hence, another contribution to the understanding of these relationships comes from the application of exchange theory (see Rhodes, 1981). State institutions and non-state institutions can be seen as linked by both reciprocal connections and more complex network relationships. Smith thus argues that:

> The notion of policy networks is a way of coming to terms with the traditionally stark state/civil society dichotomy ... State actors are also actors in civil society, they live in society and have constant contact with

groups which represent societal interests. Therefore the interests of state actors develop along with the interests of the group actors and the degree of autonomy that exists depends on the nature of policy networks. (Smith, 1993, p. 67)

Smith explores the relationship between the two concepts outlined above: 'policy networks' (the expression 'issue networks' is also used in this literature) and 'policy communities'. These are closely related ideas, between which there is *no need* to make a choice while formulating a policy theory drawing upon them. Communities are stronger versions of networks. Clearly, therefore, networks may cohere into communities and communities may disintegrate into networks. There may be some issues where communities are more likely than networks and vice versa. There may also be some institutional situations, and even societies, where one pattern is more likely than the other and so on.

Smith's analysis was developed from the work of Jordan and Richardson (1987), which tends to use the expression 'policy communities' for a range of relationships of varying stability, and that of Rhodes (1988) and Marsh and Rhodes (1992), which identifies networks of varying cohesiveness. The main features of *policy communities* are set out in Box 3.2. By contrast, *issue networks* have rather different characteristics, as set out in Box 3.3.

Box 3.2	Features of policy communities

- Shared values and frequent interaction
- Exchange of resources, with group leaders able to regulate this
- A relative balance of power among members.

Box 3.3	Characteristics of issue networks

- Large and diverse
- Fluctuating levels of contacts and lower levels of agreement than policy communities
- Varying resources and an inability to regulate their use on a collective basis
- Unequal power.

What is particularly important about this work – distinguishing networks and communities from simple pluralist clusters of organisations – is the emphasis upon the state interest in fostering them. Smith (1993), drawing on Jordan and Richardson (1987), identifies, for the British case, four reasons for this:

- Networks and communities facilitate a consultative style of government.
- They reduce policy conflict and make it possible to depoliticise issues.
- They make policy making predictable.
- They relate well to the departmental organisation of government. An example of this is the grouping associated with the development of British agricultural policy after the Second World War, which is set out in Box 3.4.

Box 3.4	The British agricultural policy 'network' or 'community'

It has been argued that this has involved close consultation between the government department responsible, the associations representing farmers' and landowners' interests and the major suppliers of fertilisers and pesticides. This grouping has been seen as working in a concerted way, resisting influences from consumer interests and anti-pollution lobbies, presenting itself as the manager of the countryside in opposition to other government departments as well as to outside pressure groups (Lowe, 1986). Between the 1940s and the 1970s this could be described as a typical policy community; more recently it has weakened and has had to consult more widely and is perhaps now more appropriately described as a policy network.

Both concepts – particularly that of policy communities – postulate a stable pattern of interest organisation, so there are some important issues that need to be addressed about how such systems change over time. Smith suggests (1993, pp. 91–8) that change may be engendered by external relationships, general economic and social change, new technology, internal divisions within networks, and challenges between networks and within communities. In the case of agriculture (outlined in Box 3.4), that change has come about partly because of Britain's membership of the European Community, partly because of the growth of a rural population with no commitment to agriculture (people working in or retired from the towns) and partly because of other events that have put consumerist and environmental issues on the political agenda.

In later work with Marsh, Smith has come back to the issues about change (Marsh and Smith, 2000). An important feature of this work has been a concern to take on board issues about networks as 'structures' and actors as 'agents' (see the discussion of the structure/agency issue in Chapter 2). This involves recognising the way in which actors change networks. Marsh and Smith then develop an examination of the impact of exogenous factors, as outlined in the last paragraph, to stress the dialectic relationship between a network, agents and the wider environment.

Other refinements of this theory have sought to be more specific about the way in which networks and communities may relate to each other. Wilks and Wright (1987) suggest the idea of a continuum from communities to networks, with the former term reserved for situations in which there is a common policy focus. Others have argued that more specific communities will often be 'nested' within larger networks (Dudley and Richardson, 1999; Chadwick, 2000).

There is a need for situations in which it is possible to test the extent to which (a) communities really are unified, as there is general agreement that communities vary in this respect, and (b) unified communities get their own way. Box 3.5 offers an exploration of this through an empirical study.

Box 3.5	**Toke and Marsh's (2003) study of policy networks and the genetically modified (GM) crops issue**

Toke and Marsh describe their study as deploying 'a dialectical model of policy networks' designed to analyse 'the interaction between agents and structure, network and context and network and outcomes to understand and explain how policy change has occurred' (p. 229).

This study explores how a policy on which there appeared to be a cohesive 'policy community' in favour of GM came under challenge. In the process of that challenge they see the policy community being transformed into a more open network in which some environmentalist groups have been incorporated and have been able to change policy towards a much more cautious approach to GM crops. It has been significant that key actors here have emerged from relatively 'establishment' pressure groups, notably the widely supported Royal Society for the Protection of Birds and from a government-supported agency English Nature. Also important has been wider public recognition of a potential 'problem' with GM crops.

In general, Marsh and Toke's study provides an example of agenda change emerging out of interest group politics. However, it does also indicate the way in which a government minister, sympathetic to the environment protection lobby, may have played a key role. What is interesting about this, however, is that he was in a comparatively junior position, with a viewpoint not supported by the Prime Minister. Here, then, we have an example of low-key policy change coming about not through a direct political initiative but through policy network transformation, yet involving a politician, and a not insignificant movement in public opinion.

There is also a danger here of getting into self-fulfilling statements, like explaining why ideas are on (or off) the policy agenda by arguing that this is because communities want them on or off. The fact that educationalists dominated the United Kingdom education system between 1945 and 1979 can just as plausibly be attributed to the fact that other powerful actors were quite content to let this happen as to the fact that the education policy community had the power to keep it that way. This leads Kisby to argue:

> In addition to the interactive relationships that exist between the socio-economic context, the structure of the network, the agents within the

network and the policy outcome, the influence of ideas upon the network may also be seen as constituting something of an interactive relationship with the agents within the network, who do not simply passively accept given ideas but who can use and develop these ideas as well as introducing new ideas themselves (2007, p. 83).

Kisby suggests that Toke and Marsh's study, cited in Box 3.5, offers stronger evidence for this viewpoint than they are prepared to acknowledge. Kisby's emphasis upon the role of ideas receives further support in the next chapter where institutional theory that extends the concept of institutions to embrace cultures and dominant ideologies will be explored.

Notwithstanding this, we can at least suggest a simpler proposition: that the policy agenda will be more organised and more predictable when unified policy communities are allowed to dominate. There may then be some interesting comparative questions about differences between societies in this respect (corporatist theory propositions are relevant here). But explaining this may be very difficult, particularly when (as seems to have happened in the United Kingdom in the last quarter of the twentieth century) quite dramatic shifts have occurred in the toleration of this policy community dominance. But the question remains why that ideology should have become so influential, and found echoes (for example in the pro-participation Left) far beyond the ranks of the leaders of the attack from the political Right. We are back here to some interesting issues about political choice, undermining social scientists' generalisations about the policy process!

The core executive

Rhodes, one of the theorists most involved in the development of network theory, has, in his work with Dunleavy, added another element to the analysis of the involvement of networks in government. Rhodes describes the term 'core executive' as referring 'to all those organisations and procedures which coordinate central government policies, and act as final arbiters of conflict between different parts of the government machine' (1995, p. 12). Efforts to define the core executive in Britain may be seen as a contribution to institutional theory (John, 1998) (see the discussion of this approach in the next chapter). However, according to Rhodes, 'The core executive is the set of networks which police the functional policy networks' (1997, p. 14). As such it needs to be seen as a refinement of network theory.

It is important to recognise how these different emphases upon networks range across a variety of policy issues and concern themselves with different aspects of the policy process. Inasmuch as network theory is an advance upon the pluralist theory of power, it concerns itself with domination (or its absence) across the policy process as a whole. But network ideas can also be found very much in evidence in relation to questions about policy implementation: in concerns about the sharing and modification of policy goals and about the determination of effective action in complex inter-organisational contexts. They have been very important for critiques of the top-down approach to the examination of implementation (see p. 203). Clearly, therefore, it is possible that network or community explanations for policy outcomes may be used for parts of policy processes where other explanations (stressing concentrations of power, or even determinist theories, or the institutional theories examined in the next chapter) are offered as prior structuring influences.

The advocacy coalition approach

Paul Sabatier has developed an approach to the analysis of the policy process that has much in common with the work of scholars who emphasise the importance of networks and policy communities. His particular contribution has been to try to refine the way the implementation process is analysed. In work with Jenkins-Smith he has developed what he calls an 'advocacy coalition' approach (see particularly Sabatier and Jenkins-Smith, 1993). This complex theory sees the policy process – from policy inception through to implementation – as involving an 'advocacy coalition' comprising actors from all parts of the policy system. Advocacy coalitions consist of 'actors from a variety of institutions who share a set of policy beliefs' (Sabatier, 1999, p. 9). Sabatier and Jenkins-Smith's approach involves the acceptance of ultimately coordinated action between actors both in favour of and against specific policy goals, and of change over time in response to events inside and outside each 'policy subsystem'. This approach can be seen to be sharing with the other approaches here the notion of a network and of the existence of a degree of consensus (coalition), but going beyond it to embody concerns about the wider political and institutional context. Sabatier, Loomis and McCarthy (1995) use this approach to some effect to explore planning decisions in the forest service in the United States. The key features of the advocacy coalition approach are set out in Box 3.6. The particular concern with 'policy learning' in this version of network theory is clearly important for the issues about inter-organisational collaboration that will be discussed in Chapter 12.

Problems with the use of network theory

It has been noted that network theory offers a way to analyse the clustering of interests in the policy process, which has advantages over both simple

| Box 3.6 | The advocacy coalition framework's key features |

Sabatier and Jenkins-Smith summarise their approach as follows:

1. Reliance upon the policy subsystem as the principal aggregate unit of analysis.
2. A model of the individual based upon (a) the possibility of complex goal structures and (b) information-processing capabilities that are limited and, most important, involve perceptual filters.
3. Concern with policy-oriented learning as an important source of policy change.
4. The concept of advocacy coalitions as a means of aggregating large numbers of actors from different institutions at multiple levels of government into a manageable number of units.
5. Conceptualizing both belief systems and public policies as sets of goals, perceptions of problems and their causes, and policy preferences that are organized in multiple tiers.
6. Coalitions that seek to manipulate governmental and other institutions to alter people's behavior and problem conditions in an effort to realize the coalitions' belief systems.

(Sabatier and Jenkins-Smith, 1999, p. 154)

pluralism and corporatist theory. Rhodes sees policy networks as 'a long-standing feature of British government' (Rhodes in Hayward and Menon, 2003, p. 65). Yet he goes on in the same essay to argue:

> To talk of the governance of Britain is to say the Westminster model is no longer acceptable and we have to tell a different story of the shift from government (the strong executive) to governance through networks. (Hayward and Menon, 2003, p. 67)

Here, then, is a potential for confusion. If one of the key justifications for the use of the term 'governance' is the importance of networks, is Rhodes saying 'we, political scientists, now see this to be the case', or is he saying that the system has changed? Probably he would reply, 'a bit of both', and of course we must remember that the categories we use influence what we see. However, there are grounds for concern that some of those who write about the contemporary importance of networks seem to take a stance on the evolution of the policy process very like that taken by earlier theorists who saw the emergence of the 'age of corporatism'. A very different stance will be taken in this book. Issues about networks as one among several 'modes of governance' will feature in many places in the book. But the author very much agrees with Lowndes and Skelcher that:

> A crude periodization of modes of governance can also carry with it the myth of progress – bureaucracy as all-bad, markets as a necessary evil and networks as the 'new Jerusalem'. (Lowndes and Skelcher, 1998, p. 331)

The account of network theory in this book differs from that of those who have seen networks as fundamental for modern 'governance' in a way which suggests that the role of the state has diminished. Rather, as Hudson and Lowe (2004, Chapter 8) argue, Smith's approach to the analysis of networks (on which the account in this chapter has heavily depended) offers the most satisfactory approach to the issue. Hudson and Lowe also commend Dutch work which approaches networks in much looser terms focusing not upon governance overall but on 'what the emergence of policy networks means for those working on the front lines of government services – how it changes their working practices, its implications for management processes and so on' (Hudson and Lowe, 2004, p. 141; key sources for the Dutch literature are Kickert, Klijn and Koppenjan, 1997 and Koppenjan and Klijn, 2004). This involves, for prescriptive approaches to policy analysis, particular concerns about the 'management' of networks; for this discussion the crucial point is that there are important empirical questions about the balance of power within networks and about the extent to which the state (or parts of it) is able to occupy a superordinate role. In a later work Hudson and his colleagues argue 'that some actors are better placed to manage *elements* of the network as a whole' (Hudson et al., 2007, p. 59) and that in this respect government actors are particularly well placed, hence: 'It is likely that such a role may provide government actors with the opportunity – contra Rhodes' claim about the autonomy of networks – to attempt to alter a network's design in order to aid the achievement of their own objectives' (ibid.).

There is, furthermore, a problem with policy community and policy network theory rather similar to that with the weaker versions of corporatist theory, that it offers a description of how policy decision processes are organised but not any explanation of why they are organised in that way. This body of theory perhaps only refers to a tendency – one of the ways relationships between the state and interest groups may be regulated. Drawing upon empirical studies it is particularly suggestive of the way in which relationships between the state and interest groups are likely to be regulated in a comparatively stable political system. Smith's (1993) book explores parallels between Britain and the United States, suggesting characteristics of the system of government in the latter that make networks more likely than communities, but he argues that a great deal still depends upon the policy sector. Studies in other societies suggest the existence of similar phenomena (see, for example, Kickert and van Vucht, 1995, on the Netherlands). But it is interesting to observe how difficult it is, despite a strong state tradition and extensive and lively interest groups, to encapsulate within any single theory the characteristics of relationships between the state and groups in France (see Box 3.7). Network theory comes out best, but it explains little.

Box 3.7	Policy networks in France

Knapp and Wright's examination of 'the state and the pressure groups in France' (2001, Chapter 11) contrasts four models:

- 'the domination-crisis model', which interprets French culture in terms of ambivalence towards authority, with the consequence that there is an endemic tendency for confrontations to arise between an often authoritarian state and intransigent interest groups;

- 'the endemic and open conflict model', which shares the characteristics of the first model but sees the conflict to be rooted in a lack of accommodating institutions;

- 'the corporatist and concerted politics model', which highlights the many ways in which interest groups and the state work together;

- 'the pluralist model', which stresses the diversity, and the importance, of interest groups.

Knapp and Wright see France as:

a State capable, at times, of considerable autonomy, even high-handedness, in its actions; interest groups often both fragmented within each sector and internally divided; the frequent resort of groups to extra-institutional action, leading, in extreme cases, to crises ... But if these features offer a distinctive view of State–group relations in France, it is far from an exhaustive one. The other two models, developed for other political systems, are important reminders of other characteristics, more banal but no less present: the free competition of pluralism, the quiet collusion of corporatism. Typical traits of all four models may be discerned in France, but in different proportions in different sectors at different times. (p. 335)

In the light of this, Knapp and Wright nevertheless suggest that policy network theory offers a 'mixed model' making a 'minimum of sense out of the apparent chaos' (p. 326), a remark which highlights both the strength and the weakness of such theory.

John argues that the crucial problem with network theory is that

the all-encompassing nature of networks creates a problem. They are both everything and nothing, and they occur in all aspects of policy-making. But the concept is hard to use as the foundation for an explanation unless the investigator incorporates other factors, such as the interests, ideas and institutions which determine how networks function. The result is an endless circle of argument whereby the network idea is extended to breaking-point to try to explain something it only describes. (John, 1998, pp. 85–6)

However, it can perhaps be said that network theory in particular describes rather little except that most activities involve networks. This is the sense in which Dowding (1995) attacks network theory as offering no more than a 'metaphor' for the policy process. A slightly less negative way in which this point may be put is to suggest that it provides a 'framework' rather than a theory. This is a point that Sabatier and Jenkins-Smith consider about their approach, agreeing that it 'started as a framework' (1999, p. 154), but they still argue that as they have worked with it they have begun to develop testable hypotheses. Network theory is not alone in this respect: indeed, a problem running through the study of the policy process is that much theory describes rather than explains. This is an issue to which we will return.

CONCLUSIONS

The emphasis upon networks and communities offers an important corrective to accounts of the political system and the operation of the state which treat them as homogenous and unified entities. But network theory lacks explanatory power. Drawing our attention to the importance of networks and policy communities tells us little about how they actually influence the policy process. Moreover, it tends to provide too stable a picture of the world of policy makers. While their protagonists recognise the fluidity of networks (indeed, the work analysing the relationships between networks and policy communities is very concerned with this issue), and that there may be overlapping networks and networks within networks, there is a difficulty in giving any sense of dynamism to the resultant processes. Recognition of the need to explore issues about networks in terms of interactions between actors, and to site them in a wider environment, helps to deal with this. But there remains a problem, one that is shared with the institutional theory that will be discussed in the next chapter.

4 Institutional theory

SYNOPSIS

This chapter explores the contribution made by institutional theory to understanding the public policy process. While some writers have argued that it is a relatively recently discovered approach, the first part of the chapter will suggest that it has deep roots in the sociological analysis of policy processes, and that it has also been influenced by institutional economics. Then will follow an exposition of the theory today, showing how the concept of 'institution' has been used very widely to embrace cultural and ideological phenomena. The next part of the chapter explores the way in which theorists have sought to address the problem that an emphasis on institutions tends to imply a stress on stability and the absence of policy change. The two main solutions to this are *either* to try to develop a way of analysing critical points at which opportunities emerge for system change *or* simply to stress, as March and Olsen (1984) have, that actually the theory does little more than assert that the organisation of political life makes a difference. This leads to a view that institutional theory faces some of the same problems as network theory, inasmuch as its explanatory uses are limited, but indicates that this in many ways simply emphasises the extent to which the analysis of the policy process is an intuitive art.

One way to solve the problems about using institutional theory may lie in comparative work in which institutional differences between countries suggest reasons for differences in policy processes. The chapter therefore ends with a brief excursion into this, so far relatively undeveloped work, to see whether it provides potentially helpful developments.

Introduction

It has been suggested that during the time in the 1950s and 1970s when academic political science developed rapidly in the United States and Britain, there was a tendency to neglect the study of state institutions (Nordlinger, 1981; March and Olsen, 1984). The claim that there was a need for work 'bringing the state back in' (Evans, Rueschemeyer and Skocpol, 1985) rather exaggerated the earlier neglect. State functionaries, including the military, figured as key concerns in elite theory, yet it was true that classical Marxist theory tended to see the state simply as a supporting player for the capitalist system and that early pluralist theory largely treated it as a neutral institution which groups in society would compete to control.

Various alternative conceptions of the state are set out in Box 4.1. While it rather exaggerates their positions, it can be said that both early pluralist theory and classical Marxist theory largely embody the first of the models set out in the box. Some elite theory, corporatist theory and some of the public choice models (to be discussed in the next chapter) tend to give the state an active but unitary character (Model 2). Network theory comes close to Model 3 inasmuch as it sees the state as containing members of more than one network or community, but it pays little attention to conflict between these. The theories discussed in this chapter particularly emphasise Model 4, but in doing so they contain elements of Models 2 and 3.

Box 4.1	Ways the state may be conceptualised

Model 1   As a passive entity to be influenced/captured
Model 2   As an active entity with interests of its own
Model 3   As containing actors with potentially conflicting interests
Model 4   As a structured system influencing and perhaps constraining action.

March and Olsen contrast institutional theory with pluralist theory as follows:

There are two conventional stories of democratic politics. The first story sees politics as a market for trades in which individual and group interests are pursued by rational actors. It emphasises the negotiation of coalition and 'voluntary' exchanges. The second story is an institutional one. It characterizes politics in a more integrative fashion, emphasizing the creation of identities and institutions as well as their structuring effects on political life. (March and Olsen, 1996, p. 248)

Their model, at least as expounded in their 1996 essay, sees the need for a fusing of the two approaches: the latter framing the former but being open to change under various circumstances.

The roots of institutional analysis of the policy process

Some writers draw distinctions between different kinds of institutional theory. Hence, John portrays institutional analysis as having a 'central place in political science, particularly during the origins of the discipline', since 'the founding scholars of political science treated institutions, such as legislatures and courts, as a key part of public life and worthy of study in their own right' (1998, p. 38). He then goes on to chart the various ways in which scholars dealt with institutions until about the 1980s, and at the same time notes how behaviourist studies paid little attention to issues about the impact of institutions. After a critique of older institutional studies John then charts the rise of 'new institutionalism' in the 1980s, which placed the 'state at the centre of analysis' with institutions as 'manifestations of the state' crucial for the explanation of outcomes' (ibid., p. 57).

The present author, while recognising (as indicated above) the importance of the revival of interest in institutions, does not consider that so clear a distinction can be made between earlier and later work. Perhaps this is because his own roots are in political sociology, and he published a book called *The Sociology of Public Administration* back in 1972. Certainly, one sociologist whose work will be discussed below, Selznick, has been a seminal figure, saying things still pertinent for modern analyses of institutions. Selznick has, reasonably, been critical of the clear line modern institutionalists have tried to draw between their work and his (1996), but then academics have to try to claim originality!

In some respects institutional analysis is fundamental for the discipline of sociology, raising questions about the extent to which human actions are structurally determined. It is then given an emphasis that is particularly important for organisational activities. The importation of ideas from organisational sociology to the study of the policy process has its roots at least as far back as Selznick's classic study of the Tennessee Valley Authority, which was published in 1949. Even earlier, Barnard (1938) stressed the need to see policy decision making in its organisational context. This theme was picked up by Simon in his *Administrative Behaviour* (1957).

A distinction is made in much of the sociological work between 'organisations' and 'institutions'. Here Selznick is a key influence, arguing:

> The term 'organization' thus suggests a certain bareness, a lean no-nonsense system of consciously coordinated activities. It refers to an expendable tool, a rational instrument engineered to do a job. An 'institution' on the other hand, is more nearly a natural product of social

needs and pressures – a responsive adaptive organism. (Selznick, 1957, p. 5)

This distinction emphasises the social world within which organisations are created, drawing attention both to the impact of the external environment and to the way people bring their own needs and affiliations into organisations which then shape the social systems that develop there. Selznick describes this phenomenon very clearly in the following observations:

> All formal organizations are moulded by forces tangential to their rationally ordered structures and stated goals. Every formal organization – trade union, political party, army, corporation etcetera – attempts to mobilize human and technical resources as means for the achievement of its ends. However, the individuals within the system tend to resist being treated as means. They interact as wholes, bringing to bear their own special problems and purposes; moreover the organization is embedded in an institutional matrix and is therefore subject to pressure upon it from its environment, to which some general adjustment must be made. As a result, the organization may be significantly viewed as an adaptive social structure, facing problems which arise simply because it exists as an organization in an institutional environment, independently of the special (economic, military, political) goals which called it into being. (Selznick, 1949, p. 251)

Selznick's approach has been criticised as too deterministic, but the general thrust of his argument remains pertinent. Later work has emphasised the need to see institutions as 'cultural rules' (Meyer and Rowan, 1977). Such an approach follows Selznick in challenging the notion that an easy distinction can be drawn between formal and informal aspects of organised life; as DiMaggio and Powell put it:

> Institutions are a phenomenological process by which certain social relationships and actions come to be taken for granted, that is they are conventions that take on a rule like status in social thought and action, which explains why sociologists find institutions everywhere from handshakes to marriages to strategic-planning departments. (1991, p. 5)

DiMaggio and Powell (1983) identify the way in which a process of 'structural isomorphism' occurs, which means that organisations working in similar 'fields' tend to develop similar characteristics. Another sociologist, Scott, writes about three 'pillars' of institutions:

- regulative, resting upon 'expedience' inasmuch as people recognise the coercive power of rule systems;
- normative, resting upon social obligations;

■ cognitive, depending upon taken for granted cultural assumptions. (Scott, 1995, p. 35)

This sociological work tackles the issues about the policy process from a rather different direction from that of the political scientists. It is not concerned with questions about how public policy develops but with how organisations work. But then policy processes are generally also organisational processes. Chapters 11 and 12 will pick up some themes from the sociology of organisations.

Another feature of the development of institutional analysis has been the recognition of the need to employ historical analysis to trace the evolution of policy over a long period of time. Some of the key theorists have described themselves as 'historical institutionalists'. They see themselves as drawing inspiration from 'a long line of theorists in political science, economics and sociology including Polanyi, Veblen and Weber' (Thelen and Steinmo, 1992, p. 3).

It is pertinent too to note some relevant work on the impact of institutional arrangements on decision making emerging from economics. To some extent this involves the development of classical economic theory to provide a foundation for the analysis of political life (a topic to be explored in the next chapter). But this can also be seen in the recognition of the competitive advantages possessed by pioneer enterprises. The classic illustration is the dominance of Microsoft, having early secured a position in which the widespread dependence on the technologies it established inhibit shifts to alternatives developed by competitors at later points in time. The concept applied to this is to speak of 'increasing returns dynamics':

> First, they pinpoint how the costs of switching from one alternative to another will, in certain social contexts, increase markedly over time. Second, and related, they draw attention to issues of timing and sequence, distinguishing formative moments or conjunctures from the periods that reinforce divergent paths. In an increasing returns process, it is not only a question of what happens but also of when it happens. Issues of temporality are at the heart of the analysis. (Pierson, 2000, p. 251)

Pierson goes on from the exploration of this phenomenon to suggest that features of political life make the reversal of institutional arrangements even more difficult than in economic life, where competitive processes may reward innovation.

Also relevant is the development within economics of an institutional perspective that challenged the relatively context-free way in which classical economics analysed market relationships, pointing out the importance of seeing these exchanges within structures with their own rules and expected practices (Coase, 1937; Williamson, 1975).

Institutional theory today

March and Olsen explain their view of the importance of the institutional approach as follows:

> Political democracy depends not only on economic and social conditions but also on the design of political institutions. The bureaucratic agency, the legislative committee, and the appellate court are arenas for contending social forces, but they are also collections of standard operating procedures and structures that define and defend interests. They are political actors in their own right. (March and Olsen, 1984, p. 738)

Hall makes a rather similar point in stressing the ways policy actors' behaviour is shaped:

> Institutional factors play two fundamental roles in this model. On the one hand, the organisation of policy-making affects the degree of power that any one set of actors has over the policy outcomes . . . On the other hand, organisational position also influences an actor's definition of his own interests, by establishing his institutional responsibilities and relationships to other actors. In this way, organizational factors affect both the degree of pressure an actor can bring to bear on policy and the likely direction of that pressure. (Hall, 1986, p. 19)

Hall's approach involves stressing institutional influences outside the formal institutions of government. He asserts that he 'ranges more widely to consider the role of institutions located within society and the economy' (ibid., p. 20). His study of economic policy making in Britain and France pays considerable attention to the ways in which economic interests are formally represented in the political process. His perspective is very close, therefore, to that of the writers on policy communities discussed in the last chapter.

The quotations above tend to project a static view of the institutional approach. They suggest that an examination of the policy process needs to be seen as occurring in organised contexts where there are established norms, values, relationships, power structures and 'standard operating procedures'. But much of the work in this tradition is also concerned with looking at how those structures were formed, and to elucidate the extent to which they impose explicit constraints or the circumstances in which they are subject to change. As March and Olsen say, 'while institutions structure politics, they ordinarily do not determine political behaviour precisely' (1996, p. 252).

Box 4.2	The use of institutional analysis in the exploration of social policy in the United States by Skocpol and her associates

In the United States in the nineteenth century, democratic political institutions (only for white males, of course) predated the elaboration of public administration. This created a situation in which patronage practices were the main form of response to political demands as opposed to distributive policies using a state bureaucracy. For example, pension provisions for Civil War veterans were extended as political favours way beyond their original intentions. Political institutions were functioning to deliver benefits to some, but to limit the scope for more fundamental state-driven reform.

In the context of a federal constitution requiring complex alliances to secure social reform, policy change was difficult to achieve. Many promising movements for reform failed to put together winning coalitions. This remained the situation until an economic crisis in the 1930s enabled the leaders of the 'New Deal' to put together a coalition of the Northern urban working class with the whites of the rural and racist South which could initiate new policies and offer a brief challenge to the older interpretation of the constitution. But the changes achieved were limited because the President still had to carry a resistant legislature.

The legacy of the policy changes in the 1930s continued into the post-war period, and into the period when emergent black groups had some success in challenging the status quo and the constitution. But such social policy legislation as had been achieved in the 1930s had added the Northern white working class, who had gained through the development of social insurance pensions, to the coalition against more radical reform. This was then a source of resistance to more radical change, particularly change favouring black people.

Skocpol (1994) and her associates (Weir, Orloff and Skocpol, 1988) have used the institutional approach to good effect to explain the long-term evolution of social policy in the United States (see Box 4.2). They show how policy change at one point in time created institutions which served as a barrier to change at a later point. As March and Olsen say:

> Programs adopted as a simple political compromise by a legislature become endowed with separate meaning and force by having an agency established to deal with them. (March and Olsen, 1984, p. 739 – drawing here upon Skocpol and Finegold, 1982)

Analysis like that set out in Box 4.2 is taking a general point, which is quite often made, about the barriers to political change imposed by the United States constitution, and expanding it into an analysis of both barriers to and opportunities for policy change in a context in which one set of changes then sets the structure for future events (and thus perhaps for nondecision-making).

Immergut (1993) has carried out a somewhat similar analysis on a comparative basis, exploring the evolution of health policy in Switzerland, France and Sweden. She writes of a policy game being played within a set of rules. In her study, other events, over a turbulent period in European history, had an influence on the 'rules'. These events had an impact in different ways in each country upon 'veto' points (where those opposed to change, principally the medical profession, could successfully challenge it) and 'access' points (where agents for change could succeed). Box 4.3 features another study which used Immergut's approach.

Box 4.3	Hwang's use of Immergut's approach to institutional analysis

In a study of health reform in Taiwan, Hwang (1995) shows how a generalised commitment to state health policy originating in the republican constitution developed on the mainland of China in the 1920s and a series of limited ad hoc social insurance developments in the period between 1950 and 1980 to help engender social support for the authoritarian regime set a framework, including access points, for rapid moves towards a national health insurance scheme as Taiwan democratised in the late 1980s and early 1990s.

If it is to work satisfactorily, the institutional approach must handle the relationship between structure and action. It is not enough just to emphasise institutional constraints. It is only too easy, as suggested above, to treat, for example, the United States' constitution as a straitjacket which effectively makes it impossible to get some issues on the agenda. An examination of the history of efforts to secure a universal health insurance scheme in that country encourages that view (see Skocpol, 1994, Chapter 9). Yet the US constitution has been amended many times, and, perhaps even more importantly for the policy process, it has been subject to reinterpretation in ways that in the 1930s widened the scope for federal action and in the 1960s opened the door for the civil rights movement. Political activity is not just a game played within rules, it also often involves efforts to renegotiate those rules. The revision or reinterpretation of those rules ('meta policy making') is important. The other point, which Skocpol's work particularly emphasises, is the way successful action then generates new constraints (rules or structures). Another way some writers talk about these processes is in terms of pathways or path dependence. Here they are picking up the notion of 'increasing returns' outlined above. In his analysis of this topic Pierson stresses that pathways may be influenced by small incremental decisions as much as by big ones.

From a study of the development of Swedish labour market policy which examines the way trade union interests were built into the policy process, Rothstein suggests that:

In some, albeit probably rare, historical cases, people actually create the very institutional circumstances under which their own as well as others' future behavior will take place. (Rothstein, 1992, p. 52)

This approach, emphasising games about rules, is central to an approach to institutional theory, critical of some of the more rigid ways in which it is applied, in a book edited by Streeck and Thelen (2005). In their introductory essay the editors point out 'the *enactment of a social rule is never perfect* ... there always is a gap between the *ideal pattern* of a rule and the *real pattern* of life under it' (p. 14, italics in original). This theme – to which we return in discussions of rules and discretion in the implementation process later in the book – leads them to a distinctive approach to the analysis of institutional change, on which more will be said below.

Institutional theory, ideas and discourses

March and Olsen draw attention to the work of Bachrach and Baratz discussed in Chapter 2, and by implication also to Lukes' and Hay's ideas, in arguing that so-called 'rules' embody implicit assumptions of exclusion:

Constitutions, laws, contracts, and customary rules of politics make many potential actions or considerations illegitimate or unnoticed; some alternatives are excluded from the agenda before politics begins ... but these constraints are not imposed full blown by an external social system; they develop within the context of political institutions. (March and Olsen, 1984, p. 740)

A related point is made by Thelen and Steinmo, who argue that the use of class differences in explaining political behaviour needs to be supplemented by exploring 'the extent to which it is reinforced through state and societal institutions – party competition, union structures, and the like' (1992, p. 11).

Clearly, the institutional approach to the study of the policy process involves interpretation. It does not suggest that outcomes can be easily 'read off' from constitutional or institutional contexts. Immergut sets out her games analogy as follows:

Institutions do not allow one to predict policy outcomes. But by establishing the rules of the game, they enable one to predict the ways in which policy conflicts will be played out. (Immergut, 1992, p. 63)

In this way, modern institutional theory embodies 'cognitive and normative frames' which 'construct "mental maps"' and 'determine practices and behaviours' (Surel, 2000, p. 498).

Hall argues that

> politicians, officials, the spokesmen for social interests, and policy experts all operate within the terms of political discourse that are current in the nation at a given time, and the terms of political discourse generally have a specific configuration that lends representative legitimacy to some social interests more than others, delineates the accepted boundaries of state action, associates contemporary political developments with particular interpretations of national history and defines the context in which many issues will be understood. (Hall, 1993, p. 289)

However, a problem remains that institutional analysis may need to lay so strong an emphasis upon specific configurations of institutional situations and actors (including ideas) that all it can offer is an account of past events, from which little generalisation is possible. Hence the next section examines efforts to apply institutional theory to the explanation of change.

Institutional theory and the explanation of change

Institutional theory faces a problem that confronts all theories that emphasise structure: they are better at explaining stability than change. If we go back to classical Marxist theory we see this difficulty being tackled with a sort of evolutionary theory which argues that contradictions within systems accumulate to the point where they force change – in that case, of course, revolutionary change. But institutional theory is not suggesting that change is impossible, nor is it simply taking us back to the sorts of functionalist theories that saw social change as going down some pre-determined pathways. Rather it is emphasising constraints on change and pathways that change may follow. However, that still leaves a problem about identifying either when those constraints are least likely to apply or when there will be shifts from apparently pre-determined pathways.

We find a variety of efforts to deal with this problem. There have been attempts to do this using concepts like 'critical junctures' (Collier and Collier, 1991) or 'performance crises' (March and Olsen, 1989). A more fully argued through exploration of this issue uses the concept of 'punctuated equilibrium' (Krasner, 1984; Baumgartner and Jones, 1993). Baumgartner and Jones explore the way in which feedback from policy decisions builds up critical problems over time, hence accelerating the process of movement from stability to crisis. This has a parallel in economic theory in terms of notions that firms with oligopolistic advantages deriving from 'increasing returns' decline in efficiency to a point at which rivals can compete with them.

Surel argues that it is necessary to see exogenous influences as important for change processes. For him, 'transformations of economic conditions, and/or a serious crisis' are crucial (Surel, 2000, p. 503). It is also possible to identify exogenous political changes (for example, the impact of the evolution of the EU on non-members such as Switzerland). Environmental changes may also be relevant, forcing the reconsideration of environmental policies. This approach still poses problems about the identification of crises and shocks. One cannot simply 'read off' policy change from such an event without placing it in context.

Another approach to the issue of the relationship between structuration and change involves the use of biological analogies. This occurs in the work of both Kingdon and John. Kingdon (whose very careful analysis of agenda setting in the policy process will be explored further in Chapter 8) sees the flowing together of forces for policy innovation into an equivalent of 'primeval soup' in which they combine together to produce change.

Warning that evolutionary theory seems to carry with it a Darwinian notion of progress and the survival of the fittest, John points out that contemporary analyses of evolution (as in the work of Dawkins, 2003) do not contain these elements. Hence he sees it as feasible to see policy change as a process in which the elements to policy systems continually interact over time. Combinations of ideas and interests constantly seek to dominate decision making and to interact with institutions, patterns of interest groups and socio-economic processes which are also slowly changing and evolving over time. The notion is that some ideas are successful in this context, but that change defines the nature of modern public policy (John, 1998, p. 195).

Approaches to institutional explanation that explore differences in the extent to which institutional arrangements are 'embedded', that is, reinforced by ideological paradigms (Hall, 1993), offer another approach to the problem of explaining change. Hall explores the rise and fall of Keynesian economic dominance in government, seeing constraints not so much in structures as in dominant ideologies and charting how these change over time (Hall, 1986). Hall presents Keynesian economic theory and then monetarist theory as successive dominant paradigms. Hence he sets out to explain a 'paradigm shift' in which the emergence of new policy options required an ideological shift, facilitated in the British case by the victory of a government disposed to encourage that. In using notions of dominant ideas or paradigms, institutional theorists face questions about the extent to which these shifts can be explained independently of other phenomena. To go back to Hall's study, were Keynesian ideas and notions of public provision so universally discredited by economic changes and related crises, or was there not perhaps a form of contagious ideological change to which we need to turn to explain what happened? In other words, surely there was a new set of ideas waiting in the wings for the opportunity to replace Keynesianism (we may note not merely that the key exponents of 'new Right' ideologies, above all Hayek, had expounded their views long before but also that much that they had to say drew upon pre-Keynesian economics). Then also, what about the political actors (in the United Kingdom, Margaret Thatcher and

Keith Joseph) who had adopted monetarist ideas in their programmes? It is this sort of objection to simple reliance on institutional explanations that has led theorists to stress the need to incorporate 'ideas' and 'agency' into institutionalist theory (see Peters, Pierre and King, 2005, for a good exposition of this point of view).

There is an issue here about whether an emphasis on the importance of ideas is an extension to institutional theory or whether it provides the basis for a critique of it. Béland argues that 'institutional scholarship can pay greater attention to ideational processes without abandoning its core assumptions (2005, p. 1), offering an approach that is superior to more pluralist related accounts of ideas that subsume them within interests. Lieberman, more cautiously, argues that 'institutional accounts of politics . . . challenge the tendency of institutional theories to take the interests and aims of political actors as given' (2002, p. 698). However, he points out that Marxist and other structuralist theories are even more limited in this respect, seeing ideas as consequences of material arrangements, and he goes on in the same article to explore ways to fuse institutional and ideational theories arguing that change arises out of ' "friction" among mismatched institutional and ideational patterns' (ibid., p. 697).

This throws the problem of explaining change on to changes in the structure of ideas, or the dominant paradigms. Béland (drawing on the work of Blyth, 2002) thus suggests that ideas have an impact upon political decisions in three ways:

- 'as "cognitive locks" that help reproduce existing institutions and policies over time' (as in Hall's policy paradigms perspective);
- 'as policy blueprints that provide political actors with a model for reform';
- as 'powerful ideological weapons' that allow actors to challenge existing policies (2007, p. 125).

But that still leaves problems about explaining how ideas affect policy change. In Béland's article quoted here the case of ideas about 'social exclusion' are explored to show how they are used both to challenge existing policy paradigms (in France) and to support the dominant neo-liberal discourse (in the UK).

A related problem here is about clarity in respect to the concept of change. Streeck and Thelen (2005, p. 8) introduce two analytical considerations to try to deal with this. First, they argue that 'we must avoid being caught in a conceptual schema that provides only for either incremental change supporting institutional continuity through reproductive adaption, or disruptive change causing institutional breakdown and innovation and thereby resulting in discontinuity'. This leads them:

- to make a distinction between 'incremental' and 'abrupt' change;
- to suggest alternative 'results of change', including the subsequent restoration of continuity but also incremental change as a gradual process (ibid., p. 9).

Second, their emphasis on the incomplete nature of institutional arrangements leads them on to suggest a range of ways in which incremental change may occur:

- *Displacement*: the 'slowly rising salience of subordinate relative to dominant institutions'.
- *Layering*: 'new elements attached to existing institutions change their status and structure'.
- *Drift*: 'neglect of institutional maintenance resulting in slippage of institutional practice on the ground'.
- *Conversion*: 'redeployment of old institutions to new purposes'.
- *Exhaustion*: 'gradual breakdown . . . of institutions over time' (ibid, p. 31).

From institutional theory to garbage cans

The last section has demonstrated how there has been extensive effort to deal with the problem of explaining change within institutional theory. Clearly, some approaches to the concept of change and to the factors that generate it are more sophisticated than others. Yet despite the sophistication the theory still has difficulty doing anything other than explaining change with the benefit of hindsight. Emphases on dramatic events and exogenous changes to which the political system needs to respond offer by contrast some bases for prediction. Yet even they offer us little that helps to explain the form political change takes. For example, changes in the world economy in the 1970s forced policy change, but it was not self-evident that those responses would take the neo-liberal form they did. In that respect it is pertinent to observe that new economic 'shocks' occurring at the time of writing are indeed precisely leading some to urge the need now to abandon neo-liberal policies. The battle of ideas goes on! These observations lead us to consider in the next section, therefore, forms of institutional theory that are much more sceptical about the feasibility of using the theory to explain events.

This is the direction in which some of the things March and Olsen had to say about the institutional approach seem to be heading:

> the new institutionalism is probably better viewed as a search for alternative ideas that simplify the subtleties of empirical wisdom in a theoretically useful way.
>
> The institutionalism we have considered is neither a theory nor a coherent critique of one. It is simply an argument that the organisation of political life makes a difference. (March and Olsen, 1984, p. 747)

There are two parts to this problem. One is that institutional theory brackets together a very wide range of potential constraints, from constitutions and laws, through institutional self-interest and standard operating procedures to dominant ideologies. To some extent this mixing of the formal and the informal is justifiable. Sociologists have rightly warned us against treating constraints built into rule books as if they are necessarily firmer than custom and practice, particularly when the latter have penetrated into our language. But in analysing policy constraints we do need to make some distinctions in order to explore what a breach of those constraints may involve.

The way in which some of the institutional theorists go far beyond emphasis on the structuring provided by formal governmental arrangements to include accepted rules, norms and even ideologies has been described as 'the big tent theory of institutions', which implies that 'today we are all institutionalists' (Frederickson and Smith, 2003, p. 69). While such a development is compatible with the usages by sociologists (see, for example, the discussion of the work of theorists like Giddens, on p. 50), it has been criticised, in much the same way as network theory has been (see pp. 49–50), for encompassing so much that it explains little or nothing. John argues:

> The main problem with the new institutionalist approach is its definition of what counts as institutional. By incorporating values and norms as part of institutions, they include too many aspects of political life under one category. The resulting amalgam of processes appears to explain change under the rubric of institutions, but in reality it disguises the variety of interactions and causal mechanisms that occur between the contrasting elements of the political system. (John, 1998, p. 64)

Similarly, the overall problem with institutional theory is well put by Thelen and Steinmo, who say it is 'that institutions explain everything until they explain nothing' (1992, p. 15). They go on to argue that their concept of 'institutional dynamism' addresses the problem by identifying situations 'in which we can observe variability in the impact of institutions over time but within countries' (ibid., p. 16). The problem remains, however, that work from this school involves the interpretation of case studies where the reader is invited to share the writer's understanding of events.

As noted above, if the object is to try to achieve theoretical parsimony, this extension of institutional influences to include ideas and ideologies may be a weakness. However, its strength is that it recognises the soft and pliable nature of institutional systems. Fischer (2003), who welcomes modern institutional theory for the attention it gives to discourses, highlights the need to see institutions in the following way:

> A political system ... is a linguistic concept discursively invented and employed to describe a set of relationships that we can only partly experience – one goes to the voting booth, appears as a witness in a court case, visits parliament, speaks with a political representative, and so on. But no

one ever sees an entire political system. While we can directly encounter parts of a political system or discover its effects, the system itself remains a set of formal and informal relationships that can be constructed and discussed only through language. (Fischer, 2003, p. 45)

Going even further down this problematical path, March and Olsen have given us, from their work with Cohen, a memorable expression to typify an extreme version of the institutional approach: 'the garbage can model'. They say, almost as if distancing themselves from their own idea:

> In the form most commonly discussed in the literature, the garbage-can model assumes that problems, solutions, decision makers, and choice opportunities are independent, exogenous streams flowing through a system. (Cohen, March and Olsen, 1972)
> They come together in a manner determined by their arrival times. Thus, solutions are linked to problems primarily by their simultaneity, relatively few problems are solved, and choices are made for the most part either before any problems are connected to them (oversight) or after the problems have abandoned one choice to associate themselves with another (flight). (March and Olsen, 1984, p. 746; see also March and Olsen, 1989)

There is a problem that once any attempt to generalise is left behind in this way, the student of the policy process is being required to take a position like that of a purist atheoretical historian, determined to let the facts speak for themselves without any principles to help organise attention or lessons to draw from the study. Or is he or she being urged to look to psychology to offer some organising principles? Certainly, there has been a whole range of policy analysis literature which suggests the need to draw upon psychology. There is obviously no objection to this. However, except in some forms of social psychology, which are very closely linked to organisational sociology in endeavouring to explain how structures influence attitudes and thus actions, the problem is that much of this literature does no more than tell us that individual attitudes, emotions, etc. will influence decisions. Parsons makes this point well about Young's (1977) essay on the 'assumptive worlds' of policy actors:

> The problem is ... how can we students of public policy actually study this 'assumptive world?' ... Surface, observable forms of politics are somewhat straightforward as compared with 'values', 'beliefs', 'assumptions', and the 'subconscious aspects of policy-making'. (Parsons, 1995, p. 379)

There is obviously a need to be sensitive to unique juxtapositions of events and the unique responses of individual actors, but if we are sitting in the 'garbage can' watching the latter deal with the former we can do little but describe what happens on each unique occasion.

There is, perhaps, one other way forward by way of comparative analysis. Peters, Pierre and King speak of modern institutional theory as adopting an 'explicitly comparative focus' (2005, p. 1280). If propositions about 'pathways' or 'critical junctures etc., are to stand up as more than observations – generally with the benefit of hindsight – about what has gone on in the 'garbage can' etc., then observations about differences in different institutional structures are needed. These may be observations about different points of time in the same country, hence the importance of historical institutionalism but generally they need to involve comparisons between different places (which normally means comparisons between nation states). The next section explores this option, and shows that there have been various efforts to categorise nations in terms of differences in institutional configurations.

The contribution of comparative studies for the exploration of the institutional perspective: introduction

It is implicit in institutional theories that if countries differ because of their different institutional configurations then their policy processes are likely to differ. Whilst it is easier to show that systems diverge rather than converge, there is, nevertheless, a sense in which institutional theory, at the very least, needs comparison to demonstrate how divergence occurs. However, some propositions from institutional theory do embody suggestions of a determinist form, claiming that there may be specific combinations of institutional influences that can be identified in certain situations, particularly, that is, situations inhibiting or assisting policy change. If such propositions have any general validity they may be expected to be applicable in more than one country. The problem then is that the starting point for much comparative analysis has been the testing of determinist theories: about the extent to which particular trends in policy can be seen as common among countries with similar social or economic characteristics (for example, the relationship between economic development and political or welfare state development). As this simple determinism has been challenged, institutional theories have come in either as alternative explanations or as necessary to modify the original propositions.

In this discussion it would not be appropriate *either* to get into an overall discussion of comparative work *or* a focus on the central preoccupations of comparative politics about the conditions under which democratic systems emerge and survive together with the exploration of the relationship between democracy and national economic success. Rather there will be attention to ideas, often difficult to separate from mainstream comparative work, that have helped, or may help, with the analysis of the specific impact of institutions upon policy processes. This discussion therefore examines briefly (1) approaches that examine institutional differences that may have differential impacts upon policy, and (2) approaches that examine policy differences and suggest how institutional differences may help to explain these. After that some attention will be given to more specific efforts to use comparative studies to deal with the issues about policy change explored earlier in the chapter.

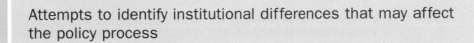

Attempts to identify institutional differences that may affect the policy process

Issues about whether nations can be compared in terms of the extent to which they are democratic have naturally led on to an exploration of the different institutional forms that allegedly democratic government may assume. The institutional focus is on *constitutional* variations. The relevant question here is whether the exploration of these can contribute to the study of the way policy processes vary from country to country.

Perhaps the most relevant comparative work on democratic systems is that of Lijphart, who argues that definitions of democracy raise the fundamental question of

> who will do the governing and to whose interests should the government be responsive when the people are in disagreement and have divergent preferences? (Lijphart, 1999, p. 1)

He goes on to contrast two answers to that question: 'the majority of the people' (the 'Westminster model') and 'as many people as possible' (the 'consensus model'). He then deploys evidence that suggests that consensual democracies (often operating through corporatist policy-making processes) are more effective and implicitly more responsive. His comparative analysis also examines variations along another dimension: that between strong federalism at one extreme and high degrees of unification at the other. Lijphart displays his comparative data in terms of these dimensions.

Lijphart is clearly engaged in a very bold attempt to produce what Lane and Ersson call 'grand social theory' (2000, p. 224). They prefer to break down their approach to the same topic into somewhat more modest attempts to produce 'middle range' generalisation. Lijphart treats the state as a very passive entity, with a fixed set of institutions to which interests can relate. Dyson's analysis (1980) of the differences between the way the state is conceptualised involves describing Britain and America as 'stateless'. This involves a rather deliberate exaggeration, and to describe societies in which the state is large and costly in this way violates common sense. His object is to emphasise both an absence of ideologies which ascribe a special role for the state in society and to show that a fragmented view of the state is dominant in the way institutions work. In this book the formulation 'strong' and 'weak' states (Katzenstein, 1977) is preferred to 'states' and 'stateless societies'. Strong states then have a tradition which involves:

a widespread sense of the legitimacy of public action . . . and . . . a willingness to define 'public power' as distinctive and to exercise it
authoritatively. (ibid., p. 256)

Such states do not necessarily have bigger governments: Dyson's proposition
is about how power is exercised. Weak states, by contrast,

are characterised by the strength of pluralism, representation and the
debating tradition in the political culture; an instrumental view of government and a pragmatic conception of politics ...; a pervasive
informality in politics ...; a preference for 'social' models of the constitution or economic analyses of politics which emphasize the role of elites
rather than institutions. (ibid., p. 52)

Both Lijphart's analysis and efforts to generalise about state power may be
taken on to help to address issues about the conditions under which effective state action will occur. It may be suggested that in the consensual
democracies, the federal states and the 'weak' states policy change will be
slower, and more subject to 'veto' by interest groups. But that does not really
take us very far towards testing of institutional theory, except as a sort of corrective perspective to pluralist theory suggesting how interest influence may
be affected.

There are dangers in using the concepts of 'strong' and 'weak' states.
Atkinson and Coleman (1989) have pointed out that their application needs
to be modified both by taking into account the extent to which there is centralisation and, even when there is not, by recognising the variations there
may be between policy sectors. Their analysis of state strength also goes on
to remind us that if the concept is used there needs to be some consideration
of the strength of the elements in society that the state is striving to influence
and regulate. Strength is a relative concept – a so-called 'strong state' may not
look so strong when it is dealing with a unified and well-organised group of
economic actors. Howlett and Ramesh, citing the work of Haggard and Moon
on South Korea (1990), go on from that point to argue that 'there is no reason
to believe that strong states will necessarily make policies that serve the
interests of society as a whole, rather than those of self-serving groups'
(Howlett and Ramesh, 2003, p. 61). In other words, do not allow usage of the
concept of the 'strong state' to lead to a begging of questions about the
respective power of the state and other groups involved in the policy process.

An examination of the UK highlights the ambiguity of the strong/weak
dichotomy. Since the arrival on the scene of the Labour Party, and the
related shift away from 'economic liberalism' by the Liberals, at the beginning of the twentieth century, the British policy-making scene has been
dominated by strong programmatic stances by the political parties. The electoral and parliamentary institutions have tended to polarise political debate
into distinctive 'Left' and 'Right' positions. Furthermore, one side in that
polarity – the Left – has tended to need to strengthen the state in order to
realise its goals. Hence, there is a need to be cautious about the typification

of Britain as a 'weak state', a point that is further exemplified by the paradox around the way in which the Thatcher government used the state to weaken the state (see Gamble, 1994).

The further general point that needs to be made here is that the importance of party politics in the British system makes the role of the state an area of controversy in a way that it is not in the United States (this is discussed further in Chapter 8). The peculiar impact of the dominance of a single party in Britain throughout much of the recent past has been highlighted in Dunleavy's analysis of 'policy disasters'. It is suggested that 'five main factors seem to be involved in generating policy disasters: scale aggregation, overly speedy legislation and policy making, political hyperactivism, the arrogance of Whitehall, and ineffective core executive checks and balances' (Dunleavy, 1995, p. 59). The first two and the last are essentially institutional factors – unitary government, a simple law-making process ('the fastest law in the west', Dunleavy says, taking this expression from a comment on the government of a smaller, similar case, New Zealand) and very centralised power. 'Political hyperactivism' can be seen as a characteristic of the contemporary ideological climate, while Dunleavy's fourth point emphasises the way in which 'political responsiveness and policy activism' (ibid., p. 62) is at a premium in the top civil service. The capacity for 'action' in the United Kingdom has been seen as making for very positive government, not weak government. The appellation 'weak' therefore draws attention to wider cultural and ideological considerations that inhibit positive government and/or undermine the legitimacy of government. On the other hand there is a very important distinction to be made between the UK and the USA which amounts not just to different positions on the unitary/federalism scale but also to the fact that the United States has a very divided system even at the centre (between President, two Houses of Congress and the Supreme Court). In the UK modern prime ministers have been described as presidential (Kavanagh and Seldon, 2001), but what is misleading about that appellation is that prime ministers have a level of control over Parliament beyond a US president's wildest dreams. In the words of Gamble, observing how the 'royal prerogatives' are now the Prime Minster's: 'the Prime Minister has no need to become a President because he is already a Monarch, a position of considerably greater scope' (2003, p. 11).

If the strong state/weak state dichotomy is of limited use, is there a satisfactory alternative in the policy styles literature, which involves a much more complex exploration of institutional differences (Richardson, 1982, see also Bovens, 't Hart and Peters, 2001). Styles are seen as varied, not merely on account of national differences, but also because of differences in the policy issues at stake. This is an approach linked to ideas about 'policy communities' (see p. 69) – hence the suggestion is that different policy styles may be manifested in different policy communities even within the same country, let alone between countries. So far this approach has been developed very little, and will not be discussed further here.

At the end of his edited book, in which this model is explored through case studies, Richardson is cautious about labelling countries in terms of policy styles. Nevertheless, Bovens, 't Hart and Peters, in introducing a study of *Success and Failure in Public Governance* (2001, pp. 18–19), offer expected 'styles' for the six countries they studied. However, they qualify their prediction by offering an alternative prediction that they may see 'roughly similar governance in each of the sectors [to be studied], and major differences between sectors even between cases set in the same country' (ibid., p. 18). Hence, we see suggestions that different national policy styles affect how policy is formulated, but this is interestingly qualified by Bovens and his colleagues with suggestions that it may very much depend upon policy area.

Explaining policy differences by institutional differences

Studies of policy differences use differences in the *characteristics* of policy (particularly those that can be quantified, such as expenditure on specific objectives and policy outputs) as *dependent variables* which may be seen as subject to influence by *independent variables*. Inevitably, the hypotheses used to determine which independent variables to examine have been influenced by the theories discussed in the earlier chapters – in particular, the extent to which outputs are determined by factors external to the national policy system (the wider social and economic environment and the impact of global forces), pressure groups and political parties. Then, as difficulties have emerged with these theories inevitably there has been a shift towards considering institutional explanations.

Whilst the comparative study of policy outputs is developing in relation to all substantive policy areas, it is in the study of social policy that a particularly sophisticated literature has grown up. This is partly because variations in levels of social policy expenditure and the way in which social policy institutions have developed are particularly salient across the more economically developed nations, with questions about whether 'welfare states' are boons or banes being particularly prominent in ideological debates. But it must also be partly attributable to the fact that social policy expenditure is a large item in the budgets of many states, and that its ingredients and implications are widely measured and reported in a variety of international databases which facilitate relatively accurate comparisons between countries. Moreover, aspects of social policy can be more easily measured for comparative purposes than, say, differences in ways of managing the economy, or conducting relations with other nations, or regulating activities and behaviour.

The most influential comparative study on this theme is Esping-Andersen's *Three Worlds of Welfare Capitalism* (1990). Esping-Andersen analyses aspects of the characteristics of social policy systems in terms of their contributions to social solidarity. This leads him to identify three regime types (see Box 4.4).

Box 4.4	Esping-Andersen's regime types

1. The '"liberal" welfare state, in which means-tested assistance, modest universal transfers, or modest social-insurance plans predominate' (Esping-Andersen, 1990, p. 26). Esping-Andersen puts Australia, the United States, New Zealand, Canada, Ireland and the United Kingdom in this category.
2. Nations where 'the historical corporatist–statist legacy was upgraded to the new "post-industrial" class structure'. In such nations 'the preservation of status differentials' is more important than either 'the liberal obsession with market efficiency' or 'the granting of social rights' (ibid., p. 27). This second category includes Italy, Japan, France, Germany, Finland, Switzerland, Austria, Belgium and the Netherlands.
3. Countries 'in which the principles of universalism and decommodification of social rights was extended also to the middle classes'; in these places 'the social democrats pursued a welfare state that would promote an equality of the highest standards' (ibid.). Denmark, Norway and Sweden are the nations in this category.

Esping-Andersen's starting point was a view that 'politics matters', using an essentially neo-pluralist perspective emphasising variations in the representation of class interests within politics. However, the notion that there may be rather different systems with different institutional and/or cultural characteristics then introduced an element of the institutional perspective. Particularly interesting here is the distinction between the second and third of the regimes outlined in Box 4.4, where differences in political representation do not seem to have sufficient explanatory power on their own. Hence the notion of 'regime types' involves a typology which highlights institutional issues but suggests a distinct clustering of institutional approaches. Esping-Andersen's work has been widely criticised yet the 'regime' concept remains dominant in comparative work on social policy. Most criticisms merely lead to reformulations of the regime model (Arts and Gelissen, 2002; Hill, 2006, Chapter 2). However, a more fundamental objection by Walker and Wong (2004) suggests that the whole regime approach embodies 'Western' ethnocentric assumptions about the role of the state and about welfare development as a product of what has been described above as 'the truce' between capital and labour. Hence there is a need for caution about using it in societies, like those of East Asia, with very different experiences.

Building on Esping-Andersen's work, Pierson's contribution (1994, 2001) is particularly important in this respect since it uses institutional theory much more explicitly, with two key features. One is that it equates regimes with institutional configurations that will channel new policy initiatives. The other is that it suggests that the relative success of interest groups will depend upon institutional arrangements. Reference was made earlier to

Immergut's comparative analysis of health policy in terms of the presence or absence of 'access points' and 'veto points' in different societies. Box 4.5 illustrates some applications of this theme, with particular reference to policy cutbacks. In general, a variety of scholars suggest that particular institutional approaches set up 'pathways' which influence future developments. Path-dependencies seem to be particularly important in income maintenance systems, where pension schemes imply long-run expectations (a theme to be explored further in Chapters 7 and 8) and often embody social insurance arrangements, which themselves build very strong, long-run political expectations and therefore obligations.

Box 4.5	Interest groups, institutional configurations and policy change

Pierson (1994) explores the way in which pressure from interest groups inhibited the cutback aspirations of Ronald Reagan in the United States and Margaret Thatcher in the United Kingdom. Béland (2001) has addressed the same theme rather differently in a study of pension reform in France and the United States, showing that the extent to which group interests are institutionalised will have an impact. His contrast is between the influence of labour unions in the two countries, and he argues that, while union membership is actually proportionately lower in France than in the United States and the control over the pensions systems is in both cases firmly in the hands of the state, nevertheless French unions have benefited from the fact that their right to be consulted about pension issues is formally embedded in the institutional arrangements. Taylor-Gooby (2001, 2002) similarly explores the impact of institutional arrangements upon social policy cuts in Europe.

This section has looked at comparative work with a specifically social policy focus. But regime theory has an equivalent, rather more tentatively developed, in theoretical work on the management of the economy, where economic activity has been seen as more coordinated, with government playing a larger role in the conservative than in the liberal systems (Hall and Soskice, 2001).

The last part of this chapter has explored, rather briefly bearing in mind the burgeoning volume of comparative work, the ways in which it may contribute to the examination of the impact of institutional differences. It must often be seen not as exploring hypotheses derived from institutional theory but as interfacing such theory with other theory (notably structural theories that emphasise economic influences on policy development and pluralist theories for which 'politics matters'). Much of the work offers no more than very general starting points for such an analysis. By the end (as exemplified in Box 4.5) we reached comparative work that addresses issues about policy pathways and institutional influences in ways quite explicitly oriented to the elaboration of institutional theory. Other examples, from other policy areas and other countries, could have been included. But it is more appropriate to use these where they relate to specific policy process analyses in the third part of this book.

CONCLUSIONS

Institutionalist writers offer a critique of other approaches to policy analysis. For example, Immergut portrays her work as 'a break with "correlational" thinking' (1992, p. 57), arguing that it goes beyond the static perspectives of interest group theory (p. 66) and asserting that 'the view that institutions are somehow congealed social structure is not especially helpful' (p. 85). But do they actually replace or supplement other theoretical approaches?

The institutionalist approach is very often operationalised through comparisons between countries, since good opportunities for looking at similar policy processes in different institutional contexts are obviously provided by national institutional differences. In looking at the relevance of comparative approaches to politics and policy in the last part of the chapter this issue was explored, leading back inevitably to the role of modern institutional theory as a corrective to earlier theoretical approaches.

5 Rational choice theory

SYNOPSIS

Rational choice theory involves the application of notions from economics (and to some extent from mathematics) to the analysis of the way in which self-interested behaviour by individuals may influence the policy process. It suggests that predictive propositions can be derived from generalisations which equate self-interest and rational behaviour and assume that they will be dominant. It assists the analysis of the policy process by reminding us of the importance of self-interest and of the extent to which public policy problems emerge from the incapacity of market mechanisms to solve many collective action problems.

The chapter starts with a comment on rational choice methodology, indicating the strengths embodied in an inductive approach to the study of the policy processes but also the biases that may follow from such an approach. Then the basic notion of the political marketplace is introduced. This is followed by a discussion of the way in which collective action problems have been analysed from an economic perspective, principally to assist with the development of prescriptive approaches, but in ways which also help with the analysis of the development of public policies. Game theory, with its roots in mathematics rather than economics, is then briefly examined as a further extension of that approach.

Finally, the economic theory of bureaucracy is examined. It is seen as a theoretical approach which contributes to insights about the behaviour of public sector bureaucrats, particularly when it is modified in ways which retain its concern to stress self-interested behaviour but show that it may lead to varied predictions of the way in which actual behavioural choices will be structured. A final note warns against the underlying determinism of theory that puts self-interest into so strong a predictive role.

Introduction

This chapter looks at a number of approaches to the analysis of the policy process which draw upon economic theory. These are given various names, but essentially they are variants of what is called rational choice theory or public choice theory. Assumptions about choices made in competitive market situations are applied to political processes. A key characteristic of this sort of theory is the way its assumptions are derived from the notion that individuals act in their own best interests. It is in this sense that the word 'rational' is used. While there are good grounds for arguing that economists have appropriated the word 'rational' for a rather particular restricted use, it will be used here since it seems now to be the term most commonly used to describe this kind of theory.

We will look here at a linked group of theories about choices in political processes, about the relationship between individual interests and collective interests and about how actors inside the policy system (particularly bureaucrats) may also have predictable interests. This kind of theoretical work offers a corrective to an idealistic view of the policy process as involving impartial problem solving, but it will be shown that it, too, suffers from problematic simplifying assumptions.

These theories are seen by some writers as providing a coherent framework for the analysis of politics, giving to political science a similar grounding to that which is claimed to exist for classical economics. This claim is contested, hence rational choice theory tends either to be rejected in totality by those who see no place for it in political science or to be accepted as a dominant perspective rendering other ones irrelevant. The position taken here will be neither of these, but rather one which sees rational choice theory as making a contribution to our understanding of the policy process, supplementing those that have been discussed already in this book. In this respect the author's perspective is a 'pick and mix' one, prepared to acknowledge ways in which rational choice theory may enhance analysis while not accepting the invitation to acknowledge the basic premises of the approach as an over-riding framework.

Hindmoor (2006, pp. 1–5) suggests that the key assumptions of rational choice theory are:

- Methodological individualism, accounting for outcomes in terms of individual choice
- Inductive methods using models to predict actions
- Behavioural rationality
- Self-interest
- Subjectivism (political individualism).

Hindmoor suggests that the fifth assumption is relatively uncontroversial, but;

The same cannot be said for the other four assumptions. Many (if not most) political scientists would argue that induction is more productive than deduction, that individuals operate with, at most, a bounded rationality . . . and that structure is either more important than agency or that structure and agency are codetermined. Finally most political scientists would join with casual observers in arguing that people are not simple, self-interested, automata (p. 4).

To explain the view taken of this work here, it is appropriate to give particular consideration at this stage in the chapter to the second of those 'assumptions': the use of inductive as opposed to deductive methods. Box 5.1 explains these two alternatives briefly.

Box 5.1	Deductive and inductive approaches

Inductive approaches start from empirical observations, try to generalise from them and thus develop theory which may then generate further testable hypotheses.

Deductive approaches start from theory and generate hypotheses, which may then be tested and fed back to improve the theory.

This book has so far explored a range of theories which, to a greater or lesser extent, provide potential deductive approaches to the study of the policy process. However, as will be argued further in the next chapter, no one approach alone provides a satisfactory approach to our subject. There is a need instead to combine theories and evidence-based observation to arrive at an appropriate analysis of the policy process. Hence there is much to be said in favour of induction, and it may be pointed out that even those who approach their work deductively tend to end up considering to what extent there are theoretical approaches that actually help to explain what they have observed. However, a theory that seeks to offer a comprehensive approach to the explanation of everything is widely regarded – in the social sciences – to claim too much. Rather there is a need to work to and fro between theory and evidence, asking which theories help to explain what happens.

Hence the problem with rational choice theory is the extent to which it purports to offer an explanatory approach intrinsically superior to others, using a set of basic assumptions about human behaviour, treating the notion of the rational self-interested actor as the basic building block (a kind of social scientist's notion of gravity) for explanation, rather than as something that may or may not be a characteristic of the actors being observed.

The problem is compounded by the fact that, whilst some rational choice theorists defend their perspective as a deductive starting point for the development of hypotheses that may or may not be sustained, others expound their explanatory model of behaviour much more dogmatically. Of course, given the difficulties in doing empirical research, there are many taken-for-granted theoretical propositions in use for which the evidence is limited in amount. However, rational choice theory attracts particular suspicion inasmuch as it has had a substantial impact upon contemporary political behaviour. To that extent it manifests itself as an ideology rather than a modest theoretical point for social science research.

This chapter will explore propositions from rational choice theory that are considered to offer useful sources for generalisations about the policy process, returning to some observations on the other controversial aspects of the theory (centring around the assumptions about self-interest) in a section just before the conclusions.

The development of the idea of the political marketplace

The idea of politics as a marketplace in which leaders compete for votes is developed in the work of Downs (1957). This perspective builds on pluralist theory by adding an element of economistic reasoning which sees self-interest as the dominant motive force in political behaviour. In the political marketplace, parties compete to win power by responding to the demands of pressure groups (see Auster and Silver, 1979; Tullock, 1976; Brittan, 1977). There is a very strong pressure upon governments to yield to those demands, and thus to enhance the role of the state as a giver of benefits (using that word in its general sense, to embrace jobs, contracts, services and tax concessions as well as direct cash benefits). This is not very effectively restrained by the fact that these benefits have to be paid for, because of the extent to which these costs can be hidden in the short run (by deficit financing) or spread in ways which lead benefits to be more readily perceived than the mechanisms to pay for them. For example, in 1991 in Britain a dramatic cut in an unpopular direct local tax (the 'poll tax') was funded by a percentage increase in an indirect sales tax rate (which had a slight and gradual impact upon prices paid by consumers). Interest groups seek specific benefits for themselves (business subsidies, welfare services, etc.) whose costs are diffused among taxpayers as a whole (Moe, 1980). The whole process involves what is often described as 'rent-seeking behaviour' in which interests secure larger gains for themselves than they would if they were competing in a free and open market (Buchanan and Tullock, 1962).

Public choice theorists argue (Tullock, 1976; Brittan, 1977) that as a result of political responses to plural demands the state grows in power and importance in ways which may be damaging to the working of the capitalist economy. They also suggest that these pluralist (or demand-side) pressures for government growth may be reinforced by monopolistic interests on the part of state suppliers, bureaucrats and professions in enhancing their 'empires'. At this point rational choice theory diverges from classical pluralist theory in giving a significant role to the state as an autonomous actor. This is a theme to which we will return below.

Another theme emerging from this school of thought has been the notion that there is a 'government business cycle' in which government expenditure, to satisfy demands and curb unemployment, is pushed up before general elections (Nordhaus, 1975; MacRae, 1977). The consequences of this are problems of inflation and adverse trade balances that will need to be dealt with in the post-election period. Hence, it is argued that political behaviour may contribute to the cyclical problems of the modern capitalist state. While it is comparatively easy to find specific examples of behaviour to support this thesis, it is less plausible as a general hypothesis. The empirical data are not conclusive (see Mosley, 1984), the feasibility of this kind of behaviour depends upon electoral systems, fitting political activities to economic trends is a difficult activity, and there have been alternative attempts to make economic rectitude a political asset (see Dearlove and Saunders, 1991, pp. 66–7). This is an example of how the widespread propagation of an alleged 'explanation' of behaviour can lead to other behaviour which contradicts it. We will also come later to the opposite kind of human response, behaviour that seems to explicitly reinforce a theoretical prediction.

Rational choice and collective action

Rational choice theory has particularly been developed by those who think it preferable to use market mechanisms to settle collective choice problems. It aims to show that public policy choices are made in ways that are no different from market choices, and that in some respects, therefore, commercial marketplaces deal with choice problems better than political marketplaces. It is argued that policy initiatives ostensibly developed to deal with the deficiencies of markets (market failure) need to take into account corresponding deficiencies of the state (state failure). In this respect, rational choice theory is more concerned with advocacy about the way public policy *should* be made than with analysis of *how* it is made. Hence, there is a close connection between rational choice theory and an economics literature which attempts to define the circumstances in which state (or at least collective) intervention may be justified, for those who believe that market systems are the right ones to settle most social distribution questions.

It may seem to be something of a digression to look at this literature inasmuch as it does not so much explain how public policy is made as examine justifications for public interventions. However, it is worth examining for the way it leads on to analyses of decision-making situations in which actors will be likely to conclude that following self-interest is problematical, and thus seek other ways of solving collective action problems.

Three key concepts are used in the discussion of this topic:

■ externalities

■ market inefficiencies

■ monopoly.

Externalities arise when market activities have consequences, either *positive* or *negative*, for people who are not party to those activities. Failure to deal with negative externalities has been described as 'the tragedy of the commons' (Hardin, 1968), referring to the collective consequences of self-interested individual decisions (see Box 5.2). Failure to give attention to externalities means that all suffer in the long run. One of the most obvious examples of this arises in relation to pollution. In the course of producing something, a manufacturer expels waste products up a chimney or into a water course. Neighbours etc. suffer the consequences of this action. Here, then, is a case for collective action, that may imply a need for state intervention: to prevent a nuisance which its producer has no incentive to prevent, given that any individual sufferer from it is likely to lack the resources to take action alone.

Box 5.2	The tragedy of the commons

Where there is common land on which peasants are entitled to graze live-stock, if there is no regulation of numbers, each individual will see it as not in their interest to restrict use. They will reason that a few more animals will not make any difference. Yet when all behave in this way the consequence is the destruction of the common pasture.

Positive externalities are not, in themselves, a source of problems. However, the difficulty in this case is that the creator of a positive externality is likely to resent the 'free riders' who will benefit from something they do not pay for. If someone builds a sea wall to protect their property from flooding, their neighbours are likely to share that benefit. There may, of course, in this case also be negative consequences somewhere else down the coast, in which case the combination of positive and negative effects further reinforces the case for collective action.

Faced with a high-cost item, and the likelihood of 'free riders', an individual is likely to try to secure agreement to collective action (the sharing of the cost among the potential beneficiaries). As far at least as the community surrounding the builder of the hypothetical sea wall are concerned, the wall constitutes what is sometimes called a 'public good'. No one can be prevented from benefiting from it. There are other examples where the benefiting community may be very much larger. Perhaps the largest example is a national – or even international – defence system. If it is true that a nuclear deterrent preserves peace then everyone benefits. The case for a state monopoly of defence (assuming acceptance of that state's legitimacy by its population) is overwhelming. There are similar issues here with regard to policing within a country.

Furthermore, whilst there have been efforts by states to delegate these tasks, states often then have to deal with severe control problems. Power has been given – in a very strong sense because weapons are involved – to a body of people who owe no ultimate allegiance to the state. Mercenaries merely have a contract to receive payment and/or spoils in return for their 'work'. It is not surprising that mercenary armies have sometimes switched allegiance, particularly when the capacity of the state to deliver on its part of the bargain has been in doubt (as it would be if the very action for which the mercenaries had been hired seemed to be failing). Some rather more modern issues also arise around the nature of the 'contract' between the state and the implementing actors, in the situations in which the latter seem to have no wider basis for 'allegiance'.

Returning, however, to the notion of externalities: how wide are the implications of positive and negative effects? Do they extend well beyond the examples given so far of environmental protection, law and order and defence? There are some other cases where the free rider problem can be brought under control: roads, bridges and parks may be provided privately, their use paid for through tolls. Then the argument for public provision lies in questions about the inefficient or inequitable use of resources.

But then the externalities argument can be widened further. For example, to what extent does everyone benefit if their fellow citizens are kept healthy? The 'external' impact of infectious diseases is clear enough, but there are other wider senses in which everyone benefits from living in a healthy community. What about education? – do not benefits similarly arise from living in an educated nation? Finally, what about 'externalities' relating to income distribution? If the elimination of extreme inequalities makes people with resources safer – from burglary, assault, revolution even – there are surely externalities which derive from income maintenance policies.

Most economic theorists would probably answer 'no' to my response to that last question, and say that this is stretching the concept too far. If they accepted the case they would probably want to discuss 'trade-offs' with other indirect consequences of state interventions. However, as stressed above, the concern here is not with the philosophical argument but rather with the fact that there has been a recognition within capitalist economies of a range of justifications for state intervention, often stretching far beyond the obvious examples of 'public goods'. Some economists have added another related concept to the list of special cases – merit goods (Musgrave, 1959), where the collectivity (state) regards it as desirable that people should have something whether they want it or not (in economists' terms this means they are prepared to and can afford to buy it). Education and health services are sometimes put into this category.

However, there may be reinforcing reasons for state action. One such reason, which lies very close to economic analysis, involves the extent to which state systems make it easier for employers to socialise costs. Public education and training systems reduce costs for employers, and reduce the disadvantage they encounter when other employers poach those upon whom they have spent training money. Help for the old and sick makes it easier for employers to discard inefficient workers. Unemployment benefits similarly may make the laying off of labour at a time of work shortage a less controversial matter, and may help those out of work to deal with their relocation problems in a more economically efficient way.

Pure economic theory is based upon assumptions of full awareness by all parties of all their options as buyers and sellers. Real-world economics concedes that there are many imperfections in the market arising from incomplete knowledge. That suggests that there may be a role for the state in helping to reduce knowledge imperfections. The case for labour market interventions, introducing buyers of labour to sellers of labour, certainly seems to have been based primarily upon this concern. That example is, however, one designed to deal with an essentially short-run problem. There are also long-term problems inasmuch as citizens may find it very difficult to act in the way the economic model presupposes (this is particularly the case when individuals are unwell or disabled). There was some recognition, even by the tough-minded theorists who designed poor law systems, that there might be individuals who could not be expected to behave like 'economic men'.

Another issue is that of monopoly, concerning principally the difficulties that competing suppliers might have in entering a market. Ironically, extreme market liberals accept a role for the state in preventing the abuse of monopoly power – the 'night-watchman state' has a duty to restrain those who try to act in restraint of the market. But another issue concerns the variety of situations in which the nature of the activity is such that it is in practice very hard to sustain competition. The crucial situation here is one in which there is a monopoly or near monopoly supplier and a competing supplier would find the costs of market entry prohibitively high. Examples of this are found in the supply of water, electricity and gas. To a lesser extent they also exist in transport systems (particularly where – like railways – they use fixed plant) and in large institutions like hospitals and schools. There is then an argument for state ownership or regulation to prevent any existing institution from exploiting its position, or perhaps (more controversially) for state intervention or subsidy to help create a second supplier.

Economic theory about externalities, incomplete knowledge and monopoly thus provides a series of justifications for public policies, both regulatory and redistributive, of a kind likely to be taken seriously by states in capitalist societies. But there are logical problems about how far to take these arguments. If it is believed that externalities are all-pervasive, incomplete knowledge is the norm and not the exception and monopoly tendencies are endemic, then the logical position reached is a state socialist one. But then, as pragmatic socialists have had to come to recognise, there are arguments to weigh on each side – setting the evidence on 'market failure' against what is sometimes called 'state failure', the incapacity of public institutions to function efficiently or equitably (see Self, 1993 for a good discussion of this issue).

It will be evident that much of the analysis in this section relates to arguments about what the state *should* do rather than about what it actually *does*. The implications of this for analysis of the policy process are (1) that justifications for intervention and for non-intervention are embodied in this literature, and (2) that, in the hands of those analysts who are convinced of the general superiority of markets, it offers rather deterministic explanations of policy problems (state failure) which arise when insufficient attention has been paid to the underlying logic.

Finally, it may be suggested that, while the evidence on the extent to which there are collective action problems that are hard to solve provides justifications for state action, it also suggests that such action may be ineffective. If we accept that there is a 'political market place' in which politicians compete to win support from interests, are there then not reasons why solutions to problems that disadvantage powerful interests will be rejected? Moreover, if on top of this we recognise that there are two levels to the 'market place', one where politicians compete within nations and another where there is self-interested competition between nations, is the difficulty not further compounded? This pessimistic view may most obviously be set out in respect of the global collective action problems arising out of pollution. The next section explores a theoretical approach that may offer an optimistic response to that.

Game theory

Game theory, while not having its roots in economic theory like the rational choice theory explored so far, has features in common with it, and contributes to the exploration of the issue of why public policy solutions to collective action problems are adopted. This theory arises from a branch of mathematics which has explored the logic of various situations in which there are conflicts of individual interests. Game theory develops a variety of models in which issues are explored about the extent to which individuals do best if they cooperate and those in which they do best if they, in the jargon of the theory, 'defect' – that is, refuse to act cooperatively. It is possible to construct scenarios in which there can only be one winner (zero sum) and games in which collaboration logically brings the best result (positive sum), but much of the relevant work of game theory focuses on games where it is not so easy to point to an obvious choice for the individual players. These games are described as 'mixed-motive games' by Scharpf, who goes on to say that in them:

> the preferences of players are partly harmonious and partly in conflict. Of these, four 'archetypal' constellations have achieved the most notoriety, even among social scientists who otherwise profess to game-theoretic illiteracy. They are known by the nicknames of 'Assurance', 'Battle of the Sexes', 'Prisoners' Dilemma' and 'Chicken'.

In discussing the implications of these mixed-motive constellations, the strategies available to both players are conventionally labelled 'cooperate' (C) and 'defect' (D) depending on whether the strategy is intended to realize the common interest of ego and alter or to maximize the advantage of ego at the expense of alter. (Scharpf, 1997, p. 73)

The best known of these games, 'The Prisoners' Dilemma', is set out in Box 5.3. While it uses what may seem a very artificial situation, it can be argued that its equivalent arises in the policy process in many situations in which conflicting actors (particularly actors that may not communicate particularly well with each other, such as nation states) are clear enough about what they have to do in their own interest and do not trust each other.

Box 5.3	The Prisoners' Dilemma

Two prisoners who conspired to commit a crime are caught. They are put in separate cells and each told that if they confess they will receive a mild punishment. The dilemma for each is the fear that, if the other confesses and they do not, this will result in a severe punishment for themselves. There are therefore four potential outcomes, as shown in the table. The optimum for both is strategy 4, but can they trust each other to stay silent in the face of the temptation to avoid a severe punishment?

It should be noted that some accounts of game theory differ from this one in according slightly different weightings which affect the likelihood of choice of the options. This does not matter, since it is a crucial feature of the way in which game theory is extended that it explores a range of situations where the benefits of self-interest may differ but ignorance of the choices of others remains a constant feature.

	Prisoner A confesses	Prisoner A does not confess
Prisoner B confesses	1. Mild punishments for both	2. Severe punishment for A, light one for B
Prisoner B does not confess	3. Severe punishment for B, light one for A	4. Possible avoidance of punishment for both

The game theory approach is thus used to explore to what extent in the real world situations emerge in which actors will be likely to move from conflicting to collaborative strategies. Particularly pertinent here will be the fact that games are rarely 'one shot' events. There are likely to be repeated interactions between actors so that experience from one game influences the next, and so on. What this leads to is the importance of the fact that games occur within structures. Hence Sharpf argues:

> ... actors ... depend on socially constructed rules to orient their actions in otherwise chaotic social environments and because, if they in fact perform this function, these rules must be "common knowledge" among the actors ... Institutions have explanatory value because sanctioned rules will reduce the range of potential behaviour by specifying required, prohibited, or permitted actions. (1997, p. 39)

This comment from Scharpf does not explore the issues about where those rules come from. The two previous chapters have explored theories that stress the relatively stable structure within which much policy decision making occurs, while also acknowledging that there are problems about explaining the processes under which networks and/or institutions are created and change. The democratic model for the creation of a system for solving collective action problems suggests, on the basis of the experience of the consequences of 'blindly' following self-interest, people will come together to create institutions. But they may equally be created by superordinate powers. The first explanation is supported by psychological research based on game theory, the second by the historical evidence that many of our institutions were imposed upon us. Today where the institutions come from may be irrelevant; the issue is about how they are used to try to solve collective action problems. That is the basis for the optimistic responses to the pessimism at the end of the last section.

The economic theory of bureaucracy

The economic theory of bureaucracy applies assumptions about self-interest to the behaviour of public officials. The rational choice theory discussed above sees competition to win political support as an activity that can be analysed like economic 'market' behaviour. This is a 'demand-side' theory about state behaviour. The economic theory of bureaucracy reinforces it by a 'supply-side' argument which is concerned with the consequences of the fact that public bureaucracies tend to be monopoly providers of goods and services. This perspective then draws upon economic theory on monopoly, which stresses the absence of constraints upon costs when these can be passed on to consumers and the extent to which in the absence of market limitations a monopolist will tend to oversupply commodities. It is thus particularly central for the notion of 'state failure'. It is argued that bureaucrats will tend, like monopolists, to enlarge their enterprises and to use resources extravagantly (Niskanen, 1971; Tullock, 1967; Buchanan and Tullock, 1962). Thus Tullock argues:

> As a general rule, a bureaucrat will find that his possibilities for promotion increase, his power, influence and public respect improve, and even the physical conditions of his office improve, if the bureaucracy in which he works expands. (Tullock, 1976, p. 29)

This theory has an intuitive plausibility, but comparatively little empirical evidence has been produced to support it. Self argues that 'these descriptions of the political process can be seen to be ... overdrawn and exaggerated' (1993, p. 58). Earlier in the same book he describes the work of the key theorist on this topic, Niskanen, as 'logically and mathematically elegant ... [but] empirically wrong in almost all its facts' (ibid., pp. 33–4). Self goes on to make the following five critical points:

1. The salary of a bureau chief is not closely related to the size of his bureau ...

2. Bureaus are not necessarily monopolistic ...

3. Political controllers are not as starved of information as Niskanen claims ...

4. In any case bureau chiefs are ... subject to the control of super bureaucrats ...

5. It is impossible to say that bureaus produce an excessive output if there is no objective way of valuing the output. (Self, 1993, p. 34)

It is not necessarily the case that bureaucratic success is measured by bureau enlargement. Brian Smith (1988, p. 167) points out how some of the most powerful and highly paid roles in civil services – in central finance departments, for example – are in small organisations. Self has observed that 'Bureaucratic self-interest takes many different forms, depending on the different career patterns and normative constraints found in different public services' (Smith, 1988, paraphrasing Self, 1985). Indeed, the political attack on big government has led to situations in which civil servants have been rewarded for their skills at cutting budgets, privatising public services and so on.

To be fair, whilst the original argument by Niskanen is put in a form that makes it a very readable polemic, even he modified it a little in a later paper (1991). Others have put the argument in various much more cautious forms. Indeed, one of Niskanen's precursors, Downs (1967), offered a typology of 'bureaucrats' with five alternatives, only the first of which closely accords with Niskanen's characterisation:

- 'Climbers' who maximise their power, income and prestige.
- 'Conservers' who maximise their security.
- 'Zealots' who promote specific policies to which they are committed.
- 'Advocates' who defend the interests of their department or the wider network of 'interests' within which it belongs.
- 'Statesmen' who have a broad commitment to the public interest.

Of course, all of these may benefit from working in monopoly situations, but one cannot make any assumptions about how they will use this.

There is a more modern and more limited formulation of the same point in Le Grand's distinction between 'knaves', motivated by self-interest, and the more public-spirited altruists, whom he calls 'knights' (1997, 2003). But then Le Grand's approach also connects this issue with the influence of structures, providing variations in the extent to which 'knavish' or 'knightly' behaviour is rewarded. In that sense he follows a position taken by institutionalist theorists (discussed in Chapter 4). For example, Thelen and Steinmo argue:

> people don't stop at every choice they make in their lives and think to themselves, 'Now what will maximise my self-interest?' Instead, most of us, most of the time, follow societally defined rules, even when so doing may not be directly in our self-interest. (Thelen and Steinmo, 1992, p. 8)

The use of an economic model to theorise about public bureaucracy is closely related to what is described as principal/agent theory, which focuses on situations in which the 'agent' – that is, the person or persons delegated authority – has motives for disregarding the instruction of 'principals' (Wood and Waterman, 1994; Horn, 1995). This goes beyond the simple proposition about bureau enlargement to explore, from a rational choice perspective, the top-down concern about control over implementation. It has led to a diligent search for situations in which 'perverse incentives' may be built into the day-to-day work of public organisations (see, for example, an influential examination of this issue in relation to the British National Health Service in Enthoven, 1985).

The model has also produced an interesting development which has rather more complex implications. Where market considerations apply, organisations are likely to try to externalise costs. Without the constraints imposed by markets, bureaucracies may also, Dunleavy has suggested (Dunleavy, 1985, 1986, 1991), internalise costs. Where theorists like Niskanen stress the negative aspects of this – it creates opportunities for the exploitation of public office – there may also be positive ones. Examples of this include: exemplary employment practices (in relation to wages, equal opportunities, employee welfare, etc.), responsiveness to clients' needs and interests (appeals procedures, opportunities for participation on policy issues, etc.) and, indeed, general openness to political intervention. Demands that bureaucracies operate as if they are private firms therefore directly challenge a variety of 'benefits' (that is, the costs that have been internalised) that have often been taken for granted as characteristics of the public service. Privatisation of such organisations, Dunleavy argues (1986), may both undermine the provision of these benefits and create situations in which there are incentives to externalise costs (pollution, income mainten-ance needs arising out of low wage policies, health consequences of employment practices, etc.).

Dunleavy accepts that bureaucrats will tend to engage in self-interested activities that are directed towards maximising their own welfare; but he shows that whether or not this will involve maximising the size of their organisations will depend upon the task of the organisation, the external (including political) pressures upon it and their own roles within the organisation. He describes their strategies as 'bureau shaping'. He sums up his position as follows:

> Rational bureaucrats therefore concentrate on developing bureau-shaping strategies designed to bring their agency into line with an ideal configuration conferring high status and agreeable work tasks, within a budgetary constraint contingent on the existing and potential shape of the agency's activities. (Dunleavy, 1991, p. 209)

Hence rational choice theory has both provided a set of arguments to support an attack on public bureaucracy *and* stimulated thinking about how we analyse organisational outputs. The attack on the public sector has taken the form of both outright privatisation and efforts to create competition between or within bureaucracies (see Olson, 1965, 1982 for the development of a rationale for this). Nevertheless, in both this theory and Dunleavy's alternative to it, it must be noted that the emphasis, as in classical economic theory, is upon what can be expected from an individual acting upon 'rational' self-interest. There remains a need to test whether actual behaviour is determined in this way.

The limitations of rational choice approaches

To a considerable extent rational choice theories build upon pluralist theories. The discussion of pluralist theories in Chapter 2 ended not only by challenging the failure of many of the early variations of pluralism for their disregard of inequalities of power but also by setting the individualistic assumptions of pluralism against arguments that identify the importance of structures. Both of these considerations also apply to rational choice theories. While rational choice theories direct us perhaps even more strongly than classical pluralist theory to attach overwhelming importance to self-interest in the explanation of public policy decision making, they do not really deal with the issues about power inequalities within the interest structures they analyse. Clearly they could do this rather more, and in this chapter a number of modifications have been noted (seeing 'games' as actually played in institutional contexts, recognising the way structures influence bureaucratic behaviour). But in general the use of an individual interest model pays little attention to the issues about the manipulation of interests that so concerns theorists like Lukes.

On the other hand, a curious feature of rational choice theory is the way in which, while it can be counterposed to theories that emphasise the determination of interests, it contains a form of determinism of its own. This has been highlighted by Hay, who argues that the 'rationalism' of rational choice theory deals with the problem of the contingency otherwise injected into social systems by agency ... by denying that agents exercise any meaningful choice at the moment of strategic deliberation. They have, if you like, a nominal choice between rationality and irrationality but, as rational actors, always opt for the former. ... It relies ... on a convenient assumption that we know to be false: that individuals in a given context will always choose the same (rational) option. In so doing it translates what would otherwise be a moment of contingency and indeterminism (at least from the political analyst's point of view) into one of complete and absolute determinism. (Hay, 2002, p. 53)

This formulation is only seeking to deal with the logic of the economic rationality assumption. Behind that, as Hay is of course fully aware, lie problems about the notion that self-interested behaviour and rational behaviour can be equated. Other theorists, although starting out from an economistic mode of reasoning, recognise that other behavioural modes may determine action. We saw that, above, for example, in Le Grand's distinction between 'knaves' and 'knights'. Jones and Cullis similarly seek to apply evidence from psychology to economic analyses of motivation (2003). Yet even with these modifications, surely Hay's strictures about determinism apply. What is merely being pointed out is that what is determined may vary.

The irony is that inasmuch as rational choice theory has been taken seriously it has had a certain self-fulfilling effect. Strategies to control bureaucrats and professionals which assume that self-interest is the crucial motivating force in their lives tend to reinforce that phenomenon (through incentive structures) and to undermine altruistic behaviour by controls which send the message that the official is not regarded as trustworthy. Self puts a related point, with particular reference to the use of insecurity as a device to control bureaucrats:

The problem of moral hazard, according to the theory, is that the bureaucrat will always tend to substitute his own personal wishes ... However a short-term contractual relationship may well increase this danger ... An official on limited contract will have less commitment to the public service and may be more disposed to use his position to establish useful contacts and opportunities in the public sector. (Self, 1993, p. 166)

Yet, earlier in the chapter we have noted, in respect of ideas about the political marketplace, how public choice theory has contributed to alternative behaviour designed to protect against the alleged 'problem' of inflation. So what we are being pointed to here is the significance of belief-systems or ideologies in influencing behaviour. In this sense the problem about rational choice theory is that, whilst it can be politically neutral, it has been widely propagated as a world view that defends market capitalism and warns us to distrust the state.

CONCLUSIONS

In the previous edition of this book rational choice theory was placed next to the chapter on theories of power, which considered pluralism and its critics, arguing that it was an extension of pluralist theory. In this edition it has been placed after chapters on network and on institutional theory. While it will have been evident that this is not because the author regards it as the most up-to-date kind of theory, its position here is logical since, while its roots may be in pluralism the most useful developments from it involve – as has been shown in the last section – combining pluralist perspectives with structural considerations. This is a theme taken forward in the next chapter.

6 Integrating theoretical approaches

SYNOPSIS

This short chapter revisits the simple representation of the main approaches to the description of the policy process provided in Figure 2.1 and suggests ways that they may be updated, on the basis of the developments in theory set out in Chapters 3–5. This includes observations on ways in which they may, to some extent, be integrated with each other, using the two policy examples explored in Chapter 1 (pp. 12–13). This discussion introduces some of the key themes to be explored further in the rest of the book.

Introduction

Chapters 2–5 have reviewed a wide range of theoretical approaches to the public policy process, pointing out the strengths and weaknesses of each. Where does that leave readers? Should they just make their own choices bearing in mind these points but guided by their own ideological predispositions? The answer is 'yes, up to a point'. However, it is important to recognise that what has been described is a succession of ideas developed over a long period of time, in the course of which some degree of consensus has developed about which are most helpful for our understanding of the policy process and which are less so. In the rest of the book connections will be made back to these theories, highlighting their usefulness where applicable. This book does not reject altogether the social-scientific search for truth, at least in the form of the view that some explanations are better than others. So it is reasonable to expect the author to 'get off the fence' and indicate his view of the validity of various perspectives.

Contrasting perspectives on the policy process updated

In Chapter 2, a simple figure (Figure 2.1) was presented to sum up the key dimensions along which accounts of the policy process differ. This is reproduced below, followed by another chart along the same lines (Figure 6.1). In the second chart the headings are omitted, but four propositions about the policy process are set out, each of which has something in common with the four in the first chart. Where the first chart may be seen as a crude formulation of the key positions, such as might have been set out before much of the modern work discussed in Chapters 2–5, the second chart offers more considered, indeed more tentative, formulations of each position that may be regarded as more up to date. What it implies is some convergence of views.

Proposition 1, as the most changed of the propositions, will be left to last. Propositions 2 and 3 in the second figure are identifiable as modified versions of the pluralist position and the elitist (or neo-Marxist) position explored in Chapter 2. It was recognised there that they have converged into formulations that reasonably comfortably combine both. Then Chapters 3 and 5 explored ways in which the pluralist position has been made more sophisticated through the recognition of (a) strategies used in the pursuit of interests, (b) the salience of interests inside government, and (c) the ways in

Figure 2.1   A simplified representation of the main approaches to the policy process

	Power structured	Power fragmented
Power distributed relatively equally	1. Representative government in which a unified executive is responsive to popular will	2. Pluralist government in which popular will prevails through competition between groups
Power distributed unequally	3. Government by an unrepresentative elite, or in the grip of external influences	4. Unpredictable and chaotic government, buffeted by multiple pressures

Figure 6.1   The simplified approach reformulated

1. The institutions of government are important, but must be regarded with scepticism. The discourses and ideologies that surround them may be more important than their formal characteristics.	2. There is extensive competition between groups to influence government and this is likely to be organised in networks in which the interests of those inside government will be involved as well as those outside.
3. Power is distributed unequally both inside and outside government, having an impact as much upon what is on the agenda and the context in which decisions are taken as on the decision process itself.	4. There is a great deal of confusion and incoherence in the policy process, but nevertheless we can identify choices made by actors, who may be able to learn from earlier events and choices.

which interests are organised in networks and policy communities. People naturally continue to differ about how unequal and how concentrated the distribution of power is, but the divergence is not as striking as it once was. This author's position is still to regard power inequalities as very salient but to be sceptical about the extent to which power is concentrated. In both cases, however, there is wide variation, both between countries and between policy areas. The latter topic will be looked at further in the next chapter.

Proposition 4 in Figure 6.1 is in many respects simply a restatement of the original statement in Figure 2.1. The important addition is the emphasis on policy choice, something that has been stressed at various points in previous chapters. Recognition of the importance of policy choice is also relevant for the rejection of the more structurally determinist positions embedded in some theoretical propositions (particularly those represented by proposition 3). A view that there is both a measure of chaos and elements of choice in the policy system does not contradict the account of power provided in the last paragraph. The chaos benefits some interests more than others (particularly the defenders of the status quo), and some actors have more opportunities to choose or to influence choice than others.

Proposition 1, in Figure 6.1, offers in place of a complacent statement about representative democracy simply an acknowledgement that institutional configurations matter (and, of course, the institutions of representative democracy are important in most of the policy process systems that are discussed in this book). Also important for the new proposition 1 is an emphasis upon what people (again, particularly the powerful) consider those institutional configurations to be. Moreover, it is through the deployment of discourses about institutions that power may be exercised. There is no necessary conflict between proposition 1 and propositions 2 and 3. But proposition 4 does seem to be rather in conflict with the other propositions, and particularly 1. It is interesting how the institutional theory discussed in Chapter 4 includes positions that emphasise both of these propositions. We find kindred theorists emphasising on the one hand structured pathways and on the other 'primeval soup' and the institutional 'garbage can'. The discussion of efforts to explain change within institutional theory indicates that there is an ongoing search for ways to handle this conflict.

However, this potential contradiction between those who emphasise the factors that contribute to stability in the system and those who emphasise the uncertainties and points at which choice is fundamental is no more than a version of the difficulties involved in reconciling the evidence of stability and the evidence of change that lie at the heart of social science discourse. Under the influence of the sociologist Giddens, perhaps the most popular contemporary exploration of this uses the terms 'structure' and 'agency' (see p. 52). Hence the issues about relating these two are well expressed by Farnsworth (2007, p. 100), with particular reference to pluralist theory, as follows:

> The biggest shift made by pluralists, in accepting the privileged interest thesis, was their recognition of the importance of structural power to

business influence on policy outcomes. Structural power (the power to influence without taking direct action) is derived from the ownership and control of capital and the uneven dependence of states and employees on capitalists. Agency power, upon which most analysis of business power tends to focus, is exercised through the actions of individual business people, firms or business associations (which themselves organise at different levels). The problem with focusing purely on agency, as classical pluralists found, is that it underplays the importance of political and economic structures, which favour some interests above others, determine the nature and extent of agency engagement and shape the expressed views and opinions of actors.

These propositions have finally to be recognised as offering an emphasis upon influences from within the nation state. There is a need not to forget the complexity of modern *governance*. This means that 'institutions of government' (proposition 1) may be international, that groups (proposition 2) may be organised outside and across individual states, that issues about inequalities of power (proposition 3) need to be analysed globally, and that choices are made by actors (proposition 4) who are increasingly conscious that they are playing on an international stage.

With the qualifications in that last paragraph added in, what is set out in Figure 6.1 are propositions about the policy process, all of which will be kept in mind during the discussion in Part 3 of the book. While there are conflicts between them, it is possible to take the view that all are important. Then, of course, there are various shades of difference of emphasis between writers on our subject, corresponding with differences in the interpretation of the relevance of the four propositions. It will also be the case that there are differences between countries, or between different points in time in the same country, or even between different policy areas, in the extent to which each of the points is relevant. Power may be more unequal, or institutional constraints may be greater, or networks may be more important, or decision processes may be more coherent, in some places or situations than in others. In this sense readers may find it helpful to explore issues by contrasting the strengths and weaknesses of different perspectives along the lines mentioned in Chapter 1 (see p. 10), where reference was made to Allison's use of contrasting lenses.

A final point about these propositions is that they may in various respects provide the theoretical foundations for hypotheses about the policy process. In this respect it is appropriate to interpose a methodological point. Some discussions of policy analysis theory (notably Hay, 2002 and Howlett and Ramesh, 2003) stress the need to distinguish inductive and deductive approaches. These were outlined in Box 5.1 and discussed a little in Chapter 5. Since each approach involves, in principle, the generation and testing of hypotheses, there is no reason, for the purposes of this discussion, to suggest that one approach should be preferred to the other. However, Howlett and Ramesh do appropriately warn us that 'many deductive-oriented researchers often seem to forget the contingent nature of their hypotheses and the need to constantly test and refine their assumptions against empirical evidence' (2003, pp. 46–7). Hay explicitly criticises the use of so-called 'rational' assumptions about self-interest in rational choice theory (see Chapter 5) in these terms. It is for this reason that public choice theory is not seen as a fifth proposition in Figure 6.1. It is seen as too closed a theoretical system, and treated instead as a source of some interesting insights and/or hypotheses, particularly in respect of the salience of interests (proposition 2). But a similar warning needs to be sounded about other deterministic theories. There is a temptation to take on board these approaches as offering a more exciting approach to generalisation about the policy process than those (which in some respects do not merit description as theories) that do no more than urge us to focus our attention on the behaviour of interest groups, the relevance of networks and communities and the salience of institutions. The stance taken here, accepting the undesirability of imposing an assumed model of the physical sciences on the study of public policy and acknowledging the very tentative nature of most generalisations on offer, means that a very pragmatic perspective will be a key influence on the discussion that follows in the rest of the book.

Examining the perspectives using examples

To illustrate the issues raised here and also to lead into the discussion to follow, let us return to the two British policy examples, explored in Chapter 1 and introduced in Boxes 1.2 and 1.3: the right to roam and the prevention of poverty among children. It was acknowledged in Chapter 1 that the first of these examples is much more susceptible to specific analysis than the second one. It concerns a very specific, rather low-profile, piece of legislation. The second by contrast, although as was pointed out in Chapter 1 it is described as a government 'policy' in the same way as the first one is, cannot be analysed without attention being given to both specific further 'policies' required to put it into action and to many other policies upon which it potentially impacts. The author has found that, while students have been able to engage in quite clear short policy process analysis exercises in respect of the issues like the first, he has had to warn students not to attempt ones like the second on the grounds that it takes them into a massive topic.

Here, therefore, whilst the issues about interpreting what happened in relation to the first example can be quite easily set out, the comments on the second will be more general and diffuse. The 'right to roam' legislation can be seen as a classic example of 'representative government' in process. The measure was promised in the 1997 Labour manifesto and what was put on the statute book largely fulfilled what was promised. It reflected a long interest among elements on the political Left, stemming from protest over problems of securing access to open moorland in the 1930s. It had precursors in earlier Labour legislation on access to the countryside, notably the National Parks Act passed in the 1940s. As far as its implementation was concerned it depended heavily on the presence at local level of an institutional system that already dealt with issues about access to the countryside, and could be expected to work with the new legislation with varying degrees of enthusiasm (an issue we return to below). Looking forward from this legislation it is not irrelevant to note that a commitment has been developed to increase access to the coast; in this sense one institutional development can be seen as a 'stepping stone' or 'pathway' towards another.

By contrast, the odd feature of the pledge to eliminate child poverty was its absence from the 1997 manifesto and its emergence from a Prime Ministerial speech. There were things in the manifesto whose enactment might have a positive impact upon child poverty, but there were also others that would have a neutral or negative impact. Most significant among these were commitments not to increase general taxation and not to go beyond the expenditure levels of existing government programmes. On the whole the traditional representative government perspective does not help very much to explain the emergence of this policy. On the other hand progress towards enactment of this policy has depended enormously upon commitments from within the institutional machinery of government, sorting out appropriate responses and vetoing other measures that might have a negative effect. Progress has in fact been modest. Choices of appropriate measures have been very significant, and here we reach another issue within institutional theory: that about the extent to which there were 'pathways' for the policy to follow. It might be expected that improvement of the existing benefits system, where the support levels offered were set at levels below the chosen poverty line, offered an obvious pathway for policy. However, the cost implications of such changes can be seen as likely to block this logical route towards the goal. Conversely the commitment of the new government to increasing the availability of work eased progress towards what has been the dominant response to the pledge: efforts to increase labour force participation by the poor. We enter here very contested territory about the extent to which 'new Labour' turned its back on the improved benefits route to poverty reduction (except in respect of tax credits explicitly linked to work force participation) in favour of the enhancement of workforce participation. Most of the existing academic narratives on this subject thus stress an ideological shift on the part of Labour. Finally, one other institutional point, the European Union use of a simple definition of poverty and the publication of indices that placed the UK in an unfavourable light may have had some impact on how the issue was played out (bearing in mind that the complex debate about how to define poverty had earlier seemed – from a political if not an academic point of view – rather deadlocked).

The right to roam policy is one which can be handled quite well in terms of a revised model of pluralism. Gainers from the policy were members of the public given greater access to the countryside. While this was not an issue about which strong public feelings could be found, those who were interested in access were strongly represented by recreational pressure groups like the Ramblers Association. Losers from the issue were landowners whose exclusive use rights were curbed slightly; they too were represented by some well-organised groups like the Country Landowners Association. Given that advocacy of a policy of this kind goes back to the 1930s it seems reasonable to suggest that initially the latter held the stronger cards (we are here in the territory of factors other than simple numbers affecting power resources). Since the 1930s various changes can be identified that would have been likely to change the balance of power:

- The decline of agriculture in the UK (see the discussion of policy communities on pp. 56–61).
- Increased leisure time and access to the countryside by the urban public.
- The declining political influence of large landowners.
- Ideological and cultural shifts away from deference to landed interests.

Notwithstanding that list it is important to bear in mind that (a) the actual loss of use by the owners was minor since only marginal land was included, (b) the Act contained measures to protect owners, and (c) implementation depended on local actors who might be influenced by local landed interests. Finally, it is important not to forget that there may be indirect interests at play in a situation like this. The measure was not cost free; significantly, arguments about administrative costs have been deployed in efforts to prevent further extensions. It was nevertheless relatively low cost, with those costs spread among a number of government agencies (the map makers and the local authorities who had to do the work on the ground). From the perspective of proposition 3 the right to roam policy is a very constrained measure, offering a minimal challenge to private interests (by contrast with the much more general Scandinavian approach to access to the countryside, let alone the land nationalisation ideas that were once formulated by socialist thinkers).

When we turn to the child poverty issue we are taken much more directly into the critique of pluralism embodied in proposition 3. The power of the poor depends crucially upon the extent to which there are specific situations in which they can threaten interest groups. This is of course a complex matter. An old but still interesting examination of this in the United States ultimately confuses by conflating fear of actual rebellion with electoral power (Piven and Cloward, 1972). A government of the Left (inasmuch as that label can be given to the Blair and Brown governments) can be seen as more likely to need votes from the poor. But the adoption of an electoral strategy directed at the median voter (a public choice proposition that nevertheless seems to sum up recent UK electoral behaviour) offers little to the poor. The concern not to be seen as a party of increased taxation has already been noted in this respect.

Moving more into the domain of theory which stresses discourses and ideologies, 'poverty' is an emotive concept inasmuch as it implies unjustifiable inequalities giving us a reason to look beyond pluralism to altruism. The latter word points us towards institutional explanations; we may observe what may be seen as a network (hesitating to use the stronger concept of a policy community here) comprising anti-poverty organisations, trade unions representing low-paid workers, public servants in the ministries and local governments that provide benefits and services to the poor, and academics (not to be over-rated in importance, but key sources of evidence). They, however, are up against alternative discourses which see the poor as responsible for their own plights or challenge the obvious redistributive remedies with arguments about incentives and requirements for economic growth.

However, unlike the right to roam policy the issue to be explained is on the one hand 'success' in putting the poverty issue on the agenda but otherwise very largely failure in pushing it forward to any great extent (a similar analysis by Katherine Smith (2007) of policy issues in respect of inequalities in health is discussed in the chapter on agenda setting, p. 159). Inasmuch as there was success, as noted above it was in respect of employment enhancement rather than the improvement of benefits. More controversially, that success is seen by some as carrying with it two prices:

- Pressure upon groups like disabled people and single parents into very poor quality work opportunities.
- Implicit in that, with its view of work as the best welfare, is an ideological perspective that tends to blame those who fail to get work for their own predicament.

Where does this take our discussion? First, let me be frank that – as for example in the last comment – we have been taken (particularly by the poverty example) into deeply-value loaded territory. Since competition between ideologies is important for the policy process, then how we explain policy processes will be influenced by our own ideologies.

Second, in using the 'catalogue' of explanations on offer different analyses are likely to apply to different issues. The two examples were, as already pointed out, chosen to enable a contrast to be made between a very precise policy issue and a very general one. Furthermore they also offer a contrast between what is contested territory in a very narrow, comparatively uncontroversial sense (even with scope for what seems to be an amicable compromise between interests) and one of the core areas of conflict in contemporary politics. The very modest nature of the movement on the poverty issue is then in many respects a measure of the consensual nature of modern party politics.

Third, and this is the point at which we look ahead to what is to come, notwithstanding the differences observed, an examination of both policies areas throws up:

- Issues about how matters get on the agenda.
- Issues about their progress once on the agenda; in the poverty case these have particular reference to the crowded policy world they entered, in the

simpler right to roam case attention can be given to the way details are formulated.

- Finally, in the right to roam case implementation obviously seems to be important; in the poverty case there are then important detailed issues – not outlined here – about the measures linked to poverty reduction (the administration of tax credits, the operation of 'welfare to work' measures) rather than the broad policy aspiration that can be examined in these terms.

The rest of this book looks at these issues; the theories explored in this section offer a variety of overall approaches to their examination.

Part

3

Analysis of the policy process

7 Looking at policy: types of policy and stages in the process

SYNOPSIS

While it is obvious that studying the policy process means studying the making of policy, we noted in Chapter 1 that policy is by no means a simple phenomenon. Furthermore, since different policies have different substantive contents it must be expected that policy will be made manifest in many different ways. Two approaches to handling this problem seem to be on offer from past literature: one of these is to use policy typologies; the other is to divide analysis into stages.

This chapter explores issues about policy differences by looking at some examples of very different policy areas, accepting the likelihood that there will be extensive differences but making no assumptions about how these might be categorised. These areas will be labelled in terms of their substantive content and explored to illustrate the diversity of public policy and highlight the very different analytical issues that emerge in each case. The policy areas that will be considered are:

- making war
- trying to control the economy
- providing income maintenance (or social security)
- providing education
- trying to prevent pollution
- reorganising local government.

This will be followed by a section comparing and contrasting these areas of policy in terms of the extent to which the stages model is applicable to their analysis.

Introduction

At the start of the part of the book where we move away from overarching theory to the examination of parts of the policy process, we need to consider how this large subject can be divided up. One way to divide the subject up is to focus upon different *kinds* of policy. There are obviously divisions in the literature in respect of policy content, often with distinct areas of scholarship in respect of foreign policy, economic policy, social policy and so on. These areas are often further subdivided: hence, for example, within social policy we find specialists on health policy, education policy, housing policy, income maintenance policy and so on. Prima facie, there are good grounds for arguing that what we have here are very different policy 'contents' and that these will have an influence on the characteristics of the policy process. We will explore this point more precisely below.

An alternative approach is to see the policy process as involving discrete stages or cycles. Some problems with this approach will be identified, particularly that the policy process takes many forms, with many feedback loops, making it undesirable to impose upon its analysis a model that has been strongly influenced by a view of the way the process should proceed rather than by analysis of the way it actually does occur. Nevertheless, it will be argued that there is a pragmatic case for the stages approach inasmuch as it offers a way to divide up a large subject. The case for the structure of the rest of the book rests upon that justification.

Introducing the different policy areas discussed

Some discussions of politics and the policy process make a distinction between the 'high politics' of managing external relations and the economy and the 'low politics' of delivering services and regulating everyday life. The first two policy areas to be explored here – making war and trying to control the economy – belong in the 'high politics' category, therefore, and the rest (generally speaking) belong in the 'low politics' category. The choice of the first two was dictated by a desire to highlight some of the characteristics of two policy areas that get little attention from the general run of discussions of policy processes and have vast, rather separate literatures of their own. The low/high distinction has been used to emphasise rather different configurations of interests. Jordan, for example, uses it in relation to those who see the European Union largely in terms of inter-governmental relations, who he says tend to emphasise the high politics, and those who stress the development of multi-level governance, who are particularly concerned with low politics issues (2001, p. 204). John (2001) mentions the way in which it has been used to indicate the policies that are particularly likely to be delegated to local government. These points are relevant to any consideration of the extent to which the policy processes in relation to making war or controlling the economy are rather different, but the point should not be exaggerated as each policy area has some distinctive characteristics of its own.

Making war

The study of policy decisions about the making of war are peculiarly absent from the mainstream policy process literature. Indeed, in political science the examination of this issue comes within the remit of international relations, a topic that is often rather hived off from the rest of the discipline. For example, the only discussion of war in Almond et al.'s *Comparative Politics Today* (2004), which is subtitled *A World View*, is a brief comparison of different national experiences of military violence (p. 146). It is thus rather risky for the present author, whose academic work has been confined to issues about domestic politics, to make comments on the study of this issue. Nevertheless, it does seem inappropriate to try to generalise about the policy process without any mention of this very important aspect.

Given the fundamental impact of war upon society, it can reasonably be argued from a prescriptive point of view that the making of war should be under democratic control. Yet probably this is unlikely to occur. The journalistic treatment of the negotiations between nations, fundamental for decisions about making war, tends to personalise the policy process. It is thus treated as being primarily about the aims and aspirations of political leaders and about the bargaining between them. In many respects this is treated as a kind of chess game of moves, gambits and bluffs. The international relations literature seems to adopt a similar approach, except that much of the personalisation of the journalists is replaced by the reification of nation states (America argues this, France did that, etc.). Hay's analysis of the various approaches to the study of international relations suggests that many of them use rational models (the chess game approach) but with varying assumptions about the idealism of the underlying goals (2002, Chapter 1).

One study about issues of war and peace (in this case the avoidance of war) that has had a great influence on the study of policy processes is Allison's (1971) study of the Cuban missile crisis. In 1962 the Russians began to install missiles in Cuba. The Americans, seeing this as a direct threat to themselves, challenged this action. After threats and fraught negotiations the Russians pulled back. This crisis, probably the most dangerous event in the history of the Cold War, since the Americans certainly contemplated using nuclear weapons, has been extensively analysed. Even a very compelling film has been made of the event. Allison's analysis of the account involves comparing three alternative models of the policy process. The details of this are set out in Box 7.1.

Box 7.1	Allison's (1971) analysis of the Cuban missile crisis, using three models

First, Allison considers the 'rational actor model', which sees actions as being formed by purposeful agents with certain goals and objectives. These agents have to choose between alternative courses of action in order to achieve their goals. Alternatives are assumed to have a set of consequences attached, and rational choice consists of selecting the best alternative in these terms. This version of the story highlights the roles of the two national leaders, Kennedy and Khrushchev, as decision makers, as do most popular accounts of the crisis.

Second, Allison considers the organisational process model which sees action not as rational choice but as the output of organisational behaviour. This behaviour is largely the enactment of established routines in which sequential attention is given to goals and standard operating procedures are adopted. The concern here is with how the decision systems worked in the two countries, a topic on which there is of course much better evidence from the United States than from Russia.

Allison's third model is the bureaucratic politics model, which sees action as neither choice nor output but as the result of bargaining between groups and individuals in the political system. Here questions are raised about the interests of the key actors in the crisis. Crucial here is the issue of the power of the military. Accounts of events in the United States suggest that Kennedy came under enormous pressure from the 'hawks' within the military, who wanted to bomb Cuba, but resisted with the support of the more cautious State Department (see also Dallek, 2003, Chapter 16).

Critics of Allison's work (Bendor and Hammond, 1992) suggest that there are not three models here but two, and that the contrast is between the 'rational actor' model and models that stress the roles of institutions.

What is significant about the Cuban missile crisis story from our point of view is that domestic political pressures (other than from within the core executive) within the United States seem to be entirely absent from the account. The early stages of the negotiations were kept very quiet and at no stage was there the kind of political debate that would have opened the decision making to any direct democratic influence. President Kennedy, ever a calculating politician, would certainly have given consideration to the impact of his decisions upon his electoral chances, but that simply implies a worry about the trade-off between having been seen to be weak on the one hand and the damage entailed in war on the other.

In this last sense we can see the politics of peace and war throughout the second half of the twentieth century as still influenced by the events that preceded the Second World War, when Hitler expanded his power rapidly while the allies sought to 'appease' him (Gilbert and Gott, 2000). Probably (though poll data from that period is not very good), appeasement was the popular (democratic) option. Such thinking seems to have continued to influence decisions about military action to this day. The 2003 war against Iraq was pursued (certainly on the part of the United Kingdom; the evidence on the United States is more ambiguous) in the face of widespread opposition both among the general public and in the ranks of the ruling United Kingdom Labour Party. The arguments of the Labour leader, Tony Blair, about the need for war certainly included a view about the need to cease to appease a dictator. It is not appropriate here to try to reach a definitive explanation of that event, but it is worthwhile mentioning a few of the explanations on offer, each of which is suggestive of the peculiar nature of the policy process when it comes to war (see Kampfner, 2003 and Shawcross, 2003 for contrasting accounts of the UK policy). These explanations are summarised in Box 7.2. Clearly, whatever explanation is used seems to testify to the relatively narrow circle of actors who played key roles in

---

| Box 7.2 | Explanations of why the UK participated in the Iraq War in 2003 |

The justification originally most used to convince those opposed to the war was that Iraq had 'weapons of mass destruction' nearly ready for use. It was substantially discredited, raising a whole range of issues about how questionable information derived from spying activities was packaged for the public. It tended then to be replaced by the argument that it was necessary to rid Iraq of an evil dictator, a problematical justification since there are other countries to which that argument would also apply but where intervention is not contemplated. This relates to a more general point about the extent to which the United States and its allies can feasibly (let alone morally) intervene directly in the internal affairs of countries suffering from oppression by a dictator. Both arguments may alternatively be seen simply as justifications to mask other motives.

A second kind of explanation for the UK role in the Iraq conflict is that Blair and some of his key supporters regarded it as essential to follow the American lead on international affairs. Here we have echoes of the argument above that sees American world dominance as a key factor in national decision making. From a UK perspective there remain questions about how essential it was that we supported our 'ally'.

The third kind of explanation goes beyond the overt political positions in both the UK and the US to suggest the continuing importance of what an American President, Eisenhower (interestingly, an old soldier and on the Right of the political spectrum), many years ago called the 'military–industrial complex', an unrepresentative network that stands to benefit from military actions. There are here also some key questions about the interests of the oil industry.

A fourth kind of explanation, much favoured by journalists, simply focuses on the personal psychology and choices of the key actors and on the relationships between them.

decisions about war and peace. In Chapter 8, when we explore issues about policy agenda setting, we will examine the role of political manifestos in that process. One thing we will not find is statements of intention to go to war. On the other hand, we *will* find generalised comments on intentions to prevent war, and, to be fair, the 'do not appease' rationale implies a willingness to risk war, or conduct small wars, to avoid worse. But the interesting thing about this is the way that evolution into war then involves an incremental process (see pp. 145–6 for a further discussion of this) in which, rather than there being an overall analysis of the options, there tends to be a process of drift as successive measures fail to prevent (or even exacerbate) conflict. A mid-twentieth-century war that provides a powerful example of this is the Vietnam War (see Box 7.3).

| Box 7.3 | The escalation of the Vietnam War – an incremental process |

After France abandoned its Vietnamese colony in the late 1950s, the United States became involved in attempting to prevent Communist dominance of the whole country. It moved incrementally from a position of simply providing military advice to the regime ruling the south of the country to providing supporting troops. Then it gradually increased the number of troops in the country to the point where it was to all intents and purposes a war between America and North Vietnam, despite the fact that America never formally declared war. Eventually, the United States withdrew and allowed the North to take over the whole country. Much political recrimination followed, but it is very difficult to point to crucial decisions that precipitated action, as opposed to a process of drift and particular leaders who took significant decisions that escalated the conflict.

Overall, then, it may be argued that the making of war is a very peculiar policy process, both in terms of separating out the influences upon it and in terms of the stages it goes through.

Trying to control the economy

The comments in the last section about the way in which international relations are given little attention in the policy process literature also applies to some extent to issues about the management of the economy (though an important exception to this is Hall, 1986). Much analysis of alternative approaches to this issue comes, of course, from economists rather than political scientists, and the fusion between the disciplines tends to come in the form of a 'political economy' literature that is particularly interested in macrotrends in the political system and in the analysis of globalism. But in the modern world the processes involved in efforts to manage the economy are of fundamental importance, both because of the importance of the issue and because of the significance of this activity for other policy processes.

The evolution of stances on how to control the economy is an important feature of modern political history. The nineteenth-century ideal of minimal government in the United States and the United Kingdom rested upon the idea of *laissez-faire*. The role of government in this field was simply to ensure that nothing interfered with the working of the market. Government expenditure in this context should be kept under control by the 'balanced budget', trying to make income and expenditure balance and minimising government borrowing. The threat to laissez-faire that was most evident to politicians at this time came from the emergent trade unions, and the legislative response to this was generally repressive. At the end of the nineteenth century, as political participation increased, the maintenance of the status quo began also to suggest (a) a slightly more conciliatory attitude towards trade unions and (b) a recognition that the other side of industry might also act in ways that damaged the market. It was for the latter reason that American legislators, in particular, developed anti-trust legislation to try to limit monopolistic tendencies in industry.

The laissez-faire view of public economic policy was not shared by many of the nations that formed and/or industrialised later than the United Kingdom. The origins of a more corporatist view of the role of government (see pp. 53–6) in various continental European nations stemmed from the recognition that government might play a more active role in the stimulation of economic development, in partnership with business (and perhaps labour).

The events that did most to challenge the laissez-faire view of the role of government were the two world wars. These forced governments into an active role in the control of the economy, into roles (which they expected to be temporary) as key managers of enterprises themselves and into the accumulation of high levels of debt. The Second World War had a particularly fundamental impact on the relationship between government and the economy. But even before it started, a search had begun for new ways in which governments might regulate economic activities. After the war a system was developed to try to stabilise relationships between national currencies. But in addition, nations began to develop new ways of managing their internal economies. In the long run the relationship between these two issues was to become critical.

Boxes 7.4 and 7.5 provide an abbreviated account of economic management in the United Kingdom between 1945 and the present day, but it should be noted that other countries developed similar measures and faced similar problems with them.

The discussion of UK economic policy in Boxes 7.4 and 7.5, whilst superficial in terms of the complexity of the issues, may seem to go a long way away from the central concerns of this book. It has been inserted to give some idea of the extent to which this crucial area of public policy involves

| Box 7.4 | UK economic management, 1945–79 |

Economic management techniques (often called Keynesian) were developed in the 20 years after the Second World War, involving manipulation of levels of government expenditure and taxation to try to retain full employment without inflation. This generated a cyclical pattern of economic (and government expenditure) growth, regularly punctuated by curbs to prevent rapid inflation. In the 1960s, despite an increasing commitment to economic planning, the cyclical pattern worsened. Inflation increased, balance of payments crises forced strong restraints to be applied to public expenditure and private incomes on a number of occasions, and, at the depressed point of the cycle, quite marked increases in unemployment occurred. In the mid-1970s, the UK faced a more severe crisis linked to worldwide increases in energy prices, in which very high inflation, a balance of payments problem and continuing high unemployment occurred all at the same time. Measures to cope with the first two by traditional means worsened the third (Dell, 1991).

Different schools of economists preached different solutions to these problems. On the Right, the 'monetarist' school of thought became increasingly influential, arguing that governments must control the money supply and let economic forces bring the system under control (Friedman, 1962, 1977). This viewpoint had some influence over policies in the 1970s, but politicians were reluctant to let bankruptcies and redundancies occur on a sufficient scale to test the monetarist hypothesis properly. More influential, and more in conformity with Keynesian orthodoxy, were those economists who argued that income restraint was necessary to bring unemployment and inflation into balance, and to prevent the UK's balance of payments becoming unmanageable as rising wages led us to import goods we could ill afford, while making it more difficult to sell things. Incomes policies were seen as crucial to solving these problems, yet over and over again governments found that political pressures made these very difficult to sustain for any length of time. The whole picture was, however, complicated by changes in the pattern of trade in the world and, particularly, by rises in prices of primary commodities, especially oil.

largely centralised decision making, in which very specialised interest groups may be consulted (particularly from both sides of industry). What is involved is a variety of complex devices, under expert control and (in the case of the delegation of powers to central banks) partly outside direct political control. The participants will include key figures from other countries and from international organisations (the European Union, the International Monetary Fund, etc.). Against the background of a policy analysis literature that emphasises processes, and sometimes stages, we have here an activity that may be compared to driving a vehicle, in which a succession of specific (and often quick) adjustments have to be made by key

Box 7.5	UK economic management, 1979–2003

After 1979, the 'monetarist' theory mentioned in Box 7.4 was more boldly put into practice by the new Conservative government. It treated the money supply, and particularly the public sector borrowing rate, as the key phenomena to keep under control. It was prepared to let unemployment rise rapidly in the war against inflation. It abandoned incomes policy in the private sector, seeking only to keep pay increases to public employees tightly under control. Initially, it found the removal of pay controls and its own taxation adjustments produced severely inflationary effects. It was subsequently successful in bringing inflation under control, but achieved that at the expense of a rapid increase in unemployment.

Later in the 1980s, the government abandoned any rigorous attempt to keep the money supply under control, concentrating attention instead on the foreign exchange value of the pound (Stephens, 1996). At this stage the European Union was moving towards the idea of a common currency. This measure would obviously eliminate currency fluctuations between its member countries. The UK, while cautious about the idea of a common currency, saw the merit of at least using controls to shadow European currency movements. That effort then failed in the UK, when currency speculation forced a dramatic currency revaluation. Meanwhile, the arrival of the Euro imposed this sort of discipline on its members.

An interesting feature of Labour's stance on the control of the economy since 1997 has been to give control over interest rates to a committee (appointed by the government) under the leadership of the nationalised Bank of England. That committee is charged to use interest rates to control inflation, an echo of monetarism but without the rigid and rather artificial element of control over the money supply. This is not a uniquely British idea – similar controls are exercised by central bankers in the United States and, most importantly for the UK, within the Euro zone by a European central bank. This measure leaves the government having to make decisions about public expenditure and about measures to prevent unemployment with a key economic regulator out of its hands. Active policies on either of these fronts may have an impact upon inflation, in which case the raising of interest rates could have a contrary effect inasmuch as private and/or public borrowing will be affected (Keegan, 2003).

At the time this book is being revised there are grounds for doubt about the efficacy of central bank control over interest rates in a global economy in which the behaviour of banks may be determined more by their inter-relationships with each other and with other independent global actors than by central bank regulation. The government is being drawn into new ways to try to control the economy, and new devices to try to protect small borrowers or lenders from the impact of problems in the world economy.

central actors. As already stressed, these decisions may be very important to other aspects of the policy process. Arguments about the right way to take them have lain at the centre of disputes between political ideologies, which may be seen as macro elements in the overall policy process.

Providing income maintenance

Turning to income maintenance, or what is often called social security or social protection policy, we come right into one of the mainstream government domestic issues and one to which a great deal of the policy process literature is seen to be applicable. Income maintenance dominates the public policy spending agendas of many states. But it is interesting to see how, when we look at all that is embraced under this rubric, we find a mixture of types of policy. Not surprisingly, there are very lively political controversies about the forms income maintenance policies should take. Income maintenance policy emerged as a major issue on the public policy agenda at the beginning of the twentieth century. Before that there were limited efforts to relieve poverty, characterised by strict tests of need and high levels of local discretion. The new income maintenance agenda arose as societies urbanised, industrialised and democratised. The idea that income inadequacies should be addressed by public policy arose both from the recognition of demands of new members of the electorate and from an awareness of the threat to public order from an increasingly organised mass population. Mass mobilisation for war increased attention to this issue. Since that time the issues on the agenda have been very much a combination of a concern for income maintenance in general with more specific issues about the relief of poverty. It is interesting to note how concerns about the difficulties that voluntary or market-based efforts encountered in dealing with the income maintenance needs of the broad mass of workers played a big part in the evolution of the policy agenda, alongside concerns about poverty. It is not without significance that in many countries pensions for soldiers and for government employees were established well before any other regularised income maintenance provisions. Such policies – and particularly pensions – imply very long-term commitments. Hence there are four crucial issues about this part of the policy agenda:

1. Income maintenance does not necessarily imply redistribution: it is to a large extent ultimately redistributively neutral inasmuch as what is involved is a form of forced savings for predicted contingencies (particularly old age).

2. Inasmuch as income maintenance policies offer benefits for the well-off as well as the poor, they may have substantial and strong electoral and pressure group support coalitions.

3. Inasmuch as income maintenance policies offer strongly supported rights to future benefits, their construction involves a distinct, staged process

from the placing of issues on the policy agenda, through the enactment of quite complex policies with elaborate rules about entitlements, to an implementation process in which officials are expected to honour claims based upon statutory rights.

4. Income maintenance structures (particularly pensions) imply long-run commitments and expectations. Hence this policy area is particularly one where pathways determined by past policies restrict opportunities for policy change.

(See Walker, 2005, for a wide ranging comparative analysis of the issues here.)

Income maintenance benefits may be designed simply to relieve poverty, whatever its causes, but more typically income maintenance systems recognise a number of contingencies to which a response is provided, the main ones being: old age, sickness and disability, unemployment, or loss of a prime family breadwinner.

Income maintenance policy can take any of the following forms (indeed, a combination of these forms characterises most systems):

- Contributory benefits
- Non-contributory but contingent benefits
- Selective, means-tested benefits
- Tax reliefs and tax credits
- Employer benefits mandated or regulated by the government.

We have already noted that income maintenance policies are not necessarily redistributive. This is particularly the case where contributory public or private pension schemes are in use. An extreme form of the non-distributive approach is offered by 'provident schemes' pioneered in Singapore, which simply involved state-enforced savings accounts.

A regulative approach to policy is directly visible where governments impose obligations upon private companies to provide schemes or expect private social security systems to abide by rules designed to protect their funds. But regulation is also in evidence in this policy area inasmuch as schemes impose obligations on claimants – to seek work or to undertake efforts to improve their health, for example. This then has implications for these other areas of public policy.

The distinction between states in which contributory benefits (social insurance) dominate income maintenance rather than selective means-tested ones, together with one concerning the extent to which policies redistribute income, dominates the regime model described in Chapter 5 (see p. 87). As was noted there, the regime model is seen to offer a route towards the interpretation of differences in access to the policy process. It also contributes to the explanation of why systems vary in their responses to cutbacks, and still diverge despite global influences which might have been expected to enhance homogeneity.

The fact that income maintenance policy is often costly for governments means policy change issues return to the agenda with great regularity.

Pension provisions were developed when life expectancies were very much less than they are today. Fluctuations in unemployment pose unanticipated burdens from time to time. Changing patterns of family behaviours have made the occurrence of single-parent families much more likely in some societies. In most countries current benefits are funded from current government income. Even most social insurance systems do not involve the accumulation of contributions in a fund but a 'pay as you go' approach, using current contributions. There are complicated reasons why this policy option was selected in the first place, which it would need a large digression to explore here. The point is that rising entitlements put pressure on income maintenance schemes, placing issues about the cutting of benefits very high on modern public policy agendas. This issue will be explored further in the next chapter, with particular reference to pensions. Finally, of course, the cost of social security implies that issues about taxation policy regularly arise in social security decision making. In this respect it is not surprising that a great deal of UK social security policy is under the direct control of the Treasury.

This section has shown that income maintenance policy in many respects dominates the public policy scene. While many of the ideas used in the analysis of public policy can easily be applied to income maintenance policy, income maintenance policies are nevertheless very diverse.

Providing education

Education has been chosen as the next area of policy to consider. It is one where public provision has dominated for a long while. It is also a policy area in which the actual characteristics of policy are very likely to be considerably influenced at the point of delivery. In other words, in many respects education policy is determined by what teachers actually do. Education policy has quite a lot in common with health policy in this respect, and to a lesser extent with other services such as social care.

There are several ways in which the government may determine or influence education:

■ as a direct provider;
■ as a funder of services provided by other autonomous or partly autonomous organisations (local governments, school boards, schools, voluntary organisations, private organisations);
■ as a regulator of privately provided services.

It is also important to recognise that there is a range of policy issues in a field like education, some of which may be given extensive attention in public policy while others may be neglected or ignored. The following list highlights some key issues, but is certainly not comprehensive:

- the funding of education
- the structuring of the system
- arrangements for control over the various parts of the system
- the content of the curriculum
- qualifications of teachers
- teaching quality
- the payment of teachers
- subsidies for students.

Comments here are based upon developments in the United Kingdom. Between the end of the Second World War and the early 1990s, the government in the UK was the main funder of state schools and exercised a loose regulatory supervision of private schools. Education was free in the state schools. Central government delegated many of the issues about the structure of the education system to local government, but increasingly intervened towards the end of the period to try to influence the organisation of secondary education. It paid remarkably little attention to the content of the curriculum. It regulated the qualifications of teachers and their pay but operated a relatively light inspection system to scrutinise the quality of their work.

Over the same period, the level of government intervention in the higher education system was even lighter. Central government funded almost the whole system, providing free places for UK students and means-tested maintenance grants towards their living costs. The universities were self-governing institutions; many other colleges were run by local government. The content of higher education was totally in the hands of the institutions, except in a few special cases where education was providing a licence to practise a publicly supported profession like medicine or teaching (though in these cases control was largely in the hands of the professions themselves). There were no required qualifications for teachers in higher education and there was no inspection system.

Since the 1990s both sectors have experienced dramatic change driven by a strong political interest in education, with strong parental pressure for raising standards and opportunities, and a political ideology, shared by Right and Left, that education must serve the economy (see Tomlinson, 2001; Ball, 2008). Change in the system has consisted of a great deal of centralisation but also some decentralisation. Centralisation has involved a substantive increase in government control over the school curriculum, and the development of a testing system and a strong inspection system to go with it. In the higher education sector central government has exercised strong control over the way the system has expanded, has developed various inspection devices and has used its control over funding to steer the system. The school system has experienced decentralisation inasmuch as local authority control has been weakened, and there has been a sort of 'hollowing out process' (see Box 12.4, p. 243) in which power has been delegated down to the schools and parents have been given more scope to choose schools for their children and to participate in the government of schools. In both sectors institutions have been given greater freedom to determine what individual teachers are paid.

While the state system has remained intact, various forms of what may be called 'quasi-marketisation' have occurred. In the school sector, funding depends on pupil numbers. Inasmuch as this interacts with parental choice (and how much the latter really exists depends upon geography), it has an impact upon whether schools succeed or fail. The publication of test results for individual schools can then further influence this process. In the higher education sector, similarly, funds follow students, and given the geographical mobility of students this can have a significant effect. A system which rations research money according to ratings of research performance, coupled with competition for other sources of funding, is contributing to the enhancement of the hierarchy within higher education institutions, with Oxbridge and some London colleges at the top and institutions recently promoted to university status at the bottom.

The overall, and necessarily simplified, objective of this brief account is to highlight the complexity of the politics of education policy. Governments come under a great deal of pressure on education policy and are engaged in much often ideologically driven change. There is a strong education policy community which is eager to influence policy, yet in the last few years this community has lost many battles against the government.

However, the complexity of the system and the subtlety of the teaching task mean that what actually happens cannot be 'read off' simply from the policy objectives that are set out by the key actors in the system. Thus Bowe and his colleagues, in their *Reforming Education and Changing Schools* (1992), have explored the complex way in which a strong, politically driven central initiative is translated into action. They describe the expression of policy as the production of a set of 'texts'. They go on to say:

> texts are generalized, written in relation to idealizations of the 'real world', and can never be exhaustive, they cannot cover all eventualities. The texts can often be contradictory ..., they use key terms differently, and they are reactive as well as expository (that is to say, the representation of policy changes in the light of events and circumstances and feedback from arenas of practice). Policy is not done and finished at the legislative moment, it evolves in and through the texts that represent it, texts have to be read in relation to the time and the particular site of their production. They also have to be read with and against one another – intertextuality is important. Second, the texts themselves are the outcome of struggle and compromise. The control of the representation of policy is problematic. (Bowe, Ball and Gold, 1992, p. 21)

As noted above, for clarity of exposition the remarks above have been confined to the UK system, but similar developments can be seen elsewhere. At the same time there are, of course, many variations in the way in which the centralisation/localisation dynamic has been handled and in the forms that marketisation takes.

Trying to prevent pollution

Pollution policy is explored here not simply because it is a very good example of a policy area where public policy is primarily regulatory but also because pollution is an issue that literally spills over national boundaries, making it a salient concern for modern *governance* (see p. 20).

Pollution comes about because of the abandonment of matter as waste and the discharge of effluents into water or air. Pollution problems are endemic in modern societies, a consequence of very many of the activities that create and sustain the levels of material prosperity enjoyed by advanced industrial societies. They need to be seen in the context of population growth, and the resultant pressure upon space and resources. They also need to be seen in relation to very high and complex levels of consumption.

In some respects pollution control policy may be regarded, particularly by those nations still struggling to raise material standards, as a luxury that is only available to those with high standards of living. If, further, the efforts of pollution policy are seen as directed towards the maintenance of an 'unspoilt' natural environment, this will particularly heighten the contrast between 'north' and 'south' (using those compass point expressions as shorthand for global conflicts of interest between developed and less developed nations). In the same way, where the problem is seen to be population growth, it will be pointed out by the nations of the 'south' that the amount of pollution generated per person is very much higher in rich countries than in poor ones. In still industrialising countries, these are bases for understandable hostility to some of the efforts to curb pollution that come from the nations whose earlier activities raised global levels of pollution to high levels in the first place.

This conflict also highlights the point that, whilst much of the attack upon environmental pollution involves a search for ways to eliminate the pollutants that are produced or to clean up after polluting activities, there is an alternative that is simpler – in the scientific if not in the political sense. This is to alter the way in which production or consumption occurs. Production techniques could be adopted that are slower and more extravagant in their use of human resources but produce fewer waste products (in particular, fewer waste products from energy use). Consumption patterns may involve simpler products, less well-packaged products, slower methods of travel and so on. There may even be a need to question whether certain forms of consumption are really necessary. These are the sorts of considerations that enter into efforts to define 'sustainable growth' (see Weale, 1992 and Cahill, 2002 for good discussions of these issues). The evidence on climate change indicates a need for governments to adopt some curbs on behaviour. This takes them into areas where they may have to make unpopular decisions, risking reactions by voters or offending powerful interest groups (curbing fuel use etc., increasing the cost of travel, making desired commodities unavailable). This both makes more difficult the politics of pollution control and brings policy issues in this area into conflict with other public policies (designed to sustain employment, encourage intensive agriculture etc.).

Another factor in the increased interest in pollution control policies is the awareness that pollution cannot be a private matter – for nations any more than for individuals. The global economic interactions that sustain the prosperity of many nations, together with tourism, contribute to the recognition that pollution is an international issue. Ecological disasters with transnational implications – like the nuclear power station explosion at Chernobyl in 1986 – reinforce this awareness. The increased attention today to a spill-over effect that is global in nature, the impact of emissions (particularly of carbon dioxide, CO_2) upon the climate of the world, intensifies the international conflict around this policy. The world faces a truly international version of the policy challenge offered by 'tragedy of the commons' analysis discussed on p. 95.

Pollution control policy development owes a great deal to scientific advances that have enabled people to perceive more clearly the damage that is being caused, and to understand how it is caused. This has also, through the contribution it makes to the understanding of long-range and long-term effects, assisted the process by which pollution has been put on the global political agenda (see Kormondy, 1989 and Brenton, 1994 for a discussion of the increasing international activity, starting largely from the Unesco conference on the biosphere of 1968 and the United Nations Stockholm conference of 1972 and carried forward by the Rio conference of 1992).

The importance of science also means that expertise is important for the identification of pollution problems. This contributes to complicated issues about the role of self-interest in relation to pollution control. In some cases democratic political participation has been seen to work against effective pollution control where actions against environmental hazards are seen as direct threats to jobs (Crenson, 1971; Blowers, 1984). In these cases it is not merely that there is the sort of insidious trade-off problem identified above; it is also the case that the trade-off is often perceived to be between a quite direct material threat and an uncertain health hazard. There are several factors which make the latter hard to perceive and interpret (these are outlined in Box 7.6).

Expertise is involved in identifying the presence of pollutants and in determining their effects; it is also involved in tracing pathways, interactions and long-term effects. Two good examples of this which have contributed to the evolution of the environmental policy agenda concern acid rain and climate change. Box 7.7 explores some key issues about the former. The issues about the impact of emissions on climate are even more complex (as noted at the end of Box 7.6). Here the potential problems are

| Box 7.6 | Issues concerning the detection and interpretation of pollution problems |

Some pollution problems are readily apparent to everyone – they can be smelt or seen or heard or even felt. But many pollution phenomena, including many of the most dangerous, are not open to straightforward sensory perception. This is the case with nuclear radiation hazards. It is also the case with many chemicals suspended in water or air, in particular metals like lead and asbestos. In these cases, measurements are needed to inform people that a pollution hazard is present. Methods may not be available to do this; but if they are, they are likely to involve the use of scientific techniques not usually available to the general public. Moreover, when such measurements are carried out, the evidence from them may not be made available to the public. The emitters are likely to want to conceal that evidence, and officials and governments may collude with this concealment.

Once measurements are taken, moreover, there may still be issues about the risks related to any particular form of pollution. Chemical suspensions in air and water are always present, and dangers exist when they are excessively concentrated. But what is an excessive concentration – how much over how long a period? The poisoning processes which occur from pollution are not generally dramatic. They occur over a long time span. The evidence that poisoning is occurring is accumulated gradually, and in circumstances in which there are reasons to argue that the resultant diseases have other causes. In the case of nuclear radiation, for example, there has been a long-standing controversy about whether a slightly raised incidence of comparatively rare diseases in particular places or among particular workforces is attributable to radiation exposure. The difficult policy issue that this raises concerns the extent to which a 'precautionary' approach is justified that curbs pollution just in case of long-run dangers or dangers that might emerge later (Barker and Peters, 1993).

The issue of climate change involves yet another dependence on scientific evidence. The public can only exceptionally, and often anecdotally, identify climate change effects for themselves. But even where effects can be identified we need scientists to examine the causal mechanisms. Changes do have other causes than increases in CO_2 emissions, and significantly there are challenges to the dominant thesis funded by interest groups whose activities would be affected by policies to check emissions. The public, and of course key policy decision makers, are bombarded with alternative interpretations of the levels of risk and alternative suggestions about how best to deal with them.

global and the adverse effects will take a long while to manifest themselves. There is still a great deal of controversy about them.

Another important issue about interaction, which is illustrated by the acid rain issue, concerns the relationships between the different strategies

| Box 7.7 | Acid rain as a cross-national pollution issue |

Initial concerns about emissions from combustion processes focused upon their impact on their immediate environment (Ashby and Anderson, 1981). Meteorological observations were necessary to identify the relationship between emissions from combustion processes and the subsequent precipitation of chemicals in rain at places separated often by considerable geographical distances. The relationship between British emissions on the one hand and tree loss and lake acidification in Scandinavia on the other, for example, had to be carefully established. Scientific complexity and national self-interest combined to make the debate about acid rain a difficult and long-drawn-out affair (Whetstone and Rosencranz, 1983).

for disposing of pollutants. There are choices about whether to disperse pollutants into the air, into water (rivers or the sea), or to bury them in the ground. Yet chemicals in the air get carried into lakes and rivers, chemicals in rivers get deposited on the land, and chemicals from landfill sites leach out into water courses. Dispersal into air or water or land, which, in the past, has been seen to be unproblematical because of the capacity of these media to absorb (and ultimately dilute) pollutants, becomes less and less satisfactory over time. Now, not only is it recognised that many rivers are carrying more pollutants than they can absorb, but worries are also emerging about strategies which involve the disposing of pollutants at sea. Some seas in particular are vulnerable as 'sinks', where matter dispersed into them and into their feeder rivers is becoming concentrated (the Mediterranean and the Baltic, for example: see Kinnersley, 1994).

These interaction effects make the determination of pollution control policies difficult. First, they make it necessary for policy strategies to be holistic – concerns about reducing air pollution, keeping rivers clear or controlling landfill activities need to be integrated, despite the fact that very different agencies, interest groups and kinds of expertise are likely to be involved. Second, it is difficult to put effective geographical boundaries around policies and regulatory agencies. Pollutants travel from one administrative area to another; in many cases, indeed, they travel from one nation state to another. Seas like the Mediterranean obviously have many nation states around them. Air basins are even more complex, and an issue like climate change is a worldwide one.

All of this discussion makes it clear that pollution control policy involves some very complex collective action problems. Individuals with resources may be able to reduce the impact of pollution upon themselves, but such strategies may be limited and may fall foul of unexpected effects. Individuals can buy bottled water, but they may find it more difficult to get access to an unpolluted lake or beach. Hence part of the case for seeing pollution control as a collective action problem lies in the difficulty individuals have in adopting strategies which protect themselves satisfactorily. Perhaps what helps to put environmental policy on the modern political agenda is the increased difficulty elites have in escaping from pollution.

However, perhaps an even more important reason why pollution control policy is seen as a collective concern lies in the fact explored on p. 95 that the pursuit of economic self-interest generates pollution but rarely generates motives to do anything about it. Production processes generate unwanted by-products. If those by-products can be pumped out into rivers and seas, blown into the air or, perhaps less commonly, dumped on waste land they will be disposed of at minimal cost to the enterprise. The owners of the enterprise may suffer no ill-effects from these actions, or, if they do worsen the quality of their own environments, the effects of their own actions upon themselves may be marginal and shared with the rest of the 'community' they have polluted. The word 'community' is put in inverted commas here: it is used very loosely, as it should be evident from the earlier discussion that this could be a very large group indeed. The overall point is that issues of this kind seldom come in a simple form. This is illustrated in Box 7.8 using the example of the disposal of waste products into a river. (It could be added to this example that some rivers cross national boundaries – a point that highlights the even greater complexity involved when emissions are into the sea or the air: see Bennett, 1992, Chapters 3 and 4 for some good case study examples).

Box 7.8	Complexity in the case of river pollution

If a single enterprise pours waste products into a river, that river may well be able to absorb those products, diluting them and transforming them into less harmful forms with no danger to the wildlife of the river or to anyone seeking to take water from the river. Modern reality is often very different. There will be many potential polluters along the banks of this hypothetical river (and before readers start to think that the author only sees industry as a polluter, it should be said that human and animal waste, agricultural chemicals and pesticides are likely to be among the sources of damage to the river quality). All waste products have to go somewhere, hence the real political issue is not about how to stop emissions, it is about how to control and/or limit them in such a way that, in the above example, for instance, (a) the river quality is maintained to an acceptable standard, and (b) the people who wish to discard by-products into the river feel that they have been fairly treated relative to others.

At the national level, the most straightforward of the policy options involves direct state action to deal with the problem or clear it up afterwards. In the case of solid and liquid waste disposal there may exist government waste disposal services. These may simply be funded out of local or national taxation, like services to remove materials from homes and business premises. There may be charges if they have to deal with large or exceptional loads. In the case of liquid waste, the common device in urban societies is simply a drainage system. Again, arrangements have to be made to deal with the exceptional. There will be problems for sewage treatment and disposal systems both if there are enterprises putting exceptional pressure upon the system or if the material being discharged is toxic and requires special treatment. Government may regulate such discharges and impose charges. Solid and liquid waste disposal responsibilities may be sub-contracted from government organisations to private firms.

Much environmental legislation gives central or local government regulatory powers. Two key distinctions concern the extent to which the powers are comprehensive ones determining the permissibility of the activity as a whole or specific ones relating to explicit activities (particularly emissions), and the extent to which powers relate solely to the start of an activity or impose continuous surveillance.

Implicit to this whole discussion are two key considerations for the policy process:

1. Pollution control is about treating collective interest as overriding individual interests.

2. Individual interests are likely to be strongly represented in the policy debate. Moreover, we are not talking here simply about some conflict between a small number of profit takers and a large public, since issues about threats to employment may be involved.

These considerations have a strong impact not merely upon the up-front politics of agenda setting but also on the way in which policy is formulated and implemented, since minimising conflict tends to involve a search for ways to tailor controls to individual situations. In pollution control policy in the UK, therefore, much attention has been given to the search for the 'best practical means' of dealing with problems while minimising their impact upon employment (Ashby and Anderson, 1981; Hill, 1983). Generalising about this issue, Hanf has written about pollution control policy as involving 'co-production' in which policy implementation is negotiated between officials and polluters (Hanf, 1993). This is a topic to which we will return in Chapter 13 (see pp. 275–6).

Overall, we may say that, whilst the control of pollution offers a good example of regulatory policy, it entails some complex issues that affect how matters get on the agenda, complicated by the extent to which pollution control is today not simply a nation-state issue. Any one country has a strong interest in how other countries deal with the problem, not merely because of externalities but also because controls have an impact upon economic competitiveness.

Reorganising local government

In this discussion of different kinds of policy it is important not to disregard policy changes that shape institutional systems. Such changes may be massive – the establishment of devolved forms of government, for example – or they may be quite slight, such as the reframing of some quite specific policy delivery arrangements (like the delegation of elements of school management from local authorities to individual schools, as discussed in the section on education policy). Moreover it must not be forgotten that governments may alter organisational arrangements in order to secure substantive policy change. For example, in the discussion of UK education policy above it was suggested that central government has become much more interested in exercising direct control; this has implied institutional changes affecting the relationship between itself and local government.

Local government reorganisation has been chosen here to illustrate institutional change policies. In dealing with this example there is a danger of getting into complexities that are inappropriate. In order to avoid that, this discussion will be shorter than has been the case with the other policy area examples.

Over the past 40 years, the United Kingdom has seen a rather frenetic succession of changes to the institutions of local government. In some societies the constraints upon organisational reform are much greater, particularly where arrangements for local government are embedded in the constitution. In the case of the United Kingdom there has been a strong tendency to see organisational reform as the key to securing more efficient policy delivery, delivering more to the public but at a lower cost. Box 7.9 provides a list of the kinds of changes that have been imposed on the English local government system *by central government* since 1970 (there have been related changes in the rest of the UK, but not necessarily at the same time).

Box 7.9	**Main changes to English local government (with dates of the key legislation in brackets – not necessarily put into operation in that year)**

- Alterations to the territorial areas covered (1972, 1985, 1992, 1998 and incrementally since)
- Alterations to the functions performed (1972, 1988)
- Alterations to the way political representation is organised (2000)
- Alterations to internal management (1970, 1989)
- Alterations to the way taxes are raised (1988, 1992)
- Alterations to the formulae governing central subventions (1980, 1982, 1984, 1992, with again a continuing process of incremental changes)
- Alterations to the way activities are supervised or inspected (1970, 1999).

Changes of this kind, particularly when put together, can make – and, in the case of the UK, certainly have made – a great difference to (a) how local services are controlled, and (b) who benefits from local services. The policy processes that introduce change are thus often contested in terms of concerns about how local democracy should work and about the extent to which they do enhance efficiency, but also in terms of their distributive consequences. On the other hand, arguments about organisational arrangements are often obscure, and the actual effects of changes may be hard to identify. The politics of organisational change lacks the popular appeal of political debates in which clear gainers and losers can be identified. But that may itself be an advantage since such change may be claimed to be an effective response to problems despite the fact these are obscure, or indeed perhaps non-existent (see Box 7.10).

Box 7.10	**Harrison and McDonald's discussion of why the British National Health Service 'is apparently forever being organised' (2008, p. 99)**

Harrison and McDonald described the NHS as 'in a perpetual state of reorganisation since the 1970s'. They see the explanation to this as partly an intended instrumental response to problems faced by policy makers' (see the discussion of issues about 'instrument choice' on pp. 176–8) but also influenced by political considerations. The latter are:

- The fact that reorganisation is something 'policy makers are generally able to achieve' within the constraints of a short period in office which offers a 'plausible-looking organisational solution' to identified policy problems.

- That reorganisations provide endless opportunities for symbolic policy making' (see p. 18 to provide reassurance that something is being done).

The suggestion here, therefore, is that there is an important category of policy processes, concerned with constituent policy, that may tend to be handled rather differently in the policy process than policy whose public impact is more direct (despite the fact that it does ultimately have an impact on 'who gets what'). This sort of policy has been called meta-policy (Dror, 1986, p. 102; see also Hupe, 1990).

Policy types

The discussion above has sought to identify some of the characteristics of different policy areas. Some clear differences between policy areas should be evident, so could the discussion have been organised using policy typologies? The most influential approach to this has been the typology developed by Lowi, who argues that 'policy may determine politics' (1972, p. 298) and goes on to specify four kinds of policy:

1. distributive policy: the distribution of new resources;
2. redistributive policy: changing the distribution of existing resources;
3. regulatory policy: regulating activities;
4. constituent policy: establishing or reorganising institutions.

Among the examples discussed above, neither the waging of war nor controlling the economy has any place in that typology. Education also fits very awkwardly into it. Providing education gives social advantages, and education policies may be (but are also often not) designed to redistribute advantages by enhancing social mobility. Education policy also involves a great deal of regulation of both public and private actors. In some respects regulation is one of the functions of education. Children are required to be sent to school where they have to be taught effectively by (normally) qualified persons. But its most obvious characteristic is as a state-provided or state-supported service.

Income maintenance seems prima facie to be an example of redistributive policy but may also involve regulatory policy. What is most important about it, however, is that much of it is not redistributive, inasmuch as social insurance is premised – to varying degrees – upon the idea of forced saving. Pollution control policy is obviously regulatory but has a variety of redistributive effects. The same is true of the example of constituent policy.

There is a logical problem with Lowi's concept of 'distributive policy'. The notion of policies being distributive without having any redistributive effects is problematical inasmuch as expenditure has to be funded and any advantages conferred on one person implicitly confer disadvantages on another. Ripley and Franklin (1982), who use the Lowi typology, seem to rest their version of the distributive/redistributive divide on the extent to which the losers can readily identify themselves. Significantly, Ripley and Franklin partly acknowledge the illogicality of this by indicating that they confine their redistributive concept to shifts of resources from advantaged to disadvantaged groups, while acknowledging that the reverse does apply. They justify this in terms of ideological perceptions in the United States (perhaps better put as the 'dominant ideology').

What Lowi was concerned with in his formulation of the typology was identifying the extent to which policy initiatives encounter resistance. But if that is to be the case, then all the policies discussed here create winners and losers, though the mechanisms by which gains and losses may occur are subtle. Clearly, it is a crucial point about the politics of policy that a great deal depends upon whether these people (and particularly losers) can identify themselves and are organised to do something about it. Wilson (1973), for example, has distinguished between 'concentrated' and 'dispersed' costs and benefits, and Hogwood (1987) suggests that policies vary in the extent to which their benefits can be distinguished. On this issue, however, it is not clear that a policy typology is much help.

We are left then, perhaps, simply with the notion that, whilst we cannot necessarily develop a typology based on these differences, policy differences matter for the way in which the policy process works.

Before we leave this point entirely it is appropriate to mention one theorist who addresses this issue, albeit in a much simpler way. Matland (see Figure 7.1) suggests two distinguishing features of policies: the extent to which they are ambiguous and the extent to which they provoke conflict. In doing this he is trying to theorise about implementation, but equally this distinction may be as much an underlying feature of a whole policy area as a specific feature of any policy as enacted.

Figure 7.1   Matland's analysis of the impact of conflict and ambiguity upon implementation

	Low conflict	High conflict
Low ambiguity	1	3
High ambiguity	2	4

Source: Adapted from Matland, 1995, p. 160, Table 4.1. By permission of Oxford University Press.

While the whole policy areas discussed in this chapter cannot, then, be neatly fitted into Matland's boxes, the high ambiguity of both education and pollution control policies in practice are evident. The extent to which policies provoke conflict hinges on the extent to which they involve creating very explicit and evident losers (as equal opportunities policy does in education or the anti-pollution measures do that threaten the economic viability of enterprises). Local government reorganisation tends to fall into the high ambiguity but low conflict category, though we have noted situations where this will not be the case. Economic intervention measures (notwithstanding that their actual economic effects will be disputed) are both relatively unambiguous and relatively unlikely to provoke conflict. War would seem to sit fairly clearly in the low ambiguity, high conflict camp, but for two crucial difficulties: that many contemporary international policing activities are very ambiguous because they may be taking nations on a path that leads to war (the Vietnam case has already been cited), and that within nations there is a strong tendency for a closing of ranks, with the effect that international conflicts may occur with a minimum of conflict within the nation.

There are quite a lot of conditional clauses in that last paragraph. Where you put policy activities on the two axes may depend upon some very complex questions. In general, while Matland, like Lowi before him, helps to sensitise us to issues about differences between policy processes, he does not progress this subject very much. Moreover, Matland's distinction perhaps becomes more workable when attention is paid to much more specific policies.

Closely related to Lowi's efforts to develop a typology of policies is a literature that examines the alternative 'policy instruments'. This term is used:

To encompass the myriad techniques at the disposal of governments to implement their public policy objectives. Sometimes referred to as 'governing instruments', these techniques range in complexity and age ... (Howlett, 1991, p. 2)

Issues about the choice of instruments have been seen to be influenced by concerns about costs and benefits. Hence, Howlett suggests, 'Instrument choice, from this perspective, is public policymaking' (ibid.). However, instrument choice – while influenced by the policy issue at stake – is much more about the selection of means to achieve policy objectives. As such it is discussed in the context of policy formulation in Chapter 9.

Policy stages

The other issue that needs to be examined in this introductory overview of how to analyse the policy process in more detail concerns the extent to which the task can be divided up in terms of a sequence of 'stages'.

The theory of representative democracy sees expressions of the popular will as an 'input' into the political system leading through various processing stages to a policy outcome as an 'output'. An influential nineteenth-century essay stressed a need for a clear distinction, during that process, between politics and administration (Wilson, 1887). The case for this is also made in arguments about the rule of law. Implicit in that concept is the notion that citizens should be able to predict the impact of the actions of the state upon themselves and secure redress when affected by illegitimate actions; hence what this implies is a coherent law-making process that then binds the subsequent actions of state officials (whether or not that process is democratic). Accordingly, what may be described as a 'stages model', or policy cycles model, was developed.

The development of the stages or policy cycle model may be seen, in part, as an elaboration of these concerns. The systems approach outlined by David Easton (1953, 1965a, 1965b) is seen as a key source for the stages model. Easton argues that political activity can be analysed in terms of a system containing a number of processes which must remain in balance if the activity is to survive. The paradigm that he employs is the biological system, whose life processes interact with each other and with the environment to produce a changing but none the less stable bodily state. Political systems are like biological systems, argues Easton, and exist in an environment which contains a variety of other systems, including social systems and ecological systems.

In Easton's model, one of the key processes of political systems is inputs, which take the form of demands and supports. Demands involve actions by individuals and groups seeking authoritative allocations of values from the authorities. Supports comprise actions such as voting, obedience to the law, and the payment of taxes. These feed into the black box of decision making, also known as the conversion process, to produce outputs, the decisions and policies of the authorities. Outputs may be distinguished from outcomes, which are the effects policies have on citizens. Easton's analysis does not end here, for within the systems framework there is allowance for feedback, through which the outputs of the political system influence future inputs into the system.

The main merit of systems theory is that it provides a way of conceptualising what are often complex political phenomena. In emphasising processes as opposed to institutions or structures, the approach is also useful in disaggregating the policy process into a number of different stages, each of which becomes amenable to more detailed analysis. For all of these reasons the systems model is of value, and this no doubt helps to account for its prominence in the literature. Other writers who do not necessarily share Easton's systems framework have also used the idea of stages in the policy process for the purposes of analysis (see Box 7.11).

Box 7.11	Variations on Easton's systems model of stages

Jenkins (1978, p. 17) elaborates the Easton model considerably, recognising complex feedback flows and identifying the following stages:

- initiation
- information
- consideration
- decision
- implementation
- evaluation
- termination.

Hogwood and Gunn (1984, p. 4) offer a more complex model in which they identify the following:

- deciding to decide
- deciding how to decide
- issue definition
- forecasting
- setting objectives and priorities
- options analysis
- policy implementation, monitoring and control
- evaluation and review
- policy maintenance, succession and termination.

The advantage of a stages model is that it offers a way of chopping up, if only for the purposes of analysis, a complex and elaborate process. It is useful as a heuristic device but potentially misleading about what actually happens (Parsons, 1995, pp. 79–81). As noted above, it is important to recognise the extent to which both the systems model and the stages 'discourse' rest upon a model of the representative democratic policy process in which politicians make decisions, senior civil servants help to translate them into specific legislation, and junior civil servants implement them. This is a widely held view of what 'should' happen. From the standpoint of this book the most important problem with this perspective is that the use of the stages model imposes upon the analysis of what actually happens a potentially distorting framework wherever what really happens is radically different from this.

From an empirical perspective, policy processes are in many respects continuous processes of evolution in which a realistic starting point may be far back in history. It was noted in considering the definitions of the term 'policy' that it is inappropriate to get into a model of the way policy processes occur which might only apply to a newly annexed desert island where nothing had been done before. Inasmuch, therefore, as it is possible to identify policy 'initiation', it may start anywhere in the system. Whilst there are grounds for seeing the stages as involving the progressive concretisation of policy (or involving a nesting of decisions in which some are logically prior to others), this offers no basis for prediction about how much will occur at any stage (in other words, while some policies may be formulated in very explicit terms early in the process, others may gradually manifest themselves as they are implemented).

Stages are not insulated from each other and there may be a succession of feedback loops between them – often the same actors are involved at different stages and the policy games they play will be carried on through different parts of the process (this remark is particularly applicable to the policy making/implementation distinction). Friedrich summed up this alternative perspective long ago when he argued: 'Public policy is being formed as it is being executed and it is likewise executed as it is being formed' (1940, p. 6).

The stages model has been discussed here because it is still widely used. This discussion has suggested, however, that its use can mislead. The problem – as John, one of the model's severest critics, has recognised – is that there is a pragmatic case for the model as it 'imposes some order on the research process' (1998, p. 36). What had to be recognised in shaping this book was that, if every process is continuously seen as interacting with every other process, there is no way to divide up discussion into separate chapters or sections. Hence, limited use is made of the stages model by recognising instead that there are somewhat different things to say about agenda setting, policy formulation and implementation respectively. At the same time, interactions are regularly stressed.

Relating the stages approach to actual policy issues

As far as the stages approach to policy analysis is concerned, there are some significant contrasts to be made. The two extremes are perhaps economic policy and income maintenance policy. In the case of economic policy, in the use of the key instruments of influence in the modern world – the exchange rate and the rate of interest – there really is no staged process at all. Specific actions or specific decisions are often made and implemented simultaneously. There will of course be some sort of agenda-setting process. Inasmuch as this may be expected to involve a public debate, political leaders may be reluctant to have one, since a debate about impending economic measures generates anticipatory actions by those likely to be affected.

As far as the device of leaving interest rate setting to a partly autonomous committee is concerned, it may be argued that such a body is merely an implementing agency working within strict parameters defined by 'policy'. But that is really playing with words, thereby illustrating the problematical nature of the policy formulation/implementation distinction. The decisions in question may have been quite closely pre-programmed, but their impact can be such that it seems inappropriate to describe them as merely implementation.

On the other hand, in the case of income maintenance policy there is likely to be not merely a prolonged, but almost certainly a public, agenda-setting process. During its later stages that agenda setting will generally take the form of the presentation of proposals to a legislature, which will then debate and perhaps amend them. Once that stage is completed (or nearing completion, as these parts of the process will overlap), work will be done to translate legislation into a rule structure that will enable individual entitlements to be identified. Once that is done the legislation will be brought into action in a form in which very explicit instructions will be given to implementers. Inasmuch as the legislation gives individuals rights, the concerns in the implementation process will be about managerial control and about ways in which people may ensure they secure those rights. Of course, discretions may be enshrined within the rules, but these will tend to be tightly structured by the legislation. Feedbacks will occur, but primarily in the interaction between legislation and more detailed formulation. Here simultaneous work on both will tend to save governments the embarrassment of having to introduce amending legislation soon after the initial legislation. Furthermore, as is the case in the UK, with what is known as the use of 'delegated legislation', flexibility for amendments based upon later experience will be built into the primary legislation. Feedbacks can often be seen as a clearly structured part of a structured process.

The only exceptions to these propositions about income maintenance policy will be some forms of means-tested benefits (with characteristics not dissimilar to the 'poor laws' of earlier ages), where high levels of policy choice have been delegated downwards (Eardley et al., 1996). On the other hand, in the cases of education policy and pollution control policy the delegation of policy choice is likely to be much more evident. Furthermore, in these two areas notions that are crucial for the characteristics of the policy are likely to be left to be settled at later stages. The UK National Curriculum for schools offers a good illustration. Beyond the specification of subjects to be studied, most of the detail of what should go into a specific curriculum has been left to officials within the education system, and even then the resulting documents leave many areas of choice for teachers. Reference was made to Bowe *et al.*'s (1992) notion of 'texts', in this case negotiated and debated up and down. Occasionally, politicians or the media have raised certain issues for national debate – such as the extent to which the history that is taught should be national history – but on the whole the detail is settled 'lower down' the system.

The equivalent to this in pollution control policy is the range of issues discussed above about different options for use of the planning system, about co-production and doctrines like 'best practical means'. These too need to be seen as matters not just for any particular level in a staged system but as the subject of interactions between the systems. A good approach to the exploration of these interactions involves seeing one level as engaged in 'mandating' others (May, 1993; and see the discussion in Chapter 12, pp. 243–4). An interesting characteristic of pollution control is the extent to which there is expectation of a tightening of control over time, using targets to be reached incrementally. Such targets even appear in international agreements. Hence there is an interesting contrast between the macro-politics of target setting (often involving supra-national bodies) and the very specific (and more local) micro-politics of determining implementation arrangements. If a stages model is used in this field of policy then it is at best going to be one in which feedback is particularly important.

The case of local government reorganisation fits less well into this discussion. A great deal depends upon the nature of the reorganisation. Also very relevant is the structural context in which it occurs, the distinction here being between the UK system, in which incremental changes are frequent, and systems in which legal constraints make change a matter for fundamental legislation, even constitutional change. In the UK, whilst legislation will be important, local government is likely to contribute to the modifications of 'bills' while they are before Parliament. Moreover, the implementation of some legislation has been made, formally speaking, subject to local referenda and other forms of public consultation.

Turning now to the making of war, here there is clearly a prolonged process which can be traced over time. But does it make any sense at all to describe, for example, the Vietnam War as involving agenda setting, formulation and then implementation, let alone to follow any even more elaborate version of the stages model? What were described above in relation to all the examples given were indeed agenda-setting processes, in which public participation was unwelcome and political elites sought (not necessarily successfully) to keep strong control over events. An interesting (dare I say sinister?) feature of the relationship between agenda setting and policy formulation is the fact that nations do not declare war until they have prepared for it. The author recalls American military supply ships massing off the shores of the United Kingdom long before war was declared on Iraq. To what extent does preparing for war make war inevitable? The evidence on the Cuban missile crisis suggests there can be a negative answer to that question, but that was a very closely run thing.

Going to war is therefore, perhaps, a very strong example of implementation as policy making. A great deal of the detail is settled incrementally in action. What makes this implementation very different from most of the examples of implementation discussed in the texts on this subject is the very high involvement of the 'top' of the political and administrative systems in the process. Once a war is in progress, policy change processes, affected by local intelligence and by local action, are likely to continue. It is an interesting paradox about military action that, whilst there is a high stress upon top-down authority and discipline, much of this is actually designed to pre-programme highly discretionary actions in situations in which those at the front have to react to unpredictable situations. This aspect of limits to control over the policy process is explored in parts of Chapters 13 and 14.

There are clearly other policy issues where a 'crisis' (in reality or as defined by the government) that requires rapid executive action creates a policy process in which separating the stages is problematical. Taylor's (2003) study of the response to the outbreak of foot and mouth disease among animals in the UK in 2001 provides a good example of this. What was involved was action that the Prime Minister and other politicians initiated quickly to supplement or replace an existing policy framework. In this case an animal disease emerged, foot and mouth, for which there was already an apparently coherent policy on the statute book, but the problem was that the disease had not manifested itself for nearly 40 years and in that time the organisation of both agriculture and the regulatory system had changed dramatically. Policy therefore had to be made 'on the hoof', as Taylor puns in his article, in a context in which very activist politicians needed quick results when a general election was pending (see Box 7.12).

The use of a stages approach: just a pragmatic matter, or something more?

The chapters in the rest of this book have labels and contents that broadly follow the specifications of the stages model. The matter could be left there, using the pragmatic case for this approach. There are, however, two threads in the case for the stages model that are regarded as important. One, to which only brief attention is appropriate (the main case has been made above) is that, while this book is an exercise in descriptive analysis rather than prescription, the prescriptive importance of the stages model (embodied in the model of representative democracy and of the rule of law)

Box 7.12	**Taylor's (2003) account of the handling of the 2001 foot and mouth disease outbreak in the UK**

The last serious outbreak of foot and mouth disease occurred in 1967–8. A sequence of recommendations was adopted after that to involve – in the UK as in the EU – the rapid diagnosis, slaughter and disposal of all animals that might have been exposed to the disease. The problem in 2001 was that agricultural and marketing arrangements had changed significantly, with very much more movement of animals around the country, hence the potential rate of spread of the disease was much increased. After such a long, almost disease-free, period, few experts had any familiarity with the disease. Furthermore, there had been substantial changes to the veterinary service at the disposal of the government, so that it was very difficult to get services into action quickly. Evidence that the disease was likely to be located in several different parts of the country and that very large numbers of animals might have been exposed to it (in all, once the picture became clear, about 2000 cases were confirmed and 4 million animals needed to be slaughtered) made it difficult to implement the standard policy. The government were seen by some as acting too slowly, by others of making unnecessarily draconian decisions about slaughter and about the movement of both people and animals. 'From a policy-making and implementation perspective, the notion of "policy on the hoof" is appropriate because that was the way in which policy proceeded during the crisis' (ibid., p. 544). This is illustrated by:

> The proposal to vaccinate and the decision to base culling on contiguous contact culling rather than contiguous premises, the decisions to reprieve Phoenix [a pet calf featured in newspaper stories] . . ., bury instead of burn carcasses, make use of retired veterinary surgeons after initially rejecting the proposal, use the army later rather than immediately and transfer major decision making to . . . [the Prime Minister's office]. (ibid.)

suggests that it is important to be aware of the extent to which processes are staged in the real world.

The other justification is a matter of logic. The author and Peter Hupe explained this in relation to implementation:

> In its most general form the act of 'implementation' presupposes a prior act, particularly the 'cognitive act' of formulating what needs to be done and making a decision on that. In everyday terms, while we may vary what we do when we take action, we very often make a decision to take action – go on a journey for example – and think about how to do it, before carrying out that action (Hill and Hupe, 2009, p. 4).

This journey analogy was used in Chapter 1 where it was suggested there will be three or four separable elements: deciding where we want to go to (agenda setting), deciding how to get there (formulation) and going (implementation). There may even be a fourth stage: evaluating what we did and how we did it.

But staying with that journey example we may also see that it is quite possible that the logic is not followed through since people may change their mind about where they want to go or how they want to get to somewhere during a journey. The point about this mundane example is then that if we want to analyse a purposive act it is surely logical to assume, *but not take for granted*, some kind of sequencing.

The journey example here involves a single actor but its logic can be extended to multiple actor situations more typical of the policy process. Here of course the conventional prescriptive position implies some sort of hierarchy, and particularly a distinction between who decides where to go and who goes on the journey. The position to be adopted here is that who does what should be regarded as an empirical question.

But, as institutional theory stresses (see Chapter 4), earlier decisions tend to structure subsequent ones. In this respect Kiser and Ostrom's (1982) notion of three related but distinct levels of analysis is useful. They thus separate decisions taken at the constitutional level, which structure the design of the context within which choices are made, from the collective choice level, at which key decisions about the management of policy are made, and the operational level, which explains the world of action. There is a 'nesting' process in which some kinds of decisions have a particularly strong impact upon the context for later ones, hence the idea of constitutional level and collective choice level decisions. The present author and Peter Hupe have adapted this idea for the examination of the implementation process, arguing that there is a need to separate the fact that there are different decision levels from the exploration of the actual organisation of governance:

> The nested character of the framework implies that, conceptually, one action level is not necessarily confined to one administrative layer. Whether, for instance, in a given policy process, a layer of government practices just 'implementation' or rather 'policy co-formation' is a difficult definitional question, resting upon interpretation of the extent of change (Hill and Hupe, 2006, p. 563).

This comment applies to the policy formation/ implementation distinction but the same argument applies (as will be shown in the next chapter) to the agenda setting/policy formation one.

CONCLUSIONS

This chapter has tried to prepare for the discussion in the rest of the book by exploring issues about differences between policies. This has been related to questions about the applicability of the stages model to the policy process and of policy types. Using a limited number of important policy areas, the limitations of the stages model and the weaknesses of simple policy typologies have been demonstrated.

The exploration of policy areas has also been designed to highlight the great diversity of policy processes. At various places in the rest of the book, discussion will return to the policy examples outlined here. The exploration of the complexities embedded in these policy areas is offered in an effort to sensitise readers to some of the key issues to be explored in the discussion to follow, in which a very limited application of the stages approach will be used to separate out some key themes in policy process analysis.

A recognition of policy diversity helps to throw light upon some of the variations in the arguments about policy process theory. Propositions about the biases in the overall structure of power are much more easily illustrated (even possibly tested) by the big political issues about war and peace and about control over the economy than they are by some of the other issues. Pollution control is interesting as an issue that has both an international and a very local dimension. Global politics increasingly determines its broad parameters but networks and local institutional arrangements need to be looked at to explain what happens at 'street level'. The clash of interest groups is much in evidence in the making of both social security policy and education policy. Evidence from these policy areas is widely used to support both rational choice theory and network theory, but institutional constraints are also in evidence (particularly in a field like pension policy). Any examination of local government reform obviously takes us into issues about the roles of institutions. While, as stressed at the end of Chapter 6, choice between theories is bound to be influenced by our value biases, it may also be affected by the substantive policy area in which we are interested.

The chapter ended with some observations indicating that, while the structure of the discussion to come can be justified in pragmatic terms, some of the notions embedded within the stages model of the policy process can be used in the analysis of the process so long as they are only seen as relating to the logical sequencing of activities, and the impact of early decisions on later ones.

8 Agenda setting

SYNOPSIS

After a brief comment on the difficulties about separating a distinct 'agenda setting' stage in the policy process, the starting point for this discussion of this will be a sociological analysis of the way in which *public* problems emerge. This points us in a very different direction from the prescriptive literature's concern about how policies *should* be made. The first challenge to the prescriptive so-called 'rational model' came from a literature that suggested that most decision making is 'incremental' in nature. The incrementalist perspective will thus be examined.

  This will be followed by considering an approach to this topic which can be said to come out of incrementalism but goes considerably further, in stressing more strongly the relative absence of a consistent or 'rational' process. This is Kingdon's model of the agenda-setting process. The strengths and weaknesses of that model are then examined.

Introduction

In the previous chapter the commonplace idea of a journey was used both to illustrate the logic of the stages model and to indicate problems with that approach. This chapter and the next two separate the analysis of the policy process along the lines suggested by the journey metaphor. The present chapter is about deciding where to go (agenda setting), the next about deciding how to get there (formulation or policy programming) and the third about going (implementation). We start therefore not merely with a warning about seeing policy making stages as neatly separable in these terms but also with the observation that readers are likely to note ways in which – in order to provide a coherent account of relevant ideas and theories – the author will have to depart from the divisions implied by the chapter headings.

The agenda setting/formulation distinction is a particularly difficult one to make, since in the modern world we very rarely see an issue that is entirely new appearing on the agenda. Moreover, where this does happen there is often a very strong and complex interaction between the initial stages of that process and those that immediately follow it as it is translated into a more concrete form. It is also important to bear in mind that in some circumstances policy may be initiated and changed without formal legislation. In the previous chapter, the examples from foreign policy and economic policy both largely fell into this category.

Sometimes agenda-setting processes and further policy formulation can be distinguished, sometimes not. The two examples used as examples of policy in Chapters 1 and 6 of this book – the right to roam and the reduction of poverty – illustrate this very clearly. The former can easily be examined in terms of a specific policy commitment (put on the agenda by a political manifesto) and subsequent rather detailed work that had to be done to translate this into action. The second on the other hand required (and indeed is still requiring) a whole range of detailed decisions about tax rates, minimum wage legislation, social benefit rules and so on. Indeed, at the time of writing, a taxation change, proclaimed at the time to be progressive in respect of the aspiration to reduce poverty, has been found (at the time it is actually being implemented) to have 'perverse' effects that increase poverty for some and has led to some complex policy adjustments with promises of more to come; even now, to use an old cliché, 'the devil resides in the details'.

What is a policy issue or problem?

It is appropriate to start examining agenda setting by taking a step back to ask: where do the issues or problems that get on the political agenda come from? No objective fact constitutes a problem in itself (Dery, 1984, p. xi; Cobb and Elder, 1983, p.172). The – social and then political – definition of a matter that needs attention always represents a collective construction directly linked to the perceptions, representations, interests and values of the actors concerned. Thus, all social reality should be understood as a historical construction, situated in time and space. It always depends on persons affected by the issue and/or those whose behaviour may need to change to solve it.

There is a need here to recognise that there are issues that may be regarded as private concerns or problems for specific individuals. These may be quite specific to the individuals themselves, or they may be problems shared with others. If we take the issue of poverty, there are two separate but related questions: (a) is that condition shared with others? (b) inasmuch as it is shared is it seen as appropriate to try to take collective action to deal with the problem? From an examination of the history of concerns about poverty we may note evidence that it is more than an isolated problem, but also a widely propagated view that it is an individual problem (explicable in terms of the moral incapacities of the individuals concerned and their lack of efforts to remedy the situation). The latter can then be observed to have been challenged ideologically by arguments that the causes of poverty lie in phenomena other than individual culpability, and practically by social movements to attack those causes. We may thereby see the translation of individual issues into social problems.

This analysis can then be taken a stage further. Gusfield (1981) makes a distinction between 'social problems' and 'public problems', noting that not all social problems necessarily become public problems, in other words the objects of political controversy. Hence, public problems represent an extension of social problems to the extent that, having emerged within civil society, they are debated within an emerging political arena. In this sense, the definition of a public problem is essentially political in nature. In other words, a problem becomes public by being put on the political agenda. At this stage of the definitional process, public actors (for example, the administration, government, parliament) recognise the need to consider a possible state solution to the identified problem.

The transfer of a problem or issue from the social sphere to the public sphere involves public actors as orchestrators of the agenda-setting process. While this attributes a proactive role to the public actors, it must, however, be stressed that the passage of a public problem is neither linear nor inevitable. Modern political history can be seen as involving the enlargement of the public agenda in this way. Many issues on the agenda today were not on it in the past. But equally there are issues that are not on the agenda that could be on it. It is interesting to observe, for example, that whilst public policy today is less concerned about issues about people's private sexual behaviour it seems to be becoming more concerned about what (or how much) we eat and drink. Questions about whether it is appropriate for certain issues to be on the agenda lie at the centre of ideological conflict in societies.

It was noted in Chapter 2 that, contrary to the pluralistic vision of democracy which assumes that every actor may access the decision-making arena to thematicise a particular problem, Bachrach and Baratz (1970) and Lukes (1974, 2005) assert that a specific form of public power consists precisely in the possibility of keeping certain social problems off the public agenda.

From the rational model of policy decision making to incrementalism

The need for a political analysis of the way in which issues get on to the agenda developed out of a disquiet with earlier models of the policy process. Here we encounter one of those issues, explored in Chapter 1, about distinguishing between a prescriptive and a descriptive approach to policy analysis. As far as agenda setting is concerned, contemporary prescriptive analysis has its roots in dissatisfaction with a prominent prescriptive model, where it was argued that it is unrealistic to analyse policy problem solving using a rational model essentially rooted in a view of what *should* happen.

Since the very beginnings of attempts to develop an academic approach to administration, efforts have been made to formulate guidance on how to secure the 'best' decisions. At the heart of this lies a perspective that does not recognise the complex relationship between problem identification and action described above. That perspective requires problem-solving behaviour to be unsullied by politics: an impartial search for the best solution. The contemporary emphasis upon 'evidence based policy' (see Davies *et al.*, 2000 for a discussion of this) seems to sum up this aspiration. Yet insightful prescriptive policy analysis recognises the problems about achieving this. Perhaps the most influential figure in this respect has been Herbert Simon (1957) who, while he is often presented as the exponent of the so called 'rational model' of policy making, in fact recognises the 'limits' upon the achievement of that ideal. What he goes on to say in this context belongs (in terms of what has already been acknowledged as a difficult boundary between agenda setting and policy formulation) rather more to the next chapter than to this one, so we return to it there. Hence, by contrast with previous editions of this book, aspects of a long-standing debate about decision making, driven by prescriptive concerns but inevitably spilling over into questions about what actually happens, will be split between this chapter and the next.

The concern here is with the way in which the rational model was challenged by an argument that it goes further than Simon is seeing it as an unrealistic view of how policy decisions are made. The key protagonist here was Charles Lindblom. His work is confusing because he revised his position several times.

Lindblom is critical of the rational-comprehensive method prescribed for decision making. In its place, he sets out an approach he calls 'successive limited comparisons' which starts from the existing situation and involves the changing of policy incrementally. Braybrooke and Lindblom note eight ways in which the rational-comprehensive model fails to adapt to the real world of policy decision making (set out in Box 8.1).

Consequently, Braybrooke and Lindblom argue, decision making in practice proceeds by successive limited comparisons. This simplifies the decision-making process not only by limiting the number of alternatives considered to those that differ in small degrees from existing policies, but also by ignoring the consequences of possible policies. Further, deciding through successive limited comparisons involves simultaneous analysis of facts and values, means and ends. As Lindblom states, 'one chooses among values and among policies at one and the same time' (1959, p. 82). That is, instead of specifying objectives and then assessing what policies would fulfil these objectives, the decision maker reaches decisions by comparing specific

Box 8.1	Braybrooke and Lindblom's eight reasons why the rational approach fails to deal with real-world decision making

1. limited human problem-solving capacities;
2. situations where there is inadequacy of information;
3. the costliness of analysis;
4. failures in constructing a satisfactory evaluative method;
5. the closeness of observed relationships between fact and value in policy making;
6. the openness of the system of variables with which it contends;
7. the analyst's need for strategic sequences of analytical moves;
8. the diverse forms in which policy problems actually arise.

(Summarised from Braybrooke and Lindblom, 1963)

policies and the extent to which these policies will result in the attainment of objectives.

Lindblom argues that incrementalism is both a good description of how policies are actually made, and a model for how decisions should be made. Prescriptively, one of the claimed advantages of what he calls 'muddling through' is that serious mistakes can be avoided if only incremental changes are made. By testing the water the decision maker can assess the wisdom of the moves he or she is undertaking and can decide whether to make further progress or to change direction. This is developed at some length by Lindblom and his collaborators. In *A Strategy of Decision* (1963), he and David Braybrooke describe in detail the strategy of disjointed incrementalism, which is a refinement of the successive limited comparisons method. This of course takes us back into the prescriptive debate, hence its features are merely summarised in Box 8.2.

Box 8.2	Disjointed incrementalism as a decision strategy

Disjointed incrementalism involves examining policies which differ from each other incrementally, and which differ incrementally from the status quo. Analysis is not comprehensive but is limited to comparisons of marginal differences in expected consequences. Using disjointed incrementalism, the decision maker keeps on returning to problems, and attempts to ameliorate those problems rather than to achieve some ideal future state. What is more, decision makers adjust objectives to available means instead of striving for a fixed set of objectives. Braybrooke and Lindblom note that disjointed incrementalism is characteristic of the United States, where 'policy-making proceeds through a series of approximations. A policy is directed at a problem; it is tried, altered, tried in its altered form, altered again, and so forth'. (Braybrooke and Lindblom, 1963, p. 73)

This theme of coordination is taken up in Lindblom's *The Intelligence of Democracy* (1965). 'Partisan mutual adjustment' is the concept Lindblom develops to describe how coordination will be achieved in the absence of a central coordinator. Partisan mutual adjustment is the process by which independent decision makers coordinate their behaviour. It involves adaptive adjustments 'in which a decision-maker simply adapts to decisions around him', and manipulated adjustments 'in which he seeks to enlist a response desired from the other decision-maker' (ibid., p. 33). Each of these forms of adjustment is further divided into a variety of more specific behaviour, including negotiation and bargaining. In a later article, Lindblom (1979) notes that, although there is no necessary connection between partisan mutual adjustment and political change by small steps, in practice the two are usually closely linked. This has been shown (by Harrison, Hunter and Pollitt, 1990, pp. 8–13) to be a weakness in Lindblom's argument since a sequence of essentially incremental changes may well occur in a context in which certain parties are dominating and therefore 'mutual adjustment' is not occurring. This, they contend, has been characteristic of change in British health policy, where medical interests have dominated.

Lindblom accepts, in his later work, that partisan mutual adjustment is only active on ordinary questions of policy. Certain grand issues such as the existence of private enterprise and private property and the distribution of income and wealth are not resolved through adjustment. Rather, because of 'a high degree of homogeneity of opinion' (1979, p. 523) grand issues are not included on the agenda. Lindblom adds that this homogeneity of opinion is heavily indoctrinated, and in *Politics and Markets* he explores the operation of ideology. Lindblom's argument is that in any stable society there is a unifying set of beliefs which are communicated to the population through the church, the media, the schools and other mechanisms (1977, Chapter 15). These beliefs appear to be spontaneous because they are so much taken for granted, but they favour, and to some extent emanate from, dominant social groups.

There is thus a shift in Lindblom's position from one in which bargaining is seen as inevitable (and desirable) to one in which ideology is seen to play a role, though essentially the latter has a limited influence upon the range of actors and options going into the bargaining process.

The rationalism/incrementalism debate is beside the point when it is party-political commitment or ideology rather than either rational planning or 'partisan mutual adjustment' that drives the policy debate. The following scenario is by no means unlikely (indeed it is not a bad summarisation of the current state of the policy process in respect of the prevention of global warming):

1. A problem arises on which it is difficult for government to develop an effective response – its causes are unknown, or beyond the reach of government action, or are phenomena with which the government is reluctant to deal (for example, economic influences upon crime).

2. Nevertheless, the key policy actors want to be seen to be 'in control', or at least doing something (they have made claims that they can manage the economy, combat crime, solve international conflicts).

3. In addition, some of the actors are driven by strong ideologies (particularly important as far as politicians are concerned).

4. The result is a series of actions that are presented as problem solving but which may equally be the thrashing around of a system that needs to be seen as active but does not really know what to do (in these circumstances it is important not to be deceived by the rational action language politicians are likely to use).

It is also vital to see agenda-setting processes in their institutional contexts. Such constraints make both 'rational' policy planning and 'partisan mutual adjustment' difficult. March and Olsen argue that 'Insofar as political actors act by making choices, they act within definitions of alternatives, consequences, preferences (interests), and strategic options that are strongly affected by the institutional context in which the actors find themselves' (March and Olsen, 1996, p. 251). We also saw that in some of their work March and Olsen seem to go even further, seeing the way policies emerge as being similar to the way rubbish accumulates in a 'garbage can' (see Chapter 4, p. 81). An alternative, institutional theory-linked approach to this issue which picks up on all the points emphasised in this paragraph is Kingdon's analysis of agenda setting.

Kingdon's model of the agenda-setting process

Kingdon originally set out his model in a book published in 1984. He updated that book in 1995. This discussion is based upon the latter book. Kingdon's work is a study of policy agenda setting in the United States. Kingdon describes his approach to the analysis of agenda setting as follows:

> Comprehensive, rational policy making is portrayed as impractical for the most part, although there are occasions where it is found. Incrementalism describes parts of the process, particularly the gradual evolution of proposals or policy changes, but does not describe the more discontinuous or sudden agenda change. Instead of these approaches, we use a revised version of the Cohen–March–Olsen garbage can model of organizational choice to understand agenda setting and alternative generation. We conceive of three process streams flowing through the system – streams of problems, policies, and politics. They are largely independent of one another, and each develops according to its own dynamics and rules. But at some critical junctures the three streams are joined, and the greatest policy changes grow out of that coupling of problems, policy proposals, and politics. (Kingdon, 1995, p. 19)

It is important to note the way in which Kingdon associates his analysis with the 'garbage can' model. He thus dissociates himself from traditional positivist American political science, which searches for universal testable propositions and sees the policy process instead as in many respects chaotic and unpredictable. In that sense the use of the term model is open to challenge by those who prefer to apply the term to something rather more precise (see Sabatier, 2007, p. 6). However, he aims to offer an approach that helps us to understand what goes on even if we cannot easily predict outcomes.

An aspect of Kingdon's approach that is widely quoted is his alternative metaphor to the 'garbage can', 'primeval soup'. This is a reference to the way in which modern explanations of the early stages of biological evolution see change occurring because genetic combinations occurred in the shapeless, soup-like environment, in which only some of them proved successful and thus led on to subsequent developments. But this is just an analogy, and one which should be treated with caution.

Rather more important for his theory is the notion that in the soup-like environment that is the modern policy process there are three streams: problems, policies and politics. Simpler explanations of the policy process have seen policies as designed to solve problems, but the weakness of such approaches is that problems themselves are socially constructed (Berger and Luckman, 1975). Kingdon suggests it can often be the case that there are policies looking for problems, that it is things key actors want to do that need justifications. He identifies the presence of what he calls 'policy entrepreneurs' who do this. These people may be politicians or civil servants or pressure group leaders with issues they want to put on the public agenda. They are, he says, like 'surfers waiting for the big wave' (Kingdon, 1995, p. 225), on the look-out for a combination of public concern about a problem and political interest in doing something about it.

Kingdon's primeval soup image is intended to convey the way in which the policy process environment is forever changing, hence opportunities for agenda setting come and go with shifting attention to issues, influenced by the short attention span of the media and the changing needs of politicians in the course of the electoral cycle (this observation echoes earlier work by Downs suggesting that there is an 'issue-attention cycle' in politics, 1972, p. 38). Kingdon shifts into yet another image here, of windows that open briefly and then close. He recognises the importance of feedback from existing policies into the agenda-setting process. He also identifies what he calls 'spillovers', the impact of one policy change on other policies. These two elements – feedback and spillovers – may be important for the problem identified with regard to both network theory and institutional theory: that despite evidence of the existence of strong forces towards stability in the policy process, there are spells of quite intense change in many systems. What may appear to involve marginal change can have major consequences.

Developments of Kingdon's approach

Birkland's research on 'focusing events' offers support for Kingdon's perspective (see Box 8.3). When the 'big wave' comes problems, policies and politics may be coupled to form the policy agenda. This is not necessarily a simple process. Kingdon makes a distinction between 'agendas' and 'alternatives', recognising that there is competition at this time.

Box 8.3	Birkland's (1998) analysis of the impact of focusing events

Birkland studied the impact of disasters (hurricanes and earthquakes) and industrial accidents (oil spills and nuclear power disasters) on the policy agenda in the United States. Interestingly, he links Kingdon's analysis of 'problems' with the network and policy communities perspective (explored in Chapter 4). He shows that focusing events may serve to bring attention to problems on the agenda, but that

> An event is more likely to be focal if an interest group or groups are available to exploit the event . . . (Birkland, 1998, p.72)

Another approach to events which create opportunities for policy change involves an emphasis on policy fiascos (Bovens and 't Hart, 1996; Gray and 't Hart (eds), 1998). Here, of course, the problems that force their attention on policy makers are the consequences of earlier policies. In this case, then, we see feedback cycles in the policy process and also a variation on Kingdon's theme of the impact of 'feedback and spillovers' on the policy process.

A related concern is with the impact of crises. Bovens, 't Hart and Peters' comparative study (2001) emphasises ways in which crises force attention to be given to problems, looking then at different ways in which governments respond to problems.

Kingdon sees his approach to the agenda-setting process as building on incrementalist theory in its rejection of the 'rational' problem-solving model. But he argues that not all change is incremental and that incrementalist theory tends to disregard issues about the way streams join and policy windows open. He sees his approach as superior to a pluralist perspective inasmuch as he is interested in the way key actors both inside and outside government come together. Similarly, for him network theory and the work on policy communities neglect issues about coupling and about variations in the extent to which behaviour is unified. His perspective can be seen as institutionalist in approach, in the light of its emphasis on the significance of actors both inside and outside government and its recognition of the impact of earlier decisions on current ones. Indeed, in his second edition he recognises the parallels between his approach and that of Baumgartner and Jones (1993) in their analysis of punctuated equilibrium (see Chapter 4, p. 76).

Kingdon's examination of the roles of policy entrepreneurs fits well with the modern developments in institutional theory that emphasise ideas. But this emphasis involves a very different perspective on the roles of experts in the policy process from that implied by those who call for more 'evidence based policy'. That emphasis has led to a concern with the circumstances under which evidence is taken seriously, whilst Kingdon's emphasis on opening windows suggests a rather more haphazard linking of (a) political contingencies and (b) unsolved policy problems. Smith (2007) has explored the issue of health inequalities (a topic closely related to the issues about poverty policy used as an example elsewhere in this book). In the UK a change of government led to a policy environment in which a case for attention to health inequalities was, in general terms, on the agenda. However, the experts Smith interviewed found it difficult to extend their engagement further into the policy process. Inasmuch as they have been successful it has been in respect of one interpretation of the causes of health inequalities – that root them in individual behaviour – that is least challenging to the political status quo. The credibility of experts seemed to rest upon factors not necessarily related to their expertise. Smith says, cautiously, 'the factors influencing an individual's credibility in policy circles are likely to be different to, and may potentially conflict with, the factors affecting credibility in academic circles (2007, p. 1447). There is a related issue here about the organisation of expert 'epistemic communities' and about their ideological compatibility with powerful political actors (Haas, 1992, 2004).

An agenda-setting example: pensions policy

It has been stressed that Kingdon's book is only about the United States (and in practice only about the federal government). It seems amazing that a book that offers a general approach to the analysis of agenda setting should have no references whatsoever to the process outside the United States. It is desirable to explore the theory further using material from elsewhere before launching into a discussion of whether Kingdon's ethnocentrism matters. This will be done in this section, using a policy issue that is on the agenda in all developed countries: pensions.

In many countries (and particularly in Europe) there have been three phases in pension policy making:

- A first phase, in which, in most countries, relatively rudimentary public pensions were provided for only some groups in the population.

- A second phase of consolidation, involving either the development of comprehensive public schemes or the formation of combinations of public and private provisions.

- A third phase, in which, while development and consolidation issues are still on the agenda, a key policy preoccupation is with cutting public pension commitments.

Tables 8.1 to 8.3 summarise the issues that influence the prospects of pension issues getting on the public policy agenda using Kingdon's key concepts.

The explanation given for the first phase in policy pension making (see Table 8.1) seems to offer a more political approach to agenda setting than there is in Kingdon's model. This seems to be dominant in historical accounts of the evolution of pension policies, though there are differences of view on the importance of the political Left (Heclo, 1974; Ashford, 1986; Baldwin, 1990). But the demographic aspect of the emergence of the problem has also been widely emphasised (Pampel and Williamson, 1989), and detailed accounts suggest the importance of policy entrepreneurs other than politicians (Gilbert, 1966; Baldwin, 1990). Furthermore, accounts of European developments make a great deal of the activities of one politician of the Right, Bismarck, who perceived an opportunity to tie the new industrial working class into the support of the state as the collector of their contributions and the guarantor of their pensions.

Table 8.1 Phase 1: Initial moves towards pension policies

Problems	An ageing population and increasing reluctance on the part of employers to keep older workers.
Politics	The emergence of democracy, a readiness to see poverty in old age as not the fault of the individual.
Policies	Either ideas derived from insurance or more universal models of public assistance for the elderly.
Policy entrepreneurs	Politicians on the Left; friendly society leaders recognising increased problems with voluntary initiatives.
Windows of opportunity	Electoral shifts to the Left.

In the consolidation period (see Table 8.2) the divergences that are a key concern of modern comparative studies really emerged between those countries that adopted more or less universal public schemes (Sweden, Norway, Denmark, for example), those that developed a more divided version of the universalist approach (Germany and France, for example) and those that settled for provisions that were a mix of public and private (the UK and Australia, for example) (Esping-Andersen, 1990). The key explanatory variables were perhaps concerns about inconsistencies and a strong universalist

Table 8.2   Phase 2: Pension policy consolidation

Problems	Poverty amongst those not in schemes; equity problems because of mixtures of different schemes; insolvency of some private schemes.
Politics	Championing of universalist solutions by the political Left.
Policies	Universal models; models involving public/private combinations.
Policy entrepreneurs	Politicians of the Left; private companies eager to secure new business or protect existing business.
Windows of opportunity	Electoral shifts to the Left; scandals about private schemes.

drive from the left of the political spectrum. But the emergence of a variety of private pension initiatives meant that the Left faced a rival agenda, with the more sophisticated of the advocates of the private model recognising the case for partnership (inasmuch as they were reluctant to take on the provision of pensions for low-income workers) and the need to secure private schemes against scandals that could discredit them.

The interesting thing about the third phase (see Table 8.3) is not so much successful agenda setting as considerable difficulties in getting cuts on the agenda (see Chapter 4, Box 4.5, also Bonoli and Shinkawa, 2005) because of the strength of the support coalition for the status quo. A peculiarity of any pension scheme is that it embodies promises made to people a long while before they reach the age of entitlement. Furthermore, if a scheme is contributory, which it is in most countries with large comprehensive schemes, then those promises for the future are being paid for in the present. The problem that prompts action is very often an expected future one rather than a current one. Policy entrepreneurs have to persuade politicians, whose time frames are short, that they should worry about long-term trends. Here the so-called 'demographic time bomb' is a good example of a socially

Table 8.3   Phase 3: Pension cutting

Problems	Substantial increases in the elderly population; threats of insolvency for both public and private schemes.
Politics	Championing of privatised solutions by the political Right.
Policies	Cuts to promised entitlements; ways to increase pre-funding.
Policy entrepreneurs	Private pension providers: international organisations.
Windows of opportunity	Electoral shifts to the Right; fiscal crises.

defined problem exaggerating the implications of demographic change (see Hill, 2007, Chapter 6). Moreover, funded pension schemes, particularly if that funding is through investment in the stock market, themselves offer uncertain promises for the future. Nevertheless, a combination of the recognition of emergent fiscal problems by governments only too aware of difficulties in raising revenues, increased commitment to privatisation and, perhaps above all, hard selling by private pension providers has succeeded in getting the case for changes on to the agenda.

This discussion has explored the issue in the group of countries that went into pension provision early in the twentieth century and consolidated schemes soon after the Second World War. The politics of pensions is very much more complicated in countries where pension provision or consolidation has only recently got on to the agenda. In these cases the conflict between the case for pension development and recognition of the strong case against open-ended and unfunded commitments made by bodies like the World Bank (1994) seriously complicates the agenda. We see here the influence of ideas, and the dominance of a belief in privatised market solutions to a problem like this.

In the case of the UK, summarised in Box 8.4, efforts at consolidation came relatively late and therefore we see complications of this kind in the agenda-setting process.

Box 8.4	Pension development in the UK

Pension schemes were set up for some citizens in the period before the First World War. Then, following the recommendations of the Beveridge Report (Beveridge, 1942), a scheme of low-level, flat rate social insurance pensions was set up which survives to this day. Beveridge expected that many people would also contribute to additional private schemes to provide more than subsistence incomes in old age. By 1963 about 48 per cent of employees were enrolled in occupational pension schemes.

In the 1950s a political debate emerged about the need for additional pensions for those not in private schemes. A complex policy-making process ensued in which concerns to improve future pensions competed with concerns about current pensions. The measure that eventually emerged was the Social Security Pensions Act of 1975, which provided an earnings related superannuation scheme, the State Earnings Related Pension Scheme (SERPS). This allowed individuals in adequate private schemes to opt out of the state scheme, but provided an enhanced inflation-proofed state superannuation scheme for all other working people. This scheme, whilst it appeared to involve funding, was, like the flat rate scheme upon which it was built, a scheme managed on a 'pay as you go' basis.

After 1979, the Conservative government sought to cut social security expenditure. The value of the original flat rate pension was significantly reduced. SERPS was deemed to involve rising costs and to impose excessive burdens on future generations. The government's initial idea was to replace it by a funded scheme, but then they recognised what heavy short-term costs the government would impose upon itself since it would lose the use of contributions to fund current benefits. Instead, they cut sharply the benefits guaranteed under SERPS. The government also gave further encouragement to the private pensions industry through tax relief and insurance contribution rebates. They abolished the requirement that any approved private scheme should be as good as SERPS. These measures unleashed a massive sales campaign by the private pensions industry which contributed to subsequent scandals about inadequate protection for some people.

By 1997, three classes of pensioners could be identified. One group, about a third of all retirees, and including public servants, had well-funded private pensions to supplement the basic Beveridge pension. At the other extreme was another group – including particularly many women and older pensioners – whose main provision came from the flat rate Beveridge scheme, which (since it remained low) they might need to supplement with means-tested benefits. In the middle there were people with modest sums from either SERPS or limited (and often fragile) private schemes to supplement the flat rate pension. The Labour government elected in 1997 initially focused reform efforts on a means-test-based 'guarantee credit' for pensioners on low incomes and on marginal improvements to the SERPS scheme (with a new name). It refused to restore the value of the contributory flat rate pension, and it made new efforts to encourage private pensions. After an extensive investigation (Pensions Commission, 2005) – the quality of which can be examined as a good example of a 'rational' approach to the solution of a policy problem – the government accepted the long-run case for increasing the value of the contributory pension (but with a timetable that put even the start of that process beyond the next election) but also set about enacting a compulsory private pension saving scheme. At the time of writing there remains a great deal of uncertainty about the progress of this policy in the light of constraints on government expenditure, weaknesses in the private saving market and the likelihood of a change of government.

Box 8.4 explores what has been going on in the UK, particularly since 1960. What has occurred has been an effort to reach a compromise between the conflicting concerns about the pension system:

- the high levels of current pensioner poverty;
- the future balance between the generations;
- the recognition that the favourable situation of many contributors to good private pension schemes is one that should be shared more widely;
- the desire of the financial market to sell pensions;

- a recognition that some marketised pensions may not be a good buy for their contributors in the long run.

What the examination of the British case highlights for an understanding of agenda setting is:

- the way in which current agendas emerge as consequences of past decisions;
- the incremental nature of change;
- the way alternative agendas come into conflict;
- the way those alternative agendas do not just arise out of conflicting interests and ideologies but also out of interrelated problems (in this case particularly the differences between the issues about current pensioner poverty and those about future comprehensive provisions)

Issues about applying Kingdon's model

Kingdon's model depicts the policy process as disorganised or haphazard. The pensions case discussed here suggests a need to question that. What has been suggested in the exploration of this issue is that it has been regularly on the agendas of many nations over a long period of time, that there has been a distinct 'politics' theme running through it and that there has been a comparative similarity, or at least a clustering, of ultimate policy responses. This politics has been analysed by a comparative study edited by Bonoli and Shinkawa (2005) that uses an approach to the analysis of that element in Kingdon's model which emphasises the significance of 'blame avoidance' by political actors. It is argued that 'politicians are motivated primarily by the desire to avoid blame for unpopular actions rather than be seeking to claim credit for popular ones' (Weaver, 1986, p. 371). Hence it can be argued that the twin dilemmas for pensions reform are that the funding of improvements will impose costs upon people who will not be immediate beneficiaries while the retrenchment necessary without those improvements 'forces tangible costs upon a limited number of people' (Shinkawa in Bonoli and Shinkawa eds, 2005, p. 165). The consequences are a search for approaches that yield benefits but hide costs and the kind of policy complexity which Box 8.4 illustrates (albeit with a lot of bewildering detail left out – see Hill, 2007 for a more extensive analysis of the issues).

There is a case for caution about the emphasis on *politics* in the case chosen here. Pension policy is perhaps a rather 'mainstream' policy issue, bound to get considerable attention and to appear regularly on policy agendas. Nevertheless, there is a need to ask whether Kingdon's American perspective leads him to underemphasise the factors that may give agenda setting a rather clearer shape, bringing it closer to the notion of a rational search for solutions to problems that he has criticised. The view that there may be differences in the way the agenda is set is explored by Cobb, Ross and Ross (1976), who distinguish between the 'outside initiation model' of liberal pluralist societies, the 'mobilisation model' of totalitarian regimes and the 'inside initiation model' where influential groups have easy access to decision makers. But this approach still seems to accept the relevance of the Kingdon model for open systems. In a book in which the emphasis is on the policy process in the United Kingdom and Europe, it seems important to consider whether the Kingdon model pays sufficient attention to institutional variations, in particular the different ways in which the political process is organised in different societies. Particular problems here are his treatment of the roles of politicians and his comments on the role of the media. The next section develops these points.

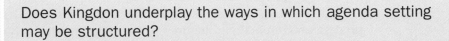

Does Kingdon underplay the ways in which agenda setting may be structured?

Essentially, the theory of representative democracy involves a model of the political process in which political parties compete to win elections, presenting manifestos between which the public may choose. There is then some expectation that the winners will implement the policies set out in their manifestos, on the basis that they have a 'mandate' for those policies. However, studies of electoral behaviour suggest that our voting choices are largely not determined in the rational way embodied in that model, and that fact may give politicians an excuse to disregard their commitments. However, despite this, the 'mandate' model operates as an important influence upon the formation of the policy agenda.

There are, then, clearly differences in the extent to which a coherent mandate can be expected. It is in the division that exists in the United States between President and Congress, and in the relatively loose programmatic bonds within parties, that we may find the basis for the relative underplaying of 'politics' in the Kingdon model. But within systems that are in formal terms more unified there may be another problem with identifying a coherent mandate: the fact that the government emerges not from the decisive victory of one party over another but from a compromise between more than one party. Notwithstanding this, it is interesting to note the continuing importance of the notion of a mandate in the very divided system in the Netherlands. A crucial stage in negotiations about the formation of a government there involves the drawing up of a *regeeraccoord* embodying an agreed policy programme.

In the last edition of this book this issue was explored through an examination of the impact of a mandate upon agenda setting in a situation in which strong effects of this kind could be expected, after a decisive victory by a single party in the 'first past the post' UK system. An examination was provided of the extent of mandate enactment by the Labour government headed by Tony Blair between the 1997 and 2001 elections. From that analysis it was argued that in this case an application of the Kingdon model would seem to rather underplay the politics dimension of agenda setting. However, the choice of the 1997 UK election probably exaggerates this since there was a dramatic shift of power (obviously influenced by the first past the post electoral system) with a new party taking power, no members of which had had any involvement in government for 18 years. It is not very easy to analyse the two subsequent general elections (2001, 2005) in the same way. The Labour manifestos for those are vaguer on pledges and tend to emphasise achievements and unfinished business. One sees then the other feature of the UK system, the impact of a strong executive, so that the emergent policies owe more than those of 1997 to work done by politicians with the assistance of civil servants. Then the structuring may be seen as an outcome of 'teamwork' involving both politicians and civil servants (a topic explored in greater detail in the next chapter).

Here then we reach one of the complex edges in an analysis of the policy process structured along the lines of the stages model. It is difficult to separate agenda setting from policy formulation when the policy production process is under the control of a strong executive in which politicians and civil servants work very closely together. But in this case it must be considered whether, where this is the case, agenda setting comes closer to the so-called rational model with the key actors engaged in a consensual process of problem solving. The answer to this question may depend upon the extent to which (a) there is a consensus about the problem and (b) there is a political system or political culture in which the achievement of consensus is prized. Hence where Smith was quoted above offering support for Kingdon's view of policy entrepreneurs, a comparative study by Eichorst and Wintermann (2006) suggests that in the Netherlands and Sweden expert advisors play an important role in the formulation of labour market policy. However, that same study reports a much more pluralist situation in respect of Germany, with competing experts linked to employers and trade union groups. Eichorst and Wintermann argue 'If government is weak for institutional reasons and policy advice rather fragmented, challenged and less policy oriented, as in the German case, policy advice cannot realize its full potential' (2006, p. 268). But that is putting the argument rather an odd way round, as if advice is normally uncontentious. It is politics that determines the consensus, not the advice.

The other issue here concerns the role of the media. Kingdon's book devotes a section to the media, within its consideration of policy entrepreneurs. However, Kingdon argues that the influence of the media on the agenda is less than might be expected, something he attributes partly to the way the media focus attention on an issue for a while and then lose interest and move on to something else. He argues that 'The media report what is going on in government ... rather than having an independent effect *on* governmental agendas' (Kingdon, 1995, p. 59). He goes on to qualify this a little with three points about the media role:

- as communicators within policy communities
- as magnifiers of movements that have occurred elsewhere
- as agencies which some actors may particularly use.

Kingdon seems here to accept a portrayal of the media role which journalists themselves propagate: as the messengers rather than as the shapers of the message. Apart from repeating the observation already made that Kingdon is of course only reporting on the United States, it is appropriate to challenge this view for its disregard of the second and third faces of power (see Chapter 2, pp. 31–6). This can be done with reference to all three of Kingdon's trilogy of problems, policy proposals and politics.

As far as 'problems' are concerned the media's limited and changing attention span is more relevant than Kingdon suggests. There is a very old joke that the journalist Claude Cockburn claimed to have won a competition at *The Times* for the dullest headline: 'Small earthquake in Chile: Not Many Dead'. It is very easy to find examples every day of news value judgements about whose accidents and disasters merit attention and whose do not. Deaths of American and British soldiers in Iraq and Afghanistan get attention, more or less one by one, while the much greater numbers of deaths of Iraqis and Afghans secure occasional references, often quoting challengeable estimates. When a natural disaster occurs in a foreign country the media tend to highlight cases of our own nationals involved. In any case, reporting of the consequences of these disasters tends to be heavy for a short time, after which it disappears from the media. Murders receive more attention than accidents, and some accidents (for example affecting planes as opposed to cars) get much more attention than others. Since this is not a book of media analysis the object here is neither to expose these issues fully, nor to examine the obvious journalistic defences of these cases of selective reporting. The points here are two-fold:

- that when and how problems are reported affects the political attention they receive;
- that media priorities are both their own priorities and reflections of what they expect public priorities to be, which can mean in both cases reinforcements of the dominant views (see Parsons, 1995, pp. 89–92 for some case study illustrations of this).

Turning then to policies, Kingdon's interpretation of the transmission role of the media is just too facile. The media tend to simplify the policies on the agenda and often highlight the simpler rather than the more complex ideas. This remark applies as much to the so-called serious press as to the mass circulation newspapers, and above all to television which works with communicable soundbites and dichotomies that can engender lively controversies. In relation to the example of pensions policy discussed above, two very complex ideas are regularly brought together by journalists in this sort of form: 'population ageing means that future pensions must be funded'. Both of the ideas are challengeable (but of course not easily in a simple soundbite; readers will have to go to my book *Pensions*, 2007, for more) inasmuch as demographic change does not necessarily imply insufficient workers for the needs of the future, and funding is a very complex business since when we save we do not just store money in the way squirrels store nuts but rather invest the money for others to use *now*.

The general point illustrated in the last paragraph is that the media shape ideas on the policy agenda in a way that promotes some perspectives and excludes others (see McCombs and Shaw, 1972, for a classic influential presentation of this view). This is particularly the case in respect of economic ideas where conventional wisdom shapes political thinking and journalists are important for the packaging of that wisdom, given the busy lives and limited attention spans of the key political actors. In this sense notions about the relative serious consequences of on the one hand rising inflation and on the other rising unemployment or about the need to limit public spending and avoid tax increases are as much the clichés of contemporary journalism as the shibboleths of contemporary politics.

In Chapter 5 it was suggested that inasmuch as rational choice theory has been taken seriously it has had a certain self-fulfilling effect. Journalists surely have had a role in propagating the simplistic generalisations of rational choice theory (see Chapter 5) as universal truths contributing to:

- Perceptions of politicians themselves as essentially self-interested actors.
- Inculcating distrust of bureaucrats, as similarly simply self-interested.
- Propagating through things like the 'median voter theorem' the view that political strategies that alienate 'middle England' (or wherever) are inherently risky.

Of course this is not agenda setting, but what it is doing is contributing to the constraints upon the agenda: discouraging innovation and political or administrative risk-taking.

This brings us to the third item in Kingdon's trilogy: 'politics'. The media are themselves part of the political process not just influences upon it. Accounts of contemporary politics draw attention to key figures among the ownership of the media, above all Rupert Murdoch and his family with their massive newspaper and television interests around the world. The views such figures take about what should or should not be on the political agenda are important, since they have the capacity to use the media to this end (see Kuhn in Seldon ed., 2007 on Blair's efforts to influence the media magnates). Again here the emphasis needs to be on the negative rather than the positive, counterbalancing Kingdon's stress on the pushing forward of ideas. But any account of the media *in politics* would be limited if it simply drew attention to the big figures with ownership powers. Journalists themselves need to be seen as members of an occupational community with views about what they should and should not do. Political journalists above all live their lives close to political elites, with privileged access to the powerful (which can be taken away if they are seen to go beyond the bounds of what the latter see as acceptable behaviour).

The qualifications to Kingdon's approach set out in this section consist essentially, notwithstanding the apparent radicalism of his approach, of suggesting that his valuable account of the dynamics of agenda setting is still too wedded to a pluralist view of the political process in which interests clash in a relatively unstructured arena. This leads him to neglect the way in which political actors can control the agenda and above all to underplay the complex role of the media in the policy process.

CONCLUSIONS

While the starting point for any consideration of agenda setting needs to be the social process that translates individual problems into social problems and then into political problems, efforts by policy analysts to theorise about agenda setting have their origins in efforts to prescribe how policy agendas should be set. This had its origins in endeavours to prescribe a 'rational' problem-solving model. But that model offers not so much an approach that helps us interpret how policy is actually made but rather an 'ideal type' against which more realistic models may be measured. The dominant approach to this realism is 'incrementalism', offered as an account of what is, but also as a more 'democratic' model for the messy world of pluralistic politics. But the analyst who really gets away from the prescriptive preoccupations of the rationalism/incrementalism debate is Kingdon.

Kingdon is not a dogmatic theorist. He speaks of himself as aiming to make progress 'in understanding . . . vague and imprecise phenomena', but finding that 'vision is still obscured' (1995, p. 208) and that he is 'trying to weave a rich tapestry' (ibid., p. 230). In this sense the fact that he gives no attention to agenda setting anywhere other than the US federal government should not be held against him. Rather, he has given us an approach – we may even say a 'toolkit' – which we can use to explore agenda setting anywhere.

Embodied in Kingdon's notion that three streams – problems, policies and politics – mingle in the 'soup' is an interesting challenge to do two related things. These are to ask questions about the extent to which agenda setting may be stabilised in practice. The discussion above, conducted by means of the example of pensions policy, where in some respects stability or shaping comes from the long-run continuity of the 'problem', has suggested that 'politics' makes a difference to national responses. From there it proceeded to look at the role of politics as a source of agenda shaping in societies that are less institutionally fragmented than the United States.

The three main approaches to the exploration of policy formulation – the rational model of decision making, incrementalism, and Kingdon's agenda-setting model – are interesting for the way in which they reflect different policy process theories. The rational model has much in common with the traditional approach to representative government, seeing policy formulation as a systematic response to authoritatively set goals. While there is not much discussion of how these may be set, the presumption is that they emerge from the democratic political process. Incrementalism's links with pluralist thinking are very evident in the writings of Lindblom. Furthermore, Lindblom's shift in perspective through his career can be seen as a response to the challenge posed to pluralism by those who stressed power inequalities. Finally, the way in which Kingdon was influenced by March and Olsen's emphasis upon system unpredictability in an institutional context shows itself in his explicit use of the concept of the 'garbage can'. Furthermore, the challenge to Kingdon's model offered by evidence that systems may be more organised than he suggests emphasises institutional arrangements and the stability of some policy networks and communities.

9 Policy formulation

SYNOPSIS

While at the beginning and the end of the chapter warnings are included about following the assumptions of the stages model too precisely, it is recognised that – as the detail in various writers' specifications of the stages suggests – there is a great deal of policy-making work that sits between successful agenda setting and implementation. The term 'policy formulation' is used to describe this, though an alternative perspective on this as 'policy programming' is also seen to be useful.

A policy example, where policy formulation might be expected to be quite simple, is used to illustrate the importance of this part of the process. This is followed by consideration of some policy process theory that focuses on 'instrument choice' – the fact that there are alternative ways of attempting to achieve policy goals.

The discussion of policy formulation leads on to a consideration of the literature on the power of civil servants, people who are likely to be particularly involved in this part of the policy process. While recognising the potential significance of wider propositions about the extent to which civil servants may be seen as the makers of policy, it will be suggested that a more plausible scenario is that civil servants will be very involved in the detailed programming of policy but that they may do this (as Page and Jenkins', 2005, study of British civil servants suggests) in a context in which they are guided by politicians' expectations or values.

Introduction

In the last chapter the distinction between it and the present chapter was set out simplistically in terms of the distinction between deciding where to go (agenda setting) and working out how to get there (formulation or policy programming). But it was noted that the agenda setting/formulation distinction is a difficult one, with a strong interaction between the two very likely. Nevertheless it is worthwhile to make the distinction and to emphasise its significance through the use of two separate chapters as the extensive range of policy-making activities that must follow on an initial policy commitment is often overlooked. A realistic approach to the study of the policy process must involve a recognition that if policies are to have real effects a great deal of detailed work has to be done. It has been suggested that much policy making is merely 'symbolic' (Edelman, 1971, 1977) consisting of gestures by politicians aimed at convincing the electorate that they care and are doing things when little is in practice being achieved. Detailed policy formulation is fundamental to the making of what may perhaps be called *real* as opposed to symbolic policy.

Attention to policy formulation is also important to avoid falling into the dichotomisation of the policy process in which just two stages are highlighted: one in which politicians *make* policy and the other in which civil servants merely *implement* it. This is of course another way of expressing the traditional distinction between politics and administration, examined in the discussion of the stages model.

Note how the two examples of the stages model by British authors, featured in Box 7.11, included, in Jenkins' formulation 'information', 'consideration' and 'decision' after 'initiation' and even more, namely 'deciding how to decide', 'issue definition', 'forecasting', 'setting objectives and priorities' and 'options analysis' after 'deciding to decide' in Hogwood and Gunn's version. We thus see these authors clustering a number of activities around agenda setting but not making the distinction between that and the formulation used in this book. Their approach takes us back to something mentioned, but given little attention, in the chapter on agenda setting: the 'rational' approach seen as using an unrealistic view of how policy decisions are made but providing a starting point for the more realistic agenda-setting model used by the incrementalists and by Kingdon. Simon argues, in his more realistic formulation of the rational approach,

> ... 'it has not been commonly recognized that a theory of administration should be concerned with the processes of decision as well as with the processes of action. This neglect perhaps stems from the notion that decision making is confined to the formulation of overall policy. On the contrary, the process of decision does not come to an end when the general purpose of an organization has been determined. The task of 'deciding' pervades the entire administrative organization quite as much as the task of 'doing' – indeed, it is integrally tied up with the latter' (1957, p. 1).

Simon attacks the notion of decision taking as external to administration, the notion that decisions are taken by politicians, leaving administrators to put those decisions into 'action'. He points out that administration involves continual decision taking. Such decisions can be seen as organised in a hierarchy, minor decisions being consequent upon major ones.

Simon presents decision making not as a process of 'maximising', as in economic theory, but as a process in which individual rationality is limited: 'The central concern of administrative theory is with the boundary between the rational and the non-rational aspects of human social behaviour. Administrative theory is peculiarly the theory of intended and bounded rationality – of the behaviour of human beings who *satisfice* because they have not the wit to *maximise* (ibid., p. xxiv).

Simon pays particular attention to the fact that decisions are based upon premises and that these premises will involve both factual and value elements. He recognises that it is often difficult to separate these elements but suggests that in ordering the hierarchy of decisions, deciding which decisions are the key ones which should form the premises for lower-order decisions, administrators should try to give priority to value premises. While from his prescriptive position he argues that the value premises should come from politicians, he explores the difficulties about making the fact/value distinction in real situations.

Simon's treatment of this issue then leads on to questions about who does this sort of work. Is it easy to make a distinction between what politicians do and what civil servants do (bearing in mind that this topic is often approached prescriptively in terms of propositions about what each should do)? Or have we here a range of activity within which that distinction is very likely to be blurred?

The relevance of the incrementalist challenge to Simon (discussed in the previous chapter) lies in the extent to which, however policy goals are selected, detailed policy formulation is a piecemeal activity too. Institutional theory, and particularly its emphasis upon pathways, suggests that this will be the case. There are moreover some activities, involving the adjustment of policy over time, that seem particularly likely to take that form. A good example here is the budgetary process. There have been various studies of the budgeting process outlining the ways in which government departments negotiate with the central finance department (including notably a classic study of the UK by Heclo and Widavsky called significantly *The Private Government of Public Money*, 1981). It is not appropriate to cite more detailed studies of the process, which of course varies from time to time and place to place. To understand what is involved, simply bear in mind what happens in voluntary organisations, large and small. On a regular basis, probably once a year, expenditure plans and income sources are reviewed. That review seldom involves wholesale reconsideration of activities. Rather the expectation is that existing activities will continue, and the existing revenue stream will remain. The questions that are then considered are about small variations in activities and small adjustments in, for example, subscriptions. Changes upwards or downwards will be *incremental*. Governmental budgetary review processes are similar, merely just more complex.

Key aspects of policy formulation

We start therefore with an examination of what policy formulation is likely to involve. This is a topic that is quite difficult to address in general terms. Consequently, the more abstract discussion of the topic will be illustrated with explicit examples largely from the author's own country. In this respect it needs to be remembered that the distinctions between the various formal policy formulation activities will vary from country to country. The contention here is merely that there will be equivalents to the UK phenomena identifiable in other countries, in respect of any policy where translation into action involves more than minimal complexity.

Knoepfel and Weidner use the term 'policy programming' (1982, see also Knoepfel, Larrue, Varone and Hill, 2007, Chapter 8) rather than formulation to address this issue and use a model that sees the detail of a policy as forming a series of layers around a policy core. These will include:

- More precise definitions of policy objectives. It was noted in relation to anti-poverty policy in Chapter 1 that the adoption of such a policy must imply a stance on the definition of poverty.
- Operational elements, which include the 'instruments' to be used to make the policy effective, a topic discussed further below.
- 'Political–administrative arrangements' which involve the specification of the authorities whose duty it will be to implement the policy; the notion that such authorities need money and other resources to do this follows self-evidently from that point.
- Procedural elements, namely the rules to be used in the implementation of the policy.

Box 9.1 illustrates these points with reference to the already used example of the 'right to roam' policy in England and Wales. What that example suggests is that, even with a relatively simple example of a public policy, the policy formulation process may be of considerable complexity. This simple Act translating a policy objective into action runs to 22 pages. It deals with important questions about overall definition of the 'right of access', of related rights and duties, of administering authorities and their tasks, of exceptions and of appeals.

The Countryside and Rights of Way Act 2000 is a British Act of Parliament. In this sense the policy formulation responsibility seems to be right where it should be in a system of representative government: with the legislature. But when we consider how detailed it is we must ask two questions: where did that detail come from, and how fully did the legislature scrutinise it? The answer – without going into what actually happened in this case – is that those 22 pages contain a great deal of material that was prepared by the executive assisted by unelected civil servants and that the

Box 9.1	The legislation to enact the 'Right to Roam' policy in England and Wales

The relevant legislation is the Countryside and Rights of Way Act of 2000, of which this measure forms the principal part (Part 1). Part of the Act, however, runs to 48 sections across 22 pages. Within it can be found:

- 'Principal definitions' including the meaning of 'access land' in the sections to come.

- Rights of the public in respect of access land, including some rules about things they may not do.

- A duty given to a public agency to prepare maps, and some specifications about how those maps should be prepared.

- Liabilities of owners of access land.

- Responsibilities of 'access authorities' – the public bodies required to administer the legislation – including powers to enable them to employ wardens.

- Conditions under which the general right of access may be withdrawn in exceptional circumstances.

- Rules about how access land can be 'accessed' – about fencing, gates, etc.

- Appeal rules in respect of various provisions.

actual legislative scrutiny may have been considerably abbreviated. We will return to this below.

However, within the Act there are other things that point to policy formulation that is likely to occur outside the legislature. The Act contains in various places a power to make further regulations. For example, it lists nine more specific issues in respect of the making of definitive maps (their form and scale, how the public shall be informed about them, how appeals about them should be handled) for which regulations may be made. There is also one more fundamental supplementary power: 'the Secretary of State (as respects England) or the Welsh Assembly (as respects Wales) may by order amend the definition of 'open country' . . . so as to include a reference to coastal land' (clause 3). In British law the issues about such regulations are complex. Technically they have to be 'laid before Parliament' but in practice there are so many regulations that only a minute quantity receives any detailed scrutiny. Once through that technical law-making process they form a substantive addition to the Act. In the past this form of law making, called delegated legislation, has been attacked by administrative lawyers as involving the taking of arbitrary powers by the government. The consensus today is that it would be impossible to deal with detailed amplification of legislation without some sort of power of this kind. For example, social security payment rates are changed regularly to allow for movements in the cost of living; Parliament would be overwhelmed if all changes of this kind needed new Acts of Parliament. On the other hand there is an implicit – but difficult – distinction to be made between detailed adjustments of policies and clauses that enable fundamental policy change without Parliamentary scrutiny.

There are, however, other clauses in the Countryside and Rights of Way Act that delegate more limited policy formulation responsibilities without even the notional requirement to involve the legislature. A central government 'agency' – the Countryside Agency has a variety of duties under the Act, including the giving of guidance to other authorities. Then lower down the system the various 'access authorities', generally local governments, may make their own arrangements about how to carry out their responsibilities. Note for example that they have 'powers', not 'duties', to employ wardens.

As noted above, it is difficult to address the subject of policy formulation without the use of examples that may be dismissed as specific to individual countries. The argument is not that legislation in other countries will have the legal shape described here, but that it may reasonably be predicted that they will have a structure that will contain most if not all of the following elements:

- Basic laws with clauses enabling later amendment.
- Provisions to make more detailed rules within the overarching legislative framework.
- Systems under which central responsible ministries will give more detailed instructions and/or advice to lower-tier agencies (including local governments).

To these may be added, in respect of forms of privatisation, the specification of much detail in contracts to non-public agencies expected to perform public functions.

This detailed formulation process involves the making of choices about ways to enact policy. This is the concern of the next section. It is followed by a section on a topic given considerable attention in the literature since the last years of the twentieth century, namely policy transfer, involving learning from other countries. Since that learning mostly involves formulation issues once a policy issue is on the agenda, it is included here rather than in the previous chapter.

Instrument choice

Knoepfel and Weidner's model of the policy formulation process has been noted as including 'instruments' within the list of operational elements. The issues about instrument choice may be very important. Howlett goes so far as to suggest that 'Instrument choice ... is public policymaking' (1991, p. 2).

Efforts to specify the key instruments have involved the provision of a list that is often quite extensive. As an appendix to his 1991 article, Howlett provides a list from other work, which contains 63 items. However, in the textbook he produced with Ramesh in 2003 he commends an approach to the delineation of policy instruments based upon Hood's listing of 'tools of government'. Hood (1986) classifies these in terms of

- 'nodality' – meaning the use of information;
- 'authority' – meaning the legal power used;
- 'treasure' – that is, the use of money;
- 'organisation' – the use of formal organisational arrangements.

It is unfortunate that Hood's fondness for acronyms leads him to use this rather odd terminology (added together they make NATO), but his approach is helpful. Howlett and Ramesh (2003) go on from this starting point to a valuable discussion of the strengths and weaknesses of various policy instruments. Key issues from their analyses are summarised in Box 9.2.

Box 9.2	**Howlett and Ramesh's (2003) analysis of policy instruments**

It is argued that instruments can be seen as within a spectrum involving increased levels of state involvement from low (at the voluntary instruments end) to high (at the compulsory instruments end). Decisions about instrument use will be influenced by the likelihood of resistance. Hence there will tend to be a preference for using low state involvement options. However, choices will be affected by the resources (as specified in Hood's list of tools) available to governments.

Howlett and Ramesh specify the following instruments (2003, p. 195):

Voluntary Instruments
Family and Community
Voluntary Organization
Private Markets

Mixed Instruments
Information and Exhortation
Subsidies
Auction of Property Rights
Tax and User Charges

Compulsory Instruments
Regulation
Public Enterprise
Direct Provision

Earlier in their book they offer a more complex formulation of this typology (p. 92).

Policy making involves choices about instrument use. Linder and Peters (1991) see policy instruments as in principle substitutable but argue that in practice choice depends upon:

- resource intensiveness
- the extent to which precise targeting of policies is required
- levels of political risk
- constraints on state activity.

Doern, on the other hand, sees instrument choice as essentially ideological, but with governments choosing the least coercive instrument. In his work with Phidd (Doern and Phidd, 1983, p. 134) he portrays instruments along a continuum rather like that provided in Box 9.2, from 'exhortation' through 'expenditure' and 'regulation' to 'public ownership'.

What the literature on instruments has made very clear is that the factors that influence instrument choice are complex. Policy type comes into play here as well as the issues about resistance to policy, but we may also see ideology influencing choice. In each specific case much depends on what is available, what has been done before, or what is already in use in a closely related policy area. Howlett argues that it is not feasible to 'develop a general theory of policy instrument types' (1991, p. 1). Rather, he suggests that issues of instrument choice need to be linked up with issues about national policy styles:

> ... there are several areas in which much more work remains to be done. First, the relationship between policy styles and policy instruments needs to be elaborated more precisely. This involves not only additional work conceptualizing and clarifying theories of policy instrument choice, but also work clarifying the concept of national policy styles. Second, much more comparative work needs to be done to add to the number of cases of instrument choice available, thus contributing to the development of studies of national styles, whether these turn out to be truly national or sectoral in nature. (ibid., p. 16)

These questions about instrument choice connect up with another theme in the discussion of the policy process, one which is widely used in association with analyses of modern approaches to public management and to governance. Various writers have developed typologies for the analysis of policy processes, stimulated by the issues on the agenda about the use of market mechanisms. Government has been seen to have choices between leaving matters to the market or imposing hierarchical systems. Then, with the development of network theory (see pp. 56–61), it has been suggested that networks offer a third alternative. Hence Thompson et al. (1991) speak of hierarchies, markets and networks as three general models of social coordination, while Ouchi (1980) distinguishes between bureaucracies, markets and clans. Bradach and Eccles (1991) and Colebatch and Larmour (1993) examine the organisation of policy action in terms of hierarchic authority (bureaucracy), individual exchanges (markets) and group activities (community). In work with Peter Hupe, the author's version of this is to propose the following distinctions for policy processes:

■ 'authority' – where rules are laid down in advance;
■ 'transaction' – where certain outputs are expected, often as specified in contracts;
■ 'persuasion' – where the essential mode of operation involves collaboration or what may be called 'co-production'. (Hill and Hupe, 2003, pp. 180–1)

Table 9.1 sets out the kinds of activities for which the different modes of accountability may be appropriate. In the second row of Table 9.1 the alternative perspectives on the management of implementation draw a distinction between top-down authority in the first column, issues about the extent to which there has been conformity with a contract in the second one, and a very mixed mode of accountability in the third column called 'co-production'. In the final row the way the actual management of the system is likely to be carried out is highlighted. This is seen in the 'Authority' column as particularly concerned with inputs, that is, questions about the extent to which resources have been appropriately applied to the performance of a task. In the 'Transaction' column it is suggested that crucial for this mode is a concern with outputs – have contractual obligations been fulfilled? By contrast with these two, the concern within the 'Persuasion' mode is with success in achieving shared goals – health or education improvement, for example – where it is real results as opposed to formally specified outputs that are crucial.

Table 9.1   Three kinds of governance

	Authority	Transaction	Persuasion
Core activity of government	Imposing Regulating Delivering goods and services	Creating frameworks Assessing results	Inviting participation Showing direction
Appropriate perspective on managing implementation	Enforcement	Performance	Co-production
Management via	Inputs	Outputs	Outcomes as shared results

There are then questions about choices between the alternatives (just as explored in the policy instruments literature). These will depend on:

■ considerations about the 'best' ways to organise any specific policy delivery process;

■ the ideologies of those who make the crucial choices (for example the strong preference for markets among many politicians of the liberal Right).

These typologies suggest that issues about instrument choice and policy delivery design will need attention in the policy formulation process. Inasmuch as they are central concerns in respect of the potential success of the policy it will of course be the case that those engaged in trying to set the policy agenda will not be indifferent to them. Then, further along the stages model, these choices will have an important impact upon the implementation process. We return at the end of this chapter to some of the issues about interactions between policy formulation and implementation.

Policy transfer

Some scholars have suggested a case for 'policy transfer theory' as a distinct and separate contribution to the study of the policy process. One aspect of globalist theory that is fairly self-evident is that in the modern world a great deal of effort is put into policy transfer. Not only do national policy makers look around at what is occurring elsewhere when they design their own policy, but it is also the case that there are a number of international organisations that are explicitly in the business of offering policy prescriptions – notably the various United Nations agencies, the World Bank and the Organisation for Economic Co-operation and Development.

'Policy transfer' is seen as a new approach to or 'framework of' policy analysis (see Dolowitz and Marsh, 1996, 2000; Dolowitz et al., 2000). It builds on Rose's work on 'policy learning' (1991, 1993). Yet since attempts to transfer policies are so widespread, a theory of 'policy transfer' either has a slightly banal quality or tends to invest too much importance in the migration of ideas as a driver of policy change. It leaves questions unanswered about how decisions are made to accept or reject ideas from elsewhere (see Box 9.3 for some of the key critical points).

There are obviously some important issues to raise about the conditions under which policy transfer occurs. There are clearly problems that arise from uncritical policy transfer. Some attention has been focused upon the role of international organisations making transfer semi-mandatory, inasmuch as continuing support is premised upon acceptance of policies (see Deacon, 1997, 2007). But the notion that a 'theory of policy transfer' can be developed must be viewed with some scepticism. On the other hand, policy transfer theory can be seen, both in terms of the general notion that new ideas and new discourses develop and are spread around the world, and in terms of its concern with circumstances in which policy transfer is or is not

Box 9.3	James and Lodge's critique of theories of lesson drawing and policy transfer (2003, p. 179)

First, can they be defined as distinctive forms of policy making separate from other, more conventional forms? 'Lesson drawing' is very similar to conventional accounts of 'rational' policy making, and it is very difficult to define 'policy transfer' distinctly from many other forms of policy making. Second, why do 'lesson drawing' and 'policy transfer' occur rather than some other form of policy making? The proponents of 'policy transfer' put a set of diverse and conflicting theories under a common framework, obscuring differences between them. Third, what are the effects of 'lesson drawing' and 'policy transfer' on policy making and how do they compare to other processes?

facilitated by existing institutional arrangements, as another contribution to institutional theory in its more wide-ranging forms.

Bulmer and Padgett use a policy transfer approach to the analysis of European Union policy. They describe the relationship between the European Union and the individual nation states as involving three distinctive forms of governance:

> Hierarchical governance is prevalent in policy areas like the single market where EU institutions exercise supranational authority leading to coercive forms of transfer. A second form of governance occurs where the European Union seeks to agree common rules or norms by common (or majority) consent. It is not uncommon to find norms modelled on those of one or more member state(s) in a form of transfer by negotiation. Finally, where member states retain sovereignty but co-ordinate policy via EU institutions (as in Justice and Home Affairs), policy transfer will take the form of unilateral voluntary exchange facilitated by the European Union (2004, p. 104).

It may be questioned whether the term 'transfer' is the right one for the first of these forms of governance (it is pertinent to note that other analysts of this phenomenon have described it as 'implementation', see Chapter 12, Box 12.2). However, the other two are pertinent to the discussion of agenda setting. With the second we see a negotiated form of the model set out by Kingdon, but with more complicated institutional arrangements. The third, on the other hand, can be seen as an important exogenous influence on policy processes largely contained within nation states.

Civil servants and policy formulation, context: the debate about the power of civil servants

We saw in Chapter 3 that a combination of politicians, civil servants and interest group representatives is implicit in the policy networks and policy communities theories. Much of the discussion of the roles of civil servants outside that framework, however, has tended to involve seeing them as alternative, even subversive, decision makers to politicians rather than as partners in a shared system (see Box 9.4). We have noted that such a perspective has been strongly influenced by the traditional preoccupation with the relationship between politics and administration. This discussion will start from that issue but aim to move away from it to a more balanced account of how these two groups interact in the policy process. In doing so it will consider, first, some of the issues about the respective roles of politicians and civil servants and then some of the issues about the compatibility of values, or ideologies, between them.

Box 9.4	**Representations of politician/civil servant relationships: fact or fiction?**

At the end of his life the prominent Labour politician of the 1940s and '50s Aneurin Bevan was reputed to have replied, when he was asked whether he had read the memoirs of one of his former Cabinet colleagues Herbert Morrison, that he 'preferred his fiction straight'. Politicians, who frequently publish memoirs, and civil servants, who occasionally do so, obviously have motives to present their relationships in ways that need to be viewed with a sceptical eye. The published diaries of one politician, Richard Crossman (1975, 1976, 1977), dealt particularly fully with his relationships with civil servants and inspired a comedy series on TV, 'Yes Minister'. That series reversed Crossman's picture of his success in securing dominance in the face of manipulative civil servants and represented the minister as the hapless dupe of the top civil servant.

While 'Yes Minister' presents a rather clear division between the two roles, in a much more recent British TV portrayal of a government office, 'In the Thick of It', it is much harder to distinguish roles. The decision making occurs in a chaotic and frenetic environment. In this case the dominant character is the press officer, and the programme is inspired by the published diaries of such a person (Campbell, 2007).

Clearly it is hard to open the 'black box' of politician/civil relationships (note Rhodes' excursion into this area by way of 'political anthropology' that is inevitably better at portraying the rituals than at exploring how decisions are actually made, 2007). We should not expect generalisation about this to be easy, and we should treat accounts designed to show who dominates as more appropriately left to the writers of fiction.

If permanent civil servants play a key role in the policy process they may tend to give continuity to the policy agenda, pursuing a departmental line regardless of political leadership. The power of the civil service and the importance of departmental agendas were emphasised in many past studies of British public administration. A particular concern of politicians and of some of the small number of outsiders brought in to support them during the Labour government of 1964–70 was civil service control over the agenda. The 'Whitehall model' has been seen as firmly established in Britain. Even though, as will be shown below, they suggest change is occurring, Campbell and Wilson say:

> politicians in few countries place as much faith in bureaucrats as do the British. The British system contrasts not only with the patronage system at the top of the executive branch in the United States but also with the continental European practice (as in Germany) of placing senior civil servants in temporary retirement if a governing party loses power . . . [t]he dependence of elected politicians on the non-partisan, permanent civil service was the core of the system that has been exported to other countries and admired by many non-British scholars. (Campbell and Wilson, 1995, p. 293)

Nevertheless, we see similar features in some other European systems. Anderweg and Irwin's (2002) account of policy making in the Netherlands suggests the importance of departmental agendas, with civil servants as the key advisors for their ministers. In respect of France, Knapp and Wright speak of 'the colonisation by the civil service of areas beyond the confines of mere administration' (2001, p. 276). Knapp and Wright's discussion of this phenomenon indicates that this came under attack but that the situation has not been changed significantly.

Obviously there will be differences between societies in how these roles are distributed. Dyson's analysis of 'strong' and 'weak' states discussed in Chapter 4 suggested that in the 'strong' state civil servants are carriers of a tradition of service to the state, which is seen as providing a context for the more temporary concerns of politicians. Much depends here upon other aspects of the constitution. If electoral systems tend to produce unified programmatic parties then there is a potential tension between the two elements in the policy-making process. Here differences between the early (agenda-setting) and later parts of the policy process are likely to be relevant. But much will depend upon the extent to which either one political party is largely dominant (as in Sweden until recently) or where there is a relatively low level of conflict between the parties (as in Germany). France is an interesting case because the constitution of the Fifth Republic gives administrators considerable autonomy. Commentators on France suggest that the period in which Mitterrand came to presidential power with innovatory socialist policies but was then forced first to water them down and then to accept 'cohabitation' with a prime minister of a different political persuasion was a crucial testing time for French democracy (Ritchie in Harrop, 1992; see also Knapp and Wright, 2001).

An alternative perspective on strong states is supplied by those where multi-party systems dominate or have dominated (the Netherlands, Belgium, the French Fourth Republic). In these the party-political input is largely seen very early in the policy process – in the issues that are contested in elections and in the compromises that occur between the elements in a coalition – after which a kind of administrator/politician accommodation seems to apply.

One of the reasons for the preoccupation in much earlier literature with questions about whether politicians or administrators dominate in the policy process arises from a concern that civil servants 'subvert' policy because they do not share the ideologies or value commitments of demo-cratically elected politicians. One possible way of dealing with this concern, the idea that civil servants should be 'representative' in a social sense, is explored in Box 9.5. The extent to which it is seen as a problem is influenced by the extent to which there are significant political or ideological divisions with regard to the policy agenda. Earlier writers on the British civil service (for example, Chapman, 1970) suggest that civil servants in Britain have strong reservations about party politics while at the same time possessing commitments to particular policies. The implication is that these officials find changes in their political masters easy to adjust to so long as they do not involve violent ideological shifts. Officials can operate most easily in a situation of political consensus. Where consensus does not exist, however,

Box 9.5	Representative bureaucracy

One response to ideological differences between politicians and civil servants has been to argue that civil servants should be, as far as possible, representative of the societies from which they are drawn. Kingsley's (1944) pioneering work on this topic looked at the British civil service, arguing that it was transformed from an aristocratic into a bourgeois organisation during that period in the nineteenth century when the commercial middle class were becoming politically dominant. The British bureaucracy was thus made representative of the dominant political class, but not, of course, of the people as a whole. To work effectively the democratic state requires a 'representative bureaucracy', Kingsley argues, thus taking up the theme, developed also by Friedrich (1940), that the power of the civil service is such that formal constitutional controls upon its activities are insufficient. Kingsley sees the recruitment of the civil service from all sectors of the population as one means of ensuring that it is a 'responsible bureaucracy'.

This issue has traditionally been explored very much in class terms (see Aberbach, Putman and Rockman, 1981). More recent work has added attention to issues about gender and about ethnic, regional or religious origins or background (Meier, Stewart and England, 1991; Selden, 1997). Much of this new work is concerned with the behaviour of 'street-level bureaucrats', and will be discussed in Chapter 13.

their role may become one of trying to create it. Graham Wallas (1948) sums this up most neatly:

> The real 'Second Chamber', the real 'constitutional check' in England, is provided, not by the House of Lords or the Monarchy, but by the existence of a permanent Civil Service, appointed on a system independent of the opinion or desires of any politician and holding office during good behaviour. (Wallas, 1948, p. 262)

In the 1960s, discontent developed on the political Left about this comfortable consensual doctrine (Thomas, 1968). A response to it was to appoint temporary political advisors to ministers. But it was on the political Right that the most robust response developed during the governments led by Margaret Thatcher in the 1980s. As a consequence, Campbell and Wilson suggest that the traditional 'Whitehall model' is being destroyed by:

- the breaking of the monopoly of the civil service as advisors to ministers;
- the development of systems to help the Prime Minister contest civil service advice;
- most importantly, 'whole generations of bureaucrats and politicians have been socialised since the 1970s into very different professional norms . . . enthusiasm for government policies has been rewarded more than honest criticism' (Campbell and Wilson, 1995, p. 296);
- 'the erosion of the belief that the civil service is an established profession, like all professions delineated from society as a whole by clear boundaries' (ibid., p. 297).

This argument was developed before Tony Blair came to power. Despite the fact that he has altered the institutions at the centre, his obsessive desire to control policy and to control the way policy is presented has done much to further these developments. This is leading to a very different attitude to the organisation of the upper reaches of the civil service, with many more temporary civil servants being recruited and much more attention being paid to the commitments of candidates for top jobs. It is interesting to note that this approach to filling top offices is now also well established in the German federal government:

> Administrative state secretaries, who are civil servants, occupy the highest grade in the Federal administration, and are regularly amongst the key figures in the ministerial policy process. They deputize for the minister in running the department, and they operate directly at the interface between politics and administration. Their special position is recognized in their status as 'political civil servants' as defined by Article 36 of the Federal Civil Service Law. It is acknowledged that they need to be in permanent basic agreement with the government's views and objectives in order to perform their task of helping to transform the government's political will into administrative action. Political civil servants, who also

include heads of division, need not be recruited from amongst career civil servants. (Goetz, 2003, pp. 27–8)

Campbell and Wilson chart some similar developments in other systems close to the 'Whitehall model' in Australia, New Zealand and Canada. In Australia, Pusey has, however, raised a rather different issue. He has explored the way in which a new ideological agenda has been pursued from within the civil service. He argues that alternative ways of managing the economy have been advanced systematically by 'economic rationalisers' who have come to dominate key roles within the civil service (Pusey, 1991). An interesting ambiguity in Pusey's analysis concerns the extent to which this has been tacitly encouraged by elected politicians, on the Labor side as much as the Liberal. A similar phenomenon has been observed in New Zealand, where a determined group of 'economic rationalisers' closely linked with the Treasury secured the support of first a Labour finance minister and later a National Party one. In respect of this case, Wallis writes of a 'conspiracy', in which the change of the agenda depended upon a concerted effort to win support in the civil service and the political parties (1997).

The evidence marshalled by Pusey and Wallis suggests that there may be a need, alongside interest in the way in which the relationship between political values and a permanent administration is managed, to look at how new ideological consensuses may be developed within a ruling elite. If, in fact, it is the case in the more unified systems, particularly those following the Westminster model, that the policy process is more controlled than Kingdon's analysis suggests, it may be beside the point to ask whether this control comes from the politicians' agenda or from a civil service-dominated policy agenda. We may, particularly when one party is in government for a long while (as in Sweden) or when the differences between the two parties are quite slight (as has been the case in the UK much of the time since 1951) or when political changes often involve slight shifts within a coalition (as in the Netherlands), be looking at control over the agenda exercised by a relatively unified community of politicians and civil servants.

The implication of the above discussion is that it may be inappropriate to polarise the distinction between politician and civil service domination. In addition, it may be important to see interest groups as part of this organised community. These issues were explored in Chapter 3, where it was suggested that some theorists, particularly those who have seen 'corporatism' as important, may have exaggerated the unification of the whole system. However, while it may be unhelpful to exaggerate the sources of policy community unification, there is a need to recognise that there may be situations in which this unification is much in evidence.

In relation to the above discussion of politics and ideology it is important to bear in mind that political parties may not be the driving forces with regard to the injection of ideological elements into the political process. Furthermore, when ideologies become dominant they may fuse all aspects of the policy process. Many writers at the end of the twentieth century gave attention to the way in which economic belief systems, stressing a need to restore market processes to a more central position in the determination of policy, secured acceptance beyond the ranks of the political 'new Right'. The case of New Zealand has attracted particular attention in this respect, since there it was a Labour government that took the crucial first steps (Kelsey, 1995; Massey, 1995). It was noted above that Wallis (1997) describes the New Zealand case as involving a 'conspiracy', inasmuch as 'an exclusive social network of policy participants' worked together to change policy (p. 1). Clearly, where 'policy communities' are able to dominate the policy process, shared ideologies may be important for this domination.

But equally important may be a commitment to collaborative working in government regardless of ideology. The political system of the Netherlands has been seen as characterised by 'consociational democracy' (Lijphart, 1975) with extensive collaboration between opposed social 'pillars' (Catholic, Protestant, secular liberal and social democratic) in both politics and administration. While there is extensive evidence that the era of pillarisation has passed (see Anderweg and Irwin, 2002), corporatist characteristics remain very persistent in the Netherlands. Success in dealing with the need for industrial restructuring has been seen as attributable to the continuation of a weak form of corporatism which has been called the 'polder model' (Visser and Hemerijk, 1997).

Civil servants and policy formulation: does the traditional debate miss the point?

Beyond this recognition of the prominence of the civil service role in general, a great deal of the discussion of the roles of civil servants seems to have become locked into the dated debate about the possibility of distinguishing policy making from administration. The position that has been taken in the first part of this chapter has been partly to challenge this but primarily to argue that it involves a very simplistic view of policy making, disregarding the complexity of the policy formulation task. However, there is still much modern writing that reverts in one way or another to simplifications about policy making roles. Huber and Shipan's *Deliberate Discretion* (2002) explores why 'politicians sometimes allow substantial discretion and at other times tell bureaucrats precisely what to do' (p. 9). The problem is that such an approach is still searching for an easy way to dichotomise roles, in this case treating rule making as what politicians do and disregarding the complexity of this task (as illustrated above, for example with the 'right to roam' legislation), which surely calls for some combination of roles. Campbell and Wilson's analysis of the changing role of the UK civil service seems similarly to miss the point when they refer to 'civil servants increasingly defining their role as policy implementers rather than policy analysts' (1995, p. 60), disregarding tasks between agenda setting and implementation. The same is true of an account of the changing civil service by someone with long experience of observing British government, Anthony King, heading a chapter 'Mandarins as Managers' and surely – again because of a disregard of detailed work – exaggerating the extent to which senior civil servants are shifting from policy-making activity to the management of implementation (2007, Chapter 9).

A study of the work of middle-ranking civil servants by Page and Jenkins (2005) supports the account of the policy formulation process set out in this chapter. It shows how civil servants, often well below the leading grades in the British civil service, play crucial roles in the formulation of policy. At the same time it challenges the view that this in any respect involves subversion of political roles. It points instead to a team-like activity in which there are close working relationships between civil servants and ministers. In some respects civil servants can be seen as paying attention to Simon's values/facts decision, showing sensitivity to issues that might concern the politicians. They identify a variety of 'cues' used for this:

- The perceived thrust of government policy
- Experience from frequent interaction with ministers
- Departmental priorities
- Reference to documents
- 'Consensus mongering' (ibid., p. 134) implying a sensitivity to contested issues.

Another crucial concept here is the notion of a 'steer', described as 'not a command' (ibid., p. 136), and even allowing for the possibility of questioning. Page and Jenkins say '...its general legitimacy as a guide to developing policy comes because it is directly or indirectly an expression of a minister's wishes' (ibid., p. 137). This study supplements an earlier one by Page in which attention was paid to the specific roles played by civil servants during the legislative process (Box 9.6 summarises the findings from this).

Page and Jenkins sum up by saying:

> Politicians are clearly at the apex of the executive structure. In comparison with the full range of tasks they oversee, ministers can at best take a close interest only in a small proportion of the decisions taken in their name. They are highly dependent upon officials working within the policy bureaucracy who work hard to fashion policies in ways they think their ministers will like (ibid., p. 184).

There is obviously an issue here about how much conclusions like this only apply to the UK. Page and Jenkins consider this issue and indicate that there are parallels in the systems used in other European countries. There are evidently variations in the extent to which outsiders are brought into play key roles close to ministers (particularly in respect of legislation). They acknowledge the likelihood of differences in the United States with the separation

Box 9.6	Page's (2003) examination of the role of the British 'civil servant as legislator'

British civil servants are drafted into 'bill teams' to work on the preparation of legislation. Such teams are typically led by civil servants drawn from the lowest grade of the 'senior' civil service. The teams tend to be formed early in the process of preparing a new policy, before it has been agreed that there will be a place for legislation in the parliamentary timetable. The decision to legislate will be a political one. However, Page shows that, in some of the cases he studied during Blair's second term in government, the identification of a need for legislation was as much a civil service activity as a political one.

Once a decision to legislate is made, teams will work on the detailed drafting of legislation. Drafting will involve the team, joined or assisted by lawyers employed by the civil service. Before being put before Parliament a draft bill will be submitted to the relevant minister or ministers, who will be responsible for steering the legislation through Parliament. To assist ministers, large briefing documents will be compiled. During the legislation process any suggested amendments will be carefully scrutinised by the team. Many will be the product of further thoughts about the legislation from within the department. Some will be inspired by pressure groups and some will come from within Parliament, but very often the aim will be to accept these in principle and secure their withdrawal so that they can be replaced by amendments compatible with the bill as a whole. Once the legislation has been steered through Parliament, the bill team is likely to move on to drafting implementing amendments and guidance on the legislation.

between executive and legislature, and the fact that accordingly key roles are played by staff working for members of Congress.

There is, as has already been acknowledged, a difficulty about drawing a line between agenda setting and formulation of policy. An interesting illustration of this comes from an apparently trivial argument between the British political parties in late 2003 and is set out in Box 9.7.

The long-standing concern to distinguish politics (or policy making) from administration, though it has its roots in an obvious issue about representative democracy, manifests itself often as a naïve demand to take politics out of medicine, or education, or whatever. In practice, these issues matter too much either for politicians to be prepared to leave them alone or for the 'administrators' (including many professional staff, a point we return to on pp. 289–90) to abdicate what they see as their responsibilities for doing the right thing. Hence there are large parts of the policy process in which political and administrative roles are inextricably mixed.

This discussion of administrative roles in the policy formulation process involves an exploration of what is perhaps the most ambiguous part of the initial policy process. It is certainly the most difficult to research, because so

Box 9.7	A 'new policy' or strengthening an old one?

The British government announced, in summer 2003, a new initiative to reduce cross-infection in hospital. The opposition argued that a 'new' policy should be brought before Parliament. The government response to this was that it was merely strengthening existing procedures. At this the opposition claimed that the government was 'spinning' news again, dressing up old initiatives as new to try to strengthen its image. An interesting further feature of the argument was that the crucial 'new' steps were being taken by a civil servant, the Chief Medical Officer, who had issued the guidance on actions that should be taken by hospitals. Here, then, is an issue about 'what is a new policy?' In the end, except to the politicians trying to score points, the answer to that question does not matter; we have here a small part of the continuous flow of activity involved in managing a system that is continually in the eye of political conflict, the National Health Service.

much of the action is private (in the UK we have to wait 30 years for the publication of official papers, and even then some items are protected for longer, some are purged, and many were never committed to paper records in the first place). The fact that there have been so many attempts to draw the politics/administration distinction or to delimit the political roles and interests of permanent officials indicates the complexity of this issue. The achievement of the ideal – that civil servants should be just 'managers' or just concerned with 'means' – is fraught with difficulty.

Dunleavy and O'Leary refer to the 'professionalisation' of government to suggest that, in areas where expertise is important, issues are pulled out of the general political arena into the more private politics of 'policy communities':

> In the professionalized state the grassroots implementation of policy, and major shifts in the overall climate of debate in each issue area, are both influenced chiefly by individual occupational groups. Professional communities act as a key forum for developing and testing knowledge, setting standards and policing the behaviour of individual policy-makers and policy implementers. Knowledge elites are crucial sources of innovations in public policy-making ... in areas where professions directly control service delivery the whole policy formulation process may be 'implementation skewed'. (Dunleavy and O'Leary, 1987, pp. 302–3)

A modern twist to all the issues about the way the politician/administrator boundary is organised comes with two approaches to government which, while they have echoes in the past and particularly in pre-democratic regimes, are currently assuming increasing importance: public/private partnerships and the delegation of public tasks to quasi-independent or independent organisations. In many respects this is a subject for the discussion of implementation. Certainly this is how governments tend to present these developments – emphasising Woodrow Wilson's politics/administration distinction or stressing that 'we' still make the 'policy', 'they' are responsible for 'operations'. Invoking the already criticised Wilson distinction indicates that this should be viewed with caution. Leaving aside the new ways in which this now brings politicians into concerns about 'implementation', it will be seen that any 'agent' with responsibilities to implement a policy is likely to develop very real concerns about the way in which the policy it operates is constructed. If confronted with something unexpectedly expensive or something unworkable, the agent is likely to lobby (probably covertly) for policy change. The 'agent' with a contract to carry out a specific task with a specific sum of money is a politically interested party (a new actor in the bargaining part of the game), and perhaps particularly likely to behave in the way predicted by public choice theory.

The policy formulation/implementation relationship

It has been suggested – in earlier discussions and at the beginning of this chapter – that just as there are problems about being precise about the agenda setting/formulation distinction so too are there problems about the formulation/implementation one. This will be discussed briefly here as a linking section between the concerns of this chapter and those of the next. In the earlier discussion support was offered to Page and Jenkins' criticism of perspectives that seem to suggest there is a distinct policy-making process that may be seen as involving rule making and then all else is implementation. But empirically speaking there may be situations in which much of the activity that creates the policy actually experienced (see the discussion of the meaning of policy on pp. 14–19) occurs during what is generally perceived as the implementation process. To return briefly to the metaphor of a journey: just as we may determine our destination during a journey, so too may we change our route during it. It is appropriate to supplement this with another 'homely' metaphor, the cooking of a meal. This will be found in Box 9.8.

In the world of public policy we find a similar range of options to those set out in Box 9.8. The first three options listed correspond with three degrees of high discretion in implementation contexts. In the more extreme cases this makes the implementer responsible for matters that in the other two options are seen as agenda setting or policy formulation. The situation of following a recipe book fits well with the classical staged model. The recipe book has identified dishes (policies) and rules formulated about how to make them; implementation consists of judgements around the aspects of the recipe that are not (and perhaps cannot be) as easily specified. But in

Box 9.8	Alternative ways in which discretionary elements occur in the policy process: a homely example

Imagine a two-person household in which one person undertakes to cook a meal to be shared with the other. There are then a variety of possibilities, of which the following are the main ones:

- That the cook is quite free to choose what to do.
- That the cook is free to choose what to do within constraints such as the size of the budget, the availability of ingredients, the amount of time available and some knowledge of the likes and dislikes of the other.
- That the ingredients were chosen in advance but that the cook still has considerable latitude about how to use them.
- That the recipe was chosen in advance, which means that what is to be done is closely prescribed (but following a recipe may still involve judgements about when elements are sufficiently well cooked, about seasoning 'to taste', etc.). A particularly problematic example here occurs with the making of a sauce, where adjustments in the course of action may be essential.
- Variants of the above but with negotiations during the process – 'Would you like this?', 'How do you think I should deal with that?', 'Taste this and tell me what you think of it' and so on.

In the author's own household versions of all these five options occur, with the last very common.

the previous example in Box 9.7 there is action, based on earlier prescriptions, but also reference back towards someone who may be seen here as in a somewhat equivalent role to those concerned with the earlier stages of the policy process. One task identified by the civil servants whom Page and Jenkins (2005) studied was giving advice on the interpretation of policy to implementers.

The point here is that much of the literature on implementation is about the various degrees of discretion accorded to those close to, or actually at, the delivery point for policy, but this means that issues inevitably arise about how the agenda setting/policy formulation/implementation distinctions have been made, or are worked out in practice. We will find that the implementation literature, like so much else in the literature on which this book has to draw, is very much influenced by efforts to prescribe how those boundaries should be drawn, and of course the politics/administration distinction raises its head again.

CONCLUSIONS

This chapter has been concerned with the fact that, whilst agenda setting and policy formulation, are closely connected, it is very clear that the translation of policy objectives into instructions for action is an extensive task often given insufficient attention in discussions of the policy process.

Various aspects of policy formulation have been identified. A recognition that much attention needs to be given to detail inevitably leads to an examination of the roles of those who do such work. It is suggested that in the British system and in many other administrative systems such work falls to full-time officials rather than to politicians or their immediate impermanent assistants. This leads the chapter into a discussion of the power of the civil service, even though much of that literature goes much wider than a concern with detailed policy formulation to postulate that civil servants often *make* policy in the strong sense of that term. Page and Jenkins' careful work on actual civil service roles brings us back to the suggestion that this postulate over-simplifies a complex team-like relationship. A fuller discussion of these relationships requires attention to implementation as well as policy formulation, the concern of the next chapter.

10 Implementation: an overview

SYNOPSIS

This chapter starts by noting how a very distinctive vein of 'implementation' studies developed towards the end of the twentieth century. It goes on to explore briefly how that work was concerned to make a clear distinction between policy formulation and implementation, and suggests that this is now a source of difficulties. This leads naturally into a consideration of the 'top-down' studies that particularly emphasised that distinction. It is followed by an exposition of the 'bottom-up' evaluation of these studies. The next section, headed 'Beyond the top-down/bottom-up debate', provides an approach which then dominates the rest of the chapter. It suggests a need for an awareness that there is a complex mix of issues to be understood about the different ways actual policies are developed, about how they may best be studied, and about the normative arguments about who should be in charge which often dominate (and obscure) discussions about implementation. Subsequent sections highlight issues about variations in the 'policy rule framework' and about 'variations in the administrative system'.

In this chapter the focus will be very much upon introducing issues about what happens during the implementation process. The chapters that follow explore aspects of the organisation of the policy process that need to be looked at in any account of that process as a whole, but in which issues about implementation loom large.

Introduction

In the United States in the early 1970s and in Europe later in that decade there emerged a wave of studies examining the implementation of public policy. Their rationale was that there had been, in the study of public policy, a 'missing link' (Hargrove, 1975) between concern with policy making and the evaluation of policy outcomes. We should perhaps be wary when academics claim to have discovered a new topic or a 'missing link', as they are very good at dressing up old concerns in new language and thereby claiming originality. The absence of theory and literature on implementation before Pressman and Wildavsky's seminal work (1973) on that topic has been exaggerated: for example, many organisational studies are de facto concerned with this phenomenon. Furthermore, a concern with the relationship between policy making and administration is as old as democratic politics (Wilson, 1887). Nevertheless, as empirical research in political science developed in the first half of the twentieth century there was perhaps a relative neglect of the study of the processes by which policies are translated into action. They were regarded as mundane and taken for granted. As Gunn (1978) argues, 'Academics have often seemed obsessed with policy formation while leaving the "practical details" of policy implementation to administrators' (p. 1).

The explosion of implementation studies therefore represents an important advance in policy analysis. Yet, like so many paradigm shifts in the social sciences, this new intellectual development has come to be seen to have its own limitations. At various places already in this book warnings have been sounded about the stages model of the policy process. At the end of the last chapter problems were examined about the distinction between policy formulation (often, indeed, called 'making') and implementation, a division particularly highlighted in stagist approaches to policy analysis.

The strength of the case for stressing the importance of implementation as distinct from the policy formulation process, and as deserving of attention in its own right, has tended to lead to an overemphasis on the distinctiveness of the two processes. There has been a tendency to treat policies as clear-cut, uncontroversial entities whose implementation can be studied quite separately. This has raised both methodological problems and problems about the extent to which the very practical concerns of implementation studies may involve, explicitly or implicitly, identification with some actors' views of what should happen.

This difficulty has been compounded by the extent to which actors regard it as important to make this distinction. We have here an argument that may be taken in two possible directions. One is to say that, inasmuch as people regard a distinction as important, in all sorts of respects it will be evident in their activities, and the empirical study of their activities must have regard to that. The other is to say that there is a need to be sceptical about a distinction that is so widely used in policy rhetoric, closely linked as it is with the notion that some actors have responsibilities to be leading decision makers (a notion often embedded in versions of democratic theory) while others have duties to carry out the policies of their 'masters'. There is in this latter case a situation in which there will be powerful people who want us to believe that the reality corresponds with the rhetoric, or will want to blame the 'implementers' when events do not correspond with original expectations.

In this book the aim is to try to have it both ways – that is, both to reflect the importance of the formulation/implementation distinction in the policy process, and to be aware of how confused it may be in practice.

The top-down model for the study of implementation

In the course of the evolution of work on implementation in the later part of the twentieth century, a debate developed between the 'top-down' and the 'bottom-up' perspectives. As in all such debates, a later resolution has been reached in which most scholars will want to avoid taking either of the extreme positions, but it is nevertheless helpful to examine this debate for the insights it gives us into some of the key issues about the study of implementation.

The top-down perspective is deeply rooted in the stages model, and involves making a clear distinction between policy formulation and policy implementation. Hence, Van Meter and Van Horn (1975) define the implementation process as 'Those actions by public or private individuals (or groups) that are directed at the achievement of objectives set forth in prior policy decisions' (p. 445).

Pressman and Wildavsky go on in a similar vein:

> Implementation to us, means just what [dictionary definitions] ... say it does: to carry out, accomplish, fulfill, produce, complete. But what is it being implemented? A policy, naturally. There must be something out there prior to implementation; otherwise there would be nothing to move toward in the process of implementation. A verb like 'implement' must have an object like 'policy'. But policies normally contain both goals and the means for achieving them. How, then, do we distinguish between a policy and its implementation? (Pressman and Wildavsky, 1973; 1984 edition: xxi)

Pressman and Wildavsky thus highlight a question that is for them of more than linguistic relevance:

> We can work neither with a definition of policy that excludes any implementation nor one that includes all implementation. There must be a starting point. If no action is begun, implementation cannot take place. There must be also an end point. Implementation cannot succeed or fail without a goal against which to judge it. (ibid., p. xxii)

There is an issue of logic here. The act of 'implementation' presupposes a prior act, particularly the act of formulating what needs to be done. Various questions follow from this: Who is the formulator? Who is the decision maker? Who is the implementer? If they are not integrated as a single actor, there is a need to identify the variety of actors involved. Then there are questions about whether the formulator or decision maker has more power, or a role that is more legitimised, than the implementer. The act of formulation and decision making may take place anywhere in the policy process. There is no necessary assumption that formulators are always at the 'top' in a political or hierarchical sense, but there is embodied in this perspective a view of the prior nature of the formulation process. This may be called the *'implementation follows formulation and decision theorem'* (Hill and Hupe, 2009, p. 4).

The pioneering implementation studies therefore highlighted the need to examine the process of putting policy into action. Their concern was to challenge those who, at that time, took it for granted that this process would be smooth and straightforward. Hence Pressman and Wildavsky gave their book a very long and often quoted subtitle: 'How Great Expectations in Washington are Dashed in Oakland; or Why It's Amazing that Federal Programs Work At All, This Being a Saga of the Economic Development Administration as told by Two Sympathetic Observers who Seek to Build Morals on a Foundation of Ruined Hopes'!

One senses here some of the frustration felt by many Americans about the failure, or limited success, of the war on poverty and the great society programmes of the late 1960s. Pressman and Wildavsky were not the first to observe this apparent gap between federal aspirations and local reality: there was a similar body of literature on the limitations of Roosevelt's reformist interventions in American society in the 1930s (see, in particular, Selznick, 1949). An important preoccupation in this work is clearly the concern with the problem of intervention from the top of a federal system; it comes through similarly in other analyses of American social policy which have less of an emphasis on implementation *per se* (see Marris and Rein, 1967; Moynihan, 1969).

However, the focus on American federalism does not destroy the value of this approach for the study of implementation in other societies. Indeed, if analysed in this manner it raises important questions about the ways in which policy transmission occurs, or fails to occur, through multi-government systems. Certainly, a great deal of the analysis in Pressman and Wildavsky's book is concerned with the extent to which successful implementation depends upon linkages between different organisations and departments at the local level. They argue that, if action depends upon a number of links in an implementation chain, then the degree of cooperation required between agencies to make those links has to be very close to 100 per cent if a situation is not to occur in which a number of small deficits cumulatively create a large shortfall. They thus introduce the idea of 'implementation deficit' and suggest that implementation may be analysed mathematically in this way. This is an important idea, but it is perhaps stated too strongly in this formulation. Bowen (1982) points out that such a formulation disregards the extent to which the interactions between these actors occur in contexts in which they rarely concern simply 'one-off' affairs; rather, these interactions are repeated and accompanied by others, in which case it can be seen that collaboration becomes much more likely.

The notion of cumulative deficit if cooperation is less than perfect has similarities to the approach to the study of administration developed in Britain by Christopher Hood (1976). He suggests:

> One way of analysing implementation problems is to begin by thinking about what 'perfect administration' would be like, comparable to the way in which economists employ the model of perfect competition. Perfect administration could be defined as a condition in which 'external' elements of resource availability and political acceptability combine with 'administration' to produce perfect policy implementation. (Hood, 1976, p. 6)

Hood goes on to develop an argument about the 'limits of administration' (his book title) which focuses not so much on the political processes that occur within the administrative system as on the inherent limits to control in complex systems. This is similarly the concern of a two-volume contribution to the subject by another British writer, Andrew Dunsire (1978a, 1978b). Hood and Dunsire, although they use examples from real situations, are concerned to link organisation theory with the study of implementation to provide an abstract model of the problems to be faced by persons attempting top-down control over the administrative system.

Criticisms of the top-down approach

The argument in this section will be complicated, since there are a number of different kinds of criticism of the top-down approach which apply differently to different representatives of that school of thought. Broadly, the arguments separate out into those about the nature of policy, those about the interrelationship between policy formulation and the implementation process, and those about the normative stance adopted by students of implementation (particularly when this is implicit rather than explicit).

Pressman and Wildavsky were quoted earlier as approaching their definition of implementation by asserting that 'implement' is a verb that must have an object: policy. In arguing in this way they surely run the risk of catching themselves in a linguistic trap of their own making. As was recognised in the third edition of their book (1984), published after Pressman's death, it is dangerous to regard it as self-evident that implementers are working with a recognisable entity that may be called a policy. In Chapter 1 it was shown that policy is indeed an extremely slippery concept. It may really only emerge through an elaborate process that is likely to include those stages that are conventionally described as implementation.

The definitions of policy quoted in Chapter 1 (see pp. 14–19) referred to its different characteristics. The two particularly different approaches to identifying policy described there – as a general stance and a rather more concrete formulation – both entail problems for implementation studies, however. These problems are, in a sense, mirror images of each other. Policies as defined as stances (Friend, Power and Yewlett, 1974) may be relatively clear-cut, political commitments to specific action. The difficulty is that they are made much more complex as they are translated into action. Policies as defined in more concrete terms are, as the definitions of Easton (1953) and Jenkins (1978) suggest, often so complex that we are unlikely to be able to identify simple goals within them. Friend's definition is really closer to the concept of policy as used in everyday speech. It refers to the goals embodied in the 'Queen's speeches' or the President's 'messages to Congress', not to the complex phenomena that emerge at the end of the legislative process. Yet it is surely the latter with which students of implementation work.

The argument so far has been that implementation studies face problems in identifying what is being implemented because policies are complex phenomena. This needs now to be taken a stage further. Perhaps policies are quite deliberately made complex, obscure, ambiguous or even meaningless. In the most extreme case the policies that are the concern of politicians may be no more than symbolic, formulated without any intention to secure implementation (Edelman, 1971, 1977). Politicians may want to be seen to be in favour of certain ideals or goals while actually doing nothing about them. Any system in which policy making and implementation are clearly separated, either by a division between legislature and executive (as in the United States) or by a division between levels of government or ministries and implementing agencies (present in most systems but most clear in federal ones), provides opportunities for the promulgation of symbolic policies. In Britain, for example, many regulatory policies require parliamentary enactment but local authority implementation. Parliament may relatively easily pass laws allowing the control of certain activities or the provision of certain services while not providing the resources to make action possible. Relatively small teams of local environmental health officials, for example, have to cope with a mountain of legislation designed to protect the public from many potential health hazards in restaurants, shops, etc. Box 10.1 sets out an example where local discretion is evident, and some would describe the legislative response as 'symbolic', but there are alternative views on the desirability of this.

Even when policies are not simply symbolic it is important to recognise that the phenomena upon which action must be based are products of negotiation and compromise. Hence, as Barrett and Hill (1981) argue, many policies:

- represent compromises between conflicting values;
- involve compromises with key interests within the implementation structure;

| Box 10.1 | Local government and litter |

In the UK there are laws to enable local governments to prosecute those who drop litter. In 2008 a television programme drew attention to the considerable variations in the extent to which prosecutions occur; whilst some authorities bring many actions many others do not prosecute at all. In defence of the inactive authorities attention was drawn to the complexity of the law and the difficulty in achieving prosecutions. Nevertheless some authorities spent considerable sums to overcome these.

In many other areas of policy, central government exercises pressures to compel local authorities to act in matters like this. A particularly important device here is requirements for statistical returns on performance. Clearly, for example, numbers of prosecutions for litter offences could be added to the list of required performance indicators. On the other hand, there are important distinctions to be drawn between litter offences, running across a continuum from casual droppings of a single item to organised disposal of rubbish (so-called 'fly tipping'). Performance indicators could easily be manipulated, with perverse effects on actual behaviour. It can be argued that it is best for local authorities to organise their own approaches to this problem, depending on local circumstances. Even further than that it is arguable that this is a localised problem where local *choice* about action is most appropriate. But alternatively, as the TV programme suggested, this may be seen as an issue on which the government has been content to provide the legislation which facilitates action, without addressing the issues about making it effective.

- involve compromises with key interests upon whom implementation will have an impact;
- are framed without attention being given to the way in which underlying forces (particularly economic ones) will undermine them. (Barrett and Hill, 1981, p. 89)

It must, then, be recognised, first, that this compromise is not a once-and-for-all process but one that may continue throughout the history of the translation of that policy into action. Second, the initial 'policy makers' may be happy to let this occur as it enables them to evade decision problems. If, then, the implementers are distanced from the original policy-framing process, and indeed perhaps even belong to separate, 'subordinate' organisations, they may be perceived as responsible for problems and inconsistencies and for unpopular resolutions of these.

A further complication for the analysis of policies is that many government actions do not involve the promulgation of explicit programmes requiring new activities. They involve adjustments to the way existing activities are to be carried out. The most common and obvious interventions of this kind are increases or decreases in the resources available for specific activities. In this way programmes are stimulated or allowed to wither away. What, however, makes implementation studies even more complex is that the relationship between resource adjustment and substantive programmes may be an indirect one. This is particularly a feature of central–local government relations in Britain where, generally, central government does not explicitly fund programmes but makes resources available to multi-purpose authorities. In some policy fields – notably education and social care – central government has become increasingly explicit about what it expects local governments to do, and has been prepared to apply sanctions to authorities considered to be ineffective implementers. Hence, whilst local authorities may still appear to have expenditure choices these are very constrained in practice.

Adjustments to the context in which decisions are made do not only come in the form of resource change; they may also come in the form of structure change. These structure changes may or may not carry implications for substantive outputs. Hence services may be transferred from one agency to another, new rules may be made on how services are to be administered, or new arrangements may be made for policy delivery. These changes are common top-down interventions in public policy, but the analysis of their effects must rest upon an elaborate study of the way in which the balance of power is changed within the implementation system. In purposive language they are concerned with means, not ends, therefore explicit goals cannot be identified, yet they may be of fundamental importance for outcomes and may embody implicit goals. The developments in Britain and elsewhere that are transforming the way policies are delivered – replacing large, bureaucratic departments by hived-off agencies, units that are placed in a quasi-market situation, or even private organisations operating as contractors for public services – must be seen not merely as restructuring the policy delivery system but also as often transforming the policies themselves (note this particular argument in writings about the NHS, in particular Pollock's *NHS plc*, 2004).

The previous chapter looked at the importance of the policy formulation process and ended by pointing out the difficulties in determining where policy formulation stops and implementation begins. That point should be emphasised further:

> to say that some policies are easier to implement than others one has to be able to identify the point at which they are packaged up ready for implementation. We may be able to say some commitments in party manifestos are easier to implement than others. We may equally be able to say that some Acts of Parliament are easier to implement than others. But in both cases such generalisation may be heavily dependent upon the extent to which aspirations have been concretised. (Hill, in Barrett and Fudge, 1981, p. 208)

The concretisation of policy continues way beyond the legislative process. There is something of a seamless web here, though it may be that it is possible to identify some decisions that are more fundamental for determining the major 'policy' issues than others. There is, however, no reason why we should always expect to find such decisions, nor is it the case that these decisions, when they exist, are invariably taken during what we conventionally define as the policy formulation process. There are, on the contrary, a number of reasons why they may be left to the implementation process, of which the following is by no means an exhaustive list:

- because conflicts cannot be resolved during the policy formulation stage;
- because it is regarded as necessary to let key decisions be made when all the facts are available to implementers;
- because it is believed that implementers (professionals, for example) are better equipped to make the key decisions than anyone else;
- because little is known in advance about the actual impact of the new measures;
- because it is recognised that day-to-day decisions will have to involve negotiation and compromise with powerful groups;
- because it is considered politically inexpedient to try to resolve the conflicts early in the policy process.

Considerations of this kind must lead us to regard the policy-making process as something which often continues during the so-called implementation phase. It may involve continuing flexibility, it may involve the concretisation of policy in action, or it may involve a process of movement back and forth between policy and action. Barrett and Fudge (1981) have stressed the need, therefore, 'to consider implementation as a policy/action continuum in which an interactive and negotiative process is taking place over time between those seeking to put policy into effect and those upon whom action depends' (p. 25).

Lane (1987) highlights some of the key issues here in a paper in which, among a variety of approaches to implementation, he identifies it as 'evolution' (p. 532; see also Majone and Wildavsky, 1978), as 'learning' (p. 534; see also Browne and Wildavsky, 1984), as 'coalition' (p. 539, with important references to the essentially collaborative implementation implicit in corporatist relationships – see Chapter 3 above), and as 'responsibility and trust' (p. 541; this is a theme which we will explore further in later chapters in relation to organisational life). All of these imply a system in which a close collaborative relationship characterises relations within the policy system, allowing policy to emerge in action.

The bottom-up alternative

These arguments lead us on to the view that a model of the policy implementation relationship in which the policy formulation process can be seen as setting 'goals', the extent of whose realisation can be measured, provides an insufficient foundation for studies of implementation. It is this that has led various students of implementation to argue for a bottom-up rather than a top-down stance for the study of implementation. Elmore has coined the term 'backward mapping', which he defines as

> 'backward reasoning' from the individual and organisational choices that are the hub of the problem to which policy is addressed, to the rules, procedures and structures that have the closest proximity to those choices, to the policy instruments available to affect those things, and hence to feasible policy objectives. (Elmore, 1981, p. 1; see also Elmore, 1980)

Focusing on individual actions as a starting point enables actions to be seen as responses to problems or issues in the form of choices between alternatives. One of Elmore's justifications for this approach derives not so much from the concern explored here about the difficulty in separating policy formulation and implementation, as from a recognition that in many policy areas in the United States (youth employment policy is Elmore's particular interest) implementation actors are forced to make choices between programmes which conflict or interact with each other.

The proponents of the bottom-up approach argue that it is, by comparison with the top-down model, relatively free of predetermining assumptions. It is less likely to imply assumptions about cause and effect, about hierarchical or any other structural relations between actors and agencies, or about what should be going on between them.

The approach is expounded even more forcefully by Hjern and his associates (Hjern and Porter, 1981; Hjern and Hull, 1982), who argue for a methodology in which researchers construct empirically the networks within which field-level, decision-making actors carry out their activities without predetermining assumptions about the structures within which these occur. The present author, in his work with Susan Barrett, has added his own support to the methodological argument for this perspective, arguing as follows:

> to understand the policy–action relationship we must get away from a single perspective of the process that reflects a normative administrative or managerial view of how the process should be, and try to find a conceptualisation that reflects better the empirical evidence of the complexity and dynamics of the interactions between individuals and groups seeking to put policy into effect, those upon whom action depends and those whose interests are affected when change is proposed. To do this, we have argued for an alternative perspective to be adopted – one that focuses on the actors and agencies themselves and their interactions, and for an action-centred or 'bottom-up' mode of analysis as a method of identifying more clearly who seems to be influencing what, how and why. (Barrett and Hill, 1981, p. 19)

These are to a large extent arguments about methodology, about how to study implementation. But they also suggest a more realistic approach to the discussion of how implementation occurs than do those propositions rooted in a concern about how implementation should be controlled. What, in many respects, is being emphasised in this more action-centred mode of analysis is that the very things that top-down theorists urge must be controlled are the elements that are difficult to bring under control. The reality, therefore, is not of imperfect control but of action as a continuous process of interaction with a *changing and changeable policy, a complex interaction structure*, an *outside world which must interfere* with implementation because government action does, and is designed to, impinge upon it, and implementing actors who are *inherently difficult to control*. Analysis is best focused upon the levels at which this is occurring, since it is not so much creating implementation deficiency as recreating policy.

This emphasis, in the bottom-up critique, upon the complexities in the concept of policy and the way it is made also suggests that implementation may itself be an ambiguous concept. Lane has argued that there is some confusion in the implementation literature between 'implementation and successful implementation as an outcome, and the implementation process or how implementation comes about' (Lane, 1987, p. 528). The classical top-down studies are principally concerned with explaining why an expected outcome does or does not occur, and to do this they need clear goal statements to work with. These may be supplied by the policy makers or imputed by the researchers. Without such yardsticks we may still study processes, but our activity is rather different. Sabatier, in an attempt to fuse the best ideas from both top-down and bottom-up processes, rightly suggests that the presence or absence of a 'dominant piece of legislation structuring the situation' (1986, p. 37) may help to determine which approach is appropriate. However, this may involve starting with a question-begging assumption that this structuring has in fact occurred. One can obviously treat a piece of legislation as dominant, but if one does so the problems for explanation, in cases of implementation failure, tend to be either what others have done to subvert it, or what is wrong with it. As the arguments above suggest, both of these may be oversimplified questions about both policy and its implementation context, and particularly about the relationship between the two.

Beyond the top-down/bottom-up debate

The methodological argument that surfaces in the discussion above can be resolved relatively simply. It may be possible to examine an implementation process in terms of what happens to goals proclaimed early in the policy process (or even in terms of imputed goals) and then look at what happened. It may also be possible to start at the output end and engage in 'backward mapping'. Both approaches will have strengths and weaknesses;

both may be biased by the prejudices of the actors, the researchers or the research funders; and choices between them need to be determined by empirical factors and contingencies. As with Allison's alternative approaches to explaining the Cuban missile crisis (see p. 120), mixed approaches, with triangulation between them, may be desirable.

Winter, in two reviews of this topic, has adopted a pragmatic response to the theoretical debate as far as implementation research is concerned (2003, 2006). He argues that 'looking for *the* overall and one for all implementation theory' is a 'utopian' objective which is not feasible, and may even inhibit the creativity that comes from diversity (ibid., p. 158). He argues that we should look for partial rather than general implementation theories.

From that point of view Winter sees implementation research as able to address concrete issues, of a kind that an obsession with all-encompassing theories will tend to inhibit. He argues that there needs to be an emphasis on exploring the determinants of policy outputs:

> (...) I suggest that we look for behavioural *output* variables to characterize the *performance* of implementers (...). The first aim of implementation research then should be to explain variation in such performance (ibid.).

While this argument is framed in terms of choice about methodolgy, what it implies is a wider need to avoid the obsession with whether the 'goals' of policy designers are achieved that characterises top-down theory. Goals are contestable and change over time. Work that focuses upon goals gets into questions about what 'the real goals' in a policy process are, and often becomes tangled up with debates about what they should be. Variation in performance can be identified without engaging with these issues.

The case for trying to ensure that normative preoccupations do not interfere with a clear analysis of the implementation process has been emphasised throughout the discussion. The issue, then, for discussion here about ways to move beyond the top-down/bottom-up debate, is about recognising that there will be various ways in which actors will attempt to exercise prior control over the implementation process. The concern is with a variety of issues about the extent to which actors impose rules upon others. The other side of this is about how discretion is structured, about how easily actors can exercise autonomy. In the last analysis these are questions about hierarchies and their legitimacy, but we want to leave these out of the discussion at this stage (we will come back to some of these points in the next three chapters).

The discussion in Chapter 7 of types of policy suggested various ways in which decisions may be structured. It also suggested that the quest for some simple policy typology that would help with the interpretation of when different structuring will occur has been fruitless. It was suggested, however, that Matland's use of 'ambiguity' and 'conflict' to typify different policy issues is helpful (see p. 140). Ambiguity tends to make the delegation of discretion likely (the need to make judgements during the process highlighted in the cookery example in Box 9.8). In the absence of conflicting goals, experimentation will be feasible. Conflict, on the other hand, implies a desire to control. Actors claiming hierarchical rights will seek to assert them, and this will be particularly evident in the absence of consensus. If low ambiguity is involved then rules will be formulated (the cookery-book approach to implementation). High conflict and high ambiguity is a difficult combination. Matland, in his original analysis, called this 'symbolic implementation'. This puts it perhaps too strongly, inasmuch as symbolic implies no effort to implement whilst what is actually being highlighted is the level of difficulty. Nevertheless, of course, there may be situations in which those attempting to dictate policy want merely to claim to have tried. Figure 7.1 is repeated here as Figure 10.1, including some examples (not taken from Matland's original text).

Figure 10.1 Matland's analysis of the impact of conflict and ambiguity upon implementation, illustrated with examples

	Low conflict	High conflict
Low ambiguity	1 Example: a social benefit like 'child benefit' where there is general acceptance of the case for it and the qualification test is simple (in the UK responsibility for a child with a right of residence in the country).	3 Example: privatisation of health and social care services where, in the face of resistance, government can nevertheless still drive through change.
High ambiguity	2 Example: localised measures to try to combat health inequalities where there is general acceptance of the case for action but uncertainty about what is effective (Matland calls this 'experimental implementation').	4 Example: equal pay legislation where definitions are based on complex comparisons of activities and are often contested.

Source: Adapted from Matland, 1995, p. 160, Table 4.1. By permission of Oxford University Press.

Matland's approach is still rather static, however, and his model of conflict rather a simple dichotomy. Many of the most controversial (and perhaps most interesting) implementation stories involve prolonged interactions in situations of considerable and very complicated multi-party conflicts, a somewhat tempestuous version of the last of the meal preparation models in Box 9.8.

This leads us on to two crucial issues for the examination of the implementation process:

■ the fact that policy processes vary greatly in the extent to which there is an attempt to prescribe a rule framework;

■ the importance of variations in the administrative framework within which the process occurs.

In terms of the cooking analogy in Box 9.8, the issues can be said to be about the extent to which there is a cookbook containing clear prescriptions, and about the relational frameworks in which that will be used (not just two persons in a household but something much more complex).

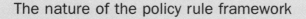

The nature of the policy rule framework

Much attention was given in Chapter 9 to the ways in which details are formulated that will govern policy implementation. At the same time it was acknowledged that there will be differences in the extent to which this takes place, from policy to policy or policy system to policy system. Crucial then for the examination of implementation is the extent to which this concretisation of policy has occurred. Whilst some policies pass out of the legislative stages with very clear rule structures, enabling implementation deficits to be easily identified, others are much less fully formed.

It can generally be argued that, in modern taxation, initiatives will reach the implementation stage with comparatively clear rule structures. These rules may be hard to implement and may be the subject of formal disputes in the courts, hence implementation deficit may be analysed, but political and social forces have taken taxation a long way from the vague

Box 10.2	Christopher Jewell's comparative analysis of the administration of social assistance (2007)

Christopher Jewell carried out case studies of social assistance officials in the United States (California), Germany (Bremen) and Sweden (Malmö). He shows that those in California work within a system with simple rules but minimal discretion, while in Bremen they are seen as the formally qualified operators of a complex legal structure and in Malmö they have high levels of discretion. There is a fascinating contrast in Jewell's book between the elaborate legal structure of the German system, where ironically high discretion emerges principally from the difficulties staff have in navigating through complex and ever changing rules, and the very loosely regulated Swedish system where high discretion is implicit and even administrative court decisions do not create precedents.

Christopher Jewell then explores the impact of growth of caseloads and pressure of work upon the three systems. Here, what he found was practice variation in all three systems arising from the impact of efforts to cut administrative costs, leading to staff shortages and staff turnover. The Swedish system seemed to be suffering least from these problems, but then it was from the outset the system in which most variation was likely. In the German case rule application seemed to have become more erratic, whilst in the American one it was 'corner cutting' by a system under great strain that was the principal source of diversity.

'tax farming' that characterised such policies in early medieval societies when implementers were charged to bring in money – to profit if they were good at it and to be punished if they were not – by rulers who cared little about how it was done.

Similar points may be made about cash benefit systems. Many income maintenance systems have evolved a long way from the decentralised 'poor law', in which a great deal of discretion was vested in local 'boards of guardians', to a modern situation in which all the main benefit systems have strong rule-based structures which facilitate computerised calculation and the operation of formal appeal mechanisms. However variations remain (see Box 10.2 on p. 207.)

There are other areas of policy where there is a complex and dynamic relationship between rule structures and their interpretation. Two British examples, both involving what have been regarded as controversial policy changes driven by political commitments, illustrate this (see Boxes 10.3 and 10.4).

Box 10.3	**Trial and error implementation: general practice fundholding in the UK**

Glennerster, Matsaganis and Owens (1994) studied the early history of a health policy initiative designed to enable primary health care doctors to secure hospital services for their own patients by entering into contracts without reference to health authorities. These 'general practitioner fundholders' were allocated budgets based upon the size of their lists and past referral practices. The initial setting of those budgets was very much a matter of 'trial and error'. Similarly the establishment of rules to regulate this activity – to prevent possible abuses of autonomy and to cope with unexpected problems – was an evolutionary process, involving collaboration between the health authorities, the national Department of Health and the 'fundholders' themselves. Glennerster and his colleagues describe this as 'Lewis and Clark planning' (adapting an idea from Schultze, 1968). They say:

> The American explorers, Lewis and Clark, were merely told to find a route to the Pacific. They did so by finding the watershed, following the rivers to the sea using their wits as they went.
>
> The implementation of fundholding can be seen as a Lewis and Clark adventure – but in this instance there was telephonic contact between the field explorers and the equivalent of Washington and regular flights back to discuss progress with other explorers. (Glennerster, Matsaganis and Owens, 1994, p. 30)

A similar process has occurred more recently when, during 2002, before the enactment of legislation, hospitals were encouraged to explore ways of enacting a new proposal to give them greater autonomy (by becoming foundation trusts). Issues from this process were fed back into the formulation of the policy.

| Box 10.4 | The National Curriculum in England and Wales: interactions in making policy aspirations a reality |

Here the issue is the development, under the 1988 Education Act, of a 'national curriculum' setting parameters for teaching in schools. In this case the legislation does little more than prescribe broad subjects to be included (Maths, English, Science, etc.) and organisations and procedures have been set up to determine more detailed content and to enforce compliance. Then, even within the implementation process there is – not surprisingly, given the complexity of the issues – considerable latitude to enable individual schools and teachers to select topics to emphasise, approaches to teaching and so on. Bowe, Ball and Gold (1992) use a concept from sociology and linguistics, 'texts' (Atkinson, 1985), to explain what is here being described as an implementation process. They argue:

> Texts carry with them both possibilities and constraints, contradictions and spaces. The reality of policy in practice depends upon the compromises and accommodations to these in particular settings. ... [o]ur conception of policy has to be set against the idea that policy is something that is simply done to people ... (Bowe, Ball and Gold, 1992, p. 15)

They go on to highlight the peculiar combination of 'Thatcherite policy-making which rides roughshod over the sensibilities of teachers', lack of public confidence in teachers and low morale on the one hand with the fact that it has depended upon a very complex interaction between education officials, advisory bodies and teachers themselves to make the National Curriculum 'work'. Thus Bowe and his colleagues argue:

> Policies ... are textual interventions but they also carry with them material constraints and possibilities. The responses to these texts have 'real' consequences. These consequences are experienced in ... the arena of practice to which policy refers ... policy is not simply received and implemented within this arena, rather it is subject to interpretation and then recreated. (ibid., pp. 21–2)

The two examples set out in Boxes 10.3 and 10.4 were selected because in both cases the authors were using new ways to try to capture the complexity of the policy/implementation relationship. Many others could have been chosen from areas where policy implementation involves complex service activities. In both cases issues about the way policy was realised during implementation are emphasised.

Similar issues arise in many areas of regulatory policy. In this area of policy, alongside the problems of complexity there may be other features which complicate implementation: in particular, the fact that the regulatee often understands the process better than the regulators, that there are difficult trade-off judgements to be made about the costs of compliance and that the ability of the regulatee to evade control puts willing compliance at a premium. This has led Hanf to see much regulatory activity as involving 'co-production' between regulator and regulatee (Hanf, 1993).

At its extreme – and this probably characterised much British pollution control until very recently – policy is essentially no more than the terms that the regulator is able to reach with the regulatee (this issue was explored a little in Chapter 7, on p. 136). In industrial air pollution control the statutory concept of the use of the 'best practicable means' to limit emissions had little meaning except in the context of such an agreement (Hill in Downing and Hanf, 1983). It certainly could not in any realistic sense be described as defined in the policy-making process. Since then, under pressure from the European Community for a more precise approach, this 'policy' has moved on a little, but the policy emphasis is still rather more upon ambient air quality targets than upon specific control over what goes up individual chimneys.

There are very important areas of policy where the policy/implementation distinction is even more blurred than in these examples from service provision and regulation. Oddly, these do not seem to have been given much attention in the implementation literature, perhaps because they concern issues at the very centre of national politics – economic and foreign policy. These issues were also discussed in Chapter 7.

If your primary aim is to understand the implementation process, a great deal is going to depend upon the activity in which you are interested. If you are looking at one in which there is a quite explicit 'top'-initiated, goal-directed activity, it may be justifiable to use a 'top-down' methodology and work with a notion such as 'implementation deficit'. This may be particularly the case where a quantifiable output is available and explicit inputs can be measured. The British experience with the Thatcher governments was of a number of examples where government goals were very clear. There were cases of very determined top-down pursuit of clearly specified objectives (the sale of local authority-owned homes to their occupiers, for example – see Forrest and Murie, 1991), cases where clear evidence of implementation problems ahead pulled the government back (the strange case of an identity cards scheme to prevent football hooliganism) and dramatic cases of implementation difficulty leading to yet further policy innovation (the classic case here was the so-called 'poll tax' – see Butler, Adonis and Travers, 1994).

Yet many other events in the policy process do not involve such clarity. Examples can be taken of complex and confusing cases where central goals were not nearly so clear, or where central goal statements should be received with great scepticism – in fields like community care, employment policy, urban renewal or the prevention of crime, for example. Furthermore, as suggested above, concern may be with an ongoing process where explicit change is not initiated from above, or where there are grounds for scepticism about whether efforts to bring about change will carry through to the 'bottom'.

The importance of variations in the administrative system

The discussion in the last section has drawn distinctions between situations in which rules for implementation are very much in evidence, situations in which implementation is very much a process of developing and elaborating initial policy frameworks and situations in which either we need to say that the implementation process *is* the policy-making process or to regard this distinction as meaningless. This variation may, of course, be influenced by the characteristics of governmental systems and by political or administrative culture.

It is perhaps not surprising that issues about the capacity of policy makers to influence implementation have been given particular attention in the United States, because of the ways in which federalism, the division of executive, legislative and judicial powers and the written constitution complicate executive action. As suggested above, ever since the New Deal in the 1930s the exploration of ways to increase Washington's influence in Oakland, or wherever, has been a key preoccupation of those Americans who regard active federal government as important for their society. In the 1960s the struggle against racial segregation in the Deep South and the efforts to develop new initiatives in welfare policy and in urban policy offered particularly salient examples.

A major factor contributing to that complexity is the fact that often intervening levels, as layers in the political-administrative system, have a legitimate claim to engage in policy formulation and decision making: Where does 'policy formation' end and 'implementation' begin? It is in recognition of this that Goggin et al. refer to federal 'messages' to states rather than of federal policies. Similarly, studies of the implementation of European Union policies (Lampinen and Uusikälä, 1998; Knill and Lenschow, 1998), indicate very distinct processes of re-formulations within individual nation states. What is called 'implementation' in these studies may in fact be seen as 'policy formation'. Chapter 12 returns to this issue.

A realistic approach to the examination of implementation in its administrative context therefore needs to give attention to the facts:

- that implementation involves complex intra-organisational interactions;
- that the analysis of those interactions must take us into issues about negotiations between actors who are at least quasi-autonomous;
- that this autonomy may be linked with claims of legitimacy which render beside the point those analyses that emphasise recalcitrance, shortfalls and deficits;
- that these complexities need to be seen as contained within different national or transnational political systems which influence the games played and the legitimacies claimed.

Modelling the influences on implementation

The discussion of the importance of giving attention to variations in the form policy takes shifts the focus a long way from approaches to the topic which see implementers simply as people who change the policy as it is put into action. It suggests that influences upon the implementation process extend from considerations about how policy is formulated through to factors that influence behaviour close to 'street-level'. They may be modelled in terms of seven categories (this categorisation owes a great deal to Van Meter and Van Horn's original modelling of the implementation process):

- policy characteristics, including issues about the way in which these have been shaped by the formulation process;
- issues about 'layers' in the policy transfer process, or what may be called 'vertical public administration', that is the issues about the relationship that so concerned Pressman and Wildavsky;
- horizontal inter-organisational relationships (relationships between parallel organisations required to collaborate in implementation);
- factors affecting the responses of implementation agencies (their organization, their disposition, and so on) – these may be subdivided into issues about the overall characteristics of the agencies and issues about the behaviour of front-line (or street level) staff;
- the impact of responses from those affected by the policy; and
- wider macro-environmental factors.

Theoretically it should be possible to try to sort out the respective impacts of these elements using, as an independent variable, policy outputs. Box 10.5 works through an example where this approach is feasible. In practice the feasibility of this depends upon a number of things. First, the extent to which distinct outputs can be identified. It is important here to bear in mind Winter's distinction between outputs and goals (see p. 205). There has been a tendency for implementation studies to use goal statements made by actors with a distinct, but contestable, view on what *they* think should be achieved. Second, a policy may have various outputs (the complexity of policy hardly needs emphasising at this stage in this book). Third, policy outputs may be hard to identify let alone quantify. Fourth, an approach of this kind depends upon being able to separate implementers (different parts of a department or different local authorities for example) in order to tease out differences; this will often not be feasible.

Box 10.5	Studying implementation: an example involving comparison of the responses of English local authorities to a central government policy initiative

In England there is a central government policy concerned with facilitating arrangements in which individuals in need of social care can be given direct payments of cash to purchase services for themselves instead of being provided with services commissioned by local authorities. Whilst some local authorities had been pioneers of this approach, central government adopted the policy and is putting increasing pressure on local governments to implement it. However, local authorities vary significantly in their enthusiasm for the policy. Hence a relatively straightforward 'dependent variable' was published in official statistics: numbers of payments made by each local authority over a period corrected to take into account variations in overall population size.

It is then possible to identify factors affecting implementation:

■ Policy characteristics – features of the policy which affect implementation (such as rules about preventing the misuse of direct payments.

■ Layers in the policy transfer process – the mechanisms that govern central/local government relationships (inspection, the collection of performance indictors etc.).

■ Horizontal inter-organisation relationships – social care direct payments may require liaison between local authorities and the health service and these vary from place to place.

■ Factors affecting responses by implementing agencies – the enthusiasm of politicians and senior officials, whether there is a 'champion' who pushes the scheme at the local level, whether street-level workers find direct payments difficult to implement or feel that they upset standard operating procedures.

■ Responses from those affected – is there a public demand or widespread suspicion of the measure? Are there local pressures groups in favour or against?

■ Wider macro-environmental factors – since direct payments often involve the employment of service workers by individuals, the local labour market may have an effect upon their availability.

(Examples based upon work on this topic by Leese and Bornat, 2006, Vick et al., 2006, Fernandez et al., 2007)

CONCLUSIONS

This chapter started with the arguments between top-down and bottom-up approaches to the study of implementation. Like all such dialectical debates in the social sciences, this one is more important in illuminating the many facets of the subject than in leading the reader to a conclusion on one side or the other.

The aim in this discussion has been first to draw attention to the import-ance of the top-down school of implementation studies initiated by Pressman and Wildavsky, stressing their role in opening up the analysis of an important, and previously rather neglected, part of the policy process. Then, secondly, it has sought to demonstrate the blind spots in such a perspective – which may be corrected by considering the alternative bottom-up approach. Whether you favour one or the other approach, some combination of the two, or one that tries to avoid either, depends very much on what you are trying to do. Clearly, they can be integrated.

Any effort to develop implementation theory – once it moves away from the attempt to develop checklists of pitfalls for the implementation process in the way described and criticised above – must face the difficulty of becoming involved with the wide range of questions that have been raised in relation to policy making and in the study of organisations. If we substitute the word 'doing' for 'implementation' we see how we are confronted by an attempt to develop a 'theory of doing' – or of action. Perhaps, therefore, that is not a very helpful way to proceed. Rather, as Susan Barrett and the present author have suggested, it is hard to go beyond the identification of the key elements that must be analysed in the study of implementation, and the recognition of the overwhelming importance of the negotiation and bargaining that occur throughout the policy process. Barrett and Hill (1981) argue:

> many so-called implementation problems arise precisely because there is a tension between the normative assumptions of government – what ought to be done and how it should happen – and the struggle and conflict between interests – the need to bargain and compromise – that represent the reality of the process by which power/influence is gained and held in order to pursue ideological goals. (Barrett and Hill, 1981, p. 145)

This general exploration of implementation – with its emphasis upon the sig-nificance of organisational complexity and upon the sources of variation in discretion in the implementation process – is now followed by chapters which look at some of these issues more fully.

11 The importance of organisational processes

SYNOPSIS

The public policy process, particularly that part of it concerned with implementation, is very largely an organisational process. It involves work within (intra-) and between (inter-) organisations. This chapter looks at the former, the next at the latter. An introductory section to this chapter shows that the pragmatic distinction between phenomena that are intra-organisational and those that are inter-organisational may at times be problematic.

Public organisations are often described as bureaucracies. A brief discussion explores the implications of the use of the word 'bureaucracy' in light of the fact that it is often given a pejorative sense. This leads into an examination of the most influential theoretical analysis of public bureaucracy, that provided by the German sociologist Max Weber, and an exploration of the way his ideas have been used by others. A brief account is provided of some other key work on the sociology of organisations that is important for understanding public sector organisations.

The section on 'rules and discretion' seems to involve a distinct change of emphasis, particularly as some of the important work analysing this has been done within academic law. However, the aim in that section, and the one that follows it on the treatment of the same theme in organisational sociology, is to show how issues about possibilities of and limits to control are of fundamental importance for understanding how policy process decision making is handled in many contexts.

Introduction

In order to determine the contents of this chapter and the next, a distinction is being drawn here between those issues about the policy process that can be seen as occurring within a single organisation and those that concern relationships between organisations.

In most respects this distinction can be understood in common-sense terms. Distinctions between what goes on, for example, within a government department and between departments are often made, and need no explanation. However, at the margins it may be difficult to make this distinction. Some sociological analyses of organisations draw attention to the way in which the boundaries between them are social constructions that may vary and may be disputed. Boundaries may be permeable and changing. This issue has become more important in the modern world of governance, two of the characteristics of which are the abandonment of simple hierarchical arrangements and the creation of hybrid organisational forms in which tasks may be subcontracted and shared. Hence, individuals may work for more than one organisation and services may depend upon collaborative arrangements. Inasmuch as this is the case, the distinction drawn here may be a misleading one. It is important, therefore, to bear this in mind as we take as our starting point a literature that has some theory about the analysis of the unitary and hierarchical nature of organisations at its very heart.

Organisation as bureaucracy

The issues about the policy process as an organisational process are emphasised in discussions of the role of bureaucracy. In the first part of the book it was shown that some of the key theories of the state – particularly elitist theories, rational choice theories and institutional theories – concern themselves with issues about bureaucratic power, often seeing it as involving the domination of the policy process by those inside the organisational system. The word 'bureaucracy' is a neutral term used to describe a complex organisation, particularly a governmental one. But it is also used in a pejorative sense to denote an impenetrable, ponderous and unimaginative organisation.

In many discussions of the role of organisations in the modern world these complex 'bureaucracies' are seen as necessary evils. As Perrow puts it, 'Without this form of social technology, the industrialized countries of the West could not have reached the heights of extravagance, wealth and pollution that they currently enjoy' (Perrow, 1972, p. 5). The emphasis upon bureaucracy as a potentially problematical form of organisation, highlighted by the frequency with which the term is used pejoratively, has two separate key concerns which can be described simply as concerns about (a) accountability and (b) efficiency and effectiveness. One tendency of critiques of bureaucracy is to stress problems with making government organisations accountable to the people. Another is to emphasise the extent to which they are unsatisfactory 'instruments' for the carrying out of policy – they are seen as increasing costs and distorting outputs.

Protagonists at both ends of the political spectrum offer solutions to the alleged problem of 'bureaucracy' in public policy. For many on the 'Right' the solution is the allocation of goods and services by way of the market, with the role of government kept to a minimum. The market offers a mechanism which is accountable, because the public are then consumers and are able to make choices about what they purchase, and efficient, because providers are in continuous competition with each other. The libertarian 'Left' alternatively sees a world in which capitalist power is overthrown as offering the possibility of free collaboration between equal citizens in meeting their needs. Both extremes embody a utopian element – in the case of the 'Right', a belief in the feasibility of a really competitive market rather than an economy in which there is a tendency for monopoly to develop and for choices to be limited and manipulated, in the case of the 'Left', a world in which big government is as unnecessary as big capitalism.

The utopianism of the 'Right' is more important for the modern political agenda than that of the 'Left', partly because of the dominance of capitalist ideology and partly because the history of communism has offered so dramatic a betrayal of its idealistic roots. Yet nearer the centre of the political debate the idealistic assertions of both camps offer key poles for debate about public policy – concerning the extent to which there are problems about organising the public sector and regulating the market sector. This takes us back to Perrow's neat aphorism. Complex organisations are needed to meet the needs of modern society because governments are engaged in a complicated combination of direct provision and market regulation. Moreover, they have to cope with trade-offs between the two. In most of the twentieth century the tendency was for governments – at least in Western Europe – to see direct provision as preferable to regulation in many areas of social and economic life. This forced attention to focus on issues about the control of their own large, bureaucratic organisations. In the final quarter of the century there was something of a reaction against this approach. But that heightens the need for attention to regulation, essentially an issue about the relationships between government organisations and private or quasi-autonomous ones. The worries about 'bureaucracy' have not been dispelled, as many within the 'neo-liberal Right' had hoped – rather, they take new forms, forcing us to reconceptualise bureaucracy in a more complex way. This reconceptualisation has been a key concern of work which sees late twentieth-century innovations in the public sector as a 'new public management' movement (Pollitt, 1990; Hood, 1991). New public management is discussed further in Chapter 14.

These normative and prescriptive arguments are not the main concerns of this book. However, some of them will emerge again in the analysis of the issues about accountability in Chapter 14. They have also coloured much theorising and research about organisational behaviour. And, as the last paragraph suggests, they have had an impact upon innovation in public policy and particularly on efforts to influence the implementation process.

Max Weber and the theory of bureaucracy

The work of a German theorist, Max Weber, active at the end of the nineteenth century and in the early years of the twentieth, was particularly important for the development of the theory of organisations. Furthermore, it was the organisation of government in the modern state that particularly concerned him. He observed the development of a powerful unified civil service in Germany, recognising its potential as an instrument of government and worrying about its implications for democratic accountability.

Weber embedded his theory of bureaucracy in a wider theory of social power. His discussion of bureaucracy is linked to an analysis of types of authority. He postulates three basic authority types: charismatic, traditional and rational–legal (see Box 11.1). He sees the last-named as characteristic of the modern state.

Box 11.1 | **Max Weber's analysis of types of authority**

Charismatic authority is based upon 'devotion to the specific and exceptional sanctity, heroism or exemplary character of an individual person' (1947, p. 328). It is a transitory phenomenon associated with periods of social turmoil; the essentially personal nature of the relationship between leader and follower makes the development of permanent institutions impossible and accordingly it succumbs to processes of 'routinisation' which transform it into one of the other types of authority.

Traditional authority, on the other hand, rests upon 'an established belief in the sanctity of immemorial traditions and the legitimacy of the status of those exercising authority under them' (ibid.). While charismatic authority's weakness lies in its instability, the weakness of traditional authority is its static nature. It is thus argued to be the case that the rational–legal type of authority is superior to either of the other two types.

Weber states that *rational-legal authority* rests upon 'a belief in the legality of patterns of normative rules, and the right of those elevated to authority under such rules to issue commands' (ibid.). The maintenance of such a system of authority rests upon the development of a bureaucratic system of administration in which permanent officials administer, and are bound by, rules.

Weber regards the development of bureaucratic administration as intimately associated with the evolution of modern industrialised society. Bureaucratisation is seen as a consequence of the development of a complex economic and political system, and also as a phenomenon that has helped to make these developments possible.

Students of Weber have differed in the extent to which they regard him as a theorist who believed that bureaucracy can be subjected to democratic control. He was clearly ambivalent on that topic. Whilst the use of 'bureaucracy' as a pejorative term (see the discussion above) clearly predates Weber, he must be seen as the theorist who effectively poses the dilemma: here is an instrument that enables much to be done that could not otherwise be done, but there is a need to be concerned about how it is used, how it is controlled and who controls it (Albrow, 1970; Beetham, 1987).

The strength of the bureaucratic form of administration, according to Weber, rests upon its formal rationality, a notion which a number of modern students of organisations have equated with efficiency. This translation of Weber's concept has led to some useful discussions of the relationship between formalism and efficiency but has also given currency to a rather unsubtle characterisation of Weber's theory. Albrow (1970) shows how this confusion arose and provides the following clarification of Weber's position:

> The real relation between formal rationality and efficiency can best be understood by considering the means by which efficiency is commonly measured, through the calculation of cost in money terms, or in time, or in energy expended. Such calculations are formal procedures which do not in themselves guarantee efficiency, but are among the conditions for determining what level of efficiency has been reached. At the heart of Weber's idea of formal rationality was the idea of correct calculation, in either numerical terms, as with the accountant, or in logical terms, as with the lawyer. This was normally a necessary though not sufficient condition for the attainment of goals; it could even conflict with material rationality. (Albrow, 1970, p. 65)

Weber's theory is seen as providing a number of simple propositions about the formal structure of organisations, a misconception that has contributed to his usefulness to students of organisations but which does not do justice to the depth of his understanding of the critical issues in organisational sociology. As he outlines the characteristics of an organisational type that is important in complex societies because of its formal rationality, he naturally stresses the strength of that type rather than its weakness. Weber's aim is to define a widespread kind of organisation and explain why it is growing in importance, offering thereby sociological analysis rather than political polemic.

Weber lists a number of characteristics which, taken together, define bureaucracy. These characteristics are set out in Box 11.2. While Weber does not see these characteristics as prescriptions for organisation, many subsequent writers have seized upon their similarity to the model prescribed by others who were searching for the best way to organise.

Perhaps the most influential figure in the search for principles of organisation before the First World War was F.W. Taylor (1911). He was an American who tried to develop scientific principles for industrial management based upon a series of generalisations which he claimed to be of

| Box 11.2 | Max Weber's delineation of the characteristics of bureaucracy |

1. A continuous organisation with a specified function, or functions, its operation bound by rules. Continuity and consistency within the organisation are ensured by the use of writing to record acts, decisions and rules.

2. The organisation of personnel is on the basis of hierarchy. The scope of authority within the hierarchy is clearly defined, and the rights and duties of the officials at each level are specified.

3. The staff are separated from ownership of the means of administration or production. They are personally free, 'subject to authority only with respect to their impersonal official obligations'.

4. Staff are appointed, not elected, on the basis of impersonal qualifications, and are promoted on the basis of merit.

5. Staff are paid fixed salaries and have fixed terms of employment. The salary scale is normally graded according to rank in the hierarchy. Employment is permanent with a certain security of tenure, and pensions are usually paid on retirement.

Based on Weber, 1947, pp. 329-41

universal application. His importance for this account is that he has been widely seen as the leading exponent of methods of organisation which rest upon treating human beings as units of labour to be used 'efficiently' without regard to their needs, attitudes and emotions (Braverman, 1974). Hence a great deal of the subsequent concern about human relations in organisations emerged from the exposure of the limitations of 'Taylorism'. Despite that exposure the influence of Taylorism lives on. Pollitt (1990) has described much modern managerialism in the public services as 'neo-Taylorism'. He argues:

> Taylorism was centrally concerned with the 'processes of determining and fixing effort levels' and can be seen as 'the bureaucratization of the structure of control but *not* the employment relationship' (Littler, 1978, pp. 199 and 185 respectively). It proceeded on the basis that ... the work process could and should be measured by management, and then used as a basis for rewarding and controlling effort ... This is not far, in principle, from the recent epidemic of electronically-mediated public-service systems of performance indicators, individual performance review and merit pay. (Pollitt, 1990, p. 16)

Taylor was working for the Ford motor company, a pioneer in mass production methods. Hence other theorists have spoken of 'Fordism' (Sabel, 1982) to describe an approach to organisation in which Taylorist methods are used to try to reduce workers to commodities, performing limited tasks in tightly regulated conditions for the lowest possible rewards. Whilst public policy implementation is seen as less likely to embody circumstances in which such mass production is feasible, Taylorism or Fordism can be seen to offer one model for the public bureaucracy (see Pollitt, 1990). It is a model, moreover, which may be seen as solving the dilemma of accountability – at least as far as routine tasks like social benefit administration are concerned – by ensuring a rigid adherence to hierarchically (and thus perhaps ultimately democratically) determined rules. This is an issue to which we will return below when we explore the relationship between rules and discretion.

But that is only one way to take the Weberian model, seeking to make it simply a compliant instrument. Other ways suggested that there were problems with this, and observed some of the tensions and contradictions in the 'ideal type'. In the 1920s and 1930s, management theory gradually began to move away from a concern with the development of formal prescriptions for organisational structure towards a better understanding of organisational life (see Box 11.3 overleaf). This development, while still firmly preoccupied with the question of how to control subordinates within the industrial enterprise, nevertheless eventually contributed to a transformation of the way organisations are understood.

The development of the sociology of organisations

As the social sciences began to grow in importance in the United States in the 1940s and 1950s, two developments in organisation theory – one stimulated by the work of Max Weber, the other influenced by the more obviously relevant findings of the Hawthorne research – began to come together. Sociologists, using Weber's work (or their understanding of it) as their starting point, set out to show the importance of patterns of informal relationships alongside formal ones. Social psychologists, on the other hand, sought to explore the conflict between human needs and the apparent requirements of formal organisations. Drawing on this work, administrative theorists sought to update the old formal prescriptive models with more flexible propositions based upon this new understanding of organisational life (Argyris, 1964; McGregor, 1960; Herzberg, 1966).

Once Weber's work became available to sociologists in the United States in the 1940s and 1950s, it was applied to organisational studies as a kind of model against which real situations might be measured. By treating it in this way sociologists began to identify problems with the rational model of bureaucracy, often unjustly alleging that Weber had not been aware of them but nevertheless usefully advancing organisational theory.

In some of this work it is suggested that there is likely to be a conflict within a bureaucratic organisation between the principle of hierarchy and

Box 11.3	The role of the Hawthorne research programme for an understanding of the importance of human relationships in organisational life

An important contribution to understanding the importance of human relationships in organisational life came from research carried out under Elton Mayo at the Hawthorne Works in Chicago during the late 1920s and early 1930s (Roethlisberger and Dickson, 1939). The researchers were influenced by research on morale carried out during the First World War. They were also well aware of the progress being made in social psychology between the wars, and in particular they were influenced by the more sophisticated approach to human motivation that Freudian psychology helped to produce. The development of a more complex approach to social structure at this time, by sociologists and anthropologists, also had an impact on their work.

The main importance of the Hawthorne researchers lies in the way they shifted the emphasis in organisation theory from a mechanical concern to discover the 'one best way' to organise work tasks to a recognition of the importance of human relationships for organisational performance. Their early research draws attention to the relevance of managerial interest in workers' activities for motivation and morale, while their later work throws light upon relationships within the work group.

The Hawthorne researchers demonstrate the need to analyse organisations as living social structures. They indicate that, just as to discover that there are such and such a number of farmers, shopkeepers and labourers living in a village and that 'x' works for 'y' and so on is not to find out a great deal of significance about the social structure of that village, so to regard an organisation as merely a pattern of formal roles is likely to make it impossible to understand fully the determinants of behaviour, even formally prescribed behaviour, within that organisation.

Although these findings relate to the shop floor, to the lowest level in an organisation's hierarchy, subsequent research has demonstrated the validity of the findings for all levels. Inter-personal relationships within groups of office workers or within management have equally been found to determine work behaviour in a way that formal organisational rules in no way anticipate.

the need to maximise the use of expertise. Gouldner (1954) makes this point in the following way:

> Weber, then, thought of bureaucracy as a Janus-faced organisation, looking two ways at once. On the one side, it was administration based on expertise: while on the other, it was administration based on discipline. (Gouldner, 1954, p. 22)

Bureaucratic organisation is founded upon the need to make the maximum use of the division of labour. Such division is based upon the need to subdivide a task either because of its size or because it is impossible for a single individual to master all its aspects. In fact, in most cases both of these reasons apply. The principle of hierarchy rests upon the notion of the delegation of responsibility to subordinates. If the superior could perform the whole of the task that is delegated, there would be no need to have subordinates. He or she will delegate part of the task either because of a lack of time to do it alone, or because he or she has neither the time nor the knowledge to perform certain parts of the task. Inasmuch as the latter is the case, it is obvious that in respect of at least part of the task the superior is less expert than the subordinate. But even in the former case this may also be true, since, particularly as far as tasks that require decision making are concerned, the subordinate will be in possession of detailed information which, in delegating responsibility, the superior has chosen not to receive. We are back here, of course, to the issues about the likelihood of discretion in action (explored in the cookery example in Box 9.8).

It is for these reasons that, as far as the detailed functioning of any organisation with complex tasks to perform is concerned, it must be recognised that expertise resides to a large extent in the lower ranks of a hierarchy. And it is for these reasons that it is inevitable that there tends to be conflict between authority based upon expertise and authority based upon hierarchy in bureaucratic organisations.

The apparent inconsistency in Weber's theory identified by Gouldner has helped to provoke several valuable studies of conflict between experts and administrators within organisations. An allied topic that has also been explored is the conflict that exists for experts between professional orientation and organisational orientation in their attitudes to their work (Gouldner, 1957–8; Reissman, 1949).

A second important theme deriving from Weber's work concerns the relationship between rationality and rigidity. One of the earliest essays on this theme was Merton's (1957) discussion of bureaucratic structure and personality. This emphasis fits with the arguments about expertise within organisations. The implications of this point and the one in the previous paragraph for the behaviour of bureaucratic employees will be explored further in Chapter 13.

All this sociological work led to an exploration of the relationship between organisational structure and organisational tasks. Thus, the question raised was whether the 'rational' structure may be well adapted to some tasks but ill adapted to others. Two British researchers, Burns and Stalker (1961), made an important contribution on this theme. They drew a distinction between 'mechanistic' and 'organic' management systems (see Box 11.4). Other sociologists began, however, to raise wider questions about the fit between organisational task and structure by examining a wide range of work situations. Some other British research played a seminal role in this development. First, Woodward (1965) developed a typology of industrial organisations based upon differences in technology. Then, later sociologists, notably a group working together at Aston University, began to argue that the varied and multi-dimensional nature of organisational arrangements is determined by a variety of 'contingencies' (see Greenwood, Hinings and Ranson, 1975 for an application of this work in public organisations). These include variables which are external to the organisation in its 'environment', variables determined by the power structure in which it operates, and variables which will depend upon 'ideology', or what Child (1972) describes as 'strategic choice'.

Box 11.4	Burns and Stalker's distinction between mechanistic and organic management systems

Mechanistic systems, involving formal structures broadly comparable to the Weberian model, are, their research suggests, most suitable for stable, unchanging tasks. Organic ones are, by contrast, best

> adapted to unstable conditions, when problems and requirements for action arise which cannot be broken down and distributed among specialist rules within a clearly defined hierarchy. Individuals have to perform their special tasks in the light of their knowledge of the tasks of the firm as a whole. Jobs lose much of their formal definition in terms of methods, duties, and powers, which have to be redefined continually by interaction with others participating in a task. Interaction runs laterally as much as vertically. Communication between people of different ranks tends to resemble lateral consultation rather than vertical command. Omniscience can no longer be imputed to the head of the concern. (Burns and Stalker, 1961, pp. 5–6)

Burns and Stalker base their dichotomy on experience of research into two contrasting industrial situations.

Organisations have thus to be recognised as being power systems in which structural features interact with, and are affected by, factors which make some participants within them more powerful than others. Hence Salaman argues:

> What occurs within organisations, the ways in which work is designed, control applied, rewards and deprivations distributed, decisions made, must be seen in terms of a constant conflict of interests, now apparent, now disguised, now overt, often implicit, which lies behind, and informs, the nature of work organisations within capitalist societies. (Salaman, 1979, p. 216; see also Clegg, 1990 and Clegg, Courpasson and Phillips, 2006, for more on these contributions to organisational theory)

These power relations within organisations are in various respects related to others outside the organisation. This issue was explored in the discussion of institutional theory in Chapter 4 (particularly pp. 69–71). We will return to this theme in the next chapter.

Rules and discretion

We need to return here to the topic of the relationship between rules, which specify the duties and obligations of officials, and discretion, which allows them freedom of choice of action. This topic, clearly very central to the accountability concerns of the top-down model of implementation, is, not surprisingly, also a preoccupation of a body of literature on public law. However, these legal preoccupations tend to involve an approach to these concepts which sees rules very much in a statutory context and discretionary actions as involving not so much individual choice of courses of action (which many will take for granted as inevitable) but as particular cases of legitimate departure from action prescribed by a legal rule structure. This is a theme to which we will return.

In any administrative system regulated by law, discretion will be embedded in a rule structure – at the very least in a form that will make it clear that only in a very specific set of circumstances can officials do what they like (probably the laws which come nearest to this form are those that give certain officials very strong powers to act in the interests of public safety or to prevent entry to the country of foreigners deemed to be a threat to the regime). This embedded character of discretion leads to a rather confusing argument between those who use broad and those who use narrow definitions of the concept. Perhaps the most influential definition of discretion is Davis's: 'A public officer has discretion wherever the effective limits on his power leave him free to make a choice among possible courses of action and inaction' (1969, p. 4). Others have used quite restrictive definitions, reserving the concept for only some of the phenomena embraced by Davis's definition. For example, Bull (1980) and Donnison (1977), in their separate discussions of social security discretion, draw a distinction between judgement, where the simple interpretation of rules is required, and discretion, where the rules give specific functionaries in particular situations the responsibility to make such decisions as they think fit. This seems to be drawing an unnecessary distinction. If all discretion is embedded to some extent in a rule structure (being what Dworkin has called 'the hole in the donut', 1977), then Bull and Donnison are merely drawing a distinction between more and less structured discretion, or between what Dworkin has called weak and strong forms (ibid., p. 31).

The approach in this book is to use the concept of discretion in the wide sense embodied in Davis's definition. This is partly influenced by a belief that social scientists should try to avoid imposing their own restrictive definitions of concepts used in everyday speech. But it is also justified by the fact that this discussion is concerned to see to what extent discretion is a useful concept with which to explore delegated decision-making processes.

The use of a wide definition like Davis's implies a concern with almost all decision-making situations since, as Jacques (1967) points out, almost all delegated tasks involve some degree of discretion. This, of course, was the point made in Box 9.8, with particular reference to cookery books. The study of discretion must involve, by implication, the study of rules, and may alternatively be defined as being concerned with the extent to which actions are determined by rules. This also means that students of discretion must be concerned with rule breaking since in real-life situations the interpretation of the extent to which rule following allows discretion merges imperceptibly into the witting or unwitting disregard of rules.

Davis's definition comes from a book in which he argues for any rule structure within which discretion is exercised to be drawn as tightly as possible. He argues: 'Our governmental and legal systems are saturated with excessive discretionary power which needs to be confined, structured and checked' (1969, p. 27). Later in the same book he argues that:

> we have to open our eyes to the reality that justice to individual parties is administered more outside courts than in them, and we have to penetrate the unpleasant areas of discretionary determinations by police and prosecutors and other administrators, where huge concentrations of injustice invite drastic reforms. (Davis, 1969, p. 215)

Davis argues that citizens' rights to procedural justice can best be achieved through earlier and more elaborate administrative rule making and in better structuring and checking of discretionary power (ibid., p. 219). He thus has a prescriptive concern about the need for the public organisation to control the discretionary power of the individual public officer, and he feels this should be primarily attempted through rules that are open to public inspection.

In Britain, Jeffrey Jowell carried forward the kind of concern about discretion shown by Davis in the United States. Jowell's definition of discretion is similar to Davis's. He defines it as 'the room for decisional manoeuvre possessed by a decision maker' (Jowell, 1973, p. 179), and argues that the key need is to ensure that decision makers cannot make arbitrary decisions. However, Jowell lays a far greater stress than Davis upon difficulties with reducing administrative discretion. In particular, he shows how many of the considerations with which decisions must be concerned are inherently difficult to specify in rules. Legislators are concerned to prevent *dangerous* driving, for example, to ensure that food is *pure*, and that factories are *safe*. The provision of clear-cut rules to define what is safe or dangerous, pure or polluted, is often difficult. It may be that legislators need the help of the experts who are to enforce the law to provide some specific rules. In this sense discretion may be limited at a later date when experience of enforcement enables explicit rules to be devised. It may be that conflict over the legislation has led to a blurring of the issues, and that legislators have evaded their responsibility to make more explicit rules. But it may be the case that the translation of standards into explicit rules is so difficult as to be practically impossible.

Jowell provides a valuable discussion of the problems of fettering discretion where concern is with the enforcement of standards. He argues that standards may be rendered more precise by criteria, facts that are to be taken into account. However, he argues that 'the feature of standards that distinguishes them from rules is their flexibility and susceptibility to change over time' (Jowell, 1973, p. 204). Box 11.5 shows how Jowell develops this point.

Box 11.5	**Jowell's (1973) analysis of the issues about standards**

Very often standards involve questions of individual taste or values. Jowell quotes with reference to this point an appeal court case in which the judge was unable 'to enforce a covenant restricting the erection of "any building of unseemly description"'. Jowell similarly suggests that situations in which unlike things have to be compared, or which are unique and non-recurring, cannot be regulated by reference to a clearly specified standard. He argues:

> It is not difficult to appreciate that it would be asking too much of the English football selectors to decide, after a public hearing and with due representation, to state reasons why the national interest would be served by having X rather than Y or Z to play centre forward in the coming match. (Jowell, 1973, p. 206)

Jowell does not accept a simple dichotomy between rules and discretion as suggested by Davis, but rather argues that discretion 'is a matter of degree, and ranges along a continuum between high and low' (1973, p. 179). At first glance, rules may appear to abolish such discretion, 'but since rules are purposively devised ... and because language is largely uncertain in its application to situations that cannot be foreseen, the applier of a rule will frequently be possessed of some degree of discretion to interpret its scope' (ibid., p. 201). This last comment suggests that any study of discretionary decision making requires a consideration of social processes internal to the organisation and a study of the attitudes and beliefs of those who have to interpret the rules.

Jowell's arguments suggest a need to relate any evaluation of discretion to the substantive issue involved. He suggests some reasons why discretion may be inevitable. His football selection example highlights not merely the issue of standards but also the relevance of expertise and the significance of 'polycentric' issues where many factors interact (Baldwin, 1995, p. 29). This suggests a need to identify types of decision situations in which discretion is more likely. This is a topic to which we return in the discussions of street-level work in Chapter 13 and of accountability in Chapter 14.

These issues have been taken up in other legal writing on discretion – hence Dworkin's (1977) distinction between strong discretion, where the decision maker creates the standards, and weak discretion, where standards set by a prior authority have to be interpreted. Galligan (1986) is similarly concerned to analyse discretion in this way, pointing out that decision makers have to apply standards to the interpretation of facts. These distinctions may seem very academic, but they are important in administrative law for drawing distinctions between decisions that are within an official's powers and ones that are not, and therefore for determining whether intervention by an appeal body is appropriate.

Issues about conflicting facts arise where evidence is ambiguous, or where individuals present different versions of the same events. One of the surprising aspects of some of the less sophisticated attacks on discretionary administration by lawyers is that, while in practising their own profession they talk of facts and law and of proof and disproof, they very often require judges and juries to decide between conflicting evidence. The proper distinction to make here is not between the precision of judicial decision making and the imprecision of much administration, but between the extent to which procedural safeguards for the individual, or due process, exist in each situation. Here again Jowell's work is helpful since he distinguishes between two approaches to the control of discretion: 'legalisation', the 'process of subjecting official decisions to predetermined rules' and thus, of course, the elimination of discretion; and 'judicialisation', involving 'submitting official decisions to adjudicative procedures' (1973, p. 178). In that sense the issue is about where ultimate decision-making power is to reside when there is conflict over official decisions.

Rules and discretion in organisational sociology

It has been argued that all work, however closely controlled and supervised, essentially involves some degree of discretion. Wherever work is delegated, the person who delegates it loses a certain amount of control. To approach the concept in this way is, of course, to examine it from the perspective of superordinate authority. Viewed the other way round, the equivalent phenomenon is rules which apparently guarantee benefits or services but nevertheless have to be interpreted by intermediaries. It is in the twin contexts of task complexity and the delegation of responsibility that the phenomenon of discretion becomes of salient importance. In complex organisational situations gaps readily emerge between intentions and outcomes. People running one-person businesses exercise discretion, of course, but the concern here is with it as a relational phenomenon. The problems about discretion are perceived, not surprisingly, as arising when one person's discretionary freedom may subvert the intentions of another.

Running through much organisation theory, and in particular through the work of those writers who are seeking to help those they see as in control of organisations to determine the right way to approach the delegation of tasks, is therefore a concern about the balance between rules and discretion, even when different words are used. Hence Simon, in his classic work *Administrative Behaviour* (1957), emphasises the importance of the various premises upon which decisions are based. Rule making and control within organisations is concerned with the specification of premises for subordinates. Simon argues:

> The behaviour of a rational person can be controlled, therefore, if the value and factual premises upon which he bases his decisions are specified for him. This control can be complete or partial – all premises can be specified, or some can be left to his discretion. Influence, then, is exercised through control over the premises of decision. (Simon, 1957, p. 223)

One reservation must be made about this statement (in addition to objecting to its gendered nature), namely that, as suggested above, the notion of total control in an organisational context is unrealistic. Otherwise this is a valuable statement of the place of discretion in a hierarchical relationship. Simon goes on to suggest that what occurs within an organisational system is that a series of areas of discretion are created in which individuals have freedom to interpret their tasks within general frameworks provided by their superiors. He quotes a military example relevant to the 'modern battlefield' (see Box 11.6), recognising the prevalence of discretion even in the most hierarchical and authoritarian of organisations. Dunsire (1978a) has seized upon the interesting reference to the 'province' of the subordinate in this context. He portrays organisational activities as

Box 11.6	Simon's example of the rules/discretion relationship on a battlefield

Simon writes:

> how does the authority of the commander extend to the soldiers in the ranks? How does he limit and guide their behaviour? He does this by specifying the general mission and objective of each unit on the next level below, and by determining such elements of time and place as will assure a proper coordination among units. The colonel assigns to each battalion in his regiment its task; the major, to each company in his battalion; the captain, to each platoon in his company. Beyond this, the officer does not ordinarily go. The internal arrangements of Army Field Services Regulations specify that 'an order should not trespass upon the province of a subordinate. It should contain everything beyond the independent authority of the subordinate, but nothing more'. (Simon, 1957, p. 224)

This example is interesting in reminding us how, in what is regarded as the most hierarchical of organisations, discretion is inevitable. The paradox here arises because in a war situation personnel at the lowest level may have to respond immediately to the unexpected. Hierarchical discipline is designed to try to make that response predictable, or at least compatible with strategy determined at higher levels. A similar point may be made about policing.

involving 'programmes within programmes'. In a hierarchy subordinate programmes are dependent upon superior ones, but they may involve very different kinds of activities. Dunsire elaborates an example of a railway closure to show that, while activities such as the rerouting of trains, the selling of railway property and, at the very end of the chain, the removal of ballast from abandoned tracks are necessarily dependent upon superior decisions about the closure of the line, the way they are carried out is not predetermined by the decisions taken at the top of the hierarchy. He argues that decisions at the higher level are of high generality, those at the bottom of high specificity. This does not mean, however, 'that a worker at a high specificity level necessarily has a smaller amount of discretion (in any of its senses) than a worker at a high generality level' (Dunsire, 1978a, p. 221). This approach helps us to make sense of the use of the concept of discretion in relation to professional hierarchies such as education or medicine. The organisational or planning activities at the top of such hierarchies set contexts for, but do not necessarily predetermine, decision making at field level, where very different tasks are performed and very different problems have to be solved.

All the writers who have been concerned with the complexity of organisations have acknowledged that there are related problems of control, coordination and communication between these different 'provinces' and linking these programmes within programmes (see Dunsire, 1978b). Attention has been drawn to the interdependence involved, and therefore to the fact that in a hierarchical situation superiors may be dependent upon subordinates. This is taken further by Gouldner (1954), who shows that the top-down presentation of hierarchical relationships with superiors promulgating rules to restrict the discretion of subordinates may sometimes be turned on its head. He draws attention to the development of rules which limit the discretionary freedom of superiors in the interests of their subordinates. The classical discussion of this occurs in Gouldner's *Patterns of Industrial Bureaucracy* (1954), in which he shows the part that workers may play in securing rules to protect their interests. Overall his emphasis is upon the appeal to rules, by either party, in a situation in which a previously obtaining relationship breaks down:

> Efforts are made to install new bureaucratic rules, or enforce old ones, when people in a given social position (i.e. management or workers) perceive those in a reciprocal position (i.e. workers or management) as failing to perform their role obligations. (Gouldner, 1954, p. 232)

Gouldner explores the many functions of rules in situations of social conflict. He draws our attention, therefore, to the extent to which rules and discretion must be studied in the context of relationships in which the parties on either side seek to influence the freedom of movement of the other.

It is important to move away from the older emphasis in organisation theory which saw the rules/discretion relationship from the perspective of superiors concerned to limit discretion, as far as acceptable, in the interests of rational management. Instead, attention should be directed towards the extent to which both rules and discretion are manipulated and bargained over within hierarchies. Fox (1974), coming to the examination of this issue from a concern with industrial relations, has interestingly related rule imposition to low-trust relationships. He picks up the top-down concern with detailed prescription and shows how this creates or reinforces low-trust relations:

> The role occupant perceives superordinates as behaving as if they believe he cannot be trusted, of his own volition, to deliver a work performance which fully accords with the goals they wish to see pursued or the values they wish to see observed. (Fox, 1974, p. 26)

A vicious circle may be expected to ensue. The subordinate who perceives that he or she is not trusted feels little commitment to the effective performance of work. This particularly affects the way the remaining discretionary parts of the work are carried out. The superior's response is to try to tighten control and further reduce the discretionary elements. The irreducible minimum of discretion that is left leaves the subordinate with some weapons against the superior: the prescribed task is performed in a rigid, unimaginative and slow way.

This means that some rather similar phenomena may emerge by different routes. One may be defined as discretion, the other as rule breaking. The former emerges from a recognition of the power and status of implementers (this word is used deliberately instead of subordinates). This is the high-trust situation described by Fox, and applies to much professional discretion within public administration. The latter is seized by low-level staff regarded as subordinates rather than implementers whom, in practice, superiors fail to control. One is legitimised, the other is regarded – by the dominant elements in the hierarchy – as illegitimate. To the member of the public on the receiving end they may be indistinguishable.

Much of the organisation theory explored here indicates that discretion and rule breaking cannot be simply contrasted. Actors may be faced with situations in which rules conflict, in which rules are ambiguous, or in which so many rules are imposed that effective action becomes impossible. In these situations choices are made between rules, or about how they are to be respected. Hence occasions arise in which subordinates can paralyse the organisation by working to rule, by obsessively following rules which under normal operating conditions everyone would tacitly recognise as only to be applied in unusual situations.

The author has discussed elsewhere (Hill, 1969) the way in which social security officials may operate when they suspect fraud. They are able to operate rules and procedures in a heavy-handed way to ensure that claims are fully investigated and claimants are made fully aware of the consequences of detection. If, however, they operate like this in more normal situations they will severely slow down the processing of claims and deter genuine applicants.

Alternatively, Blau (1955) shows how front-line bureaucrats disregard rules to enable them to relate more effectively to their peers and to the members of the public with whom they deal. In this sense rule bending or breaking operates as a substitute for discretion to generate a responsive organisation. However, there are issues here about the legitimacy of such adaptation, and the extent to which it may be used to favour some clients but not others. In Chapter 13 the discussion of Merton's (1957) portrayal of 'over-conforming' bureaucrats who create problems because they apply the letter and not the spirit of the law, and of Lipsky's (1980) work on 'street-level bureaucracy', returns to this theme.

This excursion into the treatment of discretion in organisation theory suggests, therefore, that there are a number of reasons why discretion is likely to be an important phenomenon in bureaucracies. At times, confusion arises between notions of organisation flexibility in which discretion, particularly professional discretion, is accepted as an inherent feature and notions of conflict between formal requirements and informal behaviour (or more explicitly between rule making or enforcement and rule breaking). This confusion may be a reflection of the fact that in reality these phenomena cannot be easily separated. Organisations are not simply fixed entities within which informal behaviour may develop. They are in a permanent state of change with both new rules and new forms of rule breaking occurring as conflicting interests interact. Streeck and Thelen, whose perspective on the need to appreciate the complexity of institutional arrangements was discussed in Chapter 4 (p. 75), stress:

- 'the meaning of a rule is never self-evident and always subject to and in need of interpretation' (2005, p. 14);
- rule makers have cognitive limits;
- 'rule takers do not just implement the rules . . . but also try to revise them in the process of implementation, making use of their inherent openness and under-definition' (ibid., p. 15);
- 'there are limits to the extent to which socially authorized agencies . . . can prevent an unintentional or subversive deviation from . . . rules' (ibid.).

The granting of discretion may be a conscious ingredient of the formal design at one extreme, or a reluctant concession to organisational realities at the other. Conversely, new limitations upon discretion may stem from attempts by superiors to assert their hierarchical rights, or from aspirations of subordinates to introduce greater certainty for their activities. In this last sense, therefore, there is no simple equation between rule making and hierarchical control or between the preservation of discretion and subordinate freedom.

This final point needs emphasising further. Baumgartner (1992) criticises the legal concern that discretionary behaviour is unpredictable and argues that 'social laws' make it predictable. Her essay analyses the impact of a variety of sociological features of official encounters upon their outcomes. In some respects she caricatures the legal approach – the preoccupation of people like Davis with the regulation of discretion is based as much upon a concern about the social biases that enter into it as upon its unpredictability. However, this sociological perspective is important in reminding us that 'rules' in a sociological sense may be as readily 'made' in the course of official behaviour as promulgated by policy makers and managers. These 'rules', moreover, may have characteristics which give them a power that is difficult to resist. Feldman, in an essay in the same volume as Baumgartner's, offers a clever analogy:

> The difference between the formal limits and the social context limits to discretion can be likened to the difference between a wall and a rushing stream of water. The wall is firm, clearly delineated, and it hurts when you run into it. The rushing stream ... moves; its speed varies; it is more powerful in the middle than on the edges. It does not always hurt to go into the stream; indeed it may at times be pleasurable. The wall, however, can be assaulted and broken down while the stream rushes on creating a path for itself against the mightiest resistance. (Feldman, 1992, p. 183)

Summing up on rules and discretion

In examining rules and discretion, several issues need to be given attention. First, the complex interaction of the two concepts must be emphasised. Issues about rigid rule frameworks are implicitly issues about the absence of discretion. Concerns about excessive discretion are concerns about the limitation of the rule systems within which it is embedded. Hardly ever, in the discussion of public policy, is there either absolute rule dominance or unstructured discretion.

Second, therefore, as stressed throughout this book, policy (in which rules and discretion are mixed together) must be seen in a wider social and political context, which is likely to affect the way discretion manifests itself and the attempts that are made to control it. Discretion may arise from ambiguity, sometimes deliberate, in public policy.

Third, while acknowledging political reasons why discretionary power may be conferred, the discussion has not disregarded the extent to which this phenomenon arises as a consequence of inherent *limits* to control. As Prottas (1979) argues:

> A general rule in the analysis of power is that an actor with low 'compliance observability' is relatively autonomous. If it is difficult or costly to determine how an actor behaves and the actor knows this, then he is under less compulsion to comply. (Prottas, 1979, p. 298)

Fourth, as this last observation reminds us, there is a need to analyse discretion as a facet of organisational life in a complex relationship to rule breaking. It is important to relate discretion to issues about organisational complexity, reward systems, motivation and morale.

Fifth, we should not disregard the extent to which the concern about discretion is a normative one. Under what circumstances may discretion be said to be a problem, and for whom? To what extent does the balance established between discretion and rules distribute differential advantages and disadvantages to the parties involved, and particularly to the members of the public affected by the policy?

Finally, in noting that discretion has been regarded as a problem, we should recognise that a variety of strategies of organisational control have developed to try to deal with it. The traditional approach has been to try to control it through tighter rules and procedures. More recently, identification of the ubiquitous nature of the phenomenon has led rather to attempts to structure it. This is one of the key preoccupations of the 'new public management' movement, which is explored further in Chapter 14.

CONCLUSIONS

This chapter started by examining the way in which Max Weber's theory of bureaucracy has been seen as defining a model for organisational control that has been widely adopted. We are again, as in so much of any discussion of the policy process, in a literature where issues about what *does* happen and issues about what *should* happen are often confused. The Weberian model is seen both as a way of conveying the essential character of hierarchical administration and as an ideal widely espoused by the architects of administrative systems. Organisational sociologists came along somewhat later to suggest that the reality of organisational life may be rather different. It was also the case that many of them indicated that they thought it *should* be rather different.

Nevertheless, the Weberian model was attractive to those who wanted to stress that public servants should administer impartially policies devised by politicians. In taking that view they were supported by a legal view of the desirability of rule following and a hostility to administrative discretion. The discussion of this then indicates a fascinating parallel literature to both the implementation debate and evaluation of the bureaucratic model, seeing the issues about the relationship between rules and discretion to be very complex and some forms of discretion as inevitable.

12 Inter-organisational processes

SYNOPSIS

This chapter explores the importance of inter-organisational relationships for the policy process. After an initial examination of why this subject is important the discussion is divided into two sections. The first of these looks at inter-organisational relationships in 'vertical' terms, examining the extent to which such relationships have 'top-down' characteristics. It explores the particular complications where the apparently 'lower'-tier organisations have substantial policy-making autonomy, which is particularly the case in federal or quasi-federal situations. The second section adds to these 'horizontal' relationships where collaboration is required by organisations which have no hierarchical relationship. Finally, it is noted that very often there are complex inter-organisational 'networks'.

Introduction

In Chapter 10 one of the main contributions from Pressman and Wildavsky's influential analysis of implementation was shown to be the argument that the number of links in an implementation chain can be shown, logically, to have an impact on the effectiveness of a policy transmission process. The starting point for this argument is a version of the old children's game in which a message is whispered from one end of a line to the other. Inaccuracies arise in transmission and new constructions are fabricated to try to retain the sense of the message. But of course, in the implementation process, as was noted in Chapter 10, this is not just a matter of communication. The chain or transmission line image is very often too great a simplification of the inter-organisational arrangements. Some of the links in the chain may be more complex. Imagine a complication to the children's game in which at various points in the chain two or more children had to listen to the message and then decide what its content was before passing it on. But then again, recognise that we are talking about more than mere communication when we explore inter-organisational communication in the real world, hence making sense will be influenced by roles and interests. This implies (sticking with the children's game analogy) negotiation about what they would like the message to be! There are differences of roles and interests along the 'line' and negotiations between parties. At the same time there are institutional links which may contribute to minimising dissent, or indeed in some circumstances to increasing it. In short, implementation, and indeed all aspects of the policy process, very often involves inter-organisational systems. This has been noted as a pervasive feature of modern governance.

Some efforts to solve inter-organisational collaboration problems involve integration, so that the coordination issues are contained within single organisations. Since this often involves the creation of organisations that are large and complex, it may be argued that internalising the issues makes little difference: inter-organisational problems are merely turned into intra-organisational ones. Furthermore, since collaboration issues are ubiquitous, any specific integrated arrangements may leave some coordination problems unresolved. Box 12.1 describes an ongoing English saga about efforts to coordinate personal social services which highlights these issues.

Many writers have sought to offer advice to governments on the best ways to achieve service delivery integration. Alongside the questions about where the organisational boundaries should be drawn, there are many prescriptions for inter-organisational collaboration. O'Toole summed up the problems about making policy recommendations on these issues in an article published in 1986, but the situation has not changed since then. He noted:

> The field is complex, without much cumulation or convergence. Few well-developed recommendations have been put forward by researchers, and a number of proposals are contradictory. Almost no evidence or analysis of utilization in this field has been produced. (O'Toole, 1986, p. 181)

O'Toole goes on to attribute the lack of progress to (a) 'normative disagreement' and (b) 'the state of the field's empirical theory'.

Since this book is not designed to offer recommendations but rather to explore the working of the policy process, it is tempting to leave this subject there. But it is important to try to explore some of the ways in which issues about inter-organisational collaboration are important for an understanding of the policy process.

It is appropriate to talk about inter-organisational links that are both horizontal and vertical. This is the obvious way to talk about this subject, as shown in Figure 12.1. Figure 12.1 assumes a national organisation passing policy recommendations through two regional ones to local ones. The chart

Box 12.1	Efforts to integrate social services in England

Between the 1940s and the 1960s social care services for children were supervised nationally by the Home Office and organised locally in local authority children's departments. Adult care services were the national responsibility of the Department of Health and were organised separately at the local authority level. The Seebohm Committee (1968) argued for the unification of social services 'to ensure a more co-ordinated and comprehensive approach to the problems of individuals and families and the community in which they live'. (Seebohm Report, 1968, para. 140, p. 44)

These recommendations were put into effect in 1971, with local authorities required to set up integrated social services departments.

Once the institutional change was in place effort was put into ways to ensure service integration within departments, through integrated teams. However, two things quite soon began to disrupt this development. One was experiments with 'one-stop shops' for all local government services. The other was concerns about the lack of coordination between the National Health Service (NHS) and the social care services.

The latter concern then came to play the major role in generating change. A variety of devices, often finance-led, were tried to facilitate collaboration, particularly in respect of adult services (where the social aftercare of people discharged from hospital was perhaps the dominant issue). The Health Act 1999 imposed partnership 'duties' and allowed arrangements whereby health and social services authorities could operate 'pooled budgets', transfer funds between organisations and even create new integrated organisations combining parts of both health and social care services.

As adult care services became more integrated with the NHS so they began to be split away from services for children. Then the government began to permit organisational arrangements in which local authorities broke up their social services departments. The most widely favoured arrangement involved closer integration of children's services with local education departments.

In 2003 there was a crucial change at central government level. A 'Minister of State for Children' was appointed, to belong within the Department for Education and Skills. After this the government indicated that it expected education and child protection policy to be brought together at local level too. It went on to legislate to require local authorities to create posts of Directors of Children's Services 'accountable for local authority education and children's social services'.

This change means that liaison between social services for adults and social services for children has become an inter-departmental issue. Meanwhile issues about the connections between both services and the National Health Service remain. As far as adult services are concerned, arrangements exist in some areas for integrated working in respect of, for example, mental health care services. A next development in the 'saga' could be the take-over of adult services by the health service.

We see here, then, searches for the ideal single organisation being accompanied by alternative concerns about the best ways to achieve inter-organisational collaboration. Hudson and Henwood (2002) argue that the contemporary restructuring does not necessarily offer the best way forward; rather, they suggest, issues about collaboration are essentially about behaviour at the 'street level' and are not necessarily solved by large structures.

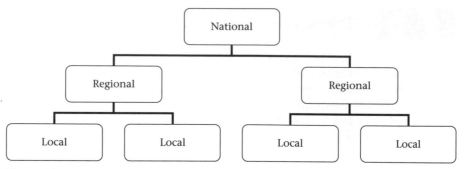

Figure 12.1   A simple organisation chart

shows hierarchical links. However, the development of policy may require horizontal links. For example, even if the organisations at each level are all-embracing, multi-purpose ones, there may be activities for which collaboration is essential. A simple example of this would be the management of a river which passes through both regions and all four local areas.

In the real world of public policy the range of possible permutations on this simple design is considerable. There may be any one of the following, singly or in combination:

- many more organisations;
- organisations with overlapping jurisdictions;
- differences of function between organisations (health/social care/ education, etc.);
- organisations with cross-cutting authority relationships (local organisations required to cooperate at the local level but accountable to different national organisations).

In addition, a chart like Figure 12.1, derived as it is from a computer package designed to help people draw organisational charts, embodies assumptions about hierarchy. Power equalities are normally implied along the horizontal dimension but not along the vertical one. The vertical dimension is normally used to convey the notion of hierarchy. In the complex world of modern governance there is a danger of falling too easily into assumptions about the existence of hierarchy. There may be various respects in which the bodies at either regional or local level in this diagram claim autonomy from central control. Conversely, whilst the bodies at the same level may be notional 'equals' there may be power inequalities. Hence even in the simple example given above of control over a river, one local authority may be a large and rich one that is reluctant to modify its policies to satisfy the demands of smaller and poorer ones.

The vertical dimension

Clearly, analysis of the vertical dimension owes a great deal to the contribution of Pressman and Wildavsky, noted above, with their subtitle highlighting the 'distance' between Washington and Oakland and emphasising the links in the implementation chain. This is a theme that has been taken up in several important American contributions to the study of implementation. In their joint book *Implementation Theory and Practice: Toward a Third Generation* (1990), Goggin, Bowman, Lester and O'Toole set out what they call a '*communications model*' for the analysis of implementation which has a very strong emphasis upon what affects the acceptance or rejection of messages between layers of government. They set out a large number of hypotheses in which 'inducements and constraints' between federal and state level and between the latter and the local level figure prominently.

Stoker (1991) identifies as a crucial flaw in the American top-down literature the extent to which it is concerned with failures to exert federal authority in a system of government that was designed to limit that authority (see also Ferman, 1990 on this theme). Stoker therefore contrasts two alternative approaches to the solution of implementation problems, and, taking his lead from Lindblom (1977), he labels these approaches 'authority' and 'exchange'. The authority approach involves suggesting ways to simplify or circumvent the barriers to compliance. The exchange approach requires the achievement of cooperation. There are problems with the exchange approach, however, since this takes us back into questions about how to distinguish policy formulation and implementation in situations in which both (or all) of the partners in the exchange relationship have the right or power to create policy. This leads him to formulate a third alternative in which there is a 'governance' role to 'manipulate the conditions of the implementation process to encourage cooperative responses to conflicts of interest' (Stoker, 1991, p. 50). This is an activity in which 'reluctant partners' are induced to collaborate. In this sense Stoker takes up an argument from Stone (1989) that it is important to give attention to 'power to' accomplish collective goals as opposed to 'power over' recalcitrant others. This leads him on to an exploration of the extent to which different 'implementation regimes' can arise, or be created. Here Stoker uses game theory, drawing particularly upon scholars who have developed this to explore relationships between nations (Axelrod, 1984; Axelrod and Keohane, 1985; Oye, 1985). What is important for Stoker is the extent to which games are repeated, and occur in contexts in which there is a 'history of interaction between participants' and 'the expectation of future interaction' (Stoker, 1991, p. 74).

Cline (2000) contrasts the theoretical contribution from Goggin and his associates with that from Stoker. Exaggerating their emphases a little, he characterises the former as seeing action as involving solving communication problems between agencies, while the latter is seen as about collaboration problems. In the first case the issue is about how to get the 'messages' right, in the second it is about the management of a bargaining process. It is clearly both.

Hence, we see an emergent concern in the implementation literature to highlight situations in which there is participation in the policy formation process by actors who, in the initial top-down formulation of the problem, were seen simply as implementers whose recalcitrance explicitly or implicitly might be the problem.

It has been noted that the development of the modern notion of governance is connected with observations about the supercession of the nation state (and about the development of federalism in Europe). But it seems confusing to mix the issues about policy or political coordination with the traditional concerns of implementation analysis. Box 12.2 provides illustrations of alternative approaches adopted to this issue.

Box 12.2	**Confusing issues about implementation with issues about inter-governmental collaboration in the context of the European Union**

Knill and Lenschow (1998) say of one of their articles that it 'analyses the roots of the widely recognized "implementation gap" of European legislation'. They go on to say: 'We define implementation effectiveness as the degree to which both the formal transposition and the practical application of supranational measures at the national level correspond to the objectives specified in the European legislation'. (Knill and Lenschow, 1998, p. 595). Cram also uses 'implementation failure' language in her discussion of national adoption of European Union policy (1997, p. 84). But note that in chapter 8 (p. 181) an approach to this issue by Bulmer and Padgett was cited that uses policy transfer theory rather than implementation theory.

From a literature review and their own research, Falkner et al. (2007) suggest that there are 'three worlds of compliance' varying from issue to issue and state to state. They distinguish 'a world of law observance' in which efforts are made to implement directives faithfully, a 'world of domestic politics' where in the face of internal political pressures 'domestic concerns dominate over the fragile aspiration to comply' (p. 405) and a 'world of transposition neglect' characterised by a neglect of EU goals stemming from what they call a 'posture of national arrogance' (ibid.). In some respects only the first of these might be called implementation. In the second case there may be policy formation involving 'transfer' with EU goals as only one influence among many. In the third case implementation discourse is rather meaningless.

We recognise that while some authors describe the issues about the adoption of European Union policies in individual nation states as about 'implementation' others do not. Earlier analyses of these issues tended to use an inter-governmental perspective which can be seen as deriving from international relations theory (Jordan, 1997, 2001). Certainly it is rather early to abandon that approach, and it is problematical to be speaking of deficits when the crucial issue is the explicit undermining of the policy thrust of an EU directive by a national government with a substantial measure of autonomy which enables it to do so.

Knill's work, notwithstanding the criticism of his use of the term 'implementation', offers an interesting perspective on the factors that influence the adoption of European Union directives by nation states. Drawing upon institutional theory he suggests that reception of new initiatives will be affected by the extent to which they are compatible with 'embedded' national administrative traditions. This can be seen as a useful contribution both to the problem of explaining change in institutional contexts and to the understanding of vertical intra-organisational relationships of all kinds. The way Knill applies his approach to issues about the adoption of European environment policy initiatives is set out in Box 12.3. The discussion of the vertical dimension so far has highlighted the special autonomies built into American

Box 12.3	Knill's (1998) analysis of the reasons for the effective adoption of EU directives by nation states

Knill explores the extent to which three states – Britain, Germany and France – have fully complied with four EU environment policy directives. The interesting feature of his analysis is his contrast between Britain and Germany (France fell between the two extremes). Given the strong German commitment to environment policy he is surprised to note poor compliance. By contrast, Britain, allegedly with a poor record of environment policy, was largely compliant. He explains this as follows:

> The distinctive characteristics of different national administrative traditions have an important impact on a country's general ability to comply with EU requirements within the national 'logic of appropriateness'. Thus, the low adaptation capability found in Germany is the result of a thick institutional core combined with low structural capacity for administrative reform. This constellation increases the potential that European legislation contradicts core administrative arrangements, which cannot effectively comply within the scope of 'appropriateness'. By contrast, adaptation capability is much higher in Britain where the general capacity for national reforms creates a potential for changing the 'logic of appropriateness' hence allowing for effective adaptation to initial core challenges. (Knill, 1998, p. 25)

In essence, the reforms challenged deeply embedded German practices whilst in the UK they benefited from the lack of formal restrictions upon government action and also from the fact that the ongoing privatisation of the water industry was stimulating regulatory reform.

federalism, and explored how far the European Union still falls short of being a federal system; however, it is not so easy to determine how to draw a line between federal arrangements and others that involve a strong measure of local autonomy. Lane and Ersson (2000), when trying to identify a classification of states in terms of whether they are federal or not, note that, while power sharing between layers of government is seen to be a key identifying characteristic of a federation, it also occurs outside federations. Hence 'one cannot simply equate federalism with a decentralized state structure, because unitary states could also harbour considerable decentralization' (p. 87). Geographical decentralisation may be seen as a continuum running from strong federalism through weak federalism, to countries where local governments have clearly entrenched autonomy, to those where it is very much weaker. In applying this to the UK today it is pertinent to suggest that devolution of power to Scotland, Wales and Northern Ireland involves a partial federalism (or taking a predictive stance inasmuch as the first steps soon led to further ones, it may be more appropriate to speak of embryonic federalism?).

Given all that, it is relevant to raise questions about the extent to which, even in apparently unitary systems, local governments are to some degree autonomous originators of policy. Some efforts have been made to distinguish local government systems in different countries, exploring issues about levels of autonomy (see, for example, Page and Goldsmith, 1987; John, 2001). But the issues here are very complex, and are becoming more so as forms of 'governance' are developed which blur hierarchical lines and bring new actors from 'civil society' into the policy process.

Many observers of British central/local government relations have observed reductions in local autonomy, charting the increasing distrust of local government by the centre across the period of Conservative rule between 1979 and 1997 (see, for example, Lansley, Goss and Wollmar, 1989). The election of a Labour government might have been expected to make a difference, yet in many respects controls over local government since 1997 have if anything increased. Janet Newman explores this theme, drawing attention to the conflicts in policy between strong central commitments and a belief in the case for decentralisation. But this is made more complicated by a desire to bring new participants and new forms of participation into the policy process. Hence she notes that 'many of the policy changes being introduced speak ' "over the heads" of local governments direct to neighbourhoods and communities' (Newman, 2001, p. 78). Box 12.4 provides an illustration of this point.

The example of the school system given in Box 12.4 highlights a further complication. When looking at potential autonomies in the policy process there are other organisational layers that need to be taken into account below local governments. There may be delegation of autonomies to schools and hospitals, for example. And 'below' that we are perforce into some of the questions about discretionary powers among street-level staff that will be addressed in the next chapter.

As an approach to this problem which does not altogether solve it, but which may help with its analysis, Peter Hupe and the present author have

| Box 12.4 | Developments in the governance of education in England |

Bache (2003) shows how since 1997 UK central government has enhanced its control over education, suggesting that the shift from government to governance in this case involves strengthening schools and bringing new actors (including private companies) into education policy in such a way that local authorities have been weakened. Of key importance there are three things:

- first, central government have modified the complex formulae governing the funding of education in ways which force increasing proportions of the money going to local government to be passed on in predetermined ways to schools;

- second, new types of publicly funded schools have been developed with higher levels of autonomy;

- third, the scrutiny of the performance of local authorities as managers of the school system, which includes powers – which have been used – to take functions away from them.

drawn a distinction between 'layers' in the administrative system and 'levels' within policy-making activities. We refer to layers as 'separate co-governments exercising authority, with a certain territorial competence and a relative autonomy' (Hill and Hupe, 2003, p. 479). But then there are levels in the policy-making systems. These were discussed on p. 148 with reference to the work of Kiser and Ostrom as 'constitutional', 'collective choice' and 'operational' levels. The notion here is that policy processes involve nesting decisions which set quasi-institutional contexts for each other. The confusion that we want to avoid by highlighting the *layers/levels* distinction is that these should not be expected to be the same. Hence, whilst in some situations it will be true that responsibility for policy structuration is delegated through a sequence of layers – nation state governments setting the main policy parameters, regional governments designing organisational arrangements and local governments dealing with policy delivery – it is fallacious to expect this neat equation to apply as a matter of course. Rather, the dynamic of relations between layers in many systems involves a succession of struggles for control over action running up and down Kiser and Ostrom's levels.

Some of the most interesting research on the issues about relationships between layers in the policy process has been done by Peter May on environment policy, in which the nature of the 'mandates' between layers of government are explored. May had carried out a range of work comparing local government responses in the United States (1993), but then he extended his work to Australia and New Zealand (1995). May and Burby (1996) compared intergovernmental policy mandates designed to prevent environmental hazards in Florida (USA) and New South Wales (Australia).

The Florida mandate involved detailed prescriptions for local planning and regulation and imposed severe sanctions on governments that disregarded the law. The New South Wales mandate used what May and Burby describe as a cooperative approach, requiring local governments to engage in a planning process and offering inducements, including promises of future funding, to encourage them to do so.

May and Burby found that the approach adopted in Florida had several advantages:

> it proved to be much more successful in securing the compliance of local governments with procedural requirements ... [and] it seems to have an edge – at least in the short run – in building commitment of elected officials to state policy objectives.

But they go on to argue that:

> The scorecard ... is not uniformly in favor of coercive intergovernmental mandates. The cooperative policy as implemented in New South Wales had the advantage of securing strong substantive compliance once different risk levels and other factors were taken into account. Stated differently, amongst the more committed and higher risk jurisdictions, the cooperative policy is at least as effective in motivating local actions in support of state policy goals. Moreover, among those complying with the prescribed processes, the quality of substantive compliance appears to be higher under cooperative policies. (May and Burby, 1996, pp. 193–4)

This sort of approach starts to tease out some of the complexities in the processes under which authorities relate to each other in a loose superordinate system. There are some intriguing unanswered questions with this research, about the extent to which there are in play here also unmeasured institutional or cultural differences between the countries. In another article produced at around the same time May reflected on the translatability of Australian and New Zealand systems of intergovernmental cooperation to the United States:

> These settings share many commonalities with the United States in terms of government roles, assignment of property rights, and other factors governing land use and environmental management. However, the American system is exceptional for its procedural and legal complexity with respect to intergovernmental regulatory programs. Breaking through these complexities and associated adversarial climate would seem to be additional challenges for success. (May, 1995, p. 113)

This exploration of the cooperation/coercion dimension is interesting since questions about the nature of central/local government relationships have been widely explored in these terms.

The policy communities literature is also relevant here, in analysing if not in explaining some of these relationships. Clearly, when disparate actors are linked together on some relatively continuous basis this may affect the likelihood of cooperation. As far as central local relationships are concerned, where there are organisations to represent local governments in their negotiations with central government they may contribute to policy coordination (Rhodes, 1981; Blom-Hansen, 1999). This point is clearly also pertinent to the issues about horizontal collaboration discussed in the next section.

Adding the horizontal dimension

Recognising the importance of collaboration between organisations, governments have been prone to argue the case for greater cooperation and tried to set up devices to facilitate joint planning. Theorists have sought to assist this task, in the process generating some very complex attempts to model the factors that affect inter-organisational collaboration. This discussion will identify some of the key themes in this literature.

It is important to recognise that collaborative relationships run along a continuum from very detached interactions to arrangements that come close to integration. In making that point it is appropriate to reiterate the one made in the introduction to this chapter, that collaboration issues occur within organisations as well as between them. Choices about organisational arrangements for policy processes need to consider what 'boundaries' there are, and what effects they have. Some writers on organisations have stressed that the very use of the concept of 'organisation' can involve an arbitrary drawing of boundaries. There are many situations in which distinctions between organisations are unclear or in which individuals belong to more than one organisation.

There is, then, a second set of issues about what collaboration may entail. Drawing upon the work of Thompson (1967), Perri 6 (2004) has suggested the taxonomy of relationships set out overleaf in Box 12.5. But he goes on to supplement these with another approach to classification that distinguishes collaboration over policy formulation, programme coordination, integration of service relationships and integration of services to individual clients (ibid., Table 3, p. 109). These distinctions remind us of two key points: (1) the danger of letting stagist thinking get in the way of understanding the complexities of intra-organisational relationships, and (2) the extent to which this subject is complicated (as analysed in relation to vertical collaboration in the last section) by issues about autonomies.

Organisation theories which focus upon the internal concerns of organisations naturally suggest that these will inhibit collaboration with others. The focus is then upon situations in which 'exchanges' are likely to be in the interest of organisations (Levine and White, 1961; for a wider discussion see

Box 12.5	A taxonomy of types of relationship

Category of relationship	Type of relationship between entities	Definition
Coordination	Taking into account	Strategy development considers the impact of/on others
	Dialogue	Exchange of information
	Joint planning	Temporary joint planning or joint working
Integration	Joint working	Temporary collaboration
	Joint venture	Long-term joint planning and joint working on major project core to the mission of at least one participating entity
	Satellite	Separate entity, jointly owned, created to serve as integrative mechanism
Increasing closeness and mutual involvement (but not necessarily greater efficacy or collective action)	Strategic alliance	Long-term joint planning and working on issues core to the mission of at least one participating entity
	Union	Formal administrative unification, maintaining some distinct identities
	Merger	Fusion to create a new structure with a single new identity

Source: 6, P., 2004, p. 108. By permission of Oxford University Press.

Hudson, 1987). It is possible to postulate a variety of situations in which exchanges will be seen to be of mutual benefit to separate organisations. Conversely, situations can be identified in which suggested exchanges will be rejected as offering no mutual benefit or as benefiting one party and not the other. Policy systems may be set up to try to increase incentives to engage in exchange relationships.

Very many organisational activities intrinsically involve relationships with others, including other organisations. Often even key public organis-ations are weak and need to engage with others to perform tasks. While the

UK has remarkably large local authorities, in countries such as the Netherlands and France there are many small authorities (particularly outside the main towns) that need to work with other local governments or with private organisations to secure quite basic services. Without exchanges many such organisations will fail. In this sense a narrow concern with internal relationships is likely to be self-defeating.

Theory on this topic tends to have been developed in relation to manufacturing firms, which need exchange relationships to provide inputs of raw materials, etc. and to secure the successful sale of outputs, or produced goods. Economic 'market' theory deals with these relationships, with price systems governing the relevant exchanges. Organisational theorists have inevitably explored the extent to which organisational exchanges in non-market situations can be seen to involve activities in which, even if money transactions are not concerned, there can be seen to be a kind of 'trading' (of power, prestige, etc.).

The criticism of public sector organisations particularly associated with the 'public choice' theory focuses on the extent to which inefficiency and a lack of accountability arise because of a lack of 'market'-type constraints (see pp. 100–3). Organisations can be inward looking and get away with it, or they may have monopoly power which enables them to control their exchange activities in their own interests.

In the exploration of market exchanges it has been recognised that one of the problems faced by emergent capitalist enterprises was control over the input and output relationships discussed above. In, for example, the emergent oil industry in the United States in the late nineteenth century, any company engaged in refining faced problems from the instabilities associated with erratic crude oil extraction on the one side and from difficulties in organising distribution on the other. The result was efforts to integrate and extend control in both directions. The classic success story in this respect was Rockefeller's Standard Oil Company. Indeed, it was such a success that the US government was pressured into breaking it up, in the interests of the enhancement of competition (Yergin, 1991). This is an example of a market organisation trying to control its environment. Notwithstanding liberal economic theory's hostility to monopoly or oligopoly, this is 'rational' behaviour from the organisation's point of view. Furthermore, even from a wider perspective the stability that monopoly imposes upon a production system may be in the public interest, reducing uncertainties and costs (see Chandler, 1977 for an economic historian's perspective on these issues).

These costs have been described as 'transaction costs' (Coase, 1937; Williamson, 1975, 1985). When separate organisations trade with each other the process of finding the best bargain is not cost free. Furthermore, when that trading needs to be on a regular basis there is likely to be a need for a 'contract' that sets out obligations on either side, lasts for a period of time and is ultimately renegotiable. Making, monitoring and revising contracts entails costs. Both sides are likely to seek long-run stability. One way of doing this is through amalgamation. That may be by agreement or, as in the case of the build-up of the Standard Oil empire, one organisation may have the market power to be able to acquire others.

Williamson has gone on to analyse these issues in terms of a contrast between 'markets' and 'hierarchies' (1975). His supposition is that, whilst in general market relationships are superior because of their flexibility and because of the role competition can play in keeping down costs, this may not apply if 'transaction costs' are high. When these are high the incorporation of suppliers, distributors, etc. into hierarchies may become a desirable strategy.

Williamson's dichotomy relates to another dichotomy, that between Fordism and post-Fordism (Piore and Sabel, 1984; Aglietta, 1987; Elam, 1990; Jessop, 1992). The heyday of the Ford motor company involved routinised production on an assembly line. It also involved the incorporation of many elements of the production and distribution processes into a single hierarchical organisation. Post-Fordism entails either or both of (a) fragmentation of activities within an organisation and (b) the hiving-off of parts of the process into separate organisations. In the business world today choices are not simple ones between 'market' and 'hierarchy'; rather they are about a range of alternative ways of controlling exchange relationships – internal markets, franchising, subcontracting, etc. Williamson's work has been generalised into forms of contingency theory (Donaldson, 1985) and has been challenged by writers who see issues of power and of control over environmental uncertainties as of greater explanatory value than Williamson's original approach (see, for example, Minzberg, 1983).

The literature on 'markets and hierarchies' suggests answers to questions about the design of systems of interacting public policy organisations. The reasons for exploring it here are thus:

1. that there are significant attempts by governments to take note of the public choice criticism of bureaucracy and to try to transform some hierarchies into markets; contracts between public organisations or between public and private organisations are becoming an increasing feature of the public policy process;

2. that even without contracts the issues about transaction costs are relevant to the exchange relations between public organisations, and there are issues about the consequences of choices between forms of organisation which incorporate many functions under one department and forms which leave them in separate bodies (see Flynn, 1993; Walsh, 1995).

However, Thelen and Steinmo, among others, argue that seeing 'institutions as efficient solutions to collective action problems, reducing transaction costs ... in order to enhance efficiency' begs 'the important questions about how political power figures into the creation and maintenance of these institutions' ... (Thelen and Steinmo, 1992, p. 10).

A general problem with the use of the concept of 'exchange' is that it tends to direct attention to comparatively equal transactions. The Standard Oil story outlined above is one of the growing capacity of one organisation to control its transactions with other organisations. Similarly, as intra-organisational relationships involve power inequalities, so too do inter-organisational ones. There is therefore a need to explore the inequalities and 'power dependencies' in organisational interactions (Kochan, 1975; Aldrich, 1976).

Analysis of this subject needs to be sited within an overall analysis of social power. One writer who has done this, Benson (1983), has criticised writers who concentrate on the problems of securing the coordination of public services and neglect the broader influences that affect coordination. Benson maintains that inter-organisational analysis is at one level concerned with examining the dependency of organisations on each other for resources such as money and authority, but that at another level it must focus on the interests built into the structure of a particular policy sector. Benson defines a policy sector as 'a cluster or complex of organisations connected to each other by resource dependencies and distinguished from other clusters or complexes by breaks in the structure of resource dependencies' (ibid., p. 3). Defined in this way, the concept of policy sectors has similarities to the policy communities discussed in Chapter 3. As well as examining the interests built into a policy sector, Benson suggests that it is necessary to examine the system of rules that governs relationships between these interests. In essence, then, there is a need to explicate the interaction between the surface level and the 'deep structure which determines within limits the range of variation of the surface levels' (ibid., p. 5).

Thus, according to Benson, a complete analysis of inter-organisational relationships needs to explore three levels in the structure of policy sectors (1983, p. 6). First, there is the administrative structure – that is, the surface level of linkages and networks between agencies held together by resource dependencies. On this Benson argues elsewhere:

> interactions at the level of service delivery are ultimately dependent upon resource acquisition. . . . It is assumed that organizational decision-makers are typically oriented to the acquisition and defence of an adequate supply of resources. Two basic types of resources are central to the political economy of inter-organisational networks. These are money and authority. (Benson, 1975, p. 231)

Second, there is the interest structure – that is, the set of groups whose interests are built into the sector either positively or negatively. These groups comprise demand groups, support groups, administrative groups, provider groups and coordinating groups. The interest structure is important because it provides the context for the administrative structure, which cannot be adequately understood except in terms of the underlying power relations manifested within the interest structure.

In turn, the interest structure has to be located within the third level – that is, 'the rules of structure formation'. In advanced societies, Benson argues, these rules are principally those that relate to the maintenance of capital accumulation. In this context we may interpret that in a slightly less Marxist way, to mean having regard to the competitiveness of business and the requirement to keep public sector costs under tight control.

Summing up these aspects of Benson's work, Ranade and Hudson say:

> The implications of his analysis are that organisational life is marked by a constant struggle for survival and domain control, and collaboration will only be entered into where there is some mutual benefit to be derived from doing so. (Ranade and Hudson, 2003, p. 39)

But Benson also puts his argument in a more structuralist form:

> For each policy sector, then, it would be necessary to explore the impact of deep rules of structure formation. These would not determine the structure of the sector in every detail. It is reasonable to assume some measure of autonomy for the other levels – administrative organisation and structural interests. In broad terms, however, the events at those levels are to be explained at the level of rules of structure formation. The rules limit and enable action at other levels. Social science accounts which do not consider these deeper rules are to varying degrees incomplete. (Benson, 1983, p. 31)

One of the issues this raises is: what precisely is the relationship between Benson's three levels? While the main thrust of Benson's argument is that action at the surface level cannot be understood without reference to the interest structure and the rules of structure formation, he is careful not to suggest that the relationship between levels is simply deterministic. Indeed, in discussing how changes might occur within sectors, he notes the possibility that the administrative structure might become independent of the structural underpinnings and that bureaucracies might develop a life and logic of their own.

Benson's theory clearly takes us back to some of the ideas about structural determinism explored in Chapter 2, particularly those ideas that derive from Marxist theory. A somewhat similar position is reached, in a way which is less determinist and draws less upon the concept of 'interests', by the institutionalist theorists discussed in Chapter 4. Thus March and Olsen argue:

> Institutional theories supplement exchange theories of political action in two primary ways: first, they emphasise the role of institutions in defining the terms of rational exchange . . . Second, without denying the reality of calculations and anticipations of consequences, institutional conceptions see such . . . as occurring within a broader framework of rules, roles and identities. (March and Olsen, 1996, p. 250)

Institutional theory is clearly relevant for the exploration of the barriers to change that are erected when efforts are made to get separate organisations to work together in new ways. If traditional bureaucratic organisations have well-established, complex institutional arrangements that include standard operating procedures, organisational cultures and value systems, then there will be resistance to ways of working with others that threaten these. There have been many efforts since 1997 to get British government departments to work together better on cross-cutting issues and problems (Flynn, 1993; Kavanagh and Richards, 2001). It has become commonplace to emphasise the 'silo' approach to government which makes inter-departmental collaboration difficult. In relation to efforts to form partnerships, 'delivering on the core business will obviously take precedence' (Ranade and Hudson, 2003, p. 41; see also Exworthy and Powell, 2004). Questions then arise, from the efforts of the institutional theorists to explain change (discussed in Chapter 4), about how 'access points' or 'critical junctions' may occur, to be seized upon by those who want to create more 'joined up government'. Inasmuch as these changes to the arrangements for 'governance' occur against a background of externally generated change or the evolution of international organisations, for example, these critical change opportunities may be occurring. Equally, success in generating change may create a platform for further change.

DiMaggio and Powell (1983) explore – in a way that rejects 'functionalist or Marxist' explanations of organisational change (p. 156) – what they call 'isomorphic processes' which tend to make organisations similar to one another. They offer a series of hypotheses on this topic – including factors like internal organisational uncertainties and external resource dependencies – to explain this convergence.

Another way into this issue without using structuralist theory is to recognise that individual members of organisations also have other affiliations. They belong to families, voluntary organisations, political parties, churches, etc. This may mean that they have commitments to other organisations which interact with the organisation that employs them. That may seem a rather trivial point, but there are circumstances in which it is definitely not. The most significant of these for public policy is where individuals are members of professional groups that extend across a number of organisations. The impact of this is then further enhanced by intra-organisational divisions, with different professional groups in separate sections or hierarchical systems. To describe this phenomenon Ouchi has added 'clans' as a third element to be looked at within organisational relationships alongside markets and bureaucracies (1980). Degeling, analysing hospitals as organisations, writes of them as often

> locales in which members of distinct authority structures are loosely linked in the provisions of services. The separateness of medicine, nursing, allied health and hotel services, recognised in the formal structure of most hospitals, attests to the past capacity of these occupational groups to stake out and preserve their control over particular aspects of treatment provision. (Degeling, 1993, p. 33)

Laffin (1986) identifies how these professional communities may have an influence upon relations between organisations, and DiMaggio and Powell (1983) argue that professional communities are important in generating convergence in organisational structures.

A related issue is the need to recognise that individual participants in organisations have careers which may spread across more than one organisation. Studies of the British civil service have suggested that Treasury dominance over the system stems, among other things, from that body's capacity to control career moves and in particular from its tendency to take promising young civil servants from other departments for a period and to bring the most successful back into its ranks later in their careers (Heclo and Wildavsky, 1981; Campbell and Wilson, 1995). This is perhaps a comparatively simple case of organisational dominance.

A less explored example, but one that is particularly pertinent to this discussion, concerns the dramatic personnel changes that occur in some of the organisations particularly affected by the establishment of a quasi-market system in Britain, which may involve fairly rapid moves between purchasers and providers or between local government and the health service. Where individuals come from and where they hope to go to must surely influence their willingness to engage with others.

Those who have explored ways to enhance inter-organisational cooperation have explicitly suggested a need for the fostering of roles which help individuals to look outwards from their own organisation (Hudson, 1987; Huxham and Macdonald, 1992). Such individuals have been described as 'reticulists' (Friend, Power and Yewlett, 1974) or 'boundary spanners' (Ranade, 1998). Questions then arise about the extent to which, given the dominant impact of intra-organisational concerns for individual careers, such roles may be created or encouraged. A variety of devices may be adopted to this end: the setting up of special joint units, the designation of collaboration as a key ingredient of a work task, the temporary secondment of staff and so on. The success of these ventures depends upon some of the considerations already discussed – the feasibility of meaningful exchanges, the overall power context, the extent to which there are shared values. But inasmuch as they must be seen in terms of individual motivation as well as organisational motivation there are key considerations to take into account about the extent to which they yield rewards – explicit or implicit, financial or psychic – for the persons involved or for the organisations from which they originate. A concern of a number of writers on this subject has been the conflict between hierarchical intra-organisational pressures and the search for inter-organisational linkages. Pollitt thus argues:

> It would not be difficult to slide into the worst of both worlds – a combination of traditional 'vertical' organizations, still carrying the principal legal responsibilities and means of delivery, and an overlay of fashionable new units or teams, which cream off the most talented staff but lack either clear lines of accountability or the implementation capacity to get things done. (Pollitt, 2003, p. 72; see also Powell, Exworthy and Berney, 2001)

A book edited by Glendinning, Powell and Rummery, *Partnerships, New Labour and the Governance of Welfare* (2002), explores contemporary evidence on many of the current issues about inter-organisational cooperation. Partnership ideas are shown to be used in a wide range of ways. In her concluding chapter, Kirstein Rummery suggests that partnerships may be characterised as involving 'interdependence' and 'trust'. The case study examples in the book show that alongside partnerships involving a great deal of reciprocity there are others that are very unequal and some that involve some very reluctant partners making minimal contributions. Since many partnerships are encouraged, supported or required by central government, elements of power and hierarchy loom large in many situations. Networks and partnerships are likely to be steered, often from above, and involve transactions and mutual exchanges characteristic of markets. Notions of voluntary compacts often have little substance without some devices, both statutory and financial, to give them substance.

In one of the essays in Glendinning et al. (2002), Hudson and Hardy, drawing particularly on their work on health and social care, ask 'What is a "successful" partnership and how can it be measured?' They make a case for the specification of six 'principles' for a successful partnership. While they claim that their principles derive from 'an extensive and extensively validated research base' (p. 62), they are perhaps more appropriately described as intuitively plausible hypotheses, supported by modest evidence, that need to be tested much more rigorously in further, more extensive empirical studies of partnerships. Their six principles are:

1. Acknowledgement of the need for partnership
2. Clarity and realism of purpose
3. Commitment and ownership
4. Development and maintenance of trust
5. Establishment of clear and robust partnership arrangements
6. Monitoring, review and organisational learning.

This of course takes the discussion in a *prescriptive* direction but may nevertheless be important for the analysis of the impact of inter-organisational arrangements.

Networks

It has already been acknowledged that in many cases both vertical and horizontal interactions between organisations are involved. In this context it is perhaps more appropriate to speak of networks, the 'net' notion here implying both directions. The contemporary importance of network theory was explored in Chapter 3. Rhodes describes governance as 'governing with and through networks, or, to employ shorthand, it refers to steering networks' (Rhodes in Hayward and Menon, 2003, p. 67). There is an interesting bringing together of potentially conflicting ideas here. Earlier, we saw network theory used to characterise the whole policy process. But to talk of 'steering' networks suggests a coordinating role for someone or something that steers. In relation to policy implementation, clearly the notion is that there is an element of hierarchical steering *from the government*.

Hence we have two alternatives here. One is to talk of networks as informally coordinated systems, in which case the general organisational theory issues discussed in the last section are sufficient for our analysis and propositions like those set out in Hudson and Hardy's list need to guide the discussion. Alternatively, there are questions to be considered about the relationship between any efforts to pull the network from 'above' and the way in which the parties relate to each other.

These issues are explored well in research by Exworthy, Berney and Powell (2002) (see Box 12.6). They show how action depends upon horizontal linkages at national level (between government departments) and vertical linkages between those departments and local agencies and then also horizontal linkages at the local level. Adapting Kingdon's analysis of policy agenda setting (discussed in Chapter 8, pp. 156–9), they suggest that in examining policy implementation in multi-organisational contexts there is a need to recognise the relationship between 'big windows' at national level and 'little windows' at local level. Decisions rest upon the successful integration of three streams (another concept from Kingdon):

Box 12.6	**Exworthy, Berney and Powell's (2002) analysis of the relevance of network linkages in British health inequalities policy**

Health inequalities policy is the kind of policy that can easily become merely symbolic if it is not firmly endorsed by key actors at all levels. It can easily be seen as an optional extra when there are mainstream policy delivery goals. The fact that action to eliminate health inequalities competes with other policy goals is significant here both in inhibiting horizontal collaboration and in blunting policy transmission between levels. Exworthy and his colleagues echo Pressman and Wildavsky's famous subtitle in one of their articles, 'How great expectations in Westminster may be dashed locally'. But in fact they do not simply endorse the top-down implications of that title. They argue:

> many local practitioners have been disappointed that, although the government had emphasised health inequalities, they had not put in place the range of initiatives that (they thought) would be necessary to effect demonstrable change. . . . [t]hey claimed that joined-up government centrally (and partnerships locally) had not been translated into better policy-making processes. The rhetoric of tackling health inequalities had not yet matched the reality for these individuals. It is not just national expectations that have foundered locally but also local expectations that have foundered centrally. (Exworthy, Berney and Powell, 2002, p. 92)

■ A policy stream concerned with goals and objectives

■ A process stream dealing with 'causal, technical and political feasibility' (ibid., p. 266)

■ A resource stream, using that concept to embrace, of course, finance but also other resources.

This perspective offers an interesting slant upon two issues which have been given much attention earlier in this book, namely the extent to which policy making cannot be seen as a 'staged' process and the limitations of the top-down model of implementation.

While we do not want to go back into a repetition of the discussion of network theory in Chapter 3, it is important to recognise how this theory is pertinent whenever action is likely to involve multi-organisational collaboration. The question is: to what extent this is a universal characteristic of public policy. Fritz Scharpf takes an extreme view:

> (...) it is unlikely, if not impossible, that public policy of any significance could result from the choice process of any single unified actor. Policy formulation and policy implementation are inevitably the result of interactions among a plurality of separate actors with separate interests, goals and strategies (1978, p. 347).

More cautiously Koppenjan and Klijn speak of 'complex problems' as 'increasingly resolved in a setting of mutual dependencies' (2004, p. 5). The expression 'wicked problem' is used in this context, with Koppenjan and Klijn arguing:

> Complex and highly undetermined types of interactions characterize wicked problem. This strategic uncertainty is not easy to reduce and can never be completely eliminated. In a complex society characterized by network formations and horizontalisation, actors have discretion to make their own choices. Unexpected strategic turns are an intrinsic characteristic of interaction processes surrounding wicked problems (ibid, p. 7).

So, is complexity an inherent feature of modern societies? Or is this particularly the case in respect of 'wicked problems', implying that there may be simpler problems where this is not the case? Many of the examples in Koppenjan and Klijn's book concern issues where a very elaborate policy process is likely to be necessary (for example, major environmental problems – flood control, pollution reduction etc.).

Is the emphasis then on the inevitability of networks, or on the need for a network approach for the management of some (argued to be frequently evident) kinds of policies? Which came first – wicked problem – or complex organisational arrangements that make those problems 'wicked'? But this is to dichotomise too simply; rather, as in Matland's analysis of the relationship between policy complexity and power conflict, a problem may be rendered wicked by difficulties in getting agreement. Then also it is quite possible that it is complex organisational arrangements that contribute to that.

In these cases the analysis of policy problem solving is largely about stages 'upstream' from implementation – such as widening the circle of those who are involved in problem solving (in other words a combination of policy formulation and decision making; or even agenda setting). Then if these complex inter-organisational structures are needed for problem solution this implies another departure from the staged model of the policy process. One cannot speak simply of implementation if organisations (with different control structures – even in some cases lying within different nation states) need to work together to solve problems like flood control. Very high levels of discretion are needed if inter-organisational negotiation is to work properly. This leads Koppenjan and Klijn on to a concern with the management of networks. While their work is largely prescriptive in this respect, what they have done is to highlight another issue about the complexity of modern governance.

CONCLUSIONS

Perri 6 comments that 'Coordination is an eternal and ubiquitous problem in public administration' (2004, p. 131). However, while not dissenting from 6's generalisation, it is important to recognise the extent to which it is a characteristic of modern governance that inter-organisational collaboration issues are very salient. The definition of governance was explored in Chapter 1 (see pp. 20–1). Writers vary in the way they stress the elements in the definition, but in the context of this chapter the gloss John puts on the terms is particularly relevant:

> Governance is a flexible pattern of public decision-making based on loose networks of individuals. The concept conveys the idea that public decisions rest less within hierarchically organized bureaucracies, but take place more in long-term relationships between key individuals located in a diverse set of organizations located at various territorial levels. (John, 2001, p. 9)

Clearly, inasmuch as that is true then – unless we are to engage in a reductionist approach to imply focusing on those 'key individuals' – the exploration of inter-organisational relationships is important for an understanding of the policy process.

A recognition of the importance of inter-organisational relationships can be seen not just as arising from the pragmatic concerns of practitioners but also from the recognition in policy process theory of the importance of networks and policy communities, and of the way in which institutional configurations influence action. It may even, as Benson argues, extend to issues about the wider structural context.

The next chapter focuses rather more on individuals, and tends in the first place to see their behaviour in the context of a single organisation, but it will be important not to lose sight of the extent to which 'street-level bureaucrats' are not just located *in* organisations but are essentially located *at their boundaries*.

13 The policy process at the street level

SYNOPSIS

Earlier chapters have paid relatively little attention to the roles of middle- and lower-level employees in public policy systems. They have presented them as working within complex, partially controlled organisations, granted various degrees of discretion and required to collaborate with others, but there has been no examination of the implications of their own dispositions and motivational structures for these situations. This chapter explores this issue. First, it examines some rather old but still relevant theory, developed by sociologists influenced by the work of Max Weber, which stresses the way in which work in bureaucratic organisations may involve the selection of (or the creation of) people who will be rigid rule followers and tend to give more attention to the means by which policy is enacted than to its ends. This will then be contrasted with the 'street-level bureaucracy' perspective of Michael Lipsky, with its particular implications for those working with relatively unroutinised service and professional roles, which stresses the many ways in which officials may actually create policy. This leads on to an examination of the issues about the roles of professionals in public sector bureaucracies. The chapter finishes with a discussion of Mashaw's analysis of issues about professional autonomy, a topic which leads towards the issues about accountability that will be examined in Chapter 14.

Bureaucratic behaviour and the bureaucratic personality

It was suggested in Chapter 11 that the administrative organisation has typically a complex structure of a kind which many writers have described as bureaucratic. For a number of commentators, however, bureaucracy implies something more than a complex organisation. For them, bureaucracies are characterised as rigid and slow, with effective action hampered by red tape.

Although the main arguments on this topic are concerned with the inherent limitations of elaborate formal procedures, several writers have sought to show that bureaucratic rigidity is in some respects a consequence either of the impact of working in a rule-bound context upon the personalities of individuals, or of a tendency for bureaucracies to recruit people with inflexible personalities.

In the study of public bureaucracy, the organisation personality theory links up with a theme that has had a place in popular mythology for many centuries, a theme which several European novelists have developed most effectively: the portrayal of the clerk in public service as an individual whose life becomes dominated by the complex rules that have to be followed in dealings with the public. A pioneering essay on organisational sociology by Merton (1957) takes up this theme and attempts to explain the conditions under which bureaucratic personalities are likely to be found. Merton argues as follows:

1. An effective bureaucracy demands reliability of response and strict devotion to regulations.
2. Such devotion to the rules leads to their transformation into absolutes; they are no longer conceived as relative to a set of purposes.
3. This interferes with ready adaptation under special conditions not clearly envisaged by those who drew up the general rules.
4. Thus, the very elements which conduce towards efficiency in general produce inefficiency in specific instances. (Merton, 1957, p. 200)

Merton goes on to suggest that the position of those in authority is markedly simplified if subordinates are submissive individuals conditioned to follow their superiors uncritically. Moreover, the implication of much managerial training is that the successful operation of a system of authority will depend upon creating bureaucratic personalities.

In his essay, Merton argues that in Weber's analysis of bureaucracy 'the positive attainments and functions of bureaucratic organisation are emphasised and the internal stresses and strains of such structures are almost wholly neglected' (1957, p. 197). He contrasts this with the popular emphasis upon the imperfections of bureaucracy. Merton argues that bureaucrats are likely to show particular attachment to rules that protect the internal system of social relationships, enhance their status by enabling them to take on the status of the organisation and protect them from conflict with clients by emphasising impersonality. Because of their function in providing security, rules of this kind are particularly likely to be transformed into absolutes. Policy goals are then distorted as means are treated as ends.

Merton's essay is applied to bureaucratic organisations in general, but there are reasons why it may be particularly applicable to public administration. First, public officials are placed in a particularly difficult position vis-à-vis their clients. They may be putting into practice political decisions with which they disagree; they are facing a public who cannot normally go elsewhere if their demands are unsatisfied, as they often can with private enterprise; and the justice of their acts is open to public scrutiny, by politicians and sometimes by courts of law. They are thus under particular pressure to ensure that their acts are in conformity with rules. Rules are bound to play a major part in their working lives.

Second, the careers of public officials are normally organised very much along the lines of Weber's bureaucratic model. Indeed, in this respect at least, state bureaucracies often come very close to Weber's ideal type. The demand for fairness in selection and promotion leads to the development of highly regularised career structures. It tends to be very difficult to justify dramatic or unconventional promotions, and therefore public service careers are likely to be oriented towards what F. Morstein Marx (1957) has called 'the economics of small chances'. Marx explains this expression in the following way:

> In the first place, the ideology of service itself minimises the unabashed display of consuming ambition. In some respects, indeed, service is its own reward. Moreover, the mass conditions to which personnel policy and procedure must be addressed in large-scale organisations cry out for recognition of the normal rather than the exceptional. Meteoric rise of the outstandingly able individual is therefore discouraged quite in the same way as favouritism and disregard of rules are discouraged. Advancement, if it is not to attract suspicious or unfriendly eyes, must generally stay in line with the 'normal'. Exceptions call for too much explaining. All this tends to make reward for accomplishment something that comes in small packages at fairly long intervals. (Marx, 1957, p. 97)

Such a career structure obviously puts an onus upon conformity, and will tend to create a situation in which, if a public official becomes conspicuous for disregarding rules, it will be more likely to hamper than enhance his or her career.

Marx's book is interesting in developing the picture of the public official as a bureaucratic personality as a result of the factors discussed above. He therefore characterises the public service as 'the settled life' in which security is valued above high rewards (ibid., p. 102). He says: 'the merit bureaucracy is not the place for those who want to make money, to rise fast, to venture far, or to stand on their own'. Marx concedes that senior public officials are usually required to be of a reasonably high calibre, but suggests that those who compete for entry will be mostly the 'solid – as contrasted with the brilliant but restive, for instance' (ibid.).

Marx goes on to suggest that the career structure he describes reinforces the pressure for uniformity within a government bureaucracy which arises from the political need for equity and consistency. Thus he claims: 'When the common rule and the common mind combine, the natural consequence is a narrowness of perspective – a weakness more aggravating than mediocrity in administrative performance' (ibid., p. 103).

Marx suggests, then, that the bureaucratic personality will be both a product of the fact that only certain types of people choose to join the public service, or indeed the fact that selection procedures may pick out certain types of people, and a product of the bureaucratic environment. The two influences upon personality operate to reinforce each other. Merton (1957) also recognises this interaction as a key problem for research. He asks:

> To what extent are particular personality types selected and modified by the various bureaucracies (private enterprise, public service, the quasi-legal political machine, religious orders)? Inasmuch as ascendancy and submission are held to be traits of personality, despite their variability in different stimulus situations, do bureaucracies select personalities of particularly submissive or ascendant tendencies? And since various studies have shown that these traits can be modified, does participation in bureaucratic office tend to increase ascendant tendencies? Do various systems of recruitment (e.g. patronage, open competition involving specialised knowledge or general mental capacity, practical experience) select different personality types? (Merton, 1957, p. 205)

There are, therefore, a number of related issues to consider here: (1) to what extent certain types of people choose to embark on bureaucratic careers; (2) the impact of selection processes in selecting certain types from among those who seek to enter bureaucratic careers; (3) the extent to which personalities who do not fit the organisational environment drop out in the course of their careers; and (4) the extent to which success or failure in climbing a career ladder is associated with personality characteristics.

Merton and Marx are, of course, attempting to analyse systematically the widely accepted stereotype of the bureaucratic official. But because it deals with a stereotype the bureaucratic personality theory runs into difficulties. On the most superficial level, the public official's role is difficult to distinguish from the role played by a very high proportion of the employed persons in a modern complex society – in which case there is nothing very special about the role of the public official. On the other hand, if an attempt is made to analyse roles more deeply it will be found that distinctions can be made both between the many different roles in a public bureaucracy, and also between alternative adjustments to formally similar roles. It is in this sense that DeHart-Davis (2007) explores the social psychology of organisational behaviour, postulating the need to recognise circumstances in which 'unbureaucratic personalities' willing to bend rules may be salient in public organisations.

The bureaucratic personality theory is both too specific, in trying to single out certain kinds of organisational roles in a context in which most people are organisational employees, and too general, in implying the existence of uniformity of roles in organisations where such uniformity does not exist.

An important contribution to organisation theory that modern management training has taken seriously recognises that there are problems about creating over-submissive subordinates, and that there are advantages to be gained from having bureaucrats who are unwilling to be excessively bound by formal rules (McGregor, 1960; Argyris, 1964). Moreover, subordinates will resist over-formalisation, and so it may be said that they will try to avoid becoming bureaucratic personalities. This tendency may be reinforced by the fact that public sector employment is less secure in the modern world.

There is a secondary criticism of the theory which can be made that there is a tendency to assume the existence of a bureaucratic personality when in practice such behaviour may be a means of protecting the individual from total involvement in the work situation. On this theme a more recent vein of writing is more relevant. It focuses on the pressures upon bureaucrats, and helps to explore, more effectively than the bureaucratic personality theory, how policies become reshaped as public officials seek to bring some order into their own lives. This is the work on street-level bureaucracy by Michael Lipsky (1980) and his associates. For these writers the issue is not the apparent total rule conformity suggested by Merton but rather the way in which officials make choices to enforce some rules, particularly those which protect them, while disregarding others.

Street-level bureaucracy

The theory of street-level bureaucracy is set out in Lipsky's book of that title. It is further developed in work by two of his former research students, Weatherley (1979) and Prottas (1979). A later book that uses a broadly similar perspective is Maynard-Moody and Musheno's *Cops, Teachers, Counsellors* (2004).

Lipsky says of his own book:

> I argue that the decisions of street-level bureaucrats, the routines they establish, and the devices they invent to cope with uncertainties and work pressures, effectively become the public policies they carry out. (Lipsky, 1980, p. xii)

He argues that this process of street-level policy making does not involve, as might be hoped, the advancement of the ideals many bring to personal service work but rather the development of practices that enable officials to cope with the pressures they face. He says:

> people often enter public employment with at least some commitment to service. Yet the very nature of this work prevents them from coming close to the ideal conception of their jobs. Large classes or huge caseloads and inadequate resources combine with the uncertainties of method and the unpredictability of clients to defeat their aspirations as service workers. (ibid.)

Lipsky argues that street-level bureaucrats develop methods of processing people in a relatively routine and stereotyped way. They adjust their work habits to reflect lower expectations of themselves and their clients. They

> often spend their work lives in a corrupted world of service. They believe themselves to be doing the best they can under adverse circumstances and they develop techniques to salvage service and decision-making values within the limits imposed upon them by the structure of work. They develop conceptions of their work and of their clients that narrow the gap between their personal and work limitations and the service ideal. (ibid., p. xii)

Thus Lipsky handles one of the paradoxes of street-level work. Such workers see themselves as cogs in a system, as oppressed by the bureaucracy within which they work. Yet they often seem to the researcher, and perhaps to their clients, to have a great deal of discretionary freedom and autonomy. This is particularly true of the many publicly employed semi-professionals – people like teachers and social workers who secure a degree of that autonomy allowed to professional workers. These are the people in whose roles Lipsky and his colleagues are particularly interested in.

Lipsky analyses the paradox suggested above in the following way. He outlines the many ways in which street-level bureaucrats are able to manipulate their clients. He stresses the non-voluntary status of clients, suggesting that they only have limited resources inasmuch as the street-level bureaucrat needs their compliance for effective action (ibid., p. 57). This is a view supported by two other American writers, Hasenfeld and Steinmetz (1981), who argue that it is appropriate to see bureaucrat–client relationships as exchanges, but that in social services agencies serving low-status clients the latter have little to offer except deference. They point out, as does Lipsky, that 'clients have a very high need for services while the availability of alternatives is exceedingly limited' (Hasenfeld and Steinmetz, 1981, pp. 84–5). Accordingly, 'the power advantage social services agencies have enables them to exercise considerable control over the lives of the recipients of their services' (ibid., p. 85). Clients have to wait for help, experience 'status degradation', have problems in securing access to information, and are taught ways to behave (ibid., pp. 89–92). They possess a generally weaker range of tactics with which to respond.

Lipsky also stresses that the street-level bureaucrat cannot readily be brought under the control of a superior. He argues:

> The essence of street-level bureaucracies is that they require people to make decisions about other people. Street-level bureaucrats have discretion because the nature of service provision calls for human judgement that cannot be programmed and for which machines cannot substitute. (Lipsky, 1980, p. 161)

In this sense Lipsky portrays the street-level bureaucrat as making policy, carrying out a political role that determines 'the allocation of particular goods and services in the society' (ibid., p. 84). Weatherley summarises this view as follows:

> a view of policy as determining frontline behaviour is insufficient for explaining what workers actually do and why, and how their activities affect clients. Of course, teachers do teach, caseworkers dispense public assistance, public defenders defend indigent clients, and doctors treat patients, and their work activities are certainly responsive to public policy. But their activities are also responsive to a number of other influences over which the policy-maker and administrator may only have limited or no control. The pyramid-shaped organisation chart depicting at the bottom the front-line worker as passively receiving and carrying out policies and procedures dispensed from above is a gross oversimplification. A more realistic model would place the front-line worker in the center of an irregularly shaped sphere with vectors of differing size directed inward. (Weatherley, 1980, p. 9)

Lipsky is widely misrepresented simply as the writer who demonstrates how difficult it is to control the activities of street-level bureaucrats. If that was actually what he had to say, he could merely be seen as someone reinforcing the top-down control-oriented perspective. In those terms he is co-opted in support of the political Right's argument for market solutions to distribution problems, to circumvent the capacity of suppliers to control public monopoly services. In fact, however, what Lipsky says is rather different, indeed much more subtle. He speaks of the street-level bureaucrat's role as an 'alienated' one (Lipsky, 1980, p. 76), stressing such classic features of alienation as that work is only on 'segments of the product', that there is no control over outcomes or over 'raw materials' (clients' circumstances), and that there is no control over the pace of work. Lipsky also emphasises the 'problem of resources': street-level bureaucrats face uncertainty about just what personal resources are necessary for their jobs, they find that work situations and outcomes are unpredictable, and they face great pressures of inadequate time in relation to limitless needs.

Is there in Lipsky's work, therefore, an element of inconsistency, or can the contradictions in his analysis be explained? Perhaps he is providing a new variant on the Marxist dictum, 'Man makes his own history, even though he does not do so under conditions of his own choosing'. This is certainly partly the case. Street-level bureaucrats make choices about the use of scarce resources under pressure; contemporary fiscal pressure upon human services makes it much easier for officials to emphasise control than to try to put into practice service ideals.

But Lipsky does not really try to link his analysis to a macro-sociological perspective which would enable him to claim that the illusory freedom of street-level bureaucrats only operates as an instrument of class oppression and manipulation, and not in any other direction. His analysis, perhaps even more pessimistically, tends to show that the street-level bureaucrat's *freedom* to make *policy* is largely used to provide a more manageable task and environment. He talks of 'defenses against discretion', emphasising, as Smith (1981) and Zimmerman (1971) have, the extent to which street-level bureaucrats develop rigid practices which may be described by the observer as involving rule conformity even though the rules are imposed upon themselves. He stresses patterns of practice as 'survival mechanisms', a perspective that is echoed in a British study of social workers which, using older American theoretical work on organisational roles by Everett Hughes (1958), has a great deal in common with Lipsky's work. This is Satyamurti's (1981) study of English urban social work teams. There she speaks of the use of 'strategies of survival' by social workers under pressure which nearly always led people with the 'best of intentions' to do 'less for clients than they might have' and often behave in 'ways that were positively damaging' (Satyamurti, 1981, p. 82). The conclusion this literature comes to is that difficult work environments lead to the abandonment of ideals and to the adoption of techniques that enable clients to be 'managed'.

Lipsky argues that there is a problem about matching limited resources to apparently much greater needs that is recognised by all sensitive members of social services agencies. Accordingly, therefore, considerable efforts are made to prioritise need and to develop rational ways to allocate resources. The problem is that 'theoretically there is no limit to the demand for free public goods' (Lipsky, 1980, p. 81). Therefore it is important to accept that welfare agencies will always feel under pressure. Lipsky says that the resource problem for street-level bureaucrats is often irresolvable 'either because the number of people treated . . . is only a fraction of the number that could be treated, or because their theoretical obligations call for higher quality treatment than it is possible to provide to individual clients' (ibid., p. 37). Adjustments to caseloads further the quality of work but leave the worry about quantity, and vice versa. It is always possible to make out a case for new resources. Marginal changes in those resources will not necessarily result in visible changes in stress for individual workers.

This equally seems to provide support for the cynical cutting of caseloads. Certainly Lipsky suggests that this is how it is sometimes seen. An agency that has great difficulty in measuring success or providing data on quantity of 'output' is inevitably vulnerable to cutting. Lipsky cogently shows how this response heightens the feeling of stress for individual workers and thus intensifies recourse to the manipulation of clients. Retrenchment and redundancy are particularly threatening to the remaining vestiges of altruism in the human services. In this sense it may be suggested that incremental growth does little to relieve stress, but incremental decline intensifies it considerably.

A substantial section of Lipsky's analysis is concerned with the way in which street-level bureaucrats categorise their clients and respond in stereotyped ways to their needs. Lipsky speaks of these as 'psychological coping mechanisms' and elaborates the importance of simplified views of the client of his or her situation and of responsibility for his or her plight to facilitate this (Lipsky, 1980, Chapter 10). Many studies of the police have shown how distinctions are made there between different kinds of citizens which enable officers to develop responses in uncertain situations. In addition, stereotyping offers short-cuts to decision making on how to approach people, how to determine whether to act on suspicion and so on (for reviews of the literature on policy discretion, see Holdaway, 1983; Grimshaw and Jefferson, 1987; Reiner, 1992). Lipsky argues that such is the need for street-level bureaucrats to differentiate clients 'that it seems as useful to assume bias (however modest) and ask why it sometimes does not occur, than to assume equality of treatment and ask why it is regularly abridged' (Lipsky, 1980, p. 111). Giller and Morris (1981) offer evidence of similar stereotyping in British social work in their essay 'What type of case is this?' An issue that is related to simplifying assumptions in categorising different kinds of clients is the adoption of stereotyped responses to clients in general. The need to stereotype in order to cope may enhance tendencies towards racist and other prejudiced behaviour. This 'management' of complex decision situations can, depending of course on your point of view, have both benign and malign effects. Box 13.1 highlights some examples.

Box 13.1	Policy evolution in the hands of street-level bureaucrats

A Californian study shows that policy reforms requiring 'welfare' recipients to increase their labour market participation were largely ignored by workers who were primarily concerned with carrying out normal eligibility interviews. We see here a point emphasised by Elmore (1980) that the implementation of a new policy often needs to be seen as a demand which people may have difficulty in accommodating with their existing view about how their work should be done.

Another interesting example of street-level bureaucrat modification of policies they find difficult to put into practice comes from two studies of the ineffectiveness of a new provision in the US AFDC ('welfare') law that expected beneficiaries to be penalised if their children did not attend school regularly. Ethridge and Percy (1993) show that the policy was premised upon a 'rational actor' theory in which quite complex linkages were expected. They set this out in terms of steps in a logical chain: parents want to maximise AFDC payments, parents are able to monitor the school attendance behaviour of their children and interpret messages about this, parents are able to control the behaviour of their children, and the threat of sanctions will lead parents to take action. They go on to show how difficult it was for staff to operationalise these in practice. Stoker and Wilson (1998) focus more precisely upon flaws in the verification process for this policy. They explore how staff encountered weaknesses with the two alternatives, one at least of which was essential for verification: the transfer of administrative information from other agencies or the production of evidence from clients that they had complied with the requirements of the legislation. Clearly, whilst from one point of view these phenomena may be seen as 'disobedience' at the street level, from another they can be regarded as the improvement of a flawed policy.

Richard Weatherley (1979) specifically applies the street-level bureaucracy perspective to the study of the implementation of special education reform in the state of Massachusetts. A new law, enacted in 1974, required schools to operate much more sophisticated procedures for assessing needs for special education and to develop individualised programmes for children. The problem for staff was that they were required to do this without significantly more resources. 'Administrators were caught between the requirements to comply with the law, which they took quite seriously ... and the certainty that their school committees would rebel against expenditures that led to increased taxes' (Weatherley and Lipsky, 1977, p. 193). Accordingly, a response to the reform was developed which accommodated the new requirements without substantially disrupting established ways of working. Implementation involved the adjustment of the law to local needs and requirements (see also Hudson, 1989 for a discussion of the applicability of Lipsky's theory to similar policy contexts in Britain).

In many situations the notions that (a) laws need to be adapted to local needs and circumstances and (b) new laws are superimposed upon already established tasks can be taken further with the recognition that much action at the street level involves trying to integrate conflicting requirements. This point was made in general terms in Chapter 10, in exploring the case for the bottom-up perspective on implementation. Box 13.2 provides an illustration of this.

Box 13.2	Conflicting policy objectives in the management of public housing at the local level

The way in which staff involved in the management of public housing have to fashion practice in ways that accommodate conflicting policies is well explored by Chris Allen (2001) in a study of a public agency, Scottish Homes. The title of Allen's article sums up the issue very well: ' "They just don't live and breathe the policy like we do ...": Policy intentions and practice dilemmas in modern social policy and implementation networks'. The article described Scottish Homes as a 'multi-functional social policy institution' which has to pursue 'community care policy goals and regeneration policy goals in relation to disadvantaged communities' (p. 150) while, at the same time, having to have regard to 'value for money' considerations in the management of the housing stock. Allen does not then arrive at the simplistic conventional view that business goals will drive out social goals, but rather argues that progress towards the latter can be achieved insofar as 'sympathetic individuals' secure key positions in the system.

This point is taken further in contemporary literature that re-visits the 'representative bureaucracy' theme (see Chapter 9, Box 9.5). Where the earlier literature had raised questions closely linked to democratic theory, postulating that – inasmuch as civil services have power – they should be socially representative, this literature explores the predispositions of street-level staff in terms of the extent to which the way they exercise their discretion carries advantages (or disadvantages) for their clientele. This means they ask what the impact is of the ethnicity, gender or social class of implementers upon their decisions. A study of equal educational opportunities argues:

> Political forces (...) were able to influence policy outputs to benefit minority students. This political influence is indirect. Black school board members influence the selection of black administrators who in turn influence the hiring of black teachers. Black teachers then mitigate the impact of bureaucratic decision rules and provide black students with better access to educational opportunities. (Meier et al., 1991, pp. 173–4; see also Pitts, 2005)

Similarly, a study of loan allocations for rural housing shows the impact of variations in the number of staff from minority groups, between different offices, upon loans to people from that group (Selden, 1997). A study by Chaney and Saltzstein (1998) shows that female representation in police forces is positively correlated with active responses to domestic violence. Riccucci and Meyers (2003), in a review of this subject, make an important distinction between 'active' and 'passive' representation. The literature on passive representation explores the social or demographic characteristics of bureaucracies while the crucial question is:

> Are passive and active representation linked? That is to say, do ascribed characteristics of an individual ... relate to or predict policy preferences, as well as actions to achieve certain policy *outcomes*? (Riccucci and Meyers, 2003, p. 585)

Notwithstanding the continuing importance of Lipsky's analysis of street-level behaviour, it must be recognised that public administration is changing with the development of new technology (see Hudson and Lowe, 2004, Chapter 5 for a discussion of this). Tasks are structured and regulated by the use of information and communication technologies (Bovens and Zouridis, 2002). Since the actual functions of these technologies in terms of standardisation are contested, the concrete consequences for discretion and autonomy will depend on the type of street-level bureaucracy – and the category of functionaries working in them. Essentially, office technology shifts discretion around rather than eliminates it. This issue has been explored by Bovens and Zouridis (2002), who suggest that issues about discretion may be transformed as

> Public servants can no longer freely take to the streets, but are always connected with the organization via the computer. Client data must be filled in, with the help of fixed templates, in electronic forms. Knowledge management systems and digital decision trees have strongly reduced the scope of administrative discretion. (Bovens and Zouridis, 2002, p. 177)

Their analysis suggests that there may be a complex shift going on here, first to what they call the 'screen level' and subsequently to the 'system level'. Box 13.3 describes their illustration of this process using the example of student grants in the Netherlands. At 'screen level' there are issues about how data are interpreted and how special cases and complaints are handled. At 'system level' discretionary power is located in system design.

Box 13.3	**From street-level discretion, through screen level to system level: a summary of Bovens and Zouridis' (2002) analysis of the development of the administration of the system of student grants and loans in the Netherlands**

In the Netherlands a system of scholarships was established early in the twentieth century to assist 'gifted young people lacking financial means'. That system was very personalised, with officials interviewing applicants and following their progress through higher education. Decisions could depend upon comparatively arbitrary views of deservingness.

In the 1960s the system was 'mechanised' and gradually computers were more and more used for processing applications. 'By the early 1980s, the leeway available to the allocating officer had largely been reduced to accepting or rejecting the decisions proposed by the computer.' Later in that decade, 'form processors replaced allocating officers'. Discretionary elements only remained when there were appeals or complaints.

In the later 1990s the system changed again, to involve a wholly automated process of form completion and decision making. This is described as the shift to 'system level'. Bovens and Zouridis note, however, that what is disputed at this stage of policy evolution is the algorithms used for this process, which brings on to the agenda issues about public access to these and the right to contest them.

This is clearly an important development. While (as has been argued in various places earlier in this book) it may be questioned whether discretion can be entirely eliminated, these developments may be making the analyses of Merton and Morstein Marx more relevant for our understanding of the work of bored officials sitting behind computer screens or in call centres. At the same time, rather more attention needs to be given to a group of bureaucrats whose work has been comparatively neglected: the junior management staff who supervise street-level work, since much of the responsibility for decisions about how detailed data collection should occur lies with them. It should also be noted that system design is often in the hands of private companies working under contract to public authorities (for example, in the UK in respect of local administration of housing benefit).

The emphasis upon 'system level' in Bovens and Zouridis' work draws attention to another issue about street-level bureaucracy theory, the fact that

– as the term 'street-level' indicates – it puts the very front line in public organisations in the spotlight. The analysis in this book of the way in which policy is likely to be elaborated in various, often interactive ways, between the 'stages' of the process, suggests that the links between street-level bureaucrats and those above them in any hierarchy must not be neglected. In some respects, in particular, the roles of the direct line managers of those in the front line tends to be have been neglected. The public management literature is now beginning to rectify this neglect, with however a distinctly prescriptive perspective on the capacity of managers to enforce hierarchically determined goals (see, for instance, Riccucci, 2005). An interesting contribution to this topic that does not start from this perspective, however, is Murray's study of child protection in Scotland. There street-level behaviour, that might be deemed to involve disregard of policy, is shown to derive from assumptions of social workers about appropriate action which are shared by their immediate managers who tacitly condone this action (Murray, 2006). Murray also suggests that the perspectives of clients – even as in the case of her study 'involuntary clients' – also shape policy outputs (Murray, 2006, pp. 221–4). We return to the latter point in a discussion of 'co-production' in the next section.

Finally, thist last example from child care social work reminds us that it is important not to lose sight here of the comments made in Chapter 7 on different types of policy. Some policies are more readily routinised than others, and there are policies where there may be strong value systems or interests that resist routinisation. In his last chapter Lipsky connects his analysis of street-level bureaucracy with some of the discussion of professionalism in bureaucracy. Are professionals different, and can the enhancement of professionalism provide a corrective to the forms of bureaucratic behaviour outlined in Lipsky's analysis? The next section will suggest that the presence of professionals in bureaucracy can make some difference to the ways in which policy is implemented, but this does not imply that the answer to the normative question posed by Lipsky is a clear 'yes'. Professional power is a sub-category of bureaucratic power in this context, with some distinctive characteristics of its own which raise equally important questions.

Professionalism in the bureaucracy

Modern emphases upon flexibility within organisations seem to offer solutions to the problems about bureaucracy outlined by Merton, Morstein Marx and Lipsky. They suggest that organisational employees should be expected to have and use expertise, and be trusted by their managers to use discretion to tackle their work tasks in an adaptive way. In short, they should be 'professionals'. The paradox in this solution is that it conflicts both with that other modern theme, rooted in public choice theory, which sees public employees as untrustworthy and professionals as the most likely of all to distort the organisation in their own interests, and with a wider body of literature (from the Left as well as the Right) which has warned against professional power. Before we look at some more specific aspects of this issue we need to look at the standard analysis of professionalism.

Sociologists have made many attempts to define professions. An influential essay by Greenwood (1957) suggests that 'all professions seem to possess: (1) systematic theory, (2) authority, (3) community sanction, (4) ethical codes, and (5) a culture' (p. 45). However, this list of the attributes of a profession mixes occupational characteristics with societal treatment of that occupation. Systematic theory, ethical codes and culture fall into the former category, authority and community sanction into the latter. An analysis of professions needs at the very least to separate the occupational characteristics that give some groups high prestige (and corresponding power if they possess scarce and needed skills) from the way in which the state and society treat them. In practice there is a very complex interaction between these two groups of factors. It is more fruitful, therefore, to see a profession as an occupation whose members have had some success in defining 'the conditions and methods of their work . . .' and in establishing 'a cognitive base and legitimation for their occupational autonomy' (DiMaggio and Powell, 1983, p. 152).

With these considerations in mind, consider the case of medicine. Of course it is true that doctors possess expertise, and that the public, in its quest for good health, values that expertise. But much medical knowledge is accessible to all. What is therefore also important about the position of the medical profession today is that the state has given that profession a monopoly over many forms of care, allowed it to control its own education and socialisation process, and in many countries created a health service or health insurance system in which its decision-making prerogatives are protected (Harrison, Hunter and Pollitt, 1990; Moran and Wood, 1993).

There is a vein of writing on professions within organisations which sees professional power and autonomy as threatened by bureaucratic employment (see Wilensky, 1964). This is misleading, since professionals may secure dominant roles within organisations. Professionalism is often a source of power *within* organisations. The core of that argument is contained in the example of the doctors quoted above. They have succeeded in persuading politicians and administrators that the public will receive the best service if their discretionary freedom is maximised, and if they are given powerful positions in the organisations that run the health services.

The arguments about expertise, linked with both the emotive nature of our concerns about health and the social status that the profession acquired before medical services were provided on any large scale by the state, have reinforced that professional claim to dominance. Other, later established, professions with a weaker base in either expertise or social status have tried to claim similar privileges – teachers and social workers, for example.

Ironically, the argument about the role professions may play in bureaucracy has been fuelled by the contrast popularly drawn between the concepts of bureaucracy and professionalism. As Friedson (1970) has argued:

> In contrast to the negative word 'bureaucracy' we have the word 'profession'. This word is almost always positive in its connotation, and is frequently used to represent a superior alternative to bureaucracy. Unlike 'bureaucracy' which is disclaimed by every organisation concerned with its public relations, 'profession' is claimed by virtually every occupation seeking to improve its public image. When the two terms are brought together, the discussion is almost always at the expense of bureaucracy and to the advantage of profession. (Friedson, 1970, pp. 129–30)

Hence, professionals stress their altruism, arguing that they are motivated by an ethic of service which would be undermined if their activities were rigidly controlled. In some respects this is a question-begging argument. If public servants are given a high degree of autonomy their actions need to be motivated by ideals of service. The maintenance of ethical standards is important if a group of people have extensive influence on the welfare of individuals. However, the ethical codes of the major professions are often more concerned with protecting members of the group from unfair competition from their colleagues, or from 'unlicensed outsiders', than with service to the public. Moreover, even the public concept of 'good health' is to a considerable extent defined for us by the medical profession: in particular, the measures necessary to sustain it, or restore it when it is absent, are largely set out in terms of the activities of the medical profession when in practice many other aspects of our lifestyles and forms of social organisation are also important (Kennedy, 1981; Illich, 1977).

We trust and respect doctors, and ask them to take responsibilities far beyond those justifiable in terms of expertise. They are allowed to take decisions on when life-support systems may be withdrawn, to ration kidney machines and abortions, to advise on where the limits of criminal responsibility may lie and so on. Such powers have emerged gradually as a complex relationship has developed between the state, society and the profession. That relationship has been legitimated partly as a result of the evolution of the medical profession's ethics and culture and partly because those with power in our society have been willing to devolve authority to it (see Johnson, 1972). The two phenomena, moreover, are closely interrelated – internal professional control has made feasible the delegation of responsibility, but equally the latter has made the former more necessary to protect professional autonomy.

In this argument may be seen an elitist or structuralist perspective (see Chapter 2) in which a professional group is part of a ruling consensus, able to secure, or alternatively granted, privileges that ensure its dominance in a specific policy area (see Harrison and McDonald, 2008, Chapter 2 for a discussion of the applicability of this idea to medicine). Occupations like medicine are not simply accorded the status of profession by virtue of their own characteristics. Professional status cannot simply be won, as some of the aspirant occupations seem to assume, by becoming more expert and devising an ethical code. It depends upon the delegation of power, and on the legitimisation process in society. In the case of doctors that legitimisation process may well owe a great deal to our fears concerning ill health and to their special expertise; nevertheless, some theorists have argued that it must also be explained in class terms. Johnson (1972) and Parry and Parry (1976) have analysed the way in which medical power was established during the nineteenth century through a developing relationship with other powerful groups in society. It is clearly relevant, therefore, to ask questions about the comparable autonomy enjoyed by other established professions whose expertise is much more accessible (lawyers, for example). Dunleavy (1981) has provided an interesting analysis of the influence on public policy of one such group, architects, tracing the close connections between conventional professional wisdom and economic interests within the building industry.

The argument in defence of professional autonomy, that they possess inaccessible expertise, is not sufficient on its own. We need to look at the situations in which that expertise is used. There are two key issues here.

The first of these is *indeterminacy*, the extent to which it is impossible to predetermine the situations in which expertise will be needed. The complexity of the situations that doctors have to face, and the solutions to medical problems, are not always of a kind that can be programmed automatically. If they were we would merely have to enter our symptoms into a computer and it could offer solutions. Of course, in very many situations this is possible. The difficulty is that judgements may be needed where the solution is not obvious or there are reasons to distrust the obvious. Paradoxically, of course, indeterminacy is most evident when expertise does not offer ready solutions.

The second issue is *invisibility*, the extent to which detailed surveillance of work is impossible. Under an anaesthetic we have to trust the surgeon to react quickly to the unexpected. We cannot debate the implications of what has been found. It is equally inappropriate to have a manager looking over the surgeon's shoulder asking for an account of what is happening, or a medical committee waiting to be convened to debate the next step.

These two issues of indeterminacy and invisibility are not peculiar to the classic cases of professional decision making, as in medicine. They apply also to the police officer alone on the beat who comes upon the unexpected around a corner. Whilst the police are not seen as 'expert' in the medical sense, there is a similar issue here about ensuring that they are as well trained as possible, to enable them to deal with the unexpected. But the case of the police reminds us of the need to go back to the issue of community sanction. Despite all that the sociologists have reminded us about the potential for collusion between powerful groups, there seems to be a sort of social contract in which the decision maker is trusted to exercise discretion in situations that are indeterminate and invisible.

This concept of 'trust' is crucial – it was explored in Chapter 11 in relation to Fox's (1974) analysis of discretion in organisations. The argument against Fordism within organisations rests fundamentally upon the idea that desired creative responses to exceptional situations occur when individuals have been trusted to exercise discretion. Where it is hoped that public officials will play an active role in developing new approaches to their tasks and more sophisticated service to the public, there may be a strong case for granting them a high degree of autonomy. In individual services there is a need to make a choice between the case for a reliable service which can only be changed by initiative from the top and a less predictable service which may nevertheless be flexible in practice. The organisation that makes extensive use of professionals is one in which there is high expertise in the lower ranks, a complex task to perform, difficulties in developing effective patterns of supervision and a need for flexibility and openness to change. A strong group of arguments for autonomy come together. In this sense professionals are street-level bureaucrats who have been able to develop special claims to autonomy. But, as suggested above, they claim to differ from other public officials in that their relationships with their clients are governed by ethical codes and by altruistic values which others lack.

Analysing professional autonomy: Mashaw's approach

These questions about autonomy are important for accountability (which will be examined in the next chapter). These themes are linked together by Mashaw's work, in which he advances the notion of three 'models' of justice (1983, Chapter 2):

- the *bureaucratic rationality* model, which demands that decisions should accurately reflect the original policy makers' objectives;
- the *professional treatment* model, which calls for the application of specialist skills in complex situations and where intuitive judgements are likely to be needed;
- the *moral judgement* model, where fairness and independence matter.

The features of these three models are set out in Table 13.1.

Table 13.1   Task diversity and models of discretionary justice

Model	Primary goal	Organisation	Example
Bureaucratic rationality	Programme implementation	Hierarchical	Income maintenance
Professional treatment	Client satisfaction	Interpersonal	Medicine
Moral judgement	Conflict resolution	Independent	Pollution control

Source: Adapted from Mashaw, 1983, p. 31

Both the 'professional treatment' model and the 'moral judgement' model are offered as justifications for high discretion; in so doing they raise issues about alternative modes of accountability to that posed by 'bureaucratic rationality', where a combination of political and legal accountability can be deemed broadly applicable. It is Mashaw's second and third models that will therefore be discussed here.

The case for regarding professional treatment – particularly medical treatment – as a special kind of public policy process has been set out above in terms of the issues of expertise, indeterminacy, invisibility and trust. The case against this is that these issues are used to obscure professional power, and used to deliver a protected work environment, occupational control and high rewards. This is a long-running argument. To what extent is its configuration changing in favour of those who seek to exercise control over professionalism?

We have seen that it is possible to show that a high percentage of professional work situations do not involve indeterminacy and do not have to be invisible. The rare and unexpected diagnostic situations, the medical or surgical emergencies where it is not possible to stop to debate or to consult a protocol, form but a small percentage of many doctors' work. Television hospital dramas give us a distorted view of a profession that is much more routine much of the time. Protocols are increasingly being developed to govern medical decision making, offering rules for many situations and yardsticks against which actions can subsequently be judged. Computerised decision models are being developed for many conditions.

The consequence is that, as has already been stressed in the discussion of discretion in Chapter 11, professional treatment involves discretion within some sort of framework of what may loosely be called 'guidance'. It is important to see guidance as a continuum, with rules at the strong end and advice at the weak end. Concepts like 'codes' and 'directives' can be found towards the strong end and ones like 'pathways' and 'protocols' towards the weak end. There are issues, then, about determinacy or indeterminacy in relation to any activity which guidance seeks to structure. Thus, in medicine there are distinctions to be drawn between the relatively strong guidelines in relation to the administering of anaesthetics or the performance of some orthopaedic operations on the one hand, and the much weaker guidelines in relation to much psychiatric medicine on the other.

An important aspect to consider when looking at the impact of guidance is where the guidance comes from. The top-down model of public policy sees such guidance as structured through a sequence of measures with an Act of Parliament at its apex. But guidance may be simply ministerial advice about 'best practice'. Then within the professional treatment model the interesting thing about notions of best practice is that the source of guidance will often be from within the profession. Guidance may thus come from either the current professional consensus on practice or from research evidence. However, since the governance arrangements for public service professionals involve professional practitioners as staff within, or advisers to, government departments, a distinction cannot necessarily be easily drawn between guidance from government and guidance from the profession.

On looking at how guidelines affect occupational practice, there is also a need to give attention to the sanctions that follow from disregarding them.

We have to recognise that there is a variety of possibilities about how adherence to guidelines may be enforced:

- requirements for immediate reporting back to a superior;
- regular collection of monitoring data;
- intermittent inspections;
- attention to whether practice followed guidelines when something has gone wrong or complaints arise.

This is certainly not an exhaustive list. Enforcement of guidelines may involve all of these phenomena, or just some of them, or of course none at all. To make sense of the impact of a guideline these issues need attention alongside issues about what the guidance is trying to regulate.

There are also issues about who enforces guidance. The argument about self-regulation by professions concerns the extent to which enforcement of good practice can be delegated to the profession. However, alongside this there are issues (particularly evident in relation to the last of the items in the list above) about either the extent to which enforcement comes through a legal process and/or about the extent to which the public customers/consumers/beneficiaries of the service may have a role in the enforcement process.

Turning now to Mashaw's third model, while there may be doubts about his label for this model, 'the moral judgement model', it draws attention to many situations where the key official role involves regulation – a form of law enforcement where the state has prescribed or is seeking to control certain activities. Much that has been said about the professional treatment model also applies to this one. These activities may in general terms be described as 'professional' but they also have much in common with criminal law enforcement. Law enforcement is particularly difficult where there is an absence of unambiguous support for the enforcing agency. Studies of the police have drawn attention to particular difficulties where there is an absence of people who regard themselves as victims (drug and alcohol offences, prostitution and traffic offences where no one is injured) or where there are groups in the community that will try to protect the criminal. Public health inspectors, pollution control officials and factory inspectors, as law enforcement agents, have to operate in a similar way to the police. The difficulties that beset the police are even more likely to apply in relation to the wide range of civil law regulatory tasks that concern officials like this – where the 'offenders' see themselves as engaged in carrying out their legitimate business, not as polluters or producers of impure food, etc.

This model particularly highlights two other conditions which often apply to these regulatory situations. First, what is being enforced by the regulator is a standard – about unreasonably high levels of pollution, etc. – that is likely to be disputed. Second, there are likely to be conflicts of interest between those who are the source of the alleged problem and those who are affected by it. On top of all this, the second alleged 'interest' is often a latent one, because:

- either the 'victims' the regulators have a duty to protect do not know they have a problem (when, for example, pollution cannot be detected by the sense of smell, etc.);

- or they regard the problem as the lesser of two evils (when they perceive it as a choice between a polluted environment and employment – see Crenson, 1971; Blowers, 1984);

- or they are quite satisfied with a situation that others consider unsatisfactory (residents suffering from dementia in a poor-quality care home, for example).

The discussion of pollution control policy in Chapter 7 explored some aspects of these issues. In some cases the conflict is between a quite specific individual interest and a very general public interest. In all these situations enforcement is likely to be controversial and the enforcers may lack clear-cut forms of public support. In many systems professionals with regulatory responsibilities therefore work not with absolute rules but with principles about best practice established by expert officials and operationalised using discretionary powers (see Hill in Downing and Hanf, eds, 1983). The relationship between rules and discretion in these situations may involve 'framework laws', with officials and regulatees negotiating to fill in the details so that gradually the law becomes more codified.

What is often involved in these cases, given that officials need to work very closely with the objects of their regulatory activities, is a process of bargaining between regulator and regulatee (Peacock, 1984; Hawkins, 1984). Such bargaining will not merely deal with costs and consequences, but will also be likely to take into account past behaviour (has the compliance record of the regulatee been satisfactory?) and the likely impact of any outcome on the behaviour of others. Hanf has described this process as one of 'co-production' in which the determinants of regulatory behaviour need to be seen as 'embedded in the social worlds within and outside the regulatory agency' (Hanf in Hill, ed., 1993, p.109; Hanf in Moran and Prosser, eds, 1994). Whilst the field of pollution control provides particularly good examples of this 'co-production', it is also evident in other cases where complex activities are being regulated – the running of a private residential care home or nursing home, for example.

In both the professional treatment and the moral judgement cases there are reasons why systems are likely to have sought to find some sort of balance between rules and discretion in which both are significant. In this discussion key issues have been stressed which tip the balance in the discretion direction: indeterminacy, standards, trust and enforcement difficulties. It was noted at the beginning of this section that Mashaw's models particularly concern the link between different administrative tasks and forms of accountability. But in that case do they cover all the possibilities? Adler has argued that they do not do this. He points out that they 'have been challenged by a *managerialist model* associated with the rise of new public management, a *consumerist model* which focuses on the increased participation of consumers in decision-making, and a *market model* which emphasizes consumer choice' (2006, p. 622). We return to this in the next chapter.

CONCLUSIONS

Since the purpose of this book is to explore how public policy is made rather than to advance propositions about alternative ways of making or controlling it, to go beyond noting the phenomenon of professional power to the exploration of the extent to which it should be seen as a 'problem' would be beyond its brief. However, in Chapter 14 issues about ways in which attempts are made to secure accountability in public policy are explored, and there it will be necessary to return to these particular issues about professional power.

In this chapter street-level officials (of all kinds) have been identified as key influences upon policy outputs. The main reasons why this is the case were, of course, explored in the examination of rules and discretion in Chapter 11. But it has also been shown that these need to be analysed within their institutional contexts. This chapter has highlighted two rather different analyses of the phenomena, one which emphasises the passivity of officials and one which emphasises their active roles. There is no necessary contradiction here. Individuals, as Selznick has stressed (see pp. 69–71), are both constrained by the structures in which they work and shape their work roles in various ways in conformity with their needs and values. An examination of the roles of street-level bureaucrats can be seen as involving an exploration of the strengths and weaknesses of institutional theory. Action at the street level makes manifest institutional constraints while also demonstrating ways in which actors who seem to be in weak roles as organisational change agents can (and sometimes have to) nevertheless operate creatively.

14 Conclusion: evaluation and accountability

SYNOPSIS

This book is about the description of the policy process and not a prescriptive text. In this concluding chapter two concepts are addressed that belong essentially to the prescriptive branches of policy analysis.

Evaluation appears as a final stage in stages models of the policy process. Yet, while for any policy process with a concrete output the other stages will have occurred in some form (however coalesced or convoluted), it will very often be the case that there is no evaluation process. And, even when evaluation does occur the literature on that subject suggests that it is often seen as an unsatisfactory and problematical process with little in the way of substantive implications for subsequent activities. On the one hand, it is seen as something important for many versions of the 'rational model' of the policy process: a process of identifying whether something that was supposed to happen actually did happen. Traditionally, the evaluation literature puts the case for rational evaluation against the rough and tumble of the political context in which it occurred. The idea that a policy process should involve the explicit identification of objectives, translated as effectively as possible into action and thus susceptible to evaluation afterwards dies hard. On the other hand, in the real world of policy that ideal is rarely attained. All that will be provided in this chapter are observations on the efforts to solve the problems in relation to this presentation of the issues about the *process*.

The wish to evaluate and accountability are logically linked. Inasmuch as there is a view that someone should be in control of a policy process it is pertinent – even perhaps necessary – to examine whether that control was successfully exercised. This is most evident in that model of democratic politics that sees the policy process as the translation into action of the will of the people, but it is by no means absent from models that adopt a more complex view of what accountability implies. Here the examination of issues about accountability, which will follow a brief section on evaluation, will look at what is involved in processes of holding public officials to account and the ways in which this is an area of dispute. It will be shown that there are many forms of accountability, including those that supplement or challenge traditional top-down approaches. Then issues about the way professionalism poses problems for these models are explored, picking up on themes developed in the previous chapter. This takes the discussion on first to the extent to which new modes of accountability are embodied in the New Public Management (NPM) movement and second to some important ideas about direct accountability to the public.

A final section explores issues about both evaluation and accountability in the context of modern governance, recognising the way in which mixed modes of accountability often co-exist and pose questions of choice for public policy decision makers. In this way it will sum up the emphasis in this book on the diversity of policy issues and of policy process contexts, which leave issues about evaluation and accountability very much areas of dispute.

Evaluation

It is understandable that questions will be asked about what specific policies have achieved. There are obvious links between the desire to ensure that policy is 'evidence based' (a fundamental feature of the 'rational model' of policy formulation as set out by Simon, see Chapter 9, pp. 172–3) and the need to see what it has achieved, with a natural feedback cycle to subsequent policy improvement. There is no wish here to argue against that ideal, rather the question is: why does this occur so rarely in practice? Discussions of evaluation offer many answers to this question.

An important group of those answers concern themselves with social science methodology. For them the problems are rooted in issues like the difficulties of formulating a positive social science and using methods that facilitate the testing of policy impact. For those subscribing to positivist social science an important problem is the difficulty in developing, in the real world, an experimental situation. The model here is the controlled trial method used in medicine, with matched groups, one of which gets the new treatment to be tested while the other does not. In practice it is rare to have situations in which entirely arbitrary distinctions (based on controlled random selection) between who gets and who does not get the benefit of a new policy can be made. Logically some policies could not be evaluated in this way (excluding some people from general benefits, like the reduction of pollution), but it is also the case that ethical objections may be raised even when such approaches are possible and politicians will be unhappy about what are seen to be arbitrary exclusions from benefits. There is then a search for alternatives that come close to that: broadly matched areas (see Walker and Duncan's discussion of the use of this in the UK, 2007, p. 176) or designs that compare matched groups of people who could, but in fact did not, secure access to the benefits of the new policy.

Alternatives to rigorous experimental designs have, however, been criticised for the difficulties they experience in controlling key variables (see Spicker, 2006, pp. 173–4). An important issue here is embodied in a distinction that many evaluation researchers make between 'outputs' and 'outcomes'. Policy objectives are often expressed in terms of desired end states: reduction in poverty, air pollution, or unemployment etc. Throughout this book arguments have been advanced about the complexity of policy, and about the need to be sceptical about proclaimed policy goals. In any case the relationship between even the most explicit and controlled policy process and its achievements may be affected by events and changes in the real world on which the policy is expected to have an impact. In theory, quasi-experimental designs may try to avoid these problems – choosing very specific policy changes and adopting statistical techniques designed to isolate external influences – but they run into severe difficulties (Pawson and Tilley, 1997).

In the context of this book it would be digressing too far from the main concerns to discuss the extent to which it is possible to develop social science methodologies that overcome these problems. Moreover, such a discussion would take us into the bigger issue of the feasibility of positivist methodologies. This is of course one of the themes that have hovered in the background in many places in the book, and was explicitly addressed in Chapter 1 (pp. 8–12). It is only appropriate to address it further here inasmuch as another problem about evaluation studies is that there are difficulties in establishing agreed outcome variables. In policy interventions desired outcomes may be disputed. The customers of services may have expectations of services that are not shared by those who deliver them. Exceptionally, services may be designed to control behaviour rather than to deliver what people want. The choice of an outcome variable may require the researcher to recognise competing policy goals, and indeed perhaps even make a choice as to 'whose side I am on'.

This is, in fact, linking together a variety of approaches at various points between positivist and outright post-modernist perspectives. One of the theorists often identified with post-modernist work on public policy, Fischer, adopts an interestingly mixed approach in his text on evaluation. He explores the evaluation of a classic American policy intervention, the Head Start programme to enhance the educational achievements of disadvantaged children, showing how different conclusions can be drawn about its results in terms of four considerations (Fischer, 2006):

- 'verification': a typical positivist evaluation measuring the achievement of stated objectives (did the test scores of children in the experiment increase more than those not in it?);
- 'validation': raising issues about the relevance of the programme in terms of definitions of the problem it claims to address (recognising that Head Start might be about more than education performance, for example about reducing cultural exclusion);
- 'vindication': asking whether the programme contributes value for

society as a whole (raising questions about whether Head Start was an appropriate response to the issues about social exclusion);

- 'social choice': raising wider ideological questions about what the programme is trying to do (suggesting that there are wider questions about social exclusion in society and about the role education plays in relation to it).

The objective here is not to explore further the methodological challenge presented by Fischer's book but rather to note that his analysis highlights the fact that evaluation is in a broad sense a 'political' activity. It is here that we see the key to the issue raised in the Introduction that there is rarely a systematic connection between evaluation and policy improvement. It is interesting then to note how Walker and Duncan in an essay that may be seen broadly as making a case for evaluation observe:

> A moment's thought reveals that policy evaluation is not a necessary concomitant of a democratic system, especially an adversarial one such as exists in Britain. Politics is a battle for minds that is won by ideas and driven by ideology and the ballot box. Hence policies have not only to 'work', but also to be seen to work; public opinion is a key ingredient in the policy process. If politicians are ideologically committed to a policy, they may be less amenable to the 'wait and see' logic inherent in prospective evaluation (2007, pp. 169–70).

This leads Walker and Duncan down the practical road of seeing evaluation as a limited activity, part of the policy development process. This is described as 'formative evaluation', defined by Spicker as

> . . . undertaken at intermediate stages in the policy cycle. Formative evaluations can take place to see whether guidelines have been followed, whether an agency is ready to start work, to see whether an agency is being properly managed, or to see whether contract terms have been complied with (2006, p. 168).

This approach offers, of course, another challenge to the stages emphasis in much earlier writing about policy, and challenges the view of evaluation as a distinctive process.

In fact, of course, inasmuch as the policy process involves (as has been argued in many places in this book) continual processes of adjustment, anything other than formative evaluation may be very difficult. Consider the policy areas explored in Chapter 7, for example. In at least three of them: 'making war', 'trying to control the economy' and 'reorganising local government', there are complex inter-related processes of policy adjustment or interventions involving interactions with other activities (or both). In respect of these – and particularly the first named – evaluation seems to be likely to involve a speculative activity like that undertaken by some historians exploring how history might have been different had some fateful decision not been taken.

We need at this point to widen consideration of this topic to ask: when talk is of the need to 'see' in the above quote from Spicker, who is doing the seeing? In other words, in a policy process in which there are contending 'actors', what may those various actors gain from an evaluation process? For Knoepfel et al. (2007, pp. 243–9) policy evaluations represent a particular form of advice. Such evaluations may be made both by governments and by their opponents. There may also be variations in the extent to which they remain in an exclusive and narrow advisory context, providing information and recommendations for action solely at the disposal of the actor/actors who commissioned them or they may be made more widely available. There may also be variations in the ways that they are used strategically to support the status quo, to attack policy developments or to support the case for further change. Later in the chapter we will see how the collection of performance indicators, which can be seen loosely as a form of evaluation, looms large in modern public management. The word 'loosely' is used since these may often be seen as rather more measures of policy system outputs than of outcomes, and are thus – along the lines outlined by Fischer – very contestable evaluation indices.

However, in this way we are reminded that evaluation is also a political process. This leads radical analyses of evaluation to stress the case for adding other actors to those 'top' ones that are typically seen as in charge of policy evaluation to seek ways of securing participation in the evaluation process (Taylor and Balloch, 2005). This recognition of alternative 'stakeholders', however, may need a view of the place of evaluation in a democracy in which power holders may be to some extent prepared to pay for uncomfortable assessments of their activities. This is where we see a key connection between the issues about evaluation and the issues about accountability, since a claim is in fact being made here for a widening of accountability.

Accountability: introduction

Accountability has been described as 'probably one of the most basic yet most intractable of political concepts' (Uhr, 1993, p. 13). Thomas, in a review of its use, argues for its restriction to describe situations 'where an authoritative relationship exists in a formal sense' (Thomas, 2003, p. 555). Yet he recognises that there is a much wider usage:

The meaning of accountability has consistently widened over the years. The term is now frequently used to describe situations where the core features of an authoritative relationship and a formal process of enforcement are not necessarily present. Certainly, the public no longer sees accountability in strictly legal and organizational terms. For them, accountability is a broader professional, ethical and moral construct that is achieved only when public officials, both elected and appointed, serve with a commitment to do the right things. (Thomas, 2003, p. 550)

This widening involves two things. One of these is recognition of the complexity of the accountability relationship in the context of modern governance, with the range of intra- and inter-organisational complexities that have been explored in earlier chapters. This is therefore something that cannot be disregarded in this discussion. The other is a confusion of 'accountability' and 'responsibility'. Criticising this confusion, Gregory says: 'accountability is a matter of political and organizational housekeeping, whereas responsibility is often about moral conflict and issues of life and death' (2003, p. 558). While Gregory goes on to suggest that there are problems with accountability systems that disregard these wider issues, it is appropriate to adopt the perspective embodied in that quotation for this chapter since the concern here is with ways in which actors in the policy process are held to account, not with these wider ethical issues.

If one's starting point is a narrow rather than a wide definition of accountability, it must be recognised that 'accountability is an unapologetic bureaucratic concept' (Kearns, 2003, p. 583) that is particularly enshrined in traditional notions of representative government. In the study of public administration the accountability theme emerged early on in the efforts to separate politics and administration, rooted in the idea that in a democratic state politics should set the goals for administration to put into practice. This idea lives on, despite all the evidence that this distinction is difficult to make in practice. Hence, there is one approach to accountability, which we may still call the dominant one, which places politics, in the form of 'top-down' representative government, in the driving seat.

This approach to accountability is accompanied by a legalistic view of what gives policy action legitimacy, that it should be within the framework of the 'rule of law'. This can involve, in some of the more philosophical approaches to this topic, notions like principles of 'natural' or 'common' law which derive from universal principles independent of the actions of governments (a view that features significantly in discussion of human rights and international legal principles). But in many cases legitimacy is seen as lying in the extent to which action is authorised by either constitutional rules or specific legislation. Both of these are in the last resort 'top-down' mandates, the product of what are seen as legitimate political processes.

Therefore, the dominant approach to accountability can be seen as a 'top-down' one, normally buttressed by some notion of representative democracy. However, if representative democracy is to be really meaningful it needs to be recognised that the ultimate accountability of governments is to the people. In the face of deficiencies in the doctrines of representative government there are claims that people should have direct control over policy processes in ways other than, or additional to, representative democracy. Embodied in these propositions is a great deal of complexity, which could take us into issues in political philosophy well beyond the brief of this book. What is clear is that, as far as policy processes are concerned, claims that functionaries should be accountable to *the government* are still very much in evidence.

Alongside the democratic challenge to top-down accountability will be found two other forms of accountability: bureaucratic and professional. Pollitt defines the former as 'accountability to the codes and norms within the bureaucratic context' and the latter as 'accountability to the standards laid down by one's professional body' (Pollitt, 2003, p. 93). Both of these have come under attack as involving a rejection of the democratic forms of accountability. The defence to this charge involves arguing that they embody apolitical notions of direct duty of service to the public. In that sense doctors, for example, may argue that they are accountable to their patients for the service they provide and to their peers who monitor those standards of service. But that brings us close to the widening of the concept of accountability to embrace responsibility as well, a moral responsibility that overrides ordinary accountability.

It is not proposed to evaluate here the justifications on offer for the various forms of accountability – the point here is to acknowledge that accountability is a complex and contested concept. Box 14.1 summarises the various forms of accountability.

All of the forms of accountability, including the direct democratic one, are often expressed in relatively simplistic top-down forms. What is meant by this is that executive bodies – prime ministers and cabinets, elected rep-

---

| Box 14.1 | Forms of accountability |

- Political – direct accountability to elected representatives (recognising that these arrangements may be complex since often there are alternatives – presidents and parliaments, central and local governments, etc.).

- Hierarchical – accountability to the 'head' of an organisation, a version of accountability that is often embodied in the political concept of accountability; but since the one does not logically embrace the other this should not be taken for granted.

- Direct democratic – direct accountability to the public (complicated by issues about who the public are in particular cases: patients, parents, pupils, tenants, etc. or everyone, and by the fact that these will be in specifically defined geographical areas).

- Legal – forms of accountability that may be secured through the courts. This may be a reinforcement to political accountability but there will be situations in which legal legitimacy overrides political legitimacy.

- Professional – governed by profession-related principles which, like some legal ones, may be considered to override political accountability.

- Bureaucratic – normally a derivative from political, hierarchical or legal accountability but may be seen in some cases to involve overriding 'responsibilities' similar to those embodied in some versions of professional accountability.

resentatives of parents, etc., supreme courts, professional governing bodies, bureau chiefs – demand that others are accountable to them. The very complexity of the policy process and of modern governance makes the achievement of any simple form of accountability difficult.

Accountability to the top: the political model

Brown sets out the importance of the top-down perspective for public administration in Britain in the following way:

> The formal characteristic of any public service is that in the last resort a lay politician carries responsibility for it to an elected assembly. There is a chain of command leading from the bedside and the local insurance office to the front bench in the House of Commons. In the personal social services the chain leads first to the committee room in county hall and then, because of his overall duty to guide the development of the service, to the secretary of state.
>
> These lines of accountability give the public, through its elected representatives, the opportunity to question and influence the operation of public services. They provide constitutional channels through which grievances can be ventilated. In the very last resort they provide a means through which the electorate can withdraw support from an administration whose policies it dislikes, and substitute one more to its liking. This is the ultimate sanction in public administration . . . (Brown, 1975, p. 247)

Brown is right to emphasise how this is the starting point for most discussions of accountability. He then, of course, goes on to recognise the limitations to this approach, saying: 'A moment's reflection, however, suggests that this needs to be supplemented in some directions and perhaps qualified in others if services are to be efficiently administered in the public interest' (ibid.). Day and Klein similarly, in an exploration of the 'career' of the concept of accountability, chart a progression from 'simple to complex models' (1987, Chapter 1).

A recognition of these complexities has characterised the analysis of public administration at least since Woodrow Wilson's classical essay (1887) on the distinction between politics and administration. While that has been seen as supporting the view that administration must be subordinate to politics, it in fact sought to prescribe a way of separating the two in the context of the realities of American politics. Wilson sought thus to combine democratic accountability with efficient administration. He was both identifying an important problem about administrative accountability and recognising that the United States faced great difficulties in coming to terms with a set of institutional arrangements that made political problem solving very difficult.

The alternative view on his politics/administration dichotomy is that this is a distinction that bears little relation to the reality of political and administrative behaviour. Evidence for this has been explored in various places in this book. But what is important about Woodrow Wilson's perspective is the way his ideal division influenced thinking about the management of government. It finds resonances not just in discussion of representative democracy but also in arguments about the 'rule of law', the concern of the next section.

The legal model of accountability and the problem of discretion

Two key ingredients in the 'rule of law' according to Wade (1982, p. 22) are:

1. 'that everything must be done according to the law', which when applied to the powers of government means that 'every act which affects the legal rights, duties or liberties of any person must be shown to have a strictly legal pedigree. The affected person may always resort to the courts of law, and if the legal pedigree is not found to be perfectly in order the court will invalidate the act, which he can then safely disregard';
2. 'that government should be conducted within a framework of recognized rules and principles which restrict discretionary power'.

The particular way those principles are enunciated by Wade may have characteristics that are peculiar to Anglo-Saxon countries, but the general thrust of the principles is accepted wherever it is claimed that governments operate within the 'rule of law'.

The importance of the 'rule of law' as a basis for legitimate rule is explored in Weber's third type of authority: 'rational-legal'. This was examined on pp. 218–20. Weber argues (in a text originally put together in the early years of the twentieth century):

> Today the most usual basis of legitimacy is the belief in legality, the readiness to conform with rules which are formally correct and have been imposed by accepted procedure. (Weber, 1947, p. 131)

Weber goes on to distinguish a social order derived from voluntary agreement from one that is imposed – but he calls this distinction 'only relative'. The first of the ideas which he sees as central to the 'effectiveness' of legal authority is:

> That any given legal norm may be established by agreement or by imposition, on grounds of expediency or rational values or both, with a claim to obedience at least on the part of the members of the corporate group. This is, however, usually extended to include all persons within the sphere of authority or of power in question – which in the case of terri-

torial bodies is the territorial area – who stand in certain social relationships or carry out forms of social action which in the order governing the
corporate group have been declared to be relevant. (ibid., p. 329)

In this rather convoluted argument, of course, lies the concept of the state.
The second idea is that:

> every body of law consists essentially in a consistent system of abstract
> rules which have been intentionally established. (ibid., p. 330)

Thus issues about the legitimacy of official rules, and the related discretions
they may explicitly or implicitly convey, may be disputed with reference to
their specific source, to their constitutional context or to wider principles.
However, this is not a simple matter.

In Britain the absence of a written constitution gives debate about public
law a peculiar shape which derives from the fact that the primary source of
law is Parliament. The central concern is with whether the rules applied by
public officials have the formal sanction of Parliament and whether depar-
tures from those rules (discretion) are formally authorised (or not formally
proscribed) by statute. A secondary concern is with the capacity of the court
system – as supplemented in the modern world by simpler grievance procedures such as tribunals and ombudsmen – to respond in situations in
which citizens (singly or in organised groups) regard official behaviour as
falling outside those statutorily determined boundaries.

The peculiarities of the British system (shared of course by some
Commonwealth countries) contrast with those of countries with written
constitutions and a supreme adjudicative body entrusted with the protection and interpretation of that constitution. In such countries, an additional
test of the legitimacy of any policy process related action will be its compatibility with the constitution. However, that contrast is not as stark as it may
seem. The absence of a written constitution should not be understood to
imply the absence of a constitution (see King, 2007). While historically
British judges have taken a very cautious view of their responsibilities in this
respect, in the last quarter of the twentieth century they began to take a
more active view. This was then reinforced by the extent to which membership of the European Union required the UK to give attention to European
law, and even more significantly by an Act of Parliament, the Human Rights
Act (1998), which incorporated the European Convention on Human Rights
into UK law, with the implication that the judges could scrutinise the compatibility of new laws with the provisions of that Act.

However, much of the detailed role of the law in dealing with accountability concerns questions about the extent to which powers exercised by
administrators have been formally authorised by government. It thus particularly deals with administrative discretion. Hence, what the law textbooks
provide is a portrait of the law as trying to keep administrative discretion
under control. In so doing the law is presented as the defender of the citizen
against the arbitrary exercise of power. Wade (1982) perceives administrative

law as an attempt to ensure that the 'whole new empires of executive power' conform to the principles of liberty and fair dealing. This perspective leads Wade to argue that the key issue is ensuring that the law can control 'the exercise of the innumerable discretionary powers which Parliament has conferred on the various authorities' (p. 4). His emphasis is on ensuring that such authorities do not act *ultra vires* by exceeding their statutory power or following the wrong procedures. Authorities cannot escape such control by being offered statutes that give them unlimited power, since 'in practice all statutory powers have statutory limits, and where the expressed limits are indefinite, the courts are all the more inclined to find that limits are implied. The notion of unlimited power has no place in the system' (ibid., p. 50). While it is clearly possible to see in this view of the rule of law a control over arbitrary government, it is largely transformed into a notion of control over arbitrary administration.

Two things further complicate this boldly stated application of the model of the 'rule of law'. One is the difficulties citizens experience in using the law to protect themselves from the executive. The other, very much within our terms of reference, is that these so-called statutory powers are very complicated. One view, abandoned by any realistic critic of the British legislative system at least 50 years ago, was that all rules should be embodied in formal Acts of Parliament. The reality is that there is a great deal of subordinate rule making – not only in 'regulations' which are hypothetically open to parliamentary scrutiny, but also in a variety of departmental guidance circulars, codes and working instructions to officials. These were a key concern of the discussion of policy formulation in Chapter 9.

The very institutional complexity of the policy system means that there is a wide range of bodies which have responsibilities to interpret and perhaps amplify their statutory mandates. Hence, it is not possible to draw a simple distinction between statutory rules deriving from the legislature and the discretion of officials. The intermediary departments, agencies, local governments and so on, which, from the old-fashioned perspective, can be seen as discretionary actors themselves, engage in subordinate rule-making processes. A considerable body of case law governs these processes.

Traditionally, British administrative law textbooks give attention to administrative discretion as a 'taken for granted' phenomenon within the political system. They point out that the concern of the courts has been with (a) whether or not the discretionary powers that are exercised have been clearly delegated by statute; (b) whether the exercise of those powers is within the boundaries of natural justice (are they exercised reasonably and with regard to due process?); and (c) the principle that if a statute grants discretionary powers then the officials using them should not devise rules which in practice fetter that discretion.

So the 'rule of law' approach to the issue of accountability primarily reinforces the top-down model of accountability, embodied in the notion of the primacy of politics in a context of representative democracy, but it may suggest that there should be wider principles to which citizens can appeal. It sets up a tension between accountability to 'Parliament' and accountability to the 'courts', which takes its most clear form in the way in which the American constitution gives the Supreme Court a superordinate role. It has led to recognition that the Supreme Court can be in some circumstances a 'policy maker'. A corresponding interesting feature in Europe is the role of the European Court, which is reinforced by an international search for ways of specifying and enforcing universal human rights.

This excursion into issues about legal control over policy introduces something else: concerns about the extent to which law may be comparatively impotent in the face of the complex issues of administrative discretion. A recognition of the limits to legal control over administration as well as the limits to top-down political control stimulates a search for other models of accountability. The debate about this has particularly centred on issues about professionalism.

Accountability, discretion and professionalism

The last chapter explored the arguments about professional discretion, showing how a case for professional autonomy has been made. That case tends to be most strongly made in relation to the role of medical doctors. Medical autonomy is traditionally defended in terms of the sanctity of the doctor/patient relationship and the needs of good medical practice. In this argument the most important form of accountability is seen as being to the patient, but it takes the paternalistic form of suggesting that the doctor's expertise enables him or her to determine what is in the patient's best interests. This is reinforced by arguments about indeterminacy in many situations and about the need for a relationship of 'trust'. A wider protection is then alleged to be offered by the fact that the doctor's behaviour is subject to scrutiny by his or her professional 'peers', who were given responsibility (by the state) for training and accreditation, and have the power to take disciplinary action against malpractice.

However, individual clinical decisions are not merely the concern of the practitioner, the profession and the patient, at least as far as publicly financed medicine is concerned. In a situation of resource constraints (which must be regarded as a normal situation for a publicly financed health service), a response to the needs of any patient involves claims on scarce resources. It must thus – taking an overall view – be to some extent at the expense of a response to others. This issue comes to the fore most poignantly where there is manifestly a lack of resources relative to an identified need – as is the case with very expensive but comparatively unused medicines, various forms of treatment for kidney disease, or in a hard-pressed emergency unit. It is also present inasmuch as there are cost differences between professionals who carry out ostensibly the same practices. Concerns about these issues are then heightened by the fact that there are often waiting lists for treatments and operations. Overall, it may be contended that there is a ubiquitous requirement for all clinical work to be planned and organised against a backcloth of resource issues, which are surely public concerns.

If the need for wider public control is conceded, the question then becomes: who is to do the controlling? Here we find, alongside straightforward top-down arguments for political and legal control, some alternatives (or some combination of them): lay managers, professionally qualified managers, other professional colleagues and patients. There are problems with accountability in respect to each of these groups.

Clearly, the standard control model for the policy process involves appointed managers working within a remit supplied by politicians. The intense need for cost control over services like health has increased the propensity to see lay managers as having a key role to play. This view has been reinforced by the availability of new technologies (computerised medical records, systems to identify the costs of 'normal' medical procedures like those offered by the identification of 'diagnosis related groups' (DRGs), etc.).

This approach to the management of professional activity is opposed by two alternatives. One is control by managers who are drawn from the ranks of the service professionals themselves. There has been a long-standing argument about this approach to the management of professionals: do these managers retain their old professional loyalties or become co-opted to the ranks of the lay managers? There seems good reason to believe, confirmed by research led by Degeling (Degeling et al., 1998, 2003) that the truth lies somewhere between these two positions. These 'managers' obviously offer scope for the development of a more sophisticated, shared accountability, but they do not, of course, open up the system to public accountability in the widest sense.

The other alternatives are variations of this. These are either the creation of a cadre of people who are involved in management but still practising their profession, or collective self-management through collegial shared participation. This is a managerial model widely favoured by professionals. However, there are well-founded suspicions that – particularly when review processes are not shared outside the professional group (medical audit, for example: Harrison and Pollitt, 1994) – this approach to management preserves traditional professional domination. There are also questions about whether this is an efficient use of members of an expert workforce.

This discussion has deliberately focused on the doctor/patient relationship, but the arguments explored are also applicable to other, similar, relationships, such as those between teacher and pupil. A view that the case of professional autonomy is weaker outside the medical profession has been embodied in arguments that in many cases it is more appropriate to speak of semi-professions rather than professions (Etzioni, 1969).

All the managerial approaches to increasing the accountability of professional service groups involve the development of performance indicators. The use of these can be seen as a particular feature of modern approaches to accountability, embodied in concepts of new public management. These will be explored next (we return to issues of direct accountability to patients, etc. later).

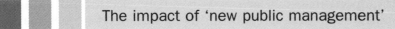

The impact of 'new public management'

It has been difficult to decide where to include a discussion of 'new public management' (NPM) in this book. Inasmuch as the NPM movement has been motivated by concerns about accountability, this is the appropriate place. However, while issues like control over professional autonomy have been one of the movement's preoccupations, this has been accompanied by a concern that the obvious alternative to this autonomy, top-down control of a bureaucratic kind, is also inadequate. In this respect, this discussion might have been included in Chapter 11, where the sociological work on the deficiencies of the top-down model was outlined, or in Chapter 13 where issues about street-level autonomy were examined. NPM is a response to dilemmas about public bureaucracy that go back at least as far as Max Weber's time, and it draws upon the sociological analysis of organisations stimulated by Weber's work and by the arguments about Taylorism or Fordism as well as the rational choice critique of organisational behaviour. In discussing it here, then, it is important to recognise the potential contradiction within NPM between a strong stress on accountability and a rejection of traditional forms of top-down control.

Hood (1995) identifies seven 'doctrines' to which 'Over the last decade, a "typical" public sector policy delivery unit in the UK, Australia, New Zealand and many other OECD [Organization for Economic Cooperation and Development] countries would be likely to have had some exposure' (p. 4). These ideas have travelled quickly from country to country, promoted by fashionable 'gurus'. Hood does not mention the United States, but perhaps the most influential of all the NPM tracts, a book by Osborne and Gaebler (1992), comes from that country. The seven doctrines Hood identifies are set out in Box 14.2.

Box 14.2 | **Hood's summary of NPM 'doctrines'**

1. 'Hands-on professional management in the public sector'
2. 'Explicit standards and measures of performance'
3. 'Greater emphasis on output controls'
4. '... disaggregation of units in the public sector'
5. '... greater competition in the public sector' (to this may be added actual privatisation)
6. '... private sector styles of management'
7. '... greater discipline and parsimony in resource use'.

Source: Based on Table 1 in Hood, 1995, pp. 104-5

In some respects the expression NPM is simply useful shorthand for a variety of innovations, widespread across the world, which are 'dominating the bureaucratic reform agenda' (Hood, 1991, p. 3). There is a danger that the use of this shorthand expression may convey the sense of a unified and compatible set of initiatives. In a later essay (1995), despite having established himself as the leading analyst of the phenomenon, Hood attacks the view that NPM is a 'new global paradigm' and highlights some of the inconsistencies within the work of its leading exponents.

Hood indicates that NPM has been attacked for its concern to place issues about efficiency before equity (Pollitt, 1990), but he argues that NPM advocates would assert that efficiency 'can be conceived in ways which do not fundamentally conflict with equity' (Hood, 1995, p. 20, citing Wilenski, 1986). This takes us into value issues which are not the concern of this discussion.

However, the issues about the relationship between efficiency and accountability *are* relevant here. Some of the NPM movement's concerns come directly from the rational choice attack (see Chapter 5) upon traditional public bureaucracy which links the two. But others – notably (1) and (4) in Hood's list – have their roots in Peters and Waterman's (1982) concerns about human relations in the organisation and the desire to create organisations where 'excellence' can be achieved by a committed workforce left to perform delegated tasks without undue surveillance. This seems to conflict with the rational choice view that public sector managers cannot be trusted to operate autonomously. A particular feature of NPM in practice has been an attack upon the traditional autonomy claims of the established professions – medicine, teaching, etc. Paradoxically, the new 'hands-on professional' managers are seen as a countervailing force to the traditional professionals (Hoggett, 1996).

If the ideas are taken together as a package, these conflicts may be resolved to the satisfaction of the New Right perspective by stressing that market discipline imposes its own accountability. Managerial autonomy does not enable managers to 'buck the market'. Others, like the 'aristocratic' old professions, it is argued, must also learn to come to terms with market discipline. But this presumes that real market discipline can be established in a public service.

Hence, for others not wedded to the New Right perspective or unconvinced about the feasibility of creating a market, this mixture of measures seems to preserve the autonomy of those 'hands-on' managers at the top while ensuring the efficiency of response by lower-level workers to their demands through the increased insecurity entailed in the combination of strict standards and competition from alternative providers (Hoggett, 1996). Relevant here is Pollitt's summary of the impact of NPM (2003, Chapter 2), in which what is particularly stressed is its emphasis upon the use of performance targets to impose accountability. In that sense NPM can be seen as an effort to secure tight controls over public organisations without recourse to traditional bureaucracy.

A characteristic of NPM in the United Kingdom (and probably in Australia and New Zealand too) is that it has been very much a 'top-down'

movement. Reform of central administration has not involved decentralisation. The 'disaggregated units' Hood refers to have been subject to tight
controls. There are grounds for arguing – with respect to the development of
quasi-autonomous agencies – that the operational freedom of these consists
merely of a freedom to take the blame. At the lower levels British local government experienced since 1985 steadily tightening financial control,
strong steering to ensure that its interpretation of NPM was compatible with
that of the government, and requirements to accept and stimulate competition that weakened its capacity to respond to local political forces (Walsh,
1995; Butcher, 2002; Hoggett, 1996; Deakin and Walsh, 1996).

Research evaluations of the key developments have been slow to emerge
and have produced equivocal findings (see Pollitt, 2003, Chapter 2). There
are grounds for believing that the achievements of NPM will be limited.
Realistic competitive 'markets' are hard to create. The evidence for this
comes from studies of the behaviour of the private sector – here the discussion of transaction costs (pp. 247–8) is relevant. There are strong reasons
why actors will try to secure long-run, stable, non-competitive relationships.

The 'search for excellence', or 'reinvented government', has involved an
attempt to put a 'post-Fordist' form of administrative organisation into place
to combat the bureaucratic 'diseases' associated with traditional hierarchies.
Yet there is a conflict between this remedy for inefficient government and
'rational choice' theory, which sees bureaucratic autonomy as a key cause of
the uncontrollable growth of government. It is also necessary to note the
conflict between the case for the flexible organisation in which staff have
high discretion and the use of rules to secure accountability.

The solution to this dilemma has been seen to involve two ideas. One of
these is that control should deal with broad general parameters, leaving
much detail to be settled at the 'street level'. This is the idea of the
loose/tight organisation of 'steering' not 'rowing' (Osborne and Gaebler,
1992). Steering is seen as involving the setting of the financial framework
and the specification of a range of incentives (Kickert, 1995, pp. 149–50). It
must be questioned how much this is really new, and how much it is
merely another approach to analysing the hierarchical structure of discretion, explored in relations to the points quoted from Simon and from
Dunsire in Chapter 11 (see also Hoggett's criticism of Kickert, 1996).
Nevertheless it does suggest the need for the co-existence of two forms of
accountability.

The other approach to control involves emphasis upon retrospective controls requiring the collection of information on performance, hence
bringing the discussion back to issues about evaluation. Rewards or sanctions are applied on the basis of such data. The crucial sanction may be the
termination of a contract if a quasi-market system is operating. Some commentators on British public policy in the 1990s have seen developments of
this kind as a retreat from accountable public administration (Baldwin,
1995). Others have seen it as a rather bogus loosening of control – taking out
some actors who might have played a role in accountability such as local
government (see Glennerster, Power and Travers, 1991) – whilst financial

constraints and fear of sanctions reinforce strong central control (Deakin and Walsh, 1996). Some forms of managerial control have been enhanced at the expense of professional autonomy, particularly where those managers hold values compatible with the pro-market 'right' (Hoggett, 1996). Clarke and Newman (1997) have seen 'new managerial regimes as producing a field of tensions', an 'unstable settlement between bureau-professional power and the new managerialism' (Newman, 2001, p. 31).

At the same time it is still necessary to draw another lesson about the use of rational devices in the control of administrative behaviour, for example management by objectives and quantitative staff assessment, from Blau's old study (1955). He demonstrates how performance indicators used in the evaluation of work may distort bureaucratic behaviour. Individuals not only set out to cook their own performance statistics but choose to emphasise those activities that will maximise the score achieved by themselves and their agency. It is through the use of output rather than outcome measures, whose collection and analysis is facilitated by computer technologies, that much retrospective control over discretion is sought. This is one of the ingredients in the curious mix of apparent neo-Fordism with a reversion to Fordism in the public sector (Pollitt, 1990; Hoggett, 1996).

Some activities are much more easily measured than others, hence performance indicators that offer a distorting impression of a public service activity as a whole may come to have an excessive influence. Allied to this issue is the fact that some of those measurements most likely to impress are those that embody data on costs or can be translated into money terms. Therefore issues about effectiveness in education have often been translated quite spuriously into indicators of 'value added' for individuals and/or the national economy (Wolf, 2002).

Measurement activities may empower another group of people: experts in measurement and other forms of auditing. Such people may be every bit as difficult to bring under accountability systems as the people whose activities they measure. Hence, Power has exposed some of the problems with auditing, raising questions about how auditors are audited (or more often, how they are not audited) (Power, 1997). Overall, what may be occurring is the enhancement, at the expense of professional service staff, of the power of those who monitor and measure their work, creating new kinds of 'professional dominance' among accountants, lawyers and managers (see Alford, 1975 and Ham 1992, on 'corporate rationalisers', and developments of this theme in Harrison, Hunter and Pollitt, 1990 and in Flynn, 1993).

The NPM movement claims to have ways to deal with these issues, but the discussion of their complexity suggests reasons to be sceptical about those claims. This is supported by Hood's analysis of the extent to which management changes under the influence of NPM produce 'side-effects and even reverse effects'. He borrows Sieber's (1981) notion of 'fatal remedies' – 'producing the opposite of the intended effect' – to analyse these (Hood, 1995, pp. 112–16). Among them the erosion of trust and the adverse effects of elaborate rule structures and reporting requirements loom large (see also Power's attack on 'the audit explosion', 1997). The next section explores an alternative way to increase sensitivity to the issues about accountability options.

Consumer control as an alternative

A set of alternative ways of conceptualising NPM have been put forward which recognise the force of the Peters and Waterman (1982) critique of bureaucracy and accept the importance of performance measures as indices to be shared with the public but reject the market orientation of much of the rest of the thinking. This approach tackles the issue of accountability not by the adoption of market devices but by trying to put bottom-up notions of accountability in place of the traditional top-down ones (Stewart and Clarke, 1987; Hoggett, 1991).

A good approach to exploring this issue is offered by Hirschman's (1970) analysis of the options available to consumers (in both public and private systems) as being 'exit, voice or loyalty'. This approach, which can be seen as related to ideas about the use of 'rational choices' by people (see Chapter 3), suggests that the exit option is the simplest. But is it easy to use and does it effectively secure accountability to consumers?

A feature of NPM that has been noted is the development of competition within public services, either through competitive arrangements within these or by allowing private providers to offer public services. It is important to note that the exit option depends not just upon the availability of alternatives but also on information about what these alternatives actually offer. Constraints are also imposed by the fact that exit carries 'transaction' costs for consumers (getting appropriate information, negotiating changes and adapting to new arrangements). Market systems are more likely to provide realistic choices at the point at which people start consuming a service – choose a doctor, a hospital or a school, for example – rather than when they are already consuming it. In this sense it is not so much 'exit' options that people have in systems of public choice as 'entry' options. These points are particularly pertinent as far as health and social care services are concerned.

'Voice', the alternative to exit, involves seeking ways to increase 'grass-roots' public accountability through forms of participation. Perhaps the chief characteristic of this approach has been to seek to establish ways of decentralising decision making to the local government level or below it (particularly where, as in the UK, local authorities are large).

This leads us to an approach to professional accountability that has been widely canvassed, one which offers a combination of political accountability and accountability to consumers by stressing localised 'political' control mechanisms. Thus Lipsky argues for a new approach to professional accountability in which there is more emphasis upon client-based evaluation of their work (Lipsky, 1980, final chapter). Similarly, Wilding (1982) writes of the need to realise 'a new relationship between professions, clients and society' (p. 149), precisely because others have so little control over them. Stewart and Clarke (1987) offer a related approach in terms of the idea of a 'public service' orientation committed to accountability to local citizens' groups.

The main, perhaps rather dismissive, point to make here is that it represents more an aspiration than a properly tried form of accountability. It comes into direct conflict with concerns about territorial justice, which emphasise the need for uniformity of services. It can also be seen as difficult to integrate with concerns about interactions between services – the demand for 'joined-up government' explored in Chapter 12 (see Newman, 2001 for an analysis of these tensions in the UK). However, as indicated at the beginning of this chapter, if accountability ultimately means accountability to citizens, then the issues about how to do this other than through representative government are bound to be on the agenda.

Accountability and governance

While academics may dismiss the political preoccupation with top-down accountability, the issue remains very much alive. It has, however, to confront the reality that new approaches to public administration – what has been described as the shift from *government* to *governance* – make the issues about control over implementation much more complicated. Central to this development was, first, the exploration of public policy delivery through private organisations using market mechanisms and public–private partnerships, followed by recognition of the importance of networks for policy delivery. This is summed up by Pollitt as follows:

> there are two sets of reasons why a simple, single accountor and single accountee model of accountability is an inadequate description of reality. First, many public managers find themselves working in partnerships or contractual relationships, where different parties are accountable for different aspects of a joint activity (multiple accountors). Second, even where a public manager is working within a single institution they will often have several lines of accountability – political, legal, professional, bureaucratic (multiple accountees). (Pollitt, 2003, p. 94)

Adler comes to this same issue with a rather different concern: that of the citizen in search of a mode of redress when dissatisfied with administrative action. The way he extends Mashaw's three models of administrative justice was noted at the end of Chapter 13. From that extension he arrives at six 'normative models' that have similarities with the forms of accountability listed in Box 14.1. These are set out in Table 14.1.

If we put Pollitt's emphasis on complex accountability and Adler's model together we may note that citizens often have choices between more than

Table 14.1   Adler's models of Administrative Justice

Model	Mode of accountability	Mode of redress
Bureaucratic	Hierarchical	Administrative review
Professional	Interpersonal	Second opinion or complaint to a professional body
Legal	Independent	Appeal to a court or tribunal
Managerial	Performance indicators and audit	Publicity
Consumerist	Consumer charters	'Voice' and/or compensation through Consumer Charters
Market	To owners and shareholders	'Exit' and/or court action (private law)

Source: Modified version of Table 3 in Adler, 2006, p. 622

one mode of redress (and of course the possibility of using two together). Earlier sections of this chapter have explored some of these combinations and interactions: the complex mix of professional and hierarchical forms of accountability, the role of a market regulated through auditing and contracts (something missing from Adler's taxonomy) and the possibility of choices between exit and voice in consumer control.

A 'realistic' approach to evaluation and accountability

The title Hogwood and Gunn used for their book on policy analysis, *Policy Analysis for the Real World*, implied a realism absent in some other work. In their concluding section, indeed, they indicate that they are 'interested in the role of policy analysis in the policy process rather than simply the academic study of the policy process' (1984, p. 268). In the first chapter of this book the latter approach was justified in terms of the argument that effective engineering needs to be grounded in a good understanding of physics rather than by drawing a distinction between an academic analysis and an analysis for the real world. In this sense the claim of realism in the heading of this section rests upon the view that these two notions, inevitably particularly important for prescriptive policy analysis – evaluation, concerned with asking what actually happened, and accountability, concerned with who is in control – need to be put in the context of the exploration of the characteristics of the policy process explored in the previous chapters of this book.

The approach adopted in books like Hogwood and Gunn's, defended as equally oriented towards assisting those in favour of or against specific policy initiatives (ibid., p. 269), is open nevertheless to the accusation that the key concepts come from ideologically or politically dominant perspectives. Throughout the present book the problems in respect of one particular dominant perspective – the stages model or policy cycle – have been emphasised. However, there are alternative problems that have to be faced by any attempt to offer a detached and value neutral account of the policy process. The physics/engineering distinction does not actually work well for the social sciences, where there is no broadly accepted framework of theory in which law-like propositions can be located. Instead, there are contending schools of thought, and there are good reasons for suggesting that social scientists cannot be detached observers of social reality. Moreover, the closer one gets to matters of fundamental ideological and political differences the more likely this will be true.

A particularly problematical area for any discussion of the policy process is the fact that some of the most challenging propositions in the field are theories deduced from general assumptions about political activity which have been subjected to little empirical testing, in a discipline in which testing is in any case a difficult activity. This issue was highlighted in the discussion of rational or public choice theory in Chapter 5. However, whilst that theory is particularly open to challenge inasmuch as it sweeps up a range of difficult explanatory problems using one over-riding assumption – that behaviour is self-interested – there are other theoretical propositions in the book that raise comparable if more limited difficulties (some of the ideas embedded in institutional theory, for example).

There are also difficulties arising from the fact that, where evidence is available to enable generalisations about the policy process to be advanced, this tends to come from studies in a single country, with its own distinctive culture and institutional system. It is then a risky undertaking to offer those generalisations outside the context in which they were developed. For example, it was noted that Kingdon's account of agenda setting which is advanced as generally useful is nevertheless based solely on careful observation in the United States. Similarly, it was shown that concerns about the working of federalism in that same country have had a major influence on the development of implementation theory.

Finally, while the objective of emphasising description rather than prescription was emphasised in Chapter 1 and has been re-emphasised elsewhere, the fact is that it has been necessary to draw upon policy analysis writings which mix these two, drawing prescriptions from observations or assumptions about 'the real world' as they see it. This brings us back to the subject matter of this chapter, concerned as it is with two questions that are of fundamental importance for prescriptive policy analysis: what happened, and how was control over the policy process exercised? These then have to be the starting points for the prescriptive questions. All participants are concerned about the issues about 'what happened'. Evaluation questions, in principle, concern us all. The interest in notions like consumer participation in evaluation and the sharing of learning from evaluation (see Taylor and Balloch, 2005) show an aspiration to embrace this perspective. On the other hand, much actual evaluation work is embedded in a traditional top-down concern that those with power to influence policy get what they want. A wide rather than a narrow view of policy accountability can operate as a counterweight to that. But the concern here has been to emphasise the way in which accountability is contested. The great virtue of the work of the early top-down theorists, eager to make prescriptions for rational policy making, was that they emphasised issues about purposive action and control over policy processes. Those issues remain important regardless of the stance one takes on who should be in control.

CONCLUSIONS

Evaluation and accountability are inevitably subjects that attract considerable controversy in discussions of public policy. In conformity with this book's concern with examining the policy process, this chapter has tried to avoid taking a stance in the debate about who should be in control and how they should do it. It has noted that the view that, in a system of representative government, the administration of public policy should be hierarchically controlled by elected representatives has dominated the literature. When a traditional top-down view of the system has been challenged, that challenge has involved either the assertion that the complexity of modern government requires that it should be supplemented by other forms of accountability or efforts to establish alternative 'democratic' legitimacy for a bottom-up perspective.

However, identification of the complexity of accountability has long involved a recognition of forms of legal accountability (normally reinforcing hierarchical political accountability but occasionally challenging it). More complexity has then been added by a recognition of ways in which the elaborate nature of many public activities involves extensive discretionary decision making. Consideration therefore needs to be given to the roles of professional groups and to the way in which forms of co-production occur. An alternative approach to these issues, coming particularly from the 'rational choice' school of thought, suggests that in various respects consumer participation can be enhanced to deal with these issues through market and quasi-market mechanisms providing 'exit' (or, as noted above, more realistically 'entry') options. An alternative is to try to strengthen 'voice' at the 'street level'.

All of this adds up to recognising that accountability in modern governance is bound to be complex. It will often be mixed, involving multiple forms of accountability to multiple groups. This has then, as noted, consequent implications for how it is evaluated. In examining these issues, attention needs to be given to the very different ways in which different public policies are made manifest, a theme that has recurred throughout this book.

It is not proposed to add a concluding chapter to this book. Many of the key themes in the book as a whole have surfaced again in this present chapter. The traditional approach to evaluation and accountability has been seen as part of that consensus about representative government within which the rational model of decision making and the top-down model of implementation also belong. This has been challenged both by an ideological pluralism which sees the need for multiple 'accountabilities' and by those who see networks and complex institutional arrangements as making any simple form of accountability difficult. In the background, and not analysed much in this chapter but emphasised in the early chapters of the book, lies another view – one which sees the structure of power as imposing severe limits on any form of popular accountability.

Throughout the book it has been stressed that there is a need to think about the policy process as a whole, even when analysis requires parts of the process to be separated out. It has also been stressed that it is important to see that the policy process is embedded in the structure of power in society. At the same time there is a need to recognise that it is not easy to generalise about the policy process, inasmuch as different policy issues emerge in different ways in different institutional contexts. The art of policy process analysis needs to involve a capacity to see connections, and to compare and contrast, while being sceptical about all-encompassing generalisations.

References

6, P. (2004) 'Joined-up government in the Western world in comparative perspective: A preliminary literature review and exploration'. *Journal of Public Administration, Research and Theory*, **14** (1), pp. 103–38.

Aberbach, J.D., Putman, R.D. and Rockman, B.A. (1981) *Bureaucrats and Politicians in Western Democracies*. Cambridge, Mass.: Harvard University Press.

Adler, M. (2006) 'Fairness in Context' *Journal of Law and Society*, **33** (4), pp. 615–38.

Aglietta, M. (1987) *A Theory of Capitalist Regulation: The US Experience*. London: Verso.

Albrow, M. (1970) *Bureaucracy*. London: Pall Mall.

Aldrich, H.E. (1976) 'Resource dependence and inter-organizational relations: Local employment service offices and social services sector organizations'. *Administration and Society*, **7** (4), pp. 419–54.

Alford, R. (1975) *Health Care Politics*. Chicago: University of Chicago Press.

Allen, C. (2001) ' "They just don't live and breathe the policy like we do . . .": Policy intentions and practice dilemmas in modern social policy and implementation networks'. *Policy Studies*, **22** (3/4), pp. 149–66.

Allison, G.T. (1971) *Essence of Decision*. Boston, Mass.: Little Brown.

Almond, G.A., Powell, G.B., Jr, Strøm, K. and Dalton, R.J. (2004) *Comparative Politics Today*, 8th edn. New York: Pearson, Longman.

Anderweg, R.B. and Irwin, G.A. (2002) *Governance and Politics in the Netherlands*, 2nd edn. Basingstoke: Palgrave Macmillan.

Argyris, C. (1964) *Integrating the Individual and the Organisation*. New York: Wiley.

Arts, W. and Gelisen, J. (2002) 'Three worlds of welfare capitalism or more?' *Journal of European Social Policy*, **12** (2), pp. 137–58.

Ashby, E. and Anderson, M. (1981) *The Politics of Clean Air*. Oxford: Clarendon Press.

Ashford, D.E. (1986) *The Emergence of the Welfare States*. Oxford: Blackwell.

Atkinson, M.M. and Coleman, W.D. (1989) 'Strong states and weak states: Sectoral policy networks in advanced capitalist economies'. *British Journal of Political Science*, 19, pp. 747–67.

Atkinson, P. (1985) *Language, Structure and Reproduction*. London: Methuen.

Auster, R.D. and Silver, M. (1979) *The State as a Firm: Economic Forces in Political Development*. The Hague: Martinus Nijhoff.

Axelrod, R. (1984) *The Evolution of Cooperation*. New York: Basic Books.

Axelrod, R. and Keohane, R. (1985) 'Achieving cooperation under anarchy: Strategies and institutions'. *World Politics*, **39** (1), pp. 226–54.

Bache, I. (2003) 'Governing through governance: Education policy control under New Labour'. *Political Studies*, **51** (2), pp. 300–14.

Bachrach, P. (1969) *The Theory of Democratic Elitism*. London: University of London Press.

Bachrach, P. and Baratz, M.S. (1962) 'Two faces of power'. *American Political Science Review*, **56**, pp. 641–51.

Bachrach, P. and Baratz, M.S. (1962) 'Decisions and nondecisions: An analytical framework'. *American Political Science Review*, **57**, pp. 947–52.

Bachrach, P. and Baratz, M.S. (1970) *Power and Poverty*. New York: Oxford University Press.

Baldwin, P. (1990) *The Politics of Social Solidarity*. Cambridge: Cambridge University Press.

Baldwin, R. (1995) *Rules and Government*. Oxford: Oxford University Press.

Ball, S.J. (2008) *The Education Debate*. Bristol: The Policy Press.

Barker, A. and Peters, B.G. (eds) (1993) *The Politics of Expert Advice*. Edinburgh: Edinburgh University Press.

Barnard, C. (1938) *The Functions of the Executive*. Cambridge, Mass.: Harvard University Press.

Barrett, M. (1980) *Women's Oppression Today*. London: Verso.

Barrett, S. and Fudge, C. (eds) (1981) *Policy and Action*. London: Methuen.

Barrett, S. and Hill, M.J. (1981) 'Report to the SSRC Central London: Methuen. Local Government Relations Panel on the "core" or theoretical component of the research on implementation' (unpublished).

Baumgartner, F. and Jones, B. (1993) *Agendas and Instability in American Politics*. Chicago: University of Chicago Press.

Baumgartner, M.P. (1992) 'The myth of discretion', in Hawkins, K. (ed.) *The Uses of Discretion*. Oxford: Clarendon Press.

Beer, S.H. (1965) *Modern British Politics*. London: Faber & Faber.

Beetham, D. (1987) *Bureaucracy*. Milton Keynes: Open University Press.

Béland, D. (2001) 'Does labor matter? Institutions, labor unions and pension reform in France and the United States'. *Journal of Public Policy*, **21** (2), pp. 153–72.

Béland, D. (2005) 'Ideas and Social Policy: An Institutionalist Perspective', *Social Policy and Administration*, **39** (1), pp. 1–18.

Béland, D. (2007) 'The social exclusion discourse: ideas and policy change'. *Policy and Politics*, **35** (1), pp. 123–40.

Bell, D. (1960) *The End of Ideology*. New York: Free Press.

Bendor, J. and Hammond, T. (1992) 'Rethinking Allison's models'. *American Political Science Review*, **86** (2), pp. 301–22.

Bennett, G. (1992) *Dilemmas: Coping with Environmental Problems*. London: Earthscan.

Benson, J.K. (1975) 'The inter-organizational network as a political economy'. *Administrative Science Quarterly*, **20** (June), pp. 229–49.

Benson, J.K. (1983) 'Interorganizational networks and policy sectors', in D. Rogers and D. Whetten (eds). *Interorganizational Coordination*. Iowa: Iowa State University Press.

Bentley, A.F. (1967) *The Process of Government*. Cambridge, Mass.: Belknap Press.

Berger, P.L. and Luckman, T. (1975) *The Social Construction of Reality*. Harmondsworth: Penguin Books.

Beveridge, W. (1942) *Social Insurance and Allied Services*. London: HMSO, Cmd. 6404.

Birkland, T.A. (1998) 'Focusing events, mobilization, and agenda setting'. *Journal of Public Policy*, **18** (1), pp. 53–74.

Blau, P.M. (1955) *The Dynamics of Bureaucracy*. Chicago: University of Chicago Press.

Blom-Hansen, J. (1999) 'Policy-making in central–local government relations: Balancing local autonomy, macroecnomic control and sectoral policy goals'. *Journal of Public Policy*, **19** (3), pp. 237–64.

Blowers, A. (1984) *Something in the Air: Corporate Power and the Environment*. London: Harper and Row.

Blyth, M. (2002) *Great Transformations: Economic ideas and institutional change in the twentieth century*. Cambridge: Cambridge University Press.

Bogason, P. (2000) *Public Policy and Local Governance*. Cheltenham: Edward Elgar.

Bonoli, G. and Shinkawa, T. (eds) (2005) *Ageing and Pension Reform Around the World*. Cheltenham: Elgar.

Booth, T. (1988) *Developing Policy Research*. Aldershot: Avebury.

Bottomore, T.B. (1966) *Elites and Society*. Harmondsworth: Penguin.

Bovens, M. and 't Hart, P. (1996) *Understanding Policy Fiascos*. Brunswick, NJ: Transaction Publishers.

Bovens, M. and Zouridis, S. (2002) 'From street-level to system-level bureaucracies: How information and communication technology is transforming administrative discretion and constitutional control'. *Public Administration Review*, **62** (2), pp. 174–84.

Bovens, M., 't Hart, P. and Peters, B.G. (eds) (2001) *Success and Failure in Public Governance*. Cheltenham: Edward Elgar.

Bowe, R., Ball, S.J. and Gold, A. (1992) *Reforming Education and Changing Schools*. London: Routledge.

Bowen, E.R. (1982) 'The Pressman–Wildavsky paradox'. *Journal of Public Policy*, **2** (1), pp. 1–21.

Bradach, J.L. and Eccles, R.G. (1991) 'Price, authority and trust: From ideal types to plural forms', in Thompson, G., Frances, J., Levacic, R. and Mitchell, J. (eds). *Markets, Hierarchies and Networks: The Coordination of Social Life*. London: Sage, pp. 277–92.

Braverman, H. (1974) *Labor and Monopoly Capital*. New York: Monthly Review Press.

Braybrooke, D. and Lindblom, C.E. (1963) *A Strategy of Decision*. New York: The Free Press.

Brenton, T. (1994) *The Greening of Machiavelli*. London: Earthscan.

Brittan, S. (1977) *The Economic Consequences of Democracy*. London: Temple Smith.

Brown, R. (1975) *The Management of Welfare*. Glasgow: Fontana/Collins.

Browne, A. and Wildavsky, A. (1984) 'Should evaluation become implementation', in Pressman, J. and Wildavsky, A. *Implementation*, 3rd edn. Berkeley: University of California Press.

Buchanan, J.M. and Tullock, G. (1962) *The Calculus of Consent*. Ann Arbor, Mich.: University of Michigan Press.

Bull, D. (1980) 'The anti-discretion movement in Britain: Fact or phantom?' *Journal of Social Welfare Law*, pp. 65–83.

Bulmer, M. (ed.) (1987) *Social Science Research and Government*. Cambridge: Cambridge University Press.

Bulmer, S. and Padgett, S. (2004) 'Policy transfer in the European Union: An Institutionalist Perspective'. *British Journal of Political Science*, **35**, pp. 103–26.

Burns, T. and Stalker, G.M. (1961) *The Management of Innovation*. London: Tavistock.

Butcher, T. (2002) *Delivering Welfare*, 2nd edn. Buckingham: Open University Press.

Butler, D., Adonis, A. and Travers, T. (1994) *Failure in British Government: The Politics of the Poll Tax*. Oxford: Oxford University Press.

Cahill, M. (2002) *The Environment and Social Policy*. London: Routledge.

Campbell, A. (2007) *The Blair Years: Extracts from the Alastair Campbell Diaries*. London: Hutchinson.

Campbell, C. and Wilson, G.K. (1995) *The End of Whitehall: Death of a Paradigm?* Oxford: Blackwell.

Chadwick, A. (2000) 'Studying political ideas: A public political discourse approach'. *Political Studies*, **48**, pp. 283–301.

Chandler, A.D. (1977) *The Visible Hand: The Managerial Revolution in American Business*. Cambridge, Mass.: Harvard University Press.

Chaney, C.K. and Saltzstein, G.H. (1998) 'Democratic control and bureaucratic responsiveness: The police and domestic violence'. *American Journal of Political Science*, **42** (3), pp. 745–68.

Chapman, R.A. (1970) *The Higher Civil Service in Britain*. London: Constable.

Child, J. (1972) 'Organization structure, environment and performance: The role of strategic choice'. *Sociology*, **6**, pp. 1–22.

Clarke, J. and Newman, J. (1997) *The Managerial State: Power, Politics and Ideology in the Remaking of Social Welfare*. London: Sage.

Clegg, S. (1990) *Modern Organizations*. London: Sage.

Clegg, S., Courpasson, D. and Phillips, N. (2006) *Power and Organizations*, London: Sage.

Cline, K.D. (2000) 'Defining the implementation problem: Organizational management versus cooperation'. *Journal of Public Administration Research and Theory*, **10** (3), pp. 551–71.

Coase, R.H. (1937) 'The nature of the firm'. *Economica*, **4**, pp. 386–405.

Cobb, R.W. and Elder, C.D. (1983) *Participation in American politics: The dynamics of agenda-building*. Baltimore, Md.: Johns Hopkins University Press.

Cobb, R.W., Ross, J.K. and Ross M.H. (1976) 'Agenda building as a comparative political process'. *American Political Science Review*, **70** (1), pp. 126–38.

Cohen, J. and Rogers, J. (1995) *Associations and Democracy*. London: Verso.

Cohen, M.D., March, J.G. and Olsen, J.P. (1972) 'A garbage can model of organizational choice'. *Administrative Science Quarterly*, **17**, pp. 1–25.

Cohen, R. (1987) *The New Helots: Migrants in the International Division of Labour*. Aldershot: Avebury.

Colebatch, H. and Larmour, P. (1993) *Market, Bureaucracy and Community*. London: Pluto.

Collier, R.B. and Collier, D. (1991) *Shaping the Political Arena: Critical Junctures, the Labour Movement and Regime Dynamics in Latin America*. Princeton, NJ: Princeton University Press.

Cox, R. (1987) *Production, Power and World Order*. New York: Columbia University Press.

Cram, L. (1997) *Policy-making in the EU*. London: Routledge.

Crenson, M.A. (1971) *The Unpolitics of Air Pollution*. Baltimore, Md.: Johns Hopkins University Press.

Crossman, R.H.S. (1975, 1976 and 1977) *Diaries of a Cabinet Minister* (three volumes.). London: Hamish Hamilton and Jonathan Cape.

Cunningham, G. (1963) 'Policy and practice'. *Public Administration*, **41**, pp. 229–38.

Dahl, R.A. (1957) 'The concept of power'. *Behavioural Science*, **2**, pp. 201–15.

Dahl, R.A. (1958) 'A critique of the ruling-elite model'. *American Political Science Review*, 52, pp. 463–9.

Dahl, R.A. (1961) *Who Governs?* New Haven, Conn.: Yale University Press.

Dahl, R.A. and Lindblom, C.E. (1953) *Politics, Economics and Welfare* (2nd edn 1976). Chicago: Chicago University Press.

Dallek, R. (2003) *John F. Kennedy: An Unfinished Life*. London: Allen Lane.

Davies, H.T.O., Nutley, S.M. and Smith, P.C. (2000) (eds) *What Works?* Bristol: The Policy Press.

Davis, K.C. (1969) *Discretionary Justice*. Baton Rouge: Louisiana State University Press.

Dawkins, R. (2003) *A Devil's Chaplain*. London: Weidenfeld and Nicolson.

Day, P. and Klein, R. (1987) *Accountabilities*. London: Tavistock.

Deacon, B. (2007) *Global Social Policy and Governance*. London, Sage.

Deacon, B. with Hulse, M. and Stubbs, P. (1997) *Global Social Policy*. London: Sage.

Deakin, N. and Walsh, K. (1996) 'The enabling state: The role of markets and contracts'. *Public Administration*, **74**, pp. 33–48.

Dearlove, J. and Saunders, P. (1991) *Introduction to British Politics*. Cambridge: Polity Press.

Degeling, P. (1993) 'Policy as the accomplishment of an implementation structure: Hospital restructuring in Australia', in Hill, M. (ed.). *New Agendas in the Study of the Policy Process*. Hemel Hempstead: Harvester Wheatsheaf.

Degeling, P. and Colebatch, H.K. (1984) 'Structure and action as constructs in the practice of public administration'. *Australian Journal of Public Administration*, **43** (4), pp. 320–31.

Degeling, P., Kennedy, J., Hill, M., Carnegie, M. and Holt, J. (1998) *Professional Sub-Cultures and Hospital Reform*. Centre for Hospital Management and Information Systems Research, University of New South Wales.

Degeling, P., Maxwell, S., Kennedy, J. and Coyle, B. (2003) 'Medicine, management and modernisation: A "danse macabre"?' *British Medical Journal*, **326**, pp. 649–52.

DeHart-Davis, L. (2007) 'The Unbureaucratic Personality'. *Public Administration Review*, Sept/Oct, pp. 892–904.

Dell, E. (1991) *A Hard Pounding: Politics and the Economic Crisis*. Oxford: Oxford University Press.

Delphy, C. (1984) *Close to Home: A Materialist Analysis of Women's Oppression*. London: Hutchinson.

Dery, D. (1984) *Problem Definition in Policy Analysis*. Lawrence: University of Kansas Press.

Dery, D. (1999) 'Policy by the way: When policy is incidental to making other policies'. *Journal of Public Policy*, **18** (2), pp. 163–76.

DiMaggio, P.J. and Powell, W. (1983) 'The iron cage revisited: Institutional isomorphism and collective rationality in organizational fields'. *American Sociological Review*, **48**, pp. 147–60.

DiMaggio, P.J. and Powell, W. (1991) *The New Institutionalism in Organizational Analysis*, Chicago, Ill.: University of Chicago Press.

Doern, G.B. and Phidd, R.W. (1983) *Canadian Public Policy*. Agincourt, Ontario: Methuen.

Dolowicz, D. and Marsh, D. (1996) 'Who learns what from whom: A review of the policy transfer literature'. *Political Studies*, **44**, pp. 343–57.

Dolowicz, D. and Marsh, D. (2000) 'Learning from abroad: The role of policy transfer in contemporary policy making'. *Governance*, **13** (1), pp. 5–24.

Dolowitz, D.P., Hulme, R., Nellis, M. and O'Neill, F. (2000) *Policy Transfer and British Social Policy: Learning from the USA?* Buckingham: Open University Press.

Donaldson, L. (1985) *In Defence of Organization Theory: A Response to the Critics*. Cambridge: Cambridge University Press.

Donnison, D.V. (1977) 'Against discretion'. *New Society*, 15 September, pp. 534–6.

Dowding, K. (1995) 'Model or metaphor? A critical review of the policy network approach'. *Political Studies*, **43**, pp. 136–58.

Downing, P.B. and Hanf, K. (eds) (1983) *International Comparisons in Implementing Pollution Laws*. Boston, Mass.: Kluwer Nijhoff.

Downs, A. (1957) *An Economic Theory of Democracy*. New York: Harper and Row.

Downs, A. (1967) *Inside Bureaucracy*. Boston: Little Brown.

Downs, A. (1972) 'Up and down with ecology – the "issue-attention cycle"'. *The Public Interest*, **28**, pp. 38–50.

Dror, Y. (1986) *Policymaking Under Adversity*. New Brunswick, NJ: Transaction Publishers.

Drysek, J.S. (1990) *Discursive Democracy*. Cambridge: Cambridge University Press.

Dudley, G. and Richardson, J. (1999) 'Competing advocacy coalitions and the process of "frame reflection": a longitudinal study of EU steel policy'. *Journal of European Public Policy*, **6** (2), pp. 225–48.

Dunleavy, P. (1981) 'Professions and policy change: notes towards a model of ideological corporatism'. *Public Administration Bulletin*, **36**, pp. 3–16.

Dunleavy, P. (1985) 'Bureaucrats, budgets and the growth of the state: Reconstructing an instrumental model'. *British Journal of Political Science*, **15**, pp. 299–328.

Dunleavy, P. (1986) 'Explaining the privatization boom: Public choice versus radical approaches'. *Public Administration*, **64** (1), pp. 13–34.

Dunleavy, P. (1991) *Democracy, Bureaucracy and Public Choice*. Hemel Hempstead: Harvester Wheatsheaf.

Dunleavy, P. (1995) 'Policy disasters: Explaining the UK's record'. *Public Policy and Administration*, **10** (2), pp. 52–69.

Dunleavy, P. and O'Leary, B. (1987) *Theories of the State*. London: Macmillan.

Dunsire, A. (1978a) *Implementation in a Bureaucracy*. Oxford: Martin Robertson.

Dunsire, A. (1978b) *Control in a Bureaucracy*. Oxford: Martin Robertson.

Dworkin, R. (1977) *Taking Rights Seriously*. London: Duckworth.

Dyson, K. (1980) *The State Tradition in Western Europe*. Oxford: Martin Robertson.

Eardley, T., Bradshaw, J., Ditch, J., Gough, I. and Whiteford, P. (1996) *Social Assistance in OECD Countries: Synthesis Report*. Department of Social Security Research Report No. 46, London: HMSO.

Easton, D. (1953) *The Political System*. New York: Knopf.

Easton, D. (1965a) *A Systems Analysis of Political Life*. New York: Wiley.

Easton, D. (1965b) *A Framework for Political Analysis*. Englewood Cliffs, NJ: Prentice Hall.

Edelman, M. (1971) *Politics as Symbolic Action*. Chicago: Markham.

Edelman, M. (1977) *Political Language: Words that Succeed and Policies that Fail*. New York: Institute for the Study of Poverty.

Edelman, M. (1988) *Constructing the Political Spectacle*. Chicago: University of Chicago Press.

Eichorst, W. and Wintermann, O. (2006) 'Generating Legitimacy for Labor Market and Welfare State Reform – The Role of Policy Advice in Germany, the Netherlands and Sweden'. *German Policy Studies*, **3** (2), pp. 268–309.

Elam, M.J. (1990) 'Puzzling out the post-Fordist debate: Technology, markets and institutions'. *Economic and Industrial Democracy*, **11**, pp. 9–38.

Ellul, J. (1964) *The Technological Society*. New York: Vintage Books.

Elmore, R. (1980) 'Backward mapping: Implementation research and policy decisions'. *Political Science Quarterly*, **94**, pp. 601–16.

Elmore, R. (1981) 'Backward mapping and youth employment' (unpublished paper prepared for the third meeting of the International Working Group on Policy Implementation).

Enthoven, A.C. (1985) *Reflections on the Management of the NHS*. London: Nuffield Provincial Hospitals Trust.

Esping-Andersen, G. (1990) *Three Worlds of Welfare Capitalism*. Cambridge: Polity Press.

Ethridge, M.E. and Percy, S.L. (1993) 'A new kind of public policy encounters disappointing results: Implementing learnfare in Wisconsin'. *Public Administration Review*, 53 (4), pp. 340–7.

Etzioni, A. (1969) *The Semi Professions and Their Organization*. New York: Free Press.

Evans, P.B., Rueschemeyer, D. and Skocpol, T. (eds) (1985) *Bringing the State Back In*. Cambridge: Cambridge University Press.

Exworthy, M. and Powell, M. (2004) 'Big windows and little windows: implementation in the 'Congested State'' *Public Administration*, 82 (2), pp. 263–81.

Exworthy, M., Berney, L. and Powell, M. (2002) '"How great expectations in Westminster may be dashed locally": The implementation of national policy on health inequalities'. *Policy and Politics*, 30 (1), pp. 79–96.

Falkner, G., Hartlapp, M. and Treib, O. (2007) 'Worlds of Compliance: Why leading approaches to European Union implementation are only "sometimes-true" theories'. *European Journal of Political Research*, 46, pp. 395–416.

Farmer, D.J. (1995) *The Language of Public Administration: Bureaucracy, Modernity and Post-modernity*. Tuscaloosa, Ala.: University of Alabama Press.

Farnsworth, K. (2007) 'Business, power, policy and politics' in Hodgson, S.M. and Irving, Z. *Policy Reconsidered: Meaning, Politics and Practices*. Bristol: The Policy Press.

Feldman, M. (1992) 'Social limits to discretion: An organizational perspective', in Hawkins, K. (ed.) *The Uses of Discretion*. Oxford: Clarendon Press.

Ferman, B. (1990) 'When failure is success: Implementation and Madisonian government', in Palumbo, D.J. and Calista, D.J. (eds). *Implementation and the Policy Process: Opening Up the Black Box*. New York: Greenwood Press, pp. 39–50.

Fernandes, J-L., Kendall, J., Davey, V. and Knapp, M. (2007) 'Direct Payments in England: Factors Linked to Variations in Local Provision', *Journal of Social Policy*, 36 (1), pp. 97–122.

Fischer, F. (2003) *Reframing Public Policy*. Oxford: Oxford University Press.

Fischer, F. (2006) *Evaluating Public Policy*. Mason, OH: Thomson Wadsworth.

Flynn, R. (1993) 'Coping with cutbacks and managing retrenchment in health'. *Journal of Social Policy*, 20 (2), pp. 215–36.

Forrest, R. and Murie, A. (1991) *Selling the Welfare State*. London: Routledge.

Foucault, M. (1980) *Power/Knowledge: Selected Interviews and Other Writings, 1972–77*. Brighton: Harvester.

Fox, A. (1974) *Beyond Contract: Work, Power and Trust Relations*. London: Faber.

Fox, C.J. and Miller, H.T. (1995) *Postmodern Public Administration: Toward Discourse*. Thousand Oaks, Cal.: Sage.

Frederickson, H.G. and Smith, K.B. (2003) *The Public Adminstration Theory Primer*. Boulder, Col.: Westview Press.

Friedman, M. (1962) *Capitalism and Freedom*. Chicago: University of Chicago Press.

Friedman, M. (1977) *Inflation and Unemployment: A New Dimension of Politics*. London: Institute of Economic Affairs.

Friedrich, C.J. (1940) 'The nature of administrative responsibility'. *Public Policy*, **1**, pp. 3–24.

Friedson, E. (1970) *Professional Dominance*. New York: Atherton.

Friend, J.K., Power, J.M. and Yewlett, C.J.L (1974) *Public Planning: The Inter-Corporate Dimension*. London: Tavistock.

Fukuyama, F. (1992) *The End of History and the Last Man*. New York: Free Press.

Galligan, D.J. (1986) *Discretionary Powers*. Oxford: Clarendon Press.

Gamble, A. (1994) *The Free Economy and the Strong State*, 2nd edn. Basingstoke: Macmillan.

Gamble, A. (2003) *Between Europe and America: The Future of British Politics*. Basingstoke: Palgrave Macmillan.

Gaventa, J. (1980) *Power and Powerlessness, Quiescence and Rebellion in an Appalachian Valley*. Oxford: Clarendon Press.

George, V. and Wilding, P. (2002) *Globalisation and Human Welfare*. Basingstoke: Palgrave.

Giddens, A. (1976) *New Rules of Sociological Method*. London: Hutchinson.

Giddens, A. (1984) *The Constitution of Society*. Cambridge: Polity Press.

Gilbert, B.B. (1966) *The Evolution of National Insurance in Great Britain*. London: Michael Joseph.

Gilbert, M. and Gott, R. (2000) *The Appeasers*. London: Weidenfeld & Nicolson.

Giller, H. and Morris, A. (1981) 'What type of case is this? Social workers' decisions about children who offend', in Adler, M. and Asquith, S. (eds). *Discretion and Welfare*. London: Heinemann.

Glendinning, C., Powell, M. and Rummery, K. (eds) (2002) *Partnerships, New Labour and the Governance of Welfare*. Bristol: The Policy Press.

Glennerster, H., Matsaganis, M. and Owens, P. (1994) *Implementing Fundholding*. Buckingham: Open University Press.

Glennerster, H., Power, A. and Travers, T. (1991) 'A new era for social policy: A new Enlightenment or a new Leviathan?' *Journal of Social Policy*, **20** (3), pp. 389–414.

Goetz, K.H. (2003) 'Government at the centre', in Padgett, S., Paterson, W.E. and Smith, G. (eds). *Developments in German Politics*, vol. 3. Basingstoke: Palgrave Macmillan.

Goggin, M.L., Bowman, A.O'M., Lester, J.P. and O'Toole, L.J., Jr (1990) *Implementation Theory and Practice: Toward a Third Generation*. Glenview: Scott Foresman/Little, Brown.

Gordon, I., Lewis, J. and Young, K. (1977) 'Perspectives on policy analysis'. *Public Administration Bulletin*, **25**, pp. 26–30.

Gough, I. (1979) *The Political Economy of the Welfare State*. London: Macmillan.

Gouldner, A.W. (1954) *Patterns of Industrial Bureaucracy*. Glencoe, Ill.: Free Press.

Gouldner, A.W. (1957–8) 'Cosmopolitans and locals: Towards an analysis of latent social roles'. *Administrative Science Quarterly*, **2**, pp. 281–306 and 444–80.

Grant, W.P. (1989) *Pressure Groups, Politics and Democracy in Britain*. London: Phillip Allan.

Gray, P.D. and 't Hart, P. (eds) (1998) *Public Policy Disasters in Europe*. London: Routledge.

Greenwood, E. (1957) 'Attributes of a profession'. *Social Work*, **2**, pp. 45–55.

Greenwood, R., Hinings, C.R. and Ranson, S. (1975) 'Contingency theory and the organisation of local authorities: Part One. Differentiation and integration'. *Public Administration*, **53**, pp. 1–24.

Gregory, R. (2003) 'Accountability in modern government', in Peters, B.G. and Pierre, J. (eds). *Handbook of Public Administration*. London: Sage.

Grimshaw, R. and Jefferson, T. (1987) *Interpreting Policework: Policy and Practice in Forms of Beat Policing*. London: Allen & Unwin.

Gunn, L. (1978) 'Why is implementation so difficult?' *Management Services in Government*, November.

Gusfield, J.R. (1981). *The culture of public problems. Drinking-driving and the symbolic order*. Chicago: The University of Chicago Press.

Haas, P. (1992) 'Introduction: Epistemic Communities and International Policy Coordination'. *International Organization*, **46** (1), pp. 1–35.

Haas, P. (2004) 'When Does Power Listen to Truth? A Constructivist Approach to the Policy Process'. *Journal of European Public Policy*, **11** (4), pp. 569–92.

Habermas, J. (1987) *The Theory of Communicative Action*. Cambridge: Polity Press.

Haggard, S. and Moon, C-I. (1990) 'Institutions and economic policy: Theory and a Korean case study'. *World Politics*, **42** (2), pp. 210–37.

Hall, P.A. (1986) *Governing the Economy: The Politics of State Intervention in Britain and France*. Cambridge: Polity Press.

Hall, P.A. (1993) 'Policy paradigms, social learning and the state: The case of economic policy making in Britain'. *Comparative Politics*, **25**, pp. 275–96.

Hall, P.A. and Soskice, D. (2001) *Varieties of Capitalism: The Institutional Foundations of Comparative Advantage*. Oxford: Oxford University Press.

Ham, C. (1992) *Health Policy in Britain*, 3rd edn. London: Macmillan.

Ham, C. and Hill, M.J. (1984) *The Policy Process in the Modern Capitalist State*. Hemel Hempstead: Harvester Wheatsheaf.

Hanf, K. (1993) 'Enforcing environmental laws: The social regulation of co-production', in Hill, M. (ed.). *New Agendas in the Study of the Policy Process*. Hemel Hempstead: Harvester Wheatsheaf.

Hardin, G. (1968) 'The tragedy of the commons'. *Science*, **162**, pp. 1243–8.

Hargrove, E.C. (1975) *The Missing Link*. Washington, DC: The Urban Institute.

Harrison, S. and McDonald, R. (2008) *The Politics of Health Care in Britain*. London: Sage.

Harrison, S. and Pollitt, C. (1994) *Controlling Health Professionals*. Buckingham: Open University Press.

Harrison, S., Hunter, D.J. and Pollitt, C. (1990) *The Dynamics of British Health Policy*. London: Unwin Hyman.

Harrop, M. (ed.) (1992) *Power and Policy in Liberal Democracies*. Cambridge: Cambridge University Press.

Hasenfeld, Y. and Steinmetz, D. (1981) 'Client–official encounters in social service agencies', in Goodsell, C.T. (ed.). *The Public Encounter*. Bloomington: Indiana University Press.

Hawkins, K. (1984) *Environment and Enforcement*. Oxford: Clarendon Press.

Hay, C. (2002) *Political Analysis: A Critical Introduction*. Basingstoke: Palgrave.

Hayek, F.A. (1944) *The Road to Serfdom*. London: Routledge and Kegan Paul.

Hayek, F.A. (1960) *The Constitution of Liberty*. London: Routledge and Kegan Paul.

Hayward, J. and Menon, A. (eds) (2003) *Governing Europe*. Oxford: Oxford University Press.

Heclo, H. (1972) 'Review article: Policy analysis'. *British Journal of Political Science*, **2**, pp. 83–108.

Heclo, H. (1974) *Modern Social Politics in Britain and Sweden*. New Haven, Conn.: Yale University Press.

Heclo, H. and Wildavsky, A. (1981) *The Private Government of Public Money*. London: Macmillan.

Herzberg, F. (1966) *Work and the Nature of Man*. New York: Staples Press.

Hill, M. (1969) 'The exercise of discretion in the National Assistance Board'. *Public Administration*, **47**, pp. 75–90.

Hill, M. (1972) *The Sociology of Public Administration*. London: Weidenfeld & Nicolson.

Hill, M. (1983) 'The role of the British Alkali and Clean Air Inspectorate in air pollution control', in Downing, P. and Hanf, K. (eds). *International Comparisons in Implementing Pollution Laws*. Dordrecht: Kluwer-Nijhoff.

Hill, M. (2006) *Social Policy in the Modern World*. Oxford: Blackwell.

Hill, M. (2007) *Pensions*. Bristol: The Policy Press.

Hill, M. (ed.) (1993) *New Agendas in the Study of the Policy Process*. Hemel Hempstead: Harvester Wheatsheaf.

Hill, M. and Hupe, P. (2003) 'The multi-layer problem in implementation research'. *Public Management Review*, **5** (4), pp. 471–90.

Hill, M. and Hupe, P. (2006) 'Analysing Policy Processes as Multiple Governance: Accountability in Social Policy'. *Policy and Politics*, **34** (3), pp. 557–73.

Hill, M. and Hupe, P. (2009) *Implementing Public Policy*. 2nd edn. London: Sage.

Hill, M., Aaronovitch, S. and Baldock, D. (1989) 'Non-decision making in pollution control in Britain: Nitrate pollution, the EEC Drinking Water Directive and agriculture'. *Policy and Politics*, **17** (3), pp. 227–40.

Hills, J. and Stewart, K. (2005) *A More Equal Society?* Bristol: The Policy Press.

Hindmoor, A. (2006) *Rational Choice*. Basingstoke: Palgrave Macmillan.

Hirschman, A.O. (1970) *Exit, Voice and Loyalty*. Cambridge, Mass.: Harvard University Press.

Hirst, P. and Thompson, G. (1992) 'The problem of "globalisation": International economic relations, national economic management and the formation of trading blocs'. *Economy and Society*, **21** (4), pp. 355–96.

Hjern, B. and Hull, C. (1982) 'Implementation research as empirical constitutionalism', in Hjern, B. and Hull, C. (eds). *Implementation Beyond Hierarchy*. Special issue of *European Journal of Political Research*.

Hjern, B. and Porter, D.O. (1981) 'Implementation structures: A new unit of administrative analysis'. *Organisational Studies*, **2**, pp. 211–27.

Hodgson, S.M. and Irving, Z. (2007) *Policy Reconsidered: Meaning, Politics and Practices*. Bristol: The Policy Press.

Hofferbert, R. (1974) *The Study of Public Policy*. Indianapolis, Ind.: Bobbs Merrill.

Hoggett, P. (1991) 'A new management for the public sector?' *Policy and Politics*, **19**, pp. 143–56.

Hoggett, P. (1996) 'New modes of control in the public service'. *Public Administration*, **74** (1), pp. 9–32.

Hogwood, B. (1987) *From Crisis to Complacency? Shaping Public Policy in Britain*. London: Oxford University Press.

Hogwood, B.W. and Gunn, L. (1981) *The Policy Orientation*. University of Strathclyde: Centre for the Study of Public Policy.

Hogwood, B.W. and Gunn, L. (1984) *Policy Analysis for the Real World*. London: Oxford University Press.

Hogwood, B.W. and Peters, B.G. (1983) *Policy Dynamics*. Brighton: Harvester.

Holdaway, S. (1983) *Inside the British Police: A Force at Work*. Oxford: Blackwell.

Hood, C. (1976) *The Limits of Administration*. Chichester: Wiley.

Hood, C. (1986) *The Tools of Government*. Chatham, NJ: Chatham House.

Hood, C. (1991) 'A public management for all seasons'. *Public Adminstration*, **69** (1), pp. 3–19.

Hood, C. (1995) 'Contemporary public management: A new global paradigm?' *Public Policy and Administration*, **10** (2), pp. 104–17.

Horn, M. (1995) *The Political Economy of Public Administration*. Cambridge: Cambridge University Press.

Howlett, M. (1991) 'Policy instruments, policy styles and policy implementation: National approaches to theories of instrument choice'. *Policy Studies Journal*, **19** (2), pp. 1–21.

Howlett, M. and Ramesh, M. (2003) *Studying Public Policy*, 2nd edn. Don Mills, Ontario: Oxford University Press.

Huber, J.D. and Shipan, C.R. (2002) *Deliberate Discretion? The Institutional Foundations of Bureaucratic Autonomy*. Cambridge: Cambridge University Press.

Hudson, B. (1987) 'Collaboration in social welfare: A framework for analysis'. *Policy and Politics*, **15** (3), pp. 175–82.

Hudson, B. (1989) 'Michael Lipsky and street-level bureaucracy: A neglected perspective', in Barton, L. (ed.). *Disability and Dependency*. Lewes: Falmer Press.

Hudson, B. and Henwood, M. (2002) 'The NHS and social care: The final countdown?' *Policy and Politics*, **30** (2), pp. 153–66.

Hudson, J. and Lowe, S. (2004) *Understanding the Policy Process*. Bristol: The Policy Press.

Hudson, J., Lowe, S., Oscroft, N. and Snell, C. (2007) 'Activating Policy Networks: A case study of local environmental policy-making in the United Kingdom'. *Policy Studies*, **28** (1), pp. 55–70.

Hughes, E.C. (1958) *Men and Their Work*. Glencoe, Ill.: Free Press.

Hunter, F. (1953) *Community Power Structure*. Chapel Hill, NC: University of North Carolina Press.

Hupe, P. (1990) 'Implementing a meta-policy: The case of decentralisation in the Netherlands'. *Policy and Politics*, **18** (3), pp. 181–91.

Hurrell, A. and Kingsbury, B. (eds) (1992) *The International Politics of the Environment*. Oxford: Oxford University Press.

Huxham, C. and Macdonald, D. (1992) 'Introducing collaborative advantage'. *Management Decision*, **30** (3), pp. 50–6.

Hwang, Yuan-shie (1995) 'Funding health care in Britain and Taiwan'. PhD diss., University of Newcastle upon Tyne.

Illich, I. (1977) *Limits to Medicine*. Harmondsworth: Penguin.

Immergut, E.M. (1992) 'The rules of the game: The logic of health policy-making in France, Switzerland and Sweden', in Steinmo, S., Thelen, K. and Longstreth, F. (eds). *Structuring Politics: Historical Institutionalism in Comparative Analysis*. Cambridge: Cambridge University Press.

Immergut, E.M. (1993) *Health Policy, Interests and Institutions in Western Europe*. Cambridge: Cambridge University Press.

Jacques, E. (1967) *Equitable Payment*. Harmondsworth: Penguin.

James, O. and Lodge, M. (2003) 'The limitations of "policy transfer" and "lesson drawing" for public policy research'. *Political Studies Review*, **1** (2), pp. 179–93.

Jenkins, R. (2007) 'The meaning of policy/policy as meaning', in Hodgson, S.M. and Irving, Z. *Policy Reconsidered: Meaning, Politics and Practices*. Bristol: The Policy Press.

Jenkins, W.I. (1978) *Policy Analysis*. London: Martin Robertson.

Jessop, B. (1992) 'Fordism and post-Fordism: A critical reformulation', in Scott, A.J. and Stormper, M. (eds). *Pathways to Industrialisation and Regional Development*. London: Routledge.

Jewell, C.J. (2007) *Agents of the Welfare State*. New York and Basingstoke: Palgrave Macmillan, 2007.

John, P. (1998) *Analysing Public Policy*. London: Pinter.

John, P. (2001) *Local Government in Western Europe*. London: Sage.

Johnson, T.J. (1972) *Professions and Power*. London: Macmillan.

Jones, P. and Cullis, J. (2003) 'Key parameters in policy design: The case of intrinsic motivation'. *Journal of Social Policy*, **32** (4), pp. 527–48.

Jordan, A. (1997) 'Overcoming the divide between comparative politics and international relations approaches to the EC: What role for "post-decisional politics"?' *West European Politics*, **20** (4), pp. 43–70.

Jordan, A. (2001) 'The European Union: An evolving system of multi-level governance ... or government?' *Policy and Politics*, **29** (2), pp. 193–208.

Jordan, A.G. (1986) 'Iron triangles, woolly corporatism and elastic nets: Images of the policy process'. *Journal of Public Policy*, **1**, pp. 95–123.

Jordan, A.G. and Richardson, J.J. (1987) *British Politics and the Policy Process*. London: Unwin Hyman.

Jowell, J. (1973) 'The legal control of administrative discretion'. *Public Law*, pp. 178–220.

Kampfner, J. (2003) *Blair's Wars*. London: Free Press.

Katzenstein, P. (1977) 'Conclusion: Domestic structures and strategies of foreign economic policy'. *International Organisation*, **31** (4), pp. 879–920.

Kavanagh, D. and Seldon, A. (2001) *The Power Behind the Prime Minister*. London: HarperCollins.

Kavanagh, G. and Richards, D. (2001) 'Departmentalism and joined-up government: Back to the future'. *Parliamentary Affairs*, **64** (1), pp. 1–18.

Kearns, K.P. (2003) 'Accountability in a seamless economy', in Peters, B.G. and Pierre, J. (eds). *Handbook of Public Administration*. London: Sage.

Keegan, W. (2003) *The Prudence of Mr Gordon Brown*. Chichester: Wiley.

Kelsey, J. (1995) *The New Zealand Experiment*. Auckland: Auckland University Press.

Kennedy, I. (1981) *The Unmasking of Medicine*. London: Allen and Unwin.

Kerr, C. (1973) *Industrialism and Industrial Man*. Harmondsworth: Penguin Books.

Kickert, W.J.M. (1995) 'Steering at a distance: A new paradigm of public governance in Dutch higher education'. *Governance*, **8** (1), pp. 135–57.

Kickert, W.J.M. and van Vucht, F.A. (eds) (1995) *Public Policy and Administration Sciences in the Netherlands*. Hemel Hempstead: Harvester Wheatsheaf.

Kickert, W.J.M., Klijn, E.H. and Koppenjan, J.F.M. (eds) (1997) *Managing Complex Networks: Strategies for the Public Sector*. London: Sage.

King, A. (2007) *The British Constitution*. Oxford: Oxford University Press.

Kingdon, J.W. (1995) *Agendas, Alternatives and Public Policies*. New York: Addison, Wesley, Longman, 2nd edn (1st edn 1984).

Kingsley, J.D. (1944) *Representative Bureaucracy*. Yellow Springs, Ohio: Antioch Press.

Kinnersley, D. (1994) *Coming Clean: The Politics of Water and the Environment*. Harmondsworth: Penguin Books.

Kisby, B. (2007) 'Analysing Policy Networks: Towards an Ideational Approach'. *Policy Studies*, **28** (1), pp. 71–90.

Kiser, L.L. and Ostrom, E. (1982) 'The three worlds of action: A metatheoretical synthesis of institutional approaches', in Ostrom, E. (ed.). *Strategies of Political Inquiry*. Beverly Hills, Cal.: Sage, pp. 179–222.

Knapp, A. and Wright, M. (2001) *The Government and Politics of France*, 4th edn. London: Routledge.

Knill, C. (1998) 'European policies: The impact of national administrative traditions'. *Journal of Public Policy*, **18** (1), pp. 1–28.

Knill, C. and Lenschow, A. (1998) 'Coping with Europe: The impact of British and German administrations on the implementation of EU environmental policy'. *Journal of European Public Policy*, **5** (4), pp. 595–614.

Knoepfel, P. and Weidner, H. (1982) 'Formulation and implementation of air quality control programmes: Patterns of interest consideration'. *Policy and Politics*, **10** (1), pp. 85–109.

Knoepfel, P., Larrue, C., Varone, F. and Hill, M. (2007) *Public Policy Analysis*. Bristol: The Policy Press.

Knoke, D. (1990) *Policy Networks: The Structural Perspective*. Cambridge: Cambridge University Press.

Kochan, T.A. (1975) 'Determinants of power boundary units in an interorganizational bargaining relation'. *Administrative Science Quarterly*, **20**, pp. 435–52.

Koppenjan, J. and Klijn, E-H. (2004) *Managing Uncertainties in Networks*. London: Routledge.

Kormondy, E.J. (ed.) (1989) *International Handbook of Pollution Control*. Westport, Conn.: Greenwood Press.

Krasner, S. (1984) 'Approaches to the state: Alternative conceptions and historical dynamics'. *Comparative Politics*, **16**, pp. 223–46.

Laffin, M. (1986) 'Professional communities and policy communities in central–local relations', in Goldsmith, M. (ed.). *New Research in Central–Local Relations*. Aldershot: Gower.

Lampinen, R. and Uusikylä, P. (1998) 'Implementation deficit – Why member states do not comply with EU directives'. *Scandinavian Political Studies*, **21** (3), pp. 231–51.

Lane, J-E. (1987) 'Implementation, accountability and trust'. *European Journal of Political Research*, **15** (5), pp. 527–46.

Lane, J-E. and Ersson, S.O. (2000) *The New Institutional Politics: Performance and Outcomes*. London: Routledge.

Lansley, S., Goss, S. and Wolmar, C. (1989) *Councils in Conflict: The Rise and Fall of the Municipal Left*. London: Macmillan.

Laski, H.J. (1925) *A Grammar of Politics*. London: Allen & Unwin.

Lasswell, H.D. (1936) *Politics: Who Gets What, When, How*. Cleveland, Ohio: Meridian Books.

Lasswell, H.D. (1951) 'The policy orientation', in Lerner, D. and Lasswell, H.D. (eds). *The Policy Sciences*. Stanford, Cal.: Stanford University Press.

Lasswell, H.D. (1968) 'The policy sciences', in *Encyclopedia of the Social Sciences*, vol. 12. New York: Macmillan.

Lasswell, H.D. (1970) 'The emerging conception of the policy sciences'. *Policy Sciences*, **1** (1) pp. 3–14.

Latham, E. (1952) *The Group Basis of Politics*. Ithaca, NY: Cornell University Press.

Le Grand, J. (1997) 'Knights, knaves and pawns? Human behaviour and social policy'. *Journal of Social Policy*, **26** (2), pp. 149–70.

Le Grand, J. (2003) *Motivation, Agency and Public Policy*. Oxford: Oxford University Press.

Leece, J. and Bornat, J. (eds) (2006) *Developments in Direct Payments*. Bristol: The Policy Press.

Lenin, V.I. (1917) *State and Revolution*. Moscow: Foreign Languages Publishing House.

Levine, S. and White, P. (1961) 'Exchange as a conceptual framework for the study of interorganisational relationships'. *Administrative Science Quarterly*, **5**, pp. 583–601.

Lieberman, R.C. (2002) 'Ideas, Institutions and Political Order: Explaining Political Change'. *American Political Science Review*, **96** (4), pp. 697–712.

Lijphart, A. (1975) *The Politics of Accommodation: Pluralism and Democracy in the Netherlands*, 2nd edn. Berkeley, Cal.: University of California Press.

Lijphart, A. (1999) *Patterns of Democracy*. New Haven, Conn.: Yale University Press.

Lindblom, C.E. (1959) 'The science of "muddling through"'. *Public Administration Review*, **19**, pp. 78–88.

Lindblom, C.E. (1965) *The Intelligence of Democracy*. New York: Free Press.

Lindblom, C.E. (1977) *Politics and Markets*. New York: Basic Books.

Lindblom, C.E. (1979) 'Still muddling, not yet through'. *Public Administration Review*, **39**, pp. 517–25.

Linder, S.H. and Peters, B.G. (1991) 'The logic of public policy design: Linking policy actors and plausible instruments'. *Knowledge in Society*, **4**, pp. 15–51.

Lipsky, M. (1980) *Street-Level Bureaucracy*. New York: Russell Sage.

Littler, C.R. (1978) 'Understanding Taylorism'. *British Journal of Sociology*, **29** (2), pp. 185–202.

Lowe, P. (1986) *Countryside Conflicts*. Aldershot: Gower.

Lowi, T.A. (1972) 'Four systems of policy, politics and choice'. *Public Administration Review*, **32**, pp. 298–310.

Lowndes, V. and Skelcher, C. (1998) 'The dynamics of multi-organizational partnerships: An analysis of changing modes of governance'. *Public Administration*, **76**, Summer, pp. 313–33.

Lukes, S. (1974) *Power: A Radical View*. London: Macmillan.

Lukes, S. (2005) *Power: A Radical View*, 2nd edn. London: Macmillan.

MacRae, C.D. (1977) 'A political model of the business cycle'. *Journal of Political Economy*, **85**, pp. 239–64.

Majone, G. and Wildavsky, A. (1978) 'Implementation as evolution', in Freeman, H. (ed.). *Policy Studies Review Annual*. Beverley Hills, Cal.: Sage.

March, J.G. and Olsen, J.P. (1984) 'The new institutionalism: Organisational factors in political life'. *American Political Science Review*, **78**, pp. 734–49.

March, J.G. and Olsen, J.P. (1989) *Rediscovering Institutions*. New York: Free Press.

March, J.G. and Olsen, J.P. (1996) 'Institutional perspectives on political institutions'. *Governance*, **9** (3), pp. 248–64.

Marris, P. and Rein, M. (1967) *Dilemmas of Social Reform*. London: Routledge & Kegan Paul.

Marsh, D. and Rhodes, R.A.W. (1992) *Policy Networks in British Government*. Oxford: Oxford University Press.

Marsh, D. and Smith, M. (2000) 'Understanding policy networks: Towards a dialectical approach'. *Political Studies*, **48** (1), pp. 4–21.

Marx, F.M. (1957) *The Administrative State*. Chicago: University of Chicago Press.

Marx, K. (1845) 'Theses on Feuerbach', reprinted in *Marx and Engels: Selected Works*, vol. 2 (1958). Moscow: Foreign Languages Publishing House.

Mashaw, J.L. (1983) *Bureaucratic Justice*. New Haven, Conn.: Yale University Press.

Massey, P. (1995) *New Zealand: Market Liberalization in a Developed Economy*. New York: St Martin's Press.

Matland, R.E. (1995) 'Synthesizing the implementation literature: The ambiguity-conflict model of policy implementation'. *Journal of Public Administration Research and Theory*, **5** (2), pp. 145–74.

May, P.J. (1993) 'Mandate design and implementation: Enhancing implementation efforts and shaping regulatory styles'. *Journal of Policy Analysis and Management*, **12** (4), pp. 634–63.

May, P.J. (1995) 'Can cooperation be mandated? Implementing intergovernmental environmental management in New South Wales and New Zealand'. *Publius*, **25** (1), pp. 89–113.

May, P.J. and Burby, R.J. (1996) 'Coercive versus cooperative policies: Comparing intergovernmental mandate performance'. *Journal of Policy Analysis and Management*, 15 (2), pp. 171–201.

Maynard-Moody, S. and Musheno, M. (2004) *Cops, Teachers, Counsellors*, Ann Arbor: University of Michigan Press.

McCombs, M. and Shaw, D.L. (1972) 'The agenda-setting function of mass media' *Public Opinion Quarterly*, **36**, pp. 176–87.

McGregor, D. (1960) *The Human Side of Enterprise*. New York: McGraw Hill.

McLellan, D. (1971) *The Thought of Karl Marx*. London: Macmillan.

Meier, K.J., Stewart, J. Jr and England, R.E. (1991) 'The politics of bureaucratic discretion: Educational access as an urban service'. *American Journal of Political Science*, **35** (1), pp. 155–77.

Merelman, R.M. (1968) 'On the neo-elitist critique of community power'. *American Political Science Review*, **62**, pp. 451–60.

Merton, R.K. (1957) *Social Theory and Social Structure*. Glencoe, Ill.: Free Press.

Meyer, J.W. and Rowan, B. (1977) 'Institutionalized organizations: Formal structure as myth and ceremony'. *American Journal of Sociology*, **83** (1), pp. 340–63.

Meynaud, J. (1965) *Technocracy*. London: Faber.

Middlemas, K. (1979) *Politics in Industrial Society*. London: Andre Deutsch.

Middlemas, K. (1986) *Power, Competition and the State*. Oxford: Blackwell.

Miliband, R. (1969) *The State in Capitalist Society*. London: Weidenfeld & Nicolson.

Millet, K. (1970) *Sexual Politics*. New York: Avon Books.

Mills, C.W. (1956) *The Power Elite*. New York: Oxford University Press.

Milward, H.B. and Francisco, R.A. (1983) 'Subsystem politics and corporatism in the United States'. *Policy and Politics*, **11** (3), pp. 273–93.

Milward, H.B., Provan, G. and Else, B.A. (1993) 'What does the "hollow state" look like?', in Bozeman, B. (ed.). *Public Management: The State of the Art.* San Francisco: Jossey-Bass, pp. 309–22.

Minzberg, H. (1983) *Power in and Around Organizations.* Englewood Cliffs, NJ: Prentice Hall.

Moe, T.M. (1980) *The Organisation of Interests.* Chicago: University of Chicago Press.

Moran, M. and Prosser, T. (eds) (1994) *Privatisation and Regulatory Change in Europe.* Buckingham: Open University Press.

Moran, M. and Wood, B. (1993) *States, Regulation and the Medical Profession.* Buckingham: Open University Press.

Mosca, C. (1939) *The Ruling Class*, trans. H.D. Kahn. London: McGraw Hill.

Mosley, P. (1984) *The Making of Economic Policy.* Brighton: Wheatsheaf.

Moynihan, D.P. (1969) *Maximum Feasible Misunderstanding.* New York: Free Press.

Murray, C. (2006) 'State Intervention and Vulnerable Children: Implementation Revisited'. *Journal of Social Policy*, **35** (2), pp. 211–28.

Musgrave, R.A. (1959) *The Theory of Public Finance.* New York: McGraw Hill.

Newman, J. (2001) *Modernising Governance.* London: Sage.

Niskanen, W. (1991) 'A Reflection on Bureaucracy and Representative Government' in Blais, A. and Dion, S. (eds). *The Budget Maximising Bureaucrat: Appraisals and Evidence.* Pittsburgh: University of Pittsburgh Press.

Niskanen, W.A. (1971) *Bureaucracy and Representative Government.* New York: Aldine-Atherton.

Nordhaus, W. (1975) 'The political business cycle'. *Review of Economic Studies*, **42**, pp. 169–90.

Nordlinger, E.A. (1981) *On the Autonomy of the Democratic State.* Cambridge, Mass.: Harvard University Press.

O'Connor, J. (1973) *The Fiscal Crisis of the State.* New York: St Martin's Press.

O'Toole, L.J. Jr (1986) 'Policy recommendations for multi-actor implementation: An assessment of the field'. *Journal of Public Policy*, **6** (2), pp. 181–210.

Olson, M. (1965) *The Logic of Collective Action.* Cambridge, Mass.: Harvard University Press.

Olson, M. (1982) *The Rise and Decline of Nations.* New Haven, Conn.: Yale University Press.

Osborne, D. and Gaebler, T. (1992) *Reinventing Government.* Reading, Mass.: Addison Wesley.

Ouchi, W.G. (1980) 'Markets, bureaucracies and clans'. *Administrative Science Quarterly*, **25**, pp. 129–41.

Oye, K. (1985) 'Explaining cooperation under anarchy: Hypotheses and strategies'. *World Politics*, **39** (1), pp. 1–24.

Page, E.C. (2003) 'The civil servant as legislator: Law making in British administration'. *Public Administration*, **81** (4), pp. 651–79.

Page, E.C. and Goldsmith, M. (1987) *Central and Local Government Relations*. Beverly Hills, Cal.: Sage.

Page, E.C. and Jenkins, B. (2005) *Policy Bureaucracy*, Oxford: Oxford University Press.

Panitch, L. (1980) 'Recent theorisations of corporatism: Reflections on a growth industry'. *British Journal of Sociology*, **31** (2), pp. 159–87.

Panitch, L. (1994) 'Globalisation and the state', in Miliband, R. and Panitch, L. (eds). *The Socialist Register, 1994*. London: Merlin.

Pareto, V. (1966) *Sociological Writings* (ed. S.E. Finer). London: Pall Mall.

Parry, N. and Parry, J. (1976) *The Rise of the Medical Profession*. London: Croom Helm.

Parsons, W. (1995) *Public Policy*. Aldershot: Edward Elgar.

Pawson, R. and Tilley, N. (1997) *Realistic Evaluation*. London: Sage.

Peacock, A. (ed.) (1984) *The Regulation Game*. Oxford: Blackwell.

Pensions Commission. (2005) *A New Pensions Settlement for the Twenty-first Century. The Second Report of the Pensions Commission*. London: The Stationery Office.

Perri 6: *see* 6, P.

Perrow, C. (1972) *Complex Organizations: A Critical Essay*. Cleanview, Ill.: Scott Foresman.

Peters, B.G. and Pierre, J. (eds) (2003) *Handbook of Public Administration*. London: Sage.

Peters, B.G. and Pierre, J. (eds) (2006) *Handbook of Public Policy*. London: Sage.

Peters, B.G., Pierre, J. and King, D.S. (2005) 'The Politics of Path Dependency: Political Conflict in Historical Institutionalism'. *The Journal of Politics*, **67** (4), pp. 1275–300.

Peters, T. and Waterman, R. (1982) *In Search of Excellence*. New York: HarperCollins.

Pierre, J. (ed.) (2000) *Debating Governance*. Oxford: Oxford University Press.

Pierre, J. and Peters, B.G. (2000) *Governance, Politics and the State*. Basingstoke: Macmillan.

Pierson, P. (1994) *Dismantling the Welfare State?* Cambridge: Cambridge University Press.

Pierson, P. (2000) 'Increasing returns, path dependence and the study of politics'. *American Political Science Review*, **92** (4), pp. 251–67.

Pierson, P. (ed.) (2001) *The New Politics of the Welfare State*. Oxford: Oxford University Press.

Piore, M. and Sabel, C.F. (1984) *The Second Industrial Divide*. New York: Basic Books.

Pitts, D. (2005) 'Diversity, representation and performance: Evidence about race and ethnicity in public organizations'. *Journal of Public Administration Research and Theory*, **15** (4), pp. 615–31.

Piven, F.F. and Cloward, R. (1993) *Regulating the Poor: The Functions of Public Welfare*. New York: Vintage Books.

Pollitt, C. (1990) *Managerialism and the Public Services*. Oxford: Blackwell.

Pollitt, C. (2003) *The Essential Public Manager*. Maidenhead: Open University Press.

Pollitt, C. and Bouckaert, G. (2000) *Public Management Reform: A Comparative Analysis*. Oxford: Oxford University Press.

Pollock, A. (2004) *NHS plc*. London: Verso.

Polsby, N.W. (1963) *Community Power and Political Theory*. New Haven, Conn.: Yale University Press.

Powell, M., Exworthy, M. and Berney, L. (2001) 'Playing the game of partnership' in Sykes, R., Bochel, C. and Ellison, N. (eds). *Social Policy Review*, pp. 39–62. Bristol: The Policy Press.

Power, M. (1997) *The Audit Explosion*. London: Demos.

Pressman, J. and Wildavsky, A. (1973 (1st edn), 1979 (2nd edn), 1984 (3rd edn)). *Implementation*. Berkeley: University of California Press.

Prottas, J.M. (1979) *People Processing: The Street-Level Bureaucrat in Public Service Bureaucracies*. Lexington, Mass.: D.C. Heath.

Pusey, M. (1991) *Economic Rationalism in Canberra*. Cambridge: Cambridge University Press.

Ranade, W. (1998) *Making Sense of Multi-Agency Groups*. Newcastle: Sustainable Cities Research Institute.

Ranade, W. and Hudson, B. (2003) 'Conceptual issues in inter-agency collaboration'. *Local Government Studies*, **29** (3), pp. 32–50.

Reiner, R. (1992) *The Politics of the Police*, 2nd edn. New York: Harvester Wheatsheaf.

Reissman, L. (1949) 'The study of role conceptions in bureaucracy'. *Social Forces*, **27**, pp. 305–10.

Rex, J. (1986) *Race and Ethnicity*. Milton Keynes: Open University Press.

Rhodes, R.A.W. (1981) *Control and Power in Central–Local Government Relations*. Farnborough: Saxon House.

Rhodes, R.A.W. (1988) *Beyond Westminster and Whitehall*. London: Unwin Hyman.

Rhodes, R.A.W. (1995) 'From prime ministerial power to core executive', in Rhodes, R.A.W. and Dunleavy, P. (eds). *Prime Minister, Cabinet and Core Executive*. Basingstoke: Macmillan.

Rhodes, R.A.W. (1996) 'The new governance: governing with government'. *Political Studies*, **44**, pp. 652–67.

Rhodes, R.A.W. (1997) *Understanding Governance: Policy Networks, Governance, Reflexivity and Accountability*. Buckingham: Open University Press.

Rhodes, R.A.W. (2003) 'What is new about governance and why does it matter?', in Hayward, J. and Menon, A. (eds). *Governing Europe*. Oxford: Oxford University Press.

Rhodes, R.A.W. (2007) 'The Everyday Life of a Minister: a Confessional and Impressionist Tale' in R.A.W. Rhodes, P. t'Hart and M. Noordegraaf (eds). *Observing Government Elites*. Basingstoke: Palgrave Macmillan.

Riccucci, N.M. (2005) *How Management Matters: Street-level Bureaucrats and Welfare Reform*. Washington, D.C.: Georgetown University Press.

Riccucci, N.M. and Meyers, M.K. (2004) 'Linking passive and active representation: the case of frontline workers in welfare agencies'. *Journal of Public Administration, Research and Theory*, **14** (4), pp. 585–97.

Richards, D. and Smith, M.J. (2002) *Governance and Public Policy in the UK*. Oxford: Oxford University Press.

Richardson, J. (ed.) (1982) *Policy Styles in Western Europe*. London: Allen and Unwin.

Richardson, J.J. and Jordan, A.G. (1979) *Governing under Pressure*. Oxford: Martin Robertson.

Ripley, R.B. and Franklin, G.A. (1982) *Bureaucracy and Policy Implementation*. Homewood: Dorsey Press.

Roethlisberger, F.J. and Dickson, W.J. (1939) *Management and the Worker*. Cambridge, Mass.: Harvard University Press.

Rose, R. (1991) 'What is lesson drawing?' *Journal of Public Policy*, **11** (1), pp. 3–30.

Rose, R. (1993) *Lesson Drawing in Public Policy*. Chatham, NJ: Chatham House.

Rothstein, B. (1992) 'Labor-market institutions and working-class strength', in Steinmo, S., Thelen, K. and Longstreth, F. (eds). *Structuring Politics: Historical Institutionalism in Comparative Analysis*. Cambridge: Cambridge University Press.

Rothstein, B. (1998) *Just Institutions Matter: The Moral and Political Logic of the Universal Welfare State*. Cambridge: Cambridge University Press.

Sabatier, P.A. (1986) 'Top-down and bottom-up approaches to implementation research: A critical analysis and suggested synthesis'. *Journal of Public Policy*, **6** (1), pp. 21–48.

Sabatier, P.A. (1999) 'The need for better theories', in Sabatier, P.A. (ed.). *Theories of the Policy Process*. Boulder, Col.: Westview Press, pp. 3–17.

Sabatier, P.A. (ed.) (1999) *Theories of the Policy Process*. Boulder, Col.: Westview Press.

Sabatier, P.A. (ed.) (2007) *Theories of the Policy Process*, 2nd edn. Boulder, Col.: Westview Press.

Sabatier, P.A. and Jenkins-Smith, H. (1999) 'The advocacy coalition framework: An assessment', in Sabatier, P.A. (ed.). *Theories of the Policy Process*. Boulder, Col.: Westview Press, pp. 117–66.

Sabatier, P.A. and Jenkins-Smith, H. (eds) (1993) *Policy Change and Learning: An Advocacy Coalition Approach*. Boulder, Col.: Westview Press.

Sabatier, P.A., Loomis, J. and McCarthy, C. (1995) 'Hierarchical controls, professional norms, local constituencies and budget maximisation: An analysis of US Forest Service planning decisions'. *American Journal of Political Science*, **39** (1), pp. 204–42.

Sabel, C.F. (1982) *Work and Politics*. Cambridge: Cambridge University Press.

Salaman, G. (1979) *Work Organisations*. London: Longman.

Salisbury, R.H. (1979) 'Why no corporatism in the United States?', in Schmitter, P.C. and Lembruch, G. (eds). *Trends Towards Corporatist Intermediation*. London: Sage.

Satyamurti, C. (1981) *Occupational Survival*. Oxford: Blackwell.

Scharpf, F.W. (1997) *Games Real Actors Play: Actor-Centered Institutionalism in Policy Research*. Boulder, Col.: Westview Press.

Schattschneider, E.E. (1960) *The Semi-Sovereign People*. New York: Holt, Rinehart and Winston.

Schmitter, P. (1974) 'Still the century of corporatism?' *Review of Politics*, **36**, pp. 85–131.

Schultze, C.L. (1968) *The Politics and Economics of Public Spending*. Washington, DC: Brookings.

Schumpeter, J. (1947) *Capitalism, Socialism and Democracy*, 2nd rev. edn. London: Allen & Unwin.

Schwarzmantel, J. (1994) *The State in Contemporary Society*. Hemel Hempstead: Harvester Wheatsheaf.

Scott, W.R. (1995) *Institutions and Organizations*. Thousand Oaks, Cal.: Sage.

Seebohm Report (1968) *Report of the Committee on Local Authority and Allied Personal Social Services*. London: HMSO, Cmnd. 3703.

Selden, S.C. (1997) 'Representative bureaucracy: Examining the linkage between passive and active representation in the farmers' home administration'. *American Review of Public Administration*, **27** (1), pp. 22–42.

Seldon, A. (2001) *The Blair Effect: The Blair Government 1997–2001*. London: Little Brown.

Seldon. A. (ed.) (2007) *Blair's Britain*. Cambridge: Cambridge University Press.

Self, P. (1985) *Political Theories of Modern Government*. London: Allen & Unwin.

Self, P. (1993) *Government by the Market?* Basingstoke: Macmillan.

Selznick, P. (1949) *TVA and the Grass Roots*. Berkeley: University of California Press.

Selznick, P. (1957) *Leadership in Administration*. New York: Harper & Row.

Selznick, P. (1996) 'Institutionalism "old" and "new"'. *Administrative Science Quarterly*, **41**, pp. 270–7.

Shambaugh, D. (1995) *Deng Xiaoping*. Oxford: Clarendon Press.

Shawcross, W. (2003) *Allies: The United States, Britain, Europe and the War with Iraq*. London: Atlantic Books.

Shinkawa, T. (2005) 'The politics of pension reform in Japan: Institutional legacies, credit claiming and blame avoidance' in Bonoli, G. and Shinkawa, T. (eds). *Ageing and Pension Reform Around the World*. Cheltenham: Elgar.

Sieber, S. (1981) *Fatal Remedies: The Ironies of Social Intervention*. New York: Plenum.

Simon, H.A. (1957) *Administrative Behaviour*, 2nd edn. New York: Macmillan.

Skocpol, T. (1994) *Social Policy in the United States*. Princeton, NJ: Princeton University Press.

Skocpol, T. and Finegold, K. (1982) 'State capacity and economic intervention in the early New Deal'. *Political Science Quarterly*, **97**, pp. 255–78.

Smith, B.C. (1976) *Policy Making in British Government*. London: Martin Robertson.

Smith, B.C. (1988) *Bureaucracy and Political Power*. Brighton: Harvester.

Smith, G. (1981) 'Discretionary decision-making in social work', in Adler, M. and Asquith, S. (eds). *Discretion and Welfare*. London: Heinemann.

Smith, K.E. (2007) 'Health inequalities in Scotland and England: the contrasting journey of ideas from research into policy'. *Social Science and Medicine*, **64**, pp. 1438–49.

Smith, M.J. (1993) *Pressure, Power and Policy*. Hemel Hempstead: Harvester Wheatsheaf.

Solomos, J., Findlay, B., Jones, S. and Gilroy, P. (1982) 'The organic crisis of British capitalism and race: The experience of the seventies', in Centre for Contemporary Cultural Studies. *The Empire Strikes Back*. London: Hutchinson.

Spicker, P. (2006) *Policy Analysis for Practice*. Bristol: The Policy Press.

Stephens, P. (1996) *Politics and the Pound*. London: Macmillan.

Stewart, J. and Clarke, M. (1987) 'The public services orientation: Issues and dilemmas'. *Public Administration*, **65**, pp. 161–77.

Stewart, K. (2007) 'Equality and Social Justice' in Seldon. A. (ed.). *Blair's Britain*. Cambridge: Cambridge University Press.

Stoker, R.P. (1991) *Reluctant Partners: Implementing Federal Policy*. Pittsburgh, Penn.: University of Pittsburgh Press.

Stoker, R.P. and Wilson, L.A. (1998) 'Verifying compliance: Social regulation and welfare reform'. *Public Administration Review*, **58** (5), pp. 395–405.

Stone, C. (1989) *Regime Politics: Governing Atlanta, 1946–1988*. Lawrence: University Press of Kansas.

Streeck, W. and Thelen, K. (eds) (2005) *Beyond Continuity: Institutional Change in Advanced Political Economies*. Oxford: Oxford University Press.

Surel, Y. (2000) 'The role of cognitive and normative frames in policy-making'. *Journal of European Public Policy*, **7** (4), pp. 495–512.

Taylor, D. and Balloch, S. (eds) (2005) *The Politics of Evaluation*. Bristol: The Policy Press.

Taylor, F.W. (1911) *The Principles of Scientific Management*. New York: Harper.

Taylor, I. (2003) 'Policy on the hoof: The handling of the foot and mouth disease outbreak in the UK, 2001'. *Policy and Politics*, **31** (4), pp. 535–46.

Taylor, M. (2003) *Public Policy in the Community*. Basingstoke: Palgrave Macmillan.

Taylor-Gooby, P. (2002) 'The silver age of the welfare state: Perspectives on resilience'. *Journal of Social Policy*, **31** (4), pp. 597–622.

Taylor-Gooby, P. (ed.) (2001) *Welfare States under Pressure*. London: Sage.

Thelen, K. and Steinmo, S. (1992) 'Historical institutionalism in comparative politics', in Steinmo, S., Thelen, K. and Longstreth, F. (eds). *Structuring Politics: Historical Institutionalism in Comparative Analysis*. Cambridge: Cambridge University Press.

Thomas, H. (ed.) (1968) *Crisis in the Civil Service*. London: Blond.

Thomas, P.G. (2003) 'Accountability: Introduction', in Peters, B.G. and Pierre, J. (eds). *Handbook of Public Administration*. London: Sage.

Thompson, G., Frances, J., Levacic, R. and Mitchell, J. (eds) (1991) *Markets, Hierarchies and Networks: The Coordination of Social Life*. London: Sage.

Thompson, J.B. (1967) *Organizations in Action: Social Science Bases of Administrative Theory*. New York: McGraw-Hill.

Thompson, J.B. (1989) 'The theory of structuration', in Held, D. and Thompson, J.B. (eds). *Social Theory of Modern Societies: Anthony Giddens and His Critics*. Cambridge: Cambridge University Press.

Thurber, J.A. (1991) 'Dynamics of policy subsystems in American politics', in Cigler, A.J. and Loomis, A. (eds). *Interest Group Politics*, 3rd edn. Washington, DC: Congressional Quarterly.

Tilly, C. (1991) 'Domination, Resistance, Compliance... Discourse', *Sociological Forum*, **6** (3), pp. 593–602.

Toke, D. and Marsh, D. (2003) 'Policy networks and the GM crops issue: assessing the utility of a dialectic model of policy networks'. *Public Administration*, **81** (2), pp. 229–51.

Tomlinson, S. (2001) *Education in a Post-Welfare Society*. Buckingham: Open University Press.

Truman, D. (1958) *The Governmental Process*. New York: Alfred Knopf.

Tullock, G. (1967) *The Politics of Bureaucracy*. New York: Public Affairs Press.

Tullock, G. (1976) *The Vote Motive*. London: Institute of Economic Affairs.

Uhr, J. (1993) 'Redesigning accountability: From muddles to maps'. *Australian Quarterly*, Winter, pp. 1–6.

Van Meter, D. and Van Horn, C.E. (1975) 'The policy implementation process, a conceptual framework'. *Administration and Society*, **6** (4), pp. 445–88.

Vick, N., Tobin, R., Swift, P., Spandler, H., Hill, M., Coldham, T., Towers, C. and Waldock, H. (2006) *An Evaluation of the Impact of the Social Care Modernisation Programme on the Implementation of Direct Payments*, unpublished report of the Health and Social Care Advisory Service to the Department of Health.

Visser, J. and Hemerijck, A. (1997) *A Dutch Miracle: Job Reform and Welfare Growth in the Netherlands*. Amsterdam: Amsterdam University Press.

Wade, H.W.R. (1982) *Administration Law*, 5th edn. Oxford: Oxford University Press.

Walker, A. and Wong, C-K. (2004) 'The ethnocentric construction of the Welfare State' in P. Kennett (ed.) *A Handbook of Comparative Social Welfare*. Cheltenham: Edward Elgar.

Walker, R. (2005) *Social Security and Welfare*. Maidenhead: Open University Press.

Walker, R. and Duncan, S. (2007) 'Policy Evaluation' in H. Bochel and S. Duncan (eds). *Making Policy in Theory and Practice*. Bristol: The Policy Press.

Wallas, G. (1948) *Human Nature in Politics*. London: Constable.

Wallerstein, I. (1979) *The Capitalist World Economy*. Cambridge: Cambridge University Press.

Wallis, J. (1997) 'Conspiracy and the policy process: A case study of the New Zealand experiment'. *Journal of Public Policy*, **17** (1), pp. 1–29.

Walsh, K. (1995) *Public Services and Market Mechanisms*. Basingstoke: Macmillan.

Walter, A. (1993) *World Power and World Money*. Hemel Hempstead: Harvester Wheatsheaf.

Weale, A. (1992) *The New Politics of Pollution*. Manchester: Manchester University Press.

Weatherley, R. (1979) *Reforming Special Education: Policy Implementation from State Level to Street Level*. Cambridge, Mass.: MIT Press.

Weatherley, R. (1980) 'Implementing social programs: The view from the front line'. Paper delivered at the annual meeting of the American Political Science Association, Washington, DC.

Weatherley, R. and Lipsky, M. (1977) 'Street-level bureaucrats and institutional innovation: Implementing special education reform'. *Harvard Educational Review*, **47** (2), pp. 171–97.

Weaver, R.K. (1986) 'The politics of blame avoidance', *Journal of Public Policy*, **6**, pp. 371–98.

Webb, A. and Wistow, G. (1982) *Whither State Welfare?* London: RIPA.

Weber, M. (1947) *The Theory of Social and Economic Organization*, trans. A.M. Henderson and T. Parsons. Glencoe, Ill.: Free Press.

Weir, M., Orloff, S. and Skocpol, T. (eds) (1988) *The Politics of Social Policy in the United States*. Princeton, NJ: Princeton University Press.

Weissert, C.S. (1994) 'Beyond the organization: The influence of community and personal values on street-level bureaucrats' responsiveness'. *Journal of Public Administration Research and Theory*, **4** (2), pp. 225–54.

Whetstone, G.S. and Rosencranz, A. (1983) *Acid Rain in Europe and North America*. Washington: Environment Law Institute.

Wildavsky, A.B. (1979) *Speaking the Truth to Power: The Art and Craft of Policy Analysis*. Boston, Mass.: Little, Brown and Co.

Wilding, P. (1982) *Professional Power and Social Welfare*. London: Routledge.

Wilenski, P. (1986) *Public Power and Public Administration*. Sydney: RAIPA.

Wilensky, H.L. (1964) 'The professionalisation of everyone'. *American Journal of Sociology*, **70**, pp. 137–58.

Wilensky, H.L. (1975) *The Welfare State and Equality*. Berkeley: University of California Press.

Wilks, S. and Wright, M. (1987) 'Conclusion: Comparing government–industry relations: States, sectors and networks', in Wilks, S. and Wright, M. (eds). *Comparative Government Industry Relations: Western Europe, the United States and Japan*. Oxford: Clarendon Press.

Williamson, O. (1975) *Markets and Hierarchies*. New York: Free Press.

Williamson, O. (1985) *The Economic Institutions of Capitalism*. New York: Free Press.

Wilson, J.Q. (1973) *Political Organizations*. Beverly Hills, Cal.: Sage.

Wilson, W. (1887) 'The study of administration'. *Political Science Quarterly*, **2**, pp. 197–222.

Winkler, J. (1976) 'Corporatism'. *Archives Européennes de Sociologie*, **17** (1), pp. 100–36.

Winter, S. C. (2003) 'Implementation Perspectives: Status and Reconsideration', in B.G. Peters and J. Pierre (eds). *Handbook of Public Administration*. London: Sage, pp. 212–22.

Winter, S.C. (2006) 'Implementation', in B.G. Peters and J. Pierre (eds). *Handbook of Public Policy*. London: Sage, pp. 151–66.

Wittfogel, K.A. (1963) *Oriental Despotism: A Comparative Study of Total Power*. New Haven, Conn.: Yale University Press.

Wolf, A. (2002) *Does Education Matter? Myths about Education and Economic Growth.* London: Penguin Books.

Wolfinger, R.E. (1971) 'Nondecisions and the study of local politics'. *American Political Science Review*, **65**, pp. 1063–80.

Woll, P. (ed.) (2003) *Public Admnistration and Policy.* New York: Harper.

Wood, D.B. and Waterman, R. (1994) *Bureaucratic Dynamics.* Boulder, Col.: Westview Press.

Woodward, J. (1965) *Industrial Organisation: Theory and Practice.* London: Oxford University Press.

World Bank (1994) *Averting the Old Age Crisis.* Oxford: Oxford University Press.

Yeates, N. (ed.) (2008) *Understanding Global Social Policy.* Bristol: The Policy Press.

Yergin, D. (1991) *The Prize: The Epic Quest for Oil, Money and Power.* London: Simon and Schuster.

Young, K. (1977) 'Values in the policy process'. *Policy and Politics*, **5** (2), pp. 1–22.

Zimmerman, D.H. (1971) 'The practicalities of rule use', in Douglas, J.D. (ed.). *Understanding Everyday Life.* London: Routledge & Kegan Paul.

Index